Financial Derivatives

New Instruments and Their Uses

Financial Derivatives

New Instruments and Their Uses

Federal Reserve Bank of Atlanta
Research Division

December 1993

Views expressed in this publication are not necessarily those of the Federal Reserve Bank of Atlanta or of the Federal Reserve System. Material may be reprinted or abstracted if this work and the individual authors are credited. Please provide the Federal Reserve Bank of Atlanta's Public Affairs Department with a copy of any publication containing reprinted material.

Additional copies are available for $15.00 (U.S.) from the Public Affairs Department, Federal Reserve Bank of Atlanta, 104 Marietta Street, NW, Atlanta, Georgia 30303-2713, telephone 404/521-8020.

ISBN 0-9624159-1-X

Printed in the United States of America

Contents

Foreword

Innovation is the hallmark of financial markets in the United States, a characteristic that has been made evident once again by the recent growth and evolution of financial derivatives. These new financial instruments have already proven to be an important tool for businesses and financial institutions that use them for risk management and as investment vehicles. The importance of derivatives can be measured by their explosive growth. In the area of interest rate derivatives alone, consider the fact that, when the Chicago Board of Trade began trading Treasury bond futures in 1977, the total volume of trades of these early financial derivatives for one month was less than 10,000. Some fifteen years later, total volume during a similar period had increased to more than 4 million.

This dramatic growth carries a special significance for financial institutions and their regulators. The complexity of these innovations poses questions about their use and management within firms. At the same time, understanding the various innovations taking place in financial markets is essential for the Federal Reserve to perform its role of fostering the safety and soundness of the financial system.

The Federal Reserve Bank of Atlanta recognized the growing importance of financial derivatives in the mid-1980s and began building a strong program of research on financial markets and instruments to supplement its traditional emphasis on banking studies. This book gathers the extensive writings on derivatives by Atlanta Fed economists, who are helping to shape the discussion of important issues in this field of financial economics.

Although the Atlanta Fed's ultimate interest in derivatives centers on the financial system as a whole, we believe that individual institutions will also find value in having a reference book that can supplement their knowledge of these instruments. The primary purpose of publishing this financial derivatives reader is to enable those at business and financial institutions who deal with risk management—especially those at the top levels of the organization—to better understand the changing nature of financial markets and these new instruments.

Robert P. Forrestal
President and Chief Executive Officer
Federal Reserve Bank of Atlanta
December 1993

Acknowledgments

We gratefully acknowledge the considerable assistance of several Atlanta Fed staff members in preparing this collection. Peter Abken's contributions to organizing the material and identifying its defining themes were invaluable, and without the able editorial, graphics, and production assistance of Joycelyn Woolfolk, Carole Starkey, and Lynn Foley, publication of this volume would not have been possible.

*I*ntroduction

This book brings together a variety of articles written by economists at the Federal Reserve Bank of Atlanta about derivative instruments and markets. Research into derivatives has been an area of specialization for the Atlanta Fed's Research Department since the mid-1980s, when we recognized that these instruments and markets were likely to become increasingly significant. In fact, there was an explosion of growth in their volume toward the end of that decade, and derivatives markets have assumed an important role in transforming the management and allocation of risk. The articles, which originally appeared in our *Economic Review*, have aimed to improve the public's understanding of derivative instruments—their benefits, their costs, and their risks—and to inform the debate on financial policy.

As their name suggests, derivatives are instruments that are linked to or derived from an underlying security or commodity. The oldest and most commonplace of these instruments are options and futures contracts. A futures contract specifies a delivery date and price of a security, or its cash value, effectively locking in a price. As the spot price for immediate delivery diverges from the futures price, the value of the futures contract fluctuates. This fluctuation provides a basis for both hedging and speculative strategies. Options are characterized by "payoffs" that depend on the difference between a security price in the future and a fixed strike price. The latter may be thought of as a

threshold price that determines whether the option is "in the money" or not.

Derivatives are related not only to underlying securities but also to each other—a key point in understanding these instruments. For example, a combination of options can be constructed to create or synthesize a futures contract. These so-called arbitrage links between instruments and markets are a central topic of many of the articles in this book. The linkages are clearly of interest to policymakers.

The banking system itself is being transformed by its involvement in derivatives markets. In recent years as their traditional lending function has languished, banks and other depository institutions have enjoyed strong earnings from derivatives activities, ranging from their long-standing participation in forward foreign exchange markets to trading in newer markets like those for swaps and exotic options. Many of the large money-center and regional banks are the chief market makers, acting as intermediaries between end users of derivatives, who frequently are other financial institutions out to "lay off" the risk of imbalances in their own positions.

The Federal Reserve is appropriately interested in the potential risks that derivatives may pose to this nation's financial system. The Fed faces the challenge of balancing social and private costs and benefits, which may be divergent. While derivatives markets have flourished as a means of more efficiently sharing risks flowing from changing asset prices and as an efficient mechanism for disseminating new information about asset prices, many derivatives are viewed as leveraged positions (that is, backed by credit) that can disrupt markets in times of rapid change or turmoil. This controversial point has been a much-debated rationale for more regulation. A more subtle concern is how the presence of a "lender of last resort"—the Federal Reserve—can affect private decisions. Whether the perception is accurate or not, if market participants believe that the Fed will step in during a crisis, institutions may choose to hold less capital as a safety cushion than they otherwise would, and in effect the Fed—and indirectly the taxpayer—is pushed to assume the cost for safeguarding derivatives (and other) financial markets. In such an environment, regulation might be appropriate as a means to protect individuals not directly involved in these markets. This issue is implicitly at the heart of current discussions about systemic risk and the markets' and regulators' responses to it.

Systemic risk arises in the following way. In the over-the-counter market, financial exchanges are bilateral transactions between contracting parties, known as counterparties. The ability of a counterparty to make good on its financial promises depends in large part on its credit standing; credit evaluation and screening are major elements of over-the-counter derivatives transactions. A failure of one counterparty to meet the terms of its contract, like making a payment to the holder of an expiring option contract, may threaten the solvency of its counterparty. The threat would be significant in a situation in which many counterparties, hit by a severe macroeconomic shock like a sudden large drop in asset prices, are unable to fulfill their obligations. In the extreme, this development could set off a domino effect of defaults that could trigger a financial panic or collapse. This domino effect is referred to as systemic risk. Derivatives traded on organized exchanges as well as on over-the-counter markets are subject to and may be sources of systemic risk.

The Federal Reserve, of course, has a keen interest in minimizing the potential for systemic problems. While banks are highly regulated, their derivatives activity is not. At the same time, because the largely unregulated derivatives industry wants to remain free to evolve and develop innovations, the industry has an incentive to police itself and build a track record of stability and safety. The Fed and other regulators face the delicate task of ensuring and promoting the stability of the financial system while not choking off a profitable line of business for many banks. The regulatory task is further complicated by the internationalization of derivatives and financial markets. Regulation that is too costly, even if well founded, could drive activity abroad to less regulated markets. Modern technology has made it easy for markets to locate virtually anywhere.

The Interdependence of Markets

This book is organized into five sections that encompass a number of instruments and markets. The first section contains articles emphasizing the interdependence of markets. The stock market crash of October 1987 crystallized investors' appreciation of the growing connections among markets domestically and internationally. This cohesion has grown even tighter in the years since the crash. Peter A. Abken's "Globalization of Stock, Futures, and Options Markets" discusses a plethora of worldwide securities and derivatives markets, which are increasingly linked by electronic networks. The impact of derivatives on other markets is highlighted in Steven P. Feinstein and William N. Goetzmann's "The Effect of the 'Triple Witching Hour' on Stock Market Volatility" and in Ira G. Kawaller, Paul D. Koch, and Timothy W. Koch's "The Relationship between the S&P 500 Index and S&P 500 Index Futures Prices." Feinstein and Goetzmann demonstrate that the simultaneous expiration of individual stock options, stock index options, and stock index futures contracts combined to have a statistically significant effect on increasing the volatility of the underlying stock index. In other words, institutional arrangements have an impact, at least temporarily, on the valuation of the underlying securities.

In a similar vein, Kawaller, Koch, and Koch examine the arbitrage link between the S&P 500 index futures and the index. Relying on transactions prices for futures and matching values for the index, they find that the "cash" and futures markets are indeed tightly connected, with the futures market responding much more quickly to new information than the stock market. The authors make careful statistical measures of the rate of adjustment in these markets based on minute-by-minute transactions data.

Swaps and Related Instruments

The second section discusses swaps and related instruments. Swaps constitute the over-the-counter instruments that have perhaps received the most attention in the financial press. One reason for such attention is that the swap market is gigantic. In terms of so-called notional principal, the total size of the worldwide interest rate and currency swaps market was roughly $5 trillion as of year-end 1992. Notional principal is the face value of the underlying financial instruments on which a swap is arranged. Although this figure overstates the cash flows involved in actual swaps, clearly the market is transforming huge amounts of securities.

The easiest way to think about swaps is as agreements to alter cash flows from fixed to variable flows and vice versa. These cash flows arise from holdings of fixed-income and floating-rate securities, commodities, and equities. The exchange of cash flows between swap counterparties can be denominated in the same currency or in different currencies. Currency swaps stipulate the rate of exchange and whether that rate is fixed or floating. Abken's "Beyond Plain Vanilla: A Taxonomy of Swaps" looks at a wide variety of swaps and their applications. In addition, Abken considers an important instance of derivatives on derivatives: options on swaps or swaptions. In "Interest-Rate Swaps: A Review of the Issues," Larry D. Wall and John J. Pringle give a detailed account of the simple fixed-for-floating or "plain vanilla" interest rate swap. They consider several reasons for the existence and popularity of swaps. The conventional wisdom on this issue—that swaps exploit debt market imperfections—fails to explain the sustained and continuing growth of the swap market. The authors present and evaluate several more plausible explanations. They also consider credit and interest rate risks associated with swaps as well as the nascent regulatory response to the emergence of this market. Finally, Abken's "Interest-Rate Caps, Collars, and Floors" discusses several close relatives of swaps that have proved to be useful in many applications, particularly those in which credit risk of a counterparty might deter others from engaging in a swap. This article concludes with a model for valuing default-risky caps, collars, and floors.

Interest Rate Instruments

The third section presents articles on interest rate instruments and their subtleties and risks. Abken's "Innovations in Modeling the Term Structure of Interest Rates" provides the background for the other articles in this area. Derivative instruments that depend on movements in interest rates or bond prices generally require a term structure model for pricing. That is, the "payoff" on interest-rate derivative instruments is determined by the future movement in interest rates. An essential part of the accurate valuation of interest-rate derivatives is the model that quantifies these movements. The article considers two seminal models in detail: the Cox, Ingersoll, and Ross general equilibrium model and the Ho and Lee arbitrage-free interest-rate movements model.

Hugh Cohen's "Beyond Duration: Measuring Interest Rate Exposure" makes the important point that using convenient shortcuts in measuring the interest-rate risk of a bond portfolio can lead to big and costly errors. The widely used shortcut he critiques is the use of a portfolio's modified duration, which assumes only parallel shifts in the term structure of interest rates, in measuring risk or actually hedging (or insuring) a portfolio against interest rate movements. Regulators, including the Federal Reserve, have been charged with the task of finding interest rate risk measures for bank portfolios to use in setting capital requirements. Cohen provides examples in which having a portfolio hedged against parallel shifts results in large losses. He suggests and illustrates an alternative simple procedure that helps preserve a portfolio's value in the face of large interest rate movements. The key point is that the alternative procedure accounts for nonparallel shifts in the term structure—reflecting the way interest rates actually move most of the time.

Stephen D. Smith's "Analyzing Risk and Return for Mortgage-Backed Securities" and James H. Gilkeson and Smith's "The Convexity Trap: Pitfalls in Financing Mortgage Portfolios and Related Securities" are not about derivatives per se. Mortgage-backed securities (MBSs), like Government National Mortgage Association passthroughs, pool individual mortgage cash flows into marketable securities. Collateralized mortgage obligations (CMOs) go a step further and repackage these cash flows to appeal to particular investors. Apart from default risk, MBSs differ from standard bonds because of the embedded option they contain, and herein lies the connection with the other derivative instruments discussed in this book. Homeowners have the right to prepay their mortgages without penalty. The rational exercise of this option depends in part on interest rate movements. (They may also prepay if, for example, they need to relocate.) If rates drop sufficiently to cover the costs of refinancing, the homeowner pays off the mortgage and the remaining mortgage principal is passed on to the mortgageholder early, thereby creating potential reinvestment risk for the investor. Valuing the prepayment option accurately is of vital importance to MBS investors like commercial banks. Compensation for prepayments takes the form of an MBS price that is lower compared with a (hypothetical) MBS price for mortgages that do not contain prepayment options for homeowners.

Smith provides a thorough examination of prepayments in relation to interest rate movements. He focuses on the so-called option adjusted spread (OAS) approach to adjusting MBS cash flows for prepayments. The spread is relative to the yield to maturity of a Treasury security of comparable duration. The positive yield spread is the compensation for bearing prepayment risk. The OAS approach relies heavily on term structure modeling to compute the present value of future cash flows. Smith makes the important point that the computed OAS does not give an indication to an investor about whether a particular MBS is under- or overvalued because the calculation does not include information about the return the individual investor requires as compensation for bearing prepayment risk.

Gilkeson and Smith, like Cohen, consider the subject of duration, but in the specific context of analyzing and hedging mortgage securities. Interest rate sensitive prepayment flows from mortgages and MBSs complicate the traditional banking practice of matching the durations of assets (MBSs) and liabilities (deposits) in order to protect the institution's net worth from interest rate fluctuations. Variable prepayment flows typically cause the durations of MBSs and the liabilities that finance them to become unmatched as interest rates fluctuate around a level at which durations were equalized. Equity can decrease and possibly become negative as a result of rate moves in either direction. The authors call this phenomenon the convexity trap and discuss ways to safeguard an institution's equity in this case.

Unusual Options

The fourth section includes a set of articles on some unusual varieties of options. The two related articles by William C. Hunter and David W. Stowe deal with path-dependent options. The first gives an introduction to these instruments, which are sometimes called exotic options because of the seeming complexity of their construction. The second takes a detailed look at the valuation of two popular types of path-dependent options, lookbacks and average-rate options. Path dependency simply means that the option payoff depends in some way on the history of the underlying asset price

during the life of the option rather than on the asset price at the time of expiration (or exercise) of the option. For example, a lookback call option entitles the holder to buy the underlying asset at the lowest price realized during the option's existence. A lookback put gives the owner the right to sell an asset at the highest price realized during that interval. (The prepayment option in MBSs is another example of a path-dependent option, as Smith discusses.) Of course, the lookback's price reflects the option market's expected assessment of the value of this flexibility. In these articles, Hunter and Stowe give numerous examples of such options and explain a number of techniques for pricing them.

Cohen's "Evaluating Embedded Options" analyzes the intricacies of embedded options using two specific examples. An embedded or implicit option, like the prepayment option discussed above, is not actually traded, and its valuation can involve extra subtleties. The first case considered is the relatively straightforward option in a callable Treasury bond. The author shows that the embedded call option can be valued separately from the underlying bond. In contrast, the "wild card" option in Treasury bond futures contracts cannot be valued separately from the futures. A careful analysis is needed to get the valuation right.

T-bond futures contracts—the most heavily traded of any futures—contain three distinct embedded options: the quality, timing, and wild card options. A trader who is "short," or who is selling, the T-bond futures contract is obligated to deliver a Treasury bond meeting the delivery criteria against the contract during its delivery month. The wild card option refers to the trader's right to decide on each day of the delivery month whether to deliver a bond during a six-hour window of time after the market closes at 2:00 P.M. The trader profits if the bond price drops below the 2:00 P.M. futures settlement price. Cohen argues that the flexibility to deliver after trading ends is of little value because exercising the wild card option (by buying a bond at a lower price than the settlement price) and thus closing out the futures position is largely offset, on average, by forgoing the marking-to-market payment the following day. Cohen's main point is that valuing the embedded wild card option separately from the futures contract, as others have done, greatly overstates its value.

Applications and Regulatory Issues

The final section presents a set of articles on miscellaneous applications of derivatives and regulatory issues. Feinstein's "Forecasting Stock-Market Volatility Using Options on Index Futures" proposes an implied volatility estimator of future stock market volatility. Stock market observers frequently try to determine the direction that the market will move over some future period, a difficult task given the (nearly) random nature of stock price movements. However, the variability of stock prices is more readily predicted, and stock-index options prices offer a market-based forecast of volatility. Roughly speaking, greater volatility would reflect greater uncertainty about asset prices, which could occur, for example, after a major shock like a stock market crash or an escalation of international political tensions.

The basic idea is to use an option-pricing model—the Black-Scholes model modified for futures contracts—to infer market volatility over a future time interval, corresponding to the life of the option. An option price is a function of the market's expectation of stock market volatility. Feinstein inverts the Black-Scholes equation to estimate the market's volatility forecast. His innovation in using this technique lies in the scheme for weighting just-out-of-the-money call options over four consecutive days, a procedure that mitigates errors in the volatility measure stemming from errors in the option prices.

Feinstein finds that his volatility estimator outperforms a naive estimator for forecasting over thirty-eight- and fifty-seven-day horizons. The naive estimator simply takes the historical volatility of the stock index over the previous twenty days as the forecast for the coming period. The implied volatility estimators were more efficient according to some standard statistical criteria that Feinstein discusses.

Abken and Feinstein in "Covered Call Options: A Proposal to Ease LDC Debt" use simple option concepts to suggest a way to help less developed countries (LDCs) raise revenue from their export commodities. The proposal is analogous to a popular method for generating income on fixed-income portfolios by writing (selling) calls on the portfolio. Countries like Mexico with large, known oil reserves could earn revenue during times of low oil prices by selling long-dated, high-strike price call options to investors in the United States and other oil-importing, industrialized countries. The options would fix a price for importers that would be attractive in high-price periods when oil revenue is also high. Essentially, the idea is to smooth an exporter's income by transferring revenue from future high-price periods to the current low-price period. When the oil price is high, the option pays off to the holder—an oil refiner in the United States, for exam-

ple. The options offer protection to the buyer when crude oil is very expensive. The hitch is the risk that the LDC option seller would default on these contracts. The authors argue that this is not a probable outcome, however.

In "Capital Requirements for Interest Rate and Foreign Exchange Hedges," Wall, Pringle, and James E. McNulty consider some important regulatory issues regarding the use of derivatives by banks and savings and loan associations. Derivatives alter the exposure of these institutions to interest rate risk and to credit risk. Regulators are only slowly coming to grips with both of these issues.

The authors review the various exchange-traded and over-the-counter derivatives and the ways in which they complement and supplement standard interest rate risk management practices used by these institutions. They then consider regulatory initiatives. Thrift Bulletin 13 of the Federal Home Loan Bank Board requires savings and loans to evaluate interest rate risk and to limit their exposure to this risk within specified bounds. The 1989 Financial Institutions Reform, Recovery, and Enforcement Act (FIRREA) extends to thrifts the regulations on risk-based capital requirements that apply to nationally chartered commercial banks.

The authors consider the provisions of the Basle Agreement of 1988, which are now in force for major derivative dealers (commercial banks) around the world. This agreement established risk-based capital standards for credit risk that includes explicit treatment of off-balance-sheet items in the determination of capital. The article details the provisions of the Basle Agreement as they relate to interest rate and currency swaps.

The derivatives industry and its regulators are re-evaluating the existing capital standards. The Basle Committee of regulators from the Group of Ten countries (Belgium, Canada, France, Germany, Italy, Japan, the Netherlands, Sweden, the United Kingdom, and the United States) along with Luxembourg and Switzerland are currently considering proposals to refine the risk-based capital standards. A central concern focuses on recognizing the derivative industry's desire to practice "close-out netting," whereby in the event of bankruptcy the outstanding value of a counterparty's swaps involving a particular counterparty would be aggregated to a single exposure, which would tend to be smaller than the sum of gross exposures for all swaps with that counterparty. Legal recognition of close-out netting by all nations participating in the Basle Agreement would reduce the amount of capital that must be held against derivatives positions. On the basis of surveys of swap dealers, the industry contends that netting would reduce capital allocated against the average swap portfolio by half (*Risk*, April 1993, 7). Although the legality of close-out netting has been affirmed by the U.S. regulatory authorities and bankruptcy courts, in many other nations netting's status is ambiguous. Legal certainty is regarded as a necessary condition for changing capital allocation from a gross to a net basis.

The wisdom of a change to a net basis for risk-based capital is an open question. Would a shift to netting increase systemic risk? Exploration of this issue is an area calling for careful academic research.

Wall, Pringle, and McNulty propose guidelines for developing a measurement of interest rate risk for setting risk-based capital. At present, capital is not allocated to cover the interest rate risk of on- and off-balance-sheet positions. Like Cohen and Gilkeson and Smith, these authors argue that duration-based measures are likely to be deficient. They suggest that regulators rely on bank's own internal risk standards and allow a trade-off in the determination of risk-based capital: banks that have less sophisticated risk-monitoring capabilities or more complex off-balance-sheet posi-

tions would have to set aside higher capital, everything else being equal, than banks with more sophisticated monitoring systems or simpler positions.

The method for including an institution's interest rate risk in a risk-based capital standard is still open. Pursuant to the requirements of FDICIA, a new proposal by the Federal Reserve, Office of the Comptroller of the Currency, and Federal Deposit Insurance Agency is essentially consistent with many of the elements of Wall, Pringle, and McNulty. Depository institutions that have the capability to monitor interest rate risk internally can rely on (or may be required to use) their own systems. Other institutions must use a simulation (or scenario) analysis prescribed by the regulators that parallels duration analysis.

Sheila L. Tschinkel
Senior Vice President and Director of Research

B. Frank King
Vice President and Associate Director of Research

Market Relationships

Globalization of Stock, Futures, and Options Markets

Peter A. Abken

This article was originally published in the Atlanta Fed's July/August 1991 Economic Review. *The author is a senior economist in the financial section of the Atlanta Fed's research department.*

Of the trendy buzzwords to emerge from the 1980s, "globalization" surely ranks high on the list of overused words in the business lexicon, but not without good reason. The word has become associated with financial markets' growing interconnections, facilitated largely by advances in communications and computer technology. Capital moves across national borders primarily as investment flows and secondarily as international trade financing. In dollar terms, global financial transactions today stand at a historically high multiple of world trade volume (John G. Heimann 1989). Record trade imbalances, however, have also contributed to financial interdependence, the most prominent example being the net current account surplus of Japan, leading to large overseas investments of the surplus, and the net deficit of the United States, necessitating borrowing from abroad.

Financial transactions' increasing volume and their decreasing costs have put strong competitive pressures on financial institutions to change the ways in which they intermediate credit and other financial flows. The financial industry has turned to automated securities trading, which is transforming and displacing the face-to-face and mouth-to-telephone methods of making financial transactions and strengthening the globalization or internationalization of securities markets in the process. Automation of trading encompasses a number of innovations that have improved the efficiency of making financial transactions. The technologies range from quotation and communications systems that facilitate traditional trading methods to so-called screen trading systems that supplant them. Their operation can be confined to one organized financial exchange, as the New York Stock Exchange's SuperDot system is, or can link many organized exchanges, as the Chicago Mercantile Exchange's Globex system does. For convenience in this discussion of the gradual automation of securities trading, these innovations will be referred to generically as automated trading systems.

This article examines currently running and proposed automated systems for many of the world's principal organized exchanges for common stock, futures, and option contracts. These exchanges are voluntary associations of members who come together to trade securities in auction markets, paying for the right to trade on an exchange—they buy a "seat" on the exchange. They generally trade for their own accounts and for outside customers. In contrast, participants in over-the-counter (OTC) markets, who are geographically dispersed, are brought together by telephone and computer lines. Over-the-counter trades go through dealers, who quote prices to buy and sell. The National Association of Securities Dealers (NASD) is one of several important OTC markets for common stocks in the United States that will be discussed below.

The article concludes with a section on market performance and regulation that takes a broader perspective on globalization. The perceived impact of globalization is closely tied to one's view of market efficiency. Integrating markets through electronic trading may reduce the magnitude of certain kinds of price shocks that propagate across markets because of a lack of information about the sources of such shocks. If markets are efficient, twenty-four-hour trading has the potential to reduce such market volatility. On the other hand, some market observers and participants, believing that markets are inefficient and excessively volatile, have proposed measures to curb speculative activity and the volatility they believe it engenders. The continuing reduction in transactions costs through technological innovation may only exacerbate market volatility. The final section considers this debate.

The Growth of International Securities Trading

Since the 1980s, securities markets of all kinds have been developing rapidly around the world. The volume of equity and bond market transactions has grown steadily, and both American purchases and sales of foreign securities and foreign purchases and sales of U.S. securities have been expanding, as Table 1 shows. A useful indicator of market activity, the growth in transactions volume coincided with in-

creases in volatility of most financial markets, which has been attributed to causes ranging from deregulation of financial markets, fiscal and trade imbalances, and so forth, to out-and-out irrationality and a gambling-casino mentality among traders. Some economists have recommended taxing securities transactions to alleviate the apparently unnecessary volatility.[1] On the other hand, there are substantive reasons for expecting that transactions volume will increase as uncertainty about "fundamentals" rises. For one thing, trading securities is necessary to adjust portfolios optimally in response to changing expected securities' payoffs.[2] In addition, volatility is a prime factor motivating financial risk management, which has spawned a variety of derivative instrument markets. Options and futures markets, for example, deal in contracts that are valued on the basis of stock, bond, and other primary securities prices. A discussion of the growth of primary and derivative securities markets follows.

Equities. Table 1 shows international equity market transactions, comparing activity for selected countries and regions in 1980 with 1990. The sum of purchases and sales, referred to here as transactions volume, measures the total transactions in equity markets by foreigners in U.S. stock markets and by Americans in foreign stock markets.[3] The dollar volume of transactions in 1980 and in 1990 was greater for foreigners transacting in U.S. markets than for Americans dealing in foreign markets. However, the overall margin of foreign volume over domestic volume diminished from 321 percent in 1980 to 43 percent in 1990.[4] The absolute levels of dollar purchases and sales have increased markedly, well in excess of the dollar's inflation rate and twice as fast as the growth of transactions volume on domestic exchanges during this period (Joseph A. Grundfest 1990, 349).

The compound annual growth rate for foreign transactions volume in U.S. securities was 17 percent, while the growth rate for U.S. transactions volume in foreign securities was 30 percent. Japanese transactions in U.S. stock markets grew at a 41 percent compound annual rate, faster than those of all other countries or regions. Japan's percentage share of the international transactions volume has correspondingly risen from 2.5 percent to 16 percent over the decade. The United Kingdom accounts for nearly half the 1990 European volume, up substantially from 1980. Much of its transactions volume probably stems from Middle Eastern and other non-United Kingdom buying and selling of U.S. stocks that occurs through London's markets, which are the preeminent financial

Table 1
Transactions Volume in Stocks

	Foreign Transactions in U.S. Securities					U.S. Transactions in Foreign Securities			
	Purchases[a]	Sales[a]	Aggregate Purchases and Sales[a]	Percentage Share of Market		Purchases[a]	Sales[a]	Aggregate Purchases and Sales[a]	Percentage Share of Market
1990									
France	5.82	7.01	12.83	3.55		6.05	5.90	11.95	4.72
Germany	5.90	6.27	12.17	3.37		6.69	7.45	14.14	5.58
United Kingdom	44.94	48.07	93.01	25.74		44.80	45.52	90.32	35.64
Total Europe	84.95	93.53	178.47	49.39		74.53	78.40	152.94	60.36
Japan	27.47	30.38	57.85	16.01		30.89	31.52	62.41	24.63
Canada	19.52	18.63	38.14	10.56		4.78	4.92	9.70	3.83
Total Worldwide	173.04	188.34	361.37	100.00		122.49	130.89	253.38	100.00
1980									
France	2.73	2.24	4.97	6.60		0.47	0.67	1.14	6.36
Germany	2.75	2.56	5.30	7.05		0.24	0.22	0.46	2.57
United Kingdom	7.44	4.94	12.38	16.44		1.38	1.36	2.75	15.38
Total Europe	24.62	21.55	46.16	61.32		3.16	3.62	6.78	37.97
Japan	0.87	1.03	1.90	2.52		0.93	1.77	2.70	15.10
Canada	6.35	5.48	11.83	15.71		3.02	3.66	6.68	37.43
Total Worldwide	40.32	34.96	75.28	100.00		7.89	9.97	17.85	100.00

Compound Annual Growth Rate, 1980-90
(percent)

	Foreign	U.S.
France	9.95	26.53
Germany	8.66	40.88
United Kingdom	22.35	41.81
Total Europe	14.48	36.56
Japan	40.73	36.92
Canada	12.42	3.80
Total Worldwide	16.98	30.38

[a] *In billions of U.S. dollars.*
Source: Derived by the Federal Reserve Bank of Atlanta from U.S. Department of the Treasury, *U.S. Treasury Bulletin* (Winter 1991), Table CM-V-5; (Winter 1981), Table CM-VI-10.

markets in Europe. From 1980 to 1990, both the United Kingdom and Japan were responsible for net inflows (cumulative excess of purchases over sales) into U.S. equity markets of about 17 billion dollars each.

U.S. transactions volume in foreign equities also grew markedly during the decade, almost twice as fast as foreign volume. This growth rate reflects the low 1980 level of U.S. purchases and sales of foreign stocks relative to foreign participation in U.S. markets. The transactions volume shares in the United Kingdom and Japan realized significant increases from 1980 to 1990, as did the corresponding compound annual growth rates. Though the share of overall volume was still relatively low in 1990, the growth rate for German stock market participation by U.S. investors was about as rapid as the rates for the United Kingdom and Japan.

Chart 1 gives another view of world equity trading, showing the dollar trading volume in major world equity markets. Clearly, the New York and Tokyo markets surpass other world markets. Each of these will be discussed further in connection with automated trading systems.

Bonds. The dollar transactions volume for bonds was approximately ten times as large as that for stocks in 1990; they were roughly comparable a decade earlier. The domestic and foreign bonds included in Table 2 exclude short-term bonds with remaining times to maturity of less than one year. Although there is considerable trading in these short-term securities, much of that trading includes government intervention in foreign exchange markets, leading in turn to sizable purchases and sales of short-term government securities such as U.S. Treasury bills. Long-term securities better gauge the growth in private cross-border capital movements. The securities included in U.S. market transactions are marketable Treasury and federally sponsored agency bonds as well as corporate bonds.

Almost all bonds are traded over-the-counter, though some are traded on organized exchanges. Somewhat less than 10 percent of all U.S. corporate bonds are traded on organized exchanges (Jack Clark Francis 1991, 87). As seen in Table 2, most foreign transactions in U.S. bond markets are in government bonds. Although the bond market is primarily

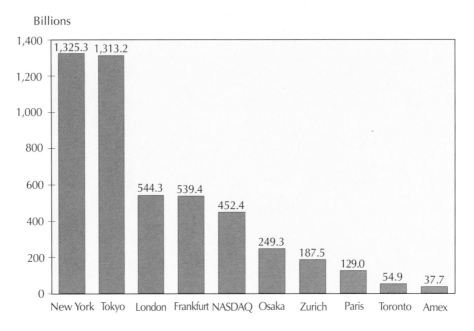

Chart 1
Dollar Trading Volume in Major World Equity Markets in 1990[a]

Billions

New York: 1,325.3
Tokyo: 1,313.2
London: 544.3
Frankfurt: 539.4
NASDAQ: 452.4
Osaka: 249.3
Zurich: 187.5
Paris: 129.0
Toronto: 54.9
Amex: 37.7

[a] *Annual trading volume is the sum of each issue's daily share volume multiplied by its closing price and aggregated over all issues and trading days in the year.*
Source: NASDAQ (1991).

Table 2
Transactions Volume in Long-Term Bonds[a]

	Foreign Transactions in U.S. Securities				U.S. Transactions in Foreign Securities			
	Purchases[b]	Sales[b]	Aggregate Purchases and Sales[b]	Percentage Share of Market	Purchases[b]	Sales[b]	Aggregate Purchases and Sales[b]	Percentage Share of Market
1990								
France	13.47	12.78	26.24	0.68	14.67	15.50	30.17	4.65
Germany	45.31	39.87	85.18	2.21	15.91	18.23	34.14	5.26
United Kingdom	564.62	555.67	1,120.29	29.08	113.95	114.16	228.10	35.12
Total Europe	804.32	773.85	1,578.17	40.97	185.46	189.78	375.25	57.77
Japan	731.08	744.96	1,476.04	38.32	36.71	43.50	80.21	12.35
Canada	66.81	69.46	136.26	3.54	54.48	56.91	111.39	17.15
Total Worldwide	1,945.19	1,906.80	3,851.99	100.00	313.58	335.93	649.50	100.00
1980								
France	0.71	0.45	1.16	0.94	0.66	0.62	1.28	3.64
Germany	2.54	5.21	7.75	6.31	0.45	0.43	0.88	2.50
United Kingdom	22.36	20.15	42.51	34.60	6.07	6.16	12.23	34.97
Total Europe	30.29	30.37	60.65	49.37	9.09	9.59	18.68	53.39
Japan	2.59	4.21	6.81	5.54	1.35	2.65	4.00	11.44
Canada	0.96	2.39	3.35	2.73	2.20	2.42	4.63	13.22
Total Worldwide	66.61	56.25	122.86	100.00	17.07	17.92	34.98	100.00

Compound Annual Growth Rate, 1980-90
(percent)

	Foreign	U.S.
France	36.66	37.22
Germany	27.09	44.24
United Kingdom	38.70	33.99
Total Europe	38.53	34.99
Japan	71.24	34.96
Canada	44.86	37.46
Total Worldwide	41.13	33.93

[a] *Bonds having maturities of one year or greater.*
[b] *In billions of U.S. dollars.*
Source: Derived by the Federal Reserve Bank of Atlanta from U.S. Department of the Treasury, *U.S. Treasury Bulletin* (Winter 1991), Table CM-V-5; (Winter 1981), Table CM-VI-10.

over-the-counter (and thus not the point of interest in this discussion), the growing number of international transactions in bonds has stimulated derivative securities markets worldwide. Increasingly, derivative securities trade in one country on underlying securities originating in another. Several examples—including the futures contracts on U.S. Treasury bonds that trade on the Tokyo Stock Exchange (TSE) and the German government bond futures that trade at the London International Financial Futures Exchange (LIFFE, pronounced "life")—will be discussed below.

The picture of globalization that emerged from the earlier consideration of equities trading comes into even sharper relief when cross-border bond trading is examined. Aside from the greater magnitude of dollar transactions volume mentioned earlier, the most striking feature is the uniformly high growth rates across countries and regions from 1980 to 1990. Equity market growth rates, particularly for French and German involvement in U.S. markets, do not show this evenness. All but one compound annual growth rate exceeds 30 percent. The transactions volume of Japanese investors in U.S. markets increased 71 percent annually! Similar to the equity data, the Japanese share in transactions volume rose over the decade from 5.5 percent to 38 percent, while the European share declined from 49 percent to 41 percent. U.S. investor participation in foreign bond markets mirrored the increased foreign activity in U.S. markets.

Futures and Options. Exchange-traded futures contracts have a long and—to some—notorious history. Commodity futures originated at the Chicago Board of Trade (CBOT) in the 1860s (see Chicago Board of Trade 1985, 1-4). Not until 1972 were the first financial futures introduced at the Chicago Mercantile Exchange (CME, or the "Merc"). The development of these currency futures reflected the anticipated hedging needs stemming from the decision allowing the dollar and other major currencies to float against one another rather than to be maintained at fixed parities. At the time agricultural contracts accounted for 97 percent of the CME's volume (William J. Brodsky 1990). Many new financial futures and options soon followed. The CBOT established the Chicago Board Options Exchange (CBOE) in 1973 to trade options on listed stocks; they created the Ginnie Mae futures contract in 1975.[5] The CME countered with its Treasury bill futures contract in 1976; the CBOT, with its Treasury bond futures contract in 1977. The latter is the most heavily traded futures contract in the world today.

In the early 1980s, these exchanges developed futures and options contracts on equity indexes, such as the Standard and Poor's (S&P) 500 futures (CME) and S&P 100 options contracts (CBOE). At the time of the market crash of October 1987, the S&P 500 futures achieved a notoriety in the minds of many investors and stock exchange members that lingers to this day. While a number of factors had contributed to the crash, the use of index futures in conjunction with so-called program trading, which uses the automated order-routing system at the New York Stock Exchange, was widely blamed. (This subject will be considered further in a later section.) In any case, many exchanges, including the New York Stock Exchange, greatly expanded capacity through automation to handle future surges in volume.

While volume in other futures contracts has remained generally flat during the 1980s, financial futures volume has grown steadily (see Robert W. Kolb 1991, 23). For example, by 1989 financial futures volume made up 91 percent of the CME's volume, with only the remaining 9 percent accounted for by commodity futures. At all U.S. futures exchanges in 1972, the total annual volume of futures trading measured by the number of contracts traded was 18.3 million. In 1990 this volume had risen to 276.5 million contracts, a compound annual growth rate of 16.3 percent. Though the U.S. exchanges are the world's most established, foreign futures markets are rapidly making inroads in the share of trading volume. For instance, since the opening of the London International Financial Futures Exchange in 1982, thirty options and futures exchanges have opened outside the United States (Brodsky 1991).

The U.S. exchanges are still dominant in the world, but, as Table 3 shows, foreign options and futures markets that emerged in the 1980s are also well represented in the top-twenty ranks. In particular, the Osaka Securities Exchange's Nikkei 225 index futures contract and Tokyo International Financial Futures Exchange's Euroyen contract surged in volume during 1990.

Automation of Equity Markets

Individual stock exchanges everywhere have adopted some degree of automation, reflecting the exigencies of competitive pressures from domestic as well as foreign exchanges. Derivative securities markets have aggressively employed the new technologies to

Table 3
Most Heavily Traded Futures and Options Contracts

Rank 1990	Rank 1989	Contract[a]	Exchanges[b]	Contract Volume 1990	Contract Volume 1989
1	1	T-bond (f)	CBOT	75,499,000	70,303,000
2	2	S&P 100 (o)	CBOE	58,845,000	58,371,000
3	3	Eurodollar (f)	CME	34,694,000	40,818,000
4	4	T-bond (o)	CBOT	27,315,000	20,784,000
5	5	Crude oil (f)	Nymex	23,687,000	20,535,000
6	6	Japanese government bond (f)	TSE	16,307,000	18,942,000
7	7	Notionnel government bond (f)	MATIF	15,996,000	15,005,000
8	30	Euroyen (f)	TIFFE	14,414,000	4,495,000
9	25	Nikkei 225 (f)	Osaka	13,589,000	5,443,000
10	8	S&P 500 (f)	CME	12,139,000	10,560,000
11	18	S&P 500 (o)	CBOE	12,089,000	6,274,000
12	11	Corn (f)	CBOT	11,423,000	9,271,000
13	10	Soybeans (f)	CBOT	10,302,000	9,635,000
14	9	Gold (f)	Comex	9,730,000	9,999,000
15	26	German bond (f)	LIFFE	9,582,000	5,330,000
16	17	Nikkei 225 (o)	Osaka	9,186,000	6,610,000
17	12	Deutsche Mark (f)	CME	9,169,000	8,186,000
18	16	Short Sterling (f)	LIFFE	8,355,000	7,131,000
19	13	Yen (f)	CME	7,437,000	7,824,000
20	15	Notionnel government bond (o)	MATIF	7,410,000	7,177,000

[a] (f) = futures contract; (o) = options contract.
[b] Nymex is the New York Mercantile Exchange; Comex is the Commodities Exchange (New York); other exchanges are described in the text.
Source: *Futures and Options World: 1991 Annual Worldwide Directory and Review* (Surrey, England: Metal Bulletin Journals Ltd., 1991), 9. Data used by permission of the publisher.

link exchanges. The discussion below considers the movement toward automated trading in equity markets and derivative markets.

New York Stock Exchange. U.S. equity markets are the largest and most liquid in the world. The biggest domestic exchange, the New York Stock Exchange (NYSE), is facing mounting competitive pressures from regional domestic exchanges and from foreign stock exchanges. The heart of the New York Stock Exchange is its specialists, charged by the exchange to maintain "fair and orderly" markets in the individual listed stocks assigned to them. The New York Stock Exchange is organized as a continuous two-sided auction market, with the specialist acting as auctioneer for incoming orders to buy or sell a particular stock. The specialist conducts an auction in the sense that he or she continually adjusts a stock's price to balance supply and demand throughout the trading day. She at times may also need to take the buy or sell side to keep prices from fluctuating too greatly. Overall about 10 percent of share purchases and 10 percent of sales on the NYSE result in specialists' staking their own capital in the trade (New York Stock Exchange 1991a, 17). This role is part of their obligation to the exchange in performing the specialist's function.

Also, the specialist has access to the computerized limit-order book, which displays orders to buy or sell if the market price reaches a specified level. Because of their knowledge, specialists have an informational advantage over traders off the exchange floor.[6] Although they may profit from their inventory position, exchange rules constrain trading for their own accounts. On every trade the specialist also receives the difference between the sale price (the ask) and the purchase price (the bid). Other market participants are willing to incur these costs in order to gain the liquidity specialists provide. However, the specialist's role is being questioned with increasing frequency: How important is it? Is the provision of liquidity worth the price?

Since the rise of institutional trading in the 1960s, the so-called upstairs market has developed, partly insulating the specialists from having to take positions in large blocks of 10,000 or more shares. Such blocks sent directly to the specialists may cause too much price fluctuation and be too risky for them to handle. Instead, block positioners match buyers and sellers and may also take positions in blocks themselves. Blocks are then sent to the specialist post for execution. Because of economies of scale, low commission rates are charged for block transactions. During the latter half of the 1980s, about half the NYSE's volume was accounted for by institutional block trading (NASDAQ 1991, 39). Preferring new, automated mechanisms that are even cheaper, institutional investors are beginning to dispense altogether with using the exchange.

More efficient handling of trading volume led to the development of the NYSE's automated routing system in 1976 called the Super Designated Order Turnaround System (SuperDot). SuperDot routes market orders of less than 2,099 shares to the specialist (or to a floor broker) for rapid execution, usually in less than a minute.[7] The system can also route large orders to the specialist. SuperDot is frequently used by program traders dealing in whole portfolios of stocks; they route lists of stocks through the system to appropriate specialists. The system handles market orders of as many as 30,099 shares and limit orders of as many as 99,999 shares of individual stocks, although the specialists are not obligated to execute these orders as rapidly as the New York Stock Exchange requires for smaller ones. Odd-lot orders of less than 100 shares are executed automatically by SuperDot at the prevailing price quote. About 75 percent of daily NYSE orders are processed through the system (New York Stock Exchange 1991a, 21).

Regionals. Regional exchanges have developed their own versions of automated order-routing and execution systems for small trades. The Midwest Stock Exchange (MSE), Pacific Stock Exchange (PSE), Philadelphia Stock Exchange (PHLX), and Boston Stock Exchange (BSE) use systems named MAX, SCOREX, PACE, and BEACON, respectively.[8] The Cincinnati Stock Exchange (CSE) is in fact an over-the-counter market with competing market makers. All trades on the CSE pass through the National Securities Trading System (NSTS), which is an order-matching system akin to the NASDAQ system to be discussed shortly (U.S. Securities and Exchange Commission 1991, 23-26).

The Securities Act amendments of 1975 mandated the Securities and Exchange Commission (SEC) to establish a national market system with the objectives of increasing competition among market makers at different exchanges and strengthening links among different exchanges (see Francis 1991, 132-33). One major change was that negotiated commissions replaced fixed commissions on securities sales and purchases. Another consequence of the act was the establishment of the "Consolidated Tape," which continuously lists the trades at seven stock exchanges and two over-the-counter markets (NASD and Instinet). Since 1978 the regional exchanges, the American Stock Exchange (Amex), NASD, and NYSE have been linked by the Intermarket Trading System (ITS), which enables a broker or specialist at one exchange to send orders to buy or sell at another exchange showing a better price.

Most of the stocks traded via the ITS communication system are NYSE-listed stocks, and a much smaller number traded are Amex-listed and regionally listed stocks. At the broker's or specialist's discretion, orders are routed to the exchange showing the best bid or offer. Once a small order is received, the BEACON, MAX, and SCOREX systems "expose" it to the specialist for fifteen seconds during which he or she may better the bid or offer price; otherwise, the order is automatically executed at the specialist's quoted bid or offer. (PACE automatically executes all small orders.) The Amex has an order-routing system called Post Execution Reporting (PER) that is very similar to the NYSE's SuperDot. Amex members can send orders for as many as 2,000 shares directly to the specialist using the system and receive an execution report for the trades (U.S. Congress 1990b, 49-50).

The regional exchanges and Amex have only a small slice of the trading-volume pie. Table 4 shows where they stand in relation to the NYSE and NASD, viewed both in terms of share volume and in terms of dollar volumes.

NASDAQ. National Association of Securities Dealers runs a telecommunications network called NASDAQ, for NASD Automated Quotations. In this over-the-counter market NASD dealers compete with one another in making bids and offers on stocks.[9] These OTC securities tend to be smaller capitalization stocks that do not meet exchange listing requirements; only a subset of them are also listed on organized exchanges.[10] To buy or sell a stock, an investor

Table 4
U.S. Equity Markets: 1990 Share and Dollar Volumes

	Share Volume		Dollar Volume	
	Millions	Percent	Millions	Percent
NASDAQ	33,380	39.2	$ 452,430	21.8
NASDAQ/OTC Trading in Listed Securities	2,589	3.0	86,494	4.2
Amex	3,329	3.9	37,715	1.8
Regionals (BSE, CSE, MSE, PSE, and PHLX)	6,208	7.3	178,139	8.5
NYSE	39,665	46.6	1,325,332	63.7
Totals	**85,171**	**100.0**	**$2,080,110**	**100.0**

Source: NASDAQ (1991).

calls a dealer, who checks NASDAQ to find the best quotation from competing dealers in a particular stock at the lowest cost (that is, lowest bid-ask spread and commission). Unlike stock exchange specialists, dealers are not obligated to provide liquidity through their own position-taking. The OTC market instead relies on interdealer competition.

About 13 percent of OTC transactions are handled by NASD's Small Order Execution System (SOES), in operation since 1985. Public buy or sell orders of as many as 1,000 shares go through SOES to the dealer offering the best price quote. However, if there are currently better price quotes on NASDAQ outside SOES, that dealer is required to fill the order at the better price.[11] In 1990 SOES added the capacity to automatically execute matching limit orders entered into the system.

Another NASDAQ system is SelectNet, which allows NASDAQ members to send buy or sell securities orders to other system members' terminals. SelectNet enables market makers to accept and execute orders partially or fully as well as to conduct price and quantity negotiations. System users are therefore not anonymous. NASDAQ securities orders must be for more than 1,000 shares.[12]

NASDAQ leads other domestic exchanges, most notably the New York Stock Exchange, in the indirect trading of foreign equities. This indirect trading is through American Depository Receipts (ADRs). Foreign corporations have American commercial or investment banks buy their equity shares and place them in a trust account, against which ADR certificates are issued. These certificates are negotiable and can be traded on exchanges and through NASDAQ. Investors find ADRs convenient because their purchase and sale and the distribution of dividend payments are entirely in dollars, not foreign currency. Foreign-currency denominated cash dividends are converted into dollars by the trustee, usually a commercial bank, and are passed on to the American Depository Receipts holders. The foreign corporation benefits by not having to comply with the SEC's disclosure requirements and other regulations enforced for domestic corporations (see Francis 1991, 62, 806-7).

In 1990 NASDAQ reached new records in ADR trading with a trading volume of 2.2 billion shares of eighty-seven ADR issues. In comparison, the NYSE had a 1.4 billion share volume for sixty-two ADR issues. NASDAQ dollar volume was 21 billion, while the dollar volume in foreign securities directly listed on NASDAQ was 7 billion.[13] NASDAQ is expanding in 1991 to offer an international quotation network based in the United Kingdom called NASDAQ International.

Instinet. NASDAQ dealers earn their livelihood from the difference in price between what they will pay for stock and their selling price, the bid-ask spread.

That spread has come under pressure to narrow because of an electronic order-execution system called Instinet, owned by Reuters Holdings PLC. Instinet is a screen trading system in that it enables subscribers to trade anonymously. These participants include not only OTC broker-dealers but also institutional investors. For example, NASDAQ dealers can trade with other NASDAQ dealers on Instinet to adjust their inventory of stocks. These trades can be accomplished within the bid-ask spread quoted on NASDAQ so that NASDAQ quotes would be unaffected. Institutional investors have also been trading actively on Instinet at much lower spreads than through NASDAQ dealers or exchange specialists. To stay competitive, dealers have had to cut their spreads.[14]

Most Instinet trades involve OTC and listed U.S. stocks, but an increasing number are in British, French, German, and other European stocks as well. The system, on-line an average of fourteen hours per day, can remain operational almost around-the-clock during periods of heavy trading.[15]

Anonymity is important to traders because a trader's identity can reveal how often and how much he or she is buying or selling, information that could move prices against the trader. For example, traders usually avoid selling large orders at once because doing so may prompt a stock's price to be bid down rapidly in the process of making the trade, on the assumption that some bad news is behind the sale. In that scenario, known as adverse selection risk, large orders will be put on the market in smaller blocks. Instinet allows traders to poll each other almost instantaneously on a prospective trade. They can send anonymous messages over the system to particular traders to negotiate quantity or price. They can see all of the bids and offers on particular stocks at a given time on the Instinet "book."

Madoff Investment Securities. This firm has set itself up in direct competition with NYSE specialists. Madoff makes a market in 350 of the S&P 500 stocks by attracting mainly retail trades from brokers, paying them a penny per share for orders. These orders are executed at prices that match the best quoted on any exchange, as reported through ITS. Madoff operates through the Cincinnati Stock Exchange's National Securities Trading System, which is essentially an over-the-counter market. Because of low overhead costs, his commission costs are much lower than for trades carried out on an exchange floor. According to a recent estimate, this firm alone generates 2 percent of the daily trading volume in NYSE listed stocks (Barbara Howard 1991, 16; William E. Sheeline 1990, 122).

Crossing Networks. To reduce transactions costs, many institutional investors have turned to so-called crossing networks, such as Instinet's The Crossing Network and Posit (Portfolio System for Institutional Trading) of Jefferies & Company, a registered broker-dealer. Many institutional investors deal in indexed equity portfolios—for example, a portfolio mimicking the S&P 500 index. These "passive" portfolio managers are not concerned about the precise timing of trade executions for individual stocks making up an index. For institutional investors seeking to trade in whole portfolios of stocks, crossing networks offer a low-cost alternative to transactions on organized stock exchanges.

The Crossing Network allows whole portfolios of stock to be bought or sold at primary markets' closing prices (for example, NYSE closing prices) and the mean of the bid-ask OTC prices. Because the trades are based on the closing price, and hence passive, there is no "market impact" on the trades themselves—that is, large buy and sell orders are matched or crossed at that price, unaffected by the unfavorable price movement such a trade might ordinarily produce. The price does not adjust to balance supply and demand, so some orders will go unmatched in a single after-hours session.

Posit is a crossing network that operates during trading hours as well as off-hours. Portfolio trades can be executed at the primary markets' opening, at prespecified times of day after the opening, or at closing prices. This system has many options that users can select; their choices affect the cost of their trades. For example, trades not matched through Posit's computer can be canceled, held for matching at a later time, sent to the primary markets for execution, or "price-guaranteed" by Jefferies (that is, Jefferies takes the other side of the trade). These alternatives entail different commission costs. The amount of information about a prospective trade, like the size of the order or identity of the investor, may be revealed or hidden from other system users (U.S. Securities and Exchange Commission 1991, 83-86).

Overseas Trading. The NYSE is also affected by the movement of institutional program trades overseas, particularly to London's over-the-counter market. A common transaction involves a stock-index futures purchase or sale on a U.S. futures exchange with a subsequent exchange-for-physicals (EFP) transaction to unwind the futures position.[16] For example, a portfolio manager who wishes to buy an S&P 500-

indexed portfolio could buy the underlying stocks on the New York Stock Exchange or alternatively buy S&P 500 contracts on the Chicago Mercantile Exchange. In the latter case, the long futures position could then be offset through an EFP over the counter in London by finding a trader (or traders) short the S&P 500 futures who holds the underlying stock portfolio. The cash prices and futures price for the EFP transaction would be determined by negotiation but typically reflect the underlying stocks' closing prices on the New York Stock Exchange, Amex, and OTC markets as well as the futures on the transaction date. The parties have traded stocks outside of the NYSE and have closed out their futures positions off the Chicago Mercantile Exchange exchange floor, saving commissions and market impact costs.[17] Similar over-the-counter program transactions also occur that do not involve index futures.

About 10 to 15 million NYSE shares currently trade after-hours in London every day (Kevin G. Salwen and Craig Torres 1991, C1). This exodus from the exchange floor was spurred in part by a postcrash NYSE rule requiring immediate display of program trades' price and volume.

SPAworks. A new system operated by R. Steven Wunsch takes after-hours trading a step further. He has designed a system, SPAworks, to trade stocks in an after-hours call market, which involves a single-price auction. This institutional arrangement was actually prevalent in the nineteenth century before the advent of continuous auction markets, and many relatively illiquid international exchanges still rely on it (see below). SPAworks has been operational since April 1991.

The system works by allowing buy and sell orders to accumulate after the NYSE closes at 4:00 P.M. (U.S. Securities and Exchange Commission 1991, 73-77; Wunsch 1991). At a predetermined time before the next day's opening, a single computerized auction of each individual stock would be held, whereby trades would be consummated at the price resulting in the largest volume of trade. Participants entering bids above or below the auction price are able to execute their trades at the auction price. Other orders go unmatched. This system saves the cost of paying for the immediate liquidity provided on the exchange floor.

Off-Hours Trading. In response to the inroads these outside trading systems have made, the NYSE announced in May 1991 that it would institute two after-hours sessions. "Crossing Session I" runs from 4:15 until 5:00 P.M. and allows investors to buy and sell at the 4:00 P.M. closing price. Once submitted by NYSE members through SuperDot, single-sided orders are

matched against others based on the times they were submitted. Matched single-sided orders and paired (prearranged) orders are then executed through Super-Dot at 5:00 P.M. "Crossing Session II," which operates from 4:00 to 5:15 P.M., specifically accommodates program traders. After the close New York Stock Exchange member firms place paired orders for programs that contain at least fifteen NYSE-listed stocks having a one-million-dollar market value or more. These coupled orders are executed as soon as they are received by the system. To make the new sessions attractive to program traders, the NYSE has granted a

---

Physical marketplaces (the trading floors) are becoming obsolete, while "virtual" marketplaces—networks of computers and computer terminals—are emerging as the "site" for transactions.

---

nine-month exemption from being required to report price and volume information for individual program trades. Only the aggregate volume and dollar value of program trades are disseminated at 5:15 P.M. Single-sided and coupled order volume are each reported separately for Crossing Session I, beginning at 5:00 P.M. (Salwen and Torres 1991, C1; U.S. Securities and Exchange Commission 1991, 36-39; New York Stock Exchange 1991b, 1-5).

Foreign Equity Markets. Many foreign stock markets are considerably less liquid than U.S. stock markets, and their institutional arrangements reflect this fact. The Austrian and Norwegian stock markets simply hold a single daily call auction. Others use a mixed system of call auctions at some times of day and continuous trading at other times. Mixed auctions are prevalent in Belgium, Denmark, France, Italy, Spain, Sweden, and Switzerland.[18] The Australian, British, Canadian, French, and Japanese markets have automated trading systems. Four of the major automated exchanges are relatively well developed.

The Toronto Stock Exchange uses the Computer Assisted Trading System (CATS), which functions as an electronic auction for less actively traded stocks and is being updated to handle more active stocks. Broker-dealers using the system can choose to have their trades executed by either a specialist or computer. CATS currently handles about 75 percent of trades on the exchange, a small volume compared with that of major American exchanges (Hansell 1989, 93; U.S. Congress 1990b, 63; Howard 1991, 15). CATS also displays the best five buy and sell limit orders along with the name of the broker making the order (Hansell 1989, 93; Howard 1991, 15).

The Paris Bourse (stock exchange) relies on a licensed version of CATS, which is also under consideration for use at exchanges in Madrid, Brussels, and Sao Paulo (Hansell 1989, 93, 98; Ian Domowitz 1990, 170). The system used by the French exchange is named CAC, for Cotation Assistée Continu. This exchange, overshadowed by the London market, is much less liquid. In fact, exchange member firms hold a single daily auction in stocks complemented by forward trading in listed stocks using both continuous trading and call auctions in forward contracts (Richard Roll 1988, 29).

The London International Stock Exchange is a dealer market very similar in operation to NASDAQ. The ISE is the most active world market in foreign (non-United Kingdom) stock trading, which makes up slightly more than half of the exchange's volume. The average daily foreign issue volume was 1.3 billion pounds sterling per day in 1990. ISE members have benefited from the migration of some U.S. program trading. The ISE's analog to the NAS-DAQ quote-display system is the Stock Exchange Automated Quotation System (SEAQ); small orders of fewer than 5,000 shares are automatically executed on the Stock Automated Exchange Facility (SAEF).

The Tokyo Stock Exchange (TSE) has a system similar to Toronto's CATS. Its Computer Assisted Order Routing and Execution System (CORES) now handles all but 150 of the exchange's most actively traded issues; however, the TSE is moving toward a fully automated system. Instead of specialists, the exchange has a group of overseers, called *saitori*, who use computer screens to monitor the trades arranged by the computer and by floor traders and to approve the prices. The saitori can also allow CORES to generate trades automatically within a specified price range. In addition, they act as human circuit breakers on the exchange floor when trading becomes too volatile; they have the authority to suspend trading briefly (Hansell 1989, 97).

*F*utures and Options Markets

Like prices of exchange-traded stocks, futures prices are established through an auction system, but one with no counterpart to the single individual, the specialist, making a market in a stock. Instead, futures prices are determined by an auction known as the open-outcry system. Exchange members—floor traders—congregate at designated trading pits and shout bids and offers at each other or use hand signals to indicate trading intentions. Exchange officials record the price and amount of each transaction. Effective in providing liquidity, this system is also subject to error and even abuse.[19]

As discussed above, international competition is forcing efficiency-enhancing automation. Many new overseas exchanges are fully or partially automated and trade many of the same contracts as American exchanges, although their volume levels are usually much lower. Systems emerging on futures and options markets harbinger the internationalization soon to come. In particular, the Chicago Mercantile Exchange's Globex (Global Exchange) system is being designed to handle volumes that exceed current open-outcry volume levels at peak trading times.

Globex. Globex, expected to be operable in early 1992, will automate *and link* participating exchanges. To date, the Chicago Board of Trade and Marché à Terme des Instruments Financiers (MATIF), the French financial futures market, are members of Globex. Other exchanges in the Far East are considering joining Globex, including Australia's Sydney Futures Exchange (SFE) and possibly Japan's Osaka Securities Exchange, or OSE (Ginger Szala and Amy Rosenbaum 1990, 44). Globex will operate after-hours, beginning at 6 P.M. Chicago time, when Japanese markets open.

The genesis of Globex lay in efforts to extend the futures trading day. In 1984 the CME established a relationship with the newly founded Singapore International Monetary Exchange (SIMEX), a relationship based mainly on mutual advantages gained from trading compatible Eurodollar and foreign currency futures contracts. The two exchanges set up a mutual offset permitting contracts opened on one exchange to be closed on the other and vice versa. This link effectively lengthened the trading day almost to twenty-four hours, helping the Chicago exchange to secure a foothold in booming East Asian financial markets. SIMEX enjoyed the benefits of the additional liquidity generated by the infusion of Chicago-based trades. Also catering to growing interest from abroad, the Merc's Chicago rival, the Chicago Board of Trade, instituted nighttime trading of its Treasury bond futures contracts in April 1987. However, this insomniac trading, as one observer termed it, and the CME's mutual offset arrangement were regarded as stopgap measures ("Futures Markets" 1988). More efficient and less error-prone electronic trading seems inevitable; the Chicago Board of Trade joined with the Chicago Mercantile Exchange as a Globex partner in 1990. Up to that point the CBOT had been developing its own after-hours system, called Aurora, that would electronically emulate open-outcry trading. (See the discussion below of LIFFE's Automated Pit Trading for a similar system).

The mechanical heart of Globex is a network of computer screens. The system is a joint venture of the "partner exchanges" (CME, CBOT, and MATIF) and Reuters Holdings PLC, which already has a large presence in over-the-counter spot foreign exchange markets. The Reuters network of computer terminals in banks and brokerage firms numbers about 180,000 worldwide. The CME emphasizes that trading via Globex is an alternate method of placing an order on its exchange or on partner exchanges (Brodsky 1990, 621). Because the exchanges do not view Globex as a new kind of futures exchange, they argue that regulatory approval of the system (particularly in Japan) should be straightforward.

Globex automatically matches and executes orders entered into the system. The system first checks the credit standing of the member firm initiating a transaction and then matches orders based on the time an order was submitted and its price. Unlike standard open-outcry trading, Globex does not allow for orders to be executed at the prevailing market price (that is, there can be no market orders); all orders must be good-until-canceled limit orders (the order stays on the book until it is executed or canceled).[20]

Trades are confirmed at participants' screens, prices and quantities are reported through the system, trades are cleared, and buyers' and sellers' accounts are adjusted. Traders on Globex deal anonymously with one another, an important consideration for most participants, as mentioned earlier. However, Globex, like other automated systems, does produce a so-called electronic audit trail, which is regarded as an improvement over the open-outcry system's less accurate recording procedures. Electronic monitoring is expected to give traders more confidence in the trading process and makes the regulator's job easier.

Although trading has not yet begun on Globex, its relative performance compared with the open-outcry auction has been assessed by Domowitz (1991). Using simulated trading experiments, he finds that Globex is the more efficient trading mechanism according to a number of measures. Globex tends to result in lower price volatility and greater market liquidity, and the differences become more pronounced as the size of the market increases.

In contrast, Merton H. Miller (1990) argues that screen trading systems, especially of the order-matching type like Globex, put traders (market makers) at a disadvantage because they cannot observe the order flow on a screen as they can from the trading pit. Traders with more current information can take advantage of previously posted traders' price quotes. For this reason Miller does not believe that electronic systems will ever attract sufficient competing market-maker participation to match the liquidity of the most active trading pits. To date, most screen trading systems have been used at low-volume exchanges or for low-volume contracts. Validation of Miller's or Domowitz's predictions will have to await actual trading through Globex as well as more extensive deployment of other screen trading systems.

Domestic Options Markets. A number of automated trading systems have been introduced to facilitate options trading. The most significant of these is the Chicago Board Options Exchange's Retail Automatic Execution System (RAES), which has been in operation since 1985. The system now handles both index options, including the heavily traded S&P 100 index option, and all CBOE equity options (on individual stocks). About 3.5 percent of contract volume is currently executed through RAES (U.S. Securities and Exchange Commission 1991, 19). The Amex uses a system called AUTO-EX for market and limit orders of as many as twenty equity contracts. The system is designed for use of Amex member firms and exchange specialists. In addition, the Amex has a mutual-offset link with the European Options Exchange in Amsterdam for the stock index options contract on the Amex's Major Market Index, or MMI (U.S. Congress 1990b, 96). The Pacific Stock Exchange has a similar system for equity options called POETS (Pacific Options Exchange Trading System). The Philadelphia Stock Exchange uses AUTOM (Automated Options Market System) for equity options. The NYSE's SuperDot also routes orders for trades on its equity and equity-index options.

Delta Government Securities, a screen-based system for trading options on U.S. Treasury bills, notes, and bonds, is operated jointly by RMJ Securities and RMJ Options, which are a registered clearing agency and registered broker-dealer, respectively. Delta always stands as the intermediary between buyer and seller using the system. It effectively operates like an electronic options exchange, issuing any options traded through the system (U.S. Securities and Exchange Commission 1991, 89).

Foreign Derivatives Markets. There is stiff competition among European futures exchanges. Marché à Terme des Instruments Financiers vies with the London International Financial Futures Exchange primarily over the three-month Euro-deutsche mark futures (a futures on the three-month rate on interbank deutsche mark-denominated deposits). MATIF, Europe's most active futures exchange, joined Globex in November 1989 and plans to list its government bond future (the Notionnel) and its short-term interest-rate future (on PIBOR—Paris Interbank Offered Rate) on the system. Part of the motivation behind MATIF's Globex membership was to boost foreign participation on the exchange and lessen London's advantage of having the offices of almost 600 international banks and brokerage firms (Janet Lewis 1990, 130).

The fact that LIFFE also offers a futures contract on the long-term German government bond, the Bund, in part spurred the creation of the first German futures market, the Deutsche Terminbörse (DTB) in 1990. A consortium of fifty-three institutions, mostly large banks, belong to the DTB. The exchange offers futures contracts to compete with LIFFE's as well as stock options on German firms (Lewis 1990, 130).

The Frankfurt-based exchange is organized as a computer network that matches and processes all trades electronically. The automated trading system employed is based on a similar system used by the Swiss Options and Financial Futures Exchange (SOFFEX), also an entirely automated order-matching system that allows member firms to be market makers, quoting bids and offers. Trades are entered anonymously, so large trades can be anonymously negotiated over the system (Hansell 1989, 93). Five fully automated futures and options exchanges now operate worldwide, as seen in Table 5.

LIFFE has a partially automated system, called Automated Pit Trading (APT), that mimics actual pit-trading (London International Financial Futures Exchange 1991). The after-hours system operates from 4:30 to 6:00 P.M. local time, with access restricted to LIFFE members. APT is not driven by quote-making

dealers but by traders who post bids and offers for specified quantities. By the touch of a computer key, any trader can instantaneously accept bids and offers that appear on the screen. This system is the analog of the open-outcry method, in which bids and offers of floor traders are valid for "as long as the breath is warm." Because the futures exchanges deal in a limited set of futures contracts, liquidity is concentrated and rapid interactions between traders can be emulated on a screen. LIFFE expanded the system in 1990 to include a central limit-order book that enables purchases and sales of futures contracts if the market price reaches the posted limit price.

In Japan financial futures were banned until 1985. Regulators and legislators have gradually been deregulating and expanding their financial and derivative markets, and the Japanese have become very active in developing futures exchanges. Japanese firms are eager to use the new contracts. They may now deal directly in securities on foreign exchanges, and foreign brokerage firms may be members of Japanese futures exchanges (see Szala and Rosenbaum 1990, 42).

The first Japanese contracts were ten- and twenty-year yen bond futures, introduced on the Tokyo Stock Exchange in 1985. As of December 1989 the TSE offered U.S. Treasury bond futures equivalent to those of the CBOT. The Japanese Ministry of Finance, however, requires higher margins to be posted against Tokyo Stock Exchange futures contracts than does the Chicago Board of Trade for comparable positions. The higher margin levels apply even for Japanese firms taking positions in CBOT contracts, so these firms have little incentive to look abroad (Szala and Rosenbaum 1990, 42).

The TSE bond contracts, now the sixth most heavily traded future in the world (see Table 3), can all be traded through CORES. The TSE stock-index future on TOPIX (Tokyo Stock Price Index) is fully automated on CORES. Fully automated trading of a three-month Euroyen contract is conducted on the new Tokyo International Financial Futures Exchange (TIFFE), which competes against SIMEX in Singapore. SIMEX is still dominant in a number of contracts, including yen-U.S. dollar futures and Eurodollar futures, but it lags in Euroyen. Unlike TIFFE, SIMEX is a traditional open-outcry exchange.

The Nikkei 225 futures, the highest-volume Japanese index futures contract, trades at the Osaka Securities Exchange (OSE). The CME has acquired the rights to offer a Nikkei 225 contract on its exchange, though it would prefer to link up with the OSE through Globex (Szala and Rosenbaum 1990,

Table 5
Automated Trading Systems

System Operator	System
Equities	
American Stock Exchange	Post Execution Reporting
Amsterdam Stock Exchange .	System based on MSE's MAX
Australian Association of Stock Exchanges	Stock Exchange Automated Trading (SEAT)
Boston Stock Exchange	BSE Automated Communication and Order Routing Network (BEACON)
Cincinnati Stock Exchange	National Securities Trading System (NSTS)
Instinet Corporation	Instinet The Crossing Network
Jefferies & Company, Inc.	Portfolio System for Institutional Trading (Posit)
London International Stock Exchange	Stock Automated Exchange Facility (SAEF)
Midwest Stock Exchange	Midwest Automated Execution (MAX)
National Association of Securities Dealers	Small Order Execution Service (SOES) SelectNet Private Offerings, Resales, and Trading through Automated Linkages (PORTAL)
New York Stock Exchange	Designated Order Turnaround system (SuperDot) Crossing Sessions I and II
Pacific Stock Exchange	Securities Communication Order Routing and Execution System (SCOREX)
Paris Bourse	Cotation Assistée en Continu (CAC)
Philadelphia Stock Exchange	Philadelphia Automated Communication and Execution System (PACE)
Tokyo Stock Exchange	Computer Assisted Order Routing and Execution System (CORES)
Toronto Stock Exchange	Computer Assisted Trading System (CATS)
Wunsch Auction Systems, Inc.	SPAworks
Futures and Options	
American Stock Exchange (equity options)	AUTO-EX
Chicago Board Options Exchange	Retail Automated Exchange System (RAES)
Chicago Board of Trade	Globex
Chicago Mercantile Exchange	Globex
Deutsche Terminbörse	Fully automated, integrated clearing
Irish Futures and Options Exchange	Fully automated, ATS-2
London International Financial Futures Exchange	Automated Pit Trading (APT)

(table continues)

Table 5 (continued)

System Operator	System
Futures and Options	
London Traded Options Market	Associated with LIFFE
Marché à Terme des Instruments Financiers	Globex
New York Stock Exchange	SuperDot
New Zealand Futures and Options Exchange	Fully automated ATS system
Pacific Stock Exchange	Pacific Options Exchange Trading System (POETS)
Philadelphia Stock Exchange	Automated Options Market System (AUTOM)
Stockholm Option Market	Integrated clearing facilities based on electronic trading and telephone brokering
Sydney Futures Exchange	Sydney Computerized Overnight Market (SYCOM)
Swiss Options and Financial Futures Exchange	Fully automated; integrated clearing
Tokyo Stock Exchange	Derivative markets fully automated CORES-F

Sources: U.S. Securities and Exchange Commission (1991); Angrist (1991); U.S. Congress (1990b); Kang and Lawton (1990); Rosenbaum (1990); Hansell (1989).

44). The CME's first overtures to the Ministry of Finance, one of the chief regulators of Japanese exchanges, were made in August 1988 and are still ongoing. The CBOT now lists a Japanese stock-index futures on the TOPIX and several Japanese government bond futures and options.

Market Performance and Regulatory Issues

Regulation of securities markets in the United States is generally intended to ensure that securities trading is conducted openly and based on publicly available information. The Securities Act of 1933 and Securities Exchange Act of 1934 mandated extensive registration and disclosure requirements for firms issuing securities to the public. However, recent policy discussions have shifted regulators' sights to safe-guarding the performance and stability of financial markets.

The Brady Commission's recommendations in the wake of the 1987 crash stand out as the most sweeping proposals for changing the ways financial markets operate and for reorganizing their regulators' responsibilities.[21] To the Brady Commission and to a large number of market observers, the crash was prima facie evidence that private financial markets can fail—spectacularly. Concerns about the flow of information and the ability of participants to act on it superseded traditional questions about fairness and honesty in the marketplace.[22] The crash underscored the potential systemic risk of market failure as trading disruptions spread from one market to another. The problems can engulf the banking system as credit demands mount, for example, because of timing differences between the receipt and disbursement of funds by clearinghouses, straining liquidity and threatening widespread defaults.[23]

An important policy challenge is determining the appropriate mix of government and private-market actions to lessen the risk of securities market failure. It is feared that the electronic globalization of financial exchanges might contribute to systemic risks. The 1987 crash broadened the concerns, touching off a debate about whether a crash in one country's markets can trigger shocks beyond domestic boundaries to other countries' markets. The desirability and feasibility of international regulatory cooperation to contain such potential problems is an open question just beginning to be addressed (see Grundfest 1990; Paul Guy 1990; and U.S. Congress 1990a).

A survey of international regulatory issues is beyond the scope of this article. Rather, the following discussion focuses on the interconnections between markets and proposals to manage the international transmission of volatility. The basic issue to be considered has to do with the source of volatility and arguments for and against counteracting it. Since the stock market crash of October 1987, and even earlier in the decade, regulators and other market observers have become concerned about market volatility and cross-market spillovers.

The increasing prevalence of cross-border trading as well as the opening of new exchanges and deepening of existing ones would seem to imply that world financial markets are becoming unified. However, the evidence of such merging is not clear-cut. In fact, the Brady Commission concluded that through 1987 correlations of price movements from different world markets provide no evidence of closer links: "The correlations between the market in the U.S. and the markets in Germany and Japan appear to form totally random series. . . . [T]here is no evidence to suggest that the association is any closer today than it was a decade ago" (Nicolas F. Brady et al. 1988, II-6). Roll (1988) has observed that the only month in the 1980s in which all major world markets moved together was October 1987.

A number of recent academic papers address the question of world financial market integration. Using a sophisticated model of global equity market equilibrium (an international capital asset pricing model with time-varying moments), Campbell R. Harvey (1991) found evidence of a lack of integration, particularly for Japanese markets with the rest of the world. The basic object of study is the reward-to-risk ratio on equities required by investors. In a world of integrated markets, the reward-to-risk ratio would be the same in every equity market. In fact, this ratio turned out to be twice as large in Japanese markets as in U.S. markets.

In other words, Japanese investors require expected returns on stocks to be double the magnitude expected by U.S. investors. Complete integration across markets would equalize differences in the reward-to-risk ratio across countries because otherwise, for example, U.S. investors would skew their portfolios toward Japanese equities offering better trade-offs between return and risk than domestic equities. Increased U.S. purchases of Japanese stocks would bid up their prices and bid down U.S. stock prices, driving Japanese expected returns down and U.S. expected returns up. There are many subtleties and qualifications in this analysis, but the preponderance of evidence is against the simple hypothesis that world markets have become integrated.

The empirical work of David Neumark, P.A. Tinsley, and Suzanne Tosini reveals that price movements for U.S. stocks listed on New York, Tokyo, and London exchanges are more highly correlated during periods of high volatility than during times of low volatility because "only larger price changes pierce the transaction cost barriers between markets" (1991, 160). These authors noted that ordinarily the stock price volatility for this group of U.S. stocks (which are contained in the Dow Jones Industrial Average) is three times greater during New York trading hours than during London or Tokyo trading hours. In their view, this phenomenon occurs because the largest share of news relevant to the determination of the stock prices is disseminated during New York trading hours. This pattern was disrupted in the aftermath of the October 1987 crash when, in the authors' judgment, news was more globally dispersed and had mostly to do with "the volatile behavior of other investors" (176).

Yasushi Hamao, Ronald W. Masulis, and Victor Ng (1990) conducted another detailed study of intermarket linkages focusing on what they term price "volatility spillovers" among the New York, London, and Tokyo stock markets. For a subperiod that excludes the 1987 crash, they found that, while there was no significant transmission of volatility from Tokyo to either London or New York, the latter two cities' volatility did spill over to trading in Tokyo. When the post-1987 period is included, evidence indicates that all three markets were shocked by "volatility surprises," although Tokyo markets still did not affect New York's.

Mervyn A. King and Sushil Wadhwani (1990) have examined the market events surrounding October 1987 and offer a hypothesis about the worldwide scope of the market crash. To investigate the conundrum of what change in market fundamentals could explain a 23 percent drop in the Dow and similar gigantic declines in other markets around the globe, the authors developed a model in which rational traders in one market have less information about stocks than traders in the home market and must infer information partly from stock price movements abroad. This situation leads to the possibility of price movement "contagion" from one market to another, which will be particularly severe during periods of high market volatility. A sharp decline in a foreign price index is a (noisy) signal of bad news, some of which home market traders may not know from other sources. While the authors' hypothesis does not shed light on the "news" that triggered the October 1987 crash, it does explain why the crash was so uniform around the world despite important differences in markets and economic circumstances.

Gerard Gennotte and Hayne Leland (1990) have also developed a model in which rational traders' lack of information can precipitate a crash. Their concern is with informationless trading associated with hedging strategies like portfolio insurance. Formal portfolio insurance techniques systematically increase exposure to the market as stock prices rise and reduce it as stock prices fall (by shifting a portfolio's mix between index stocks and bonds or by adjusting the size of a short index futures hedge against a stock index portfolio). Although portfolio insurance-related selling is strictly passive, responding to declining stock prices, it could be mistaken for selling based on adverse information, and other traders look to prices and price changes as a way to glean information that they may lack. If nonpassive traders knew that they were taking the buy side of an informationless trade, they would more likely be willing to do so and would thereby supply liquidity to the market.

Gennotte and Leland's model shows how unobserved hedging programs, though only a small proportion of total trading, can destabilize a market. The disturbance may then propagate to other world markets. Their recommendation is that informationless trades should be preannounced and that "[e]lectronic 'open books' should be a seriously considered reform [to show the buy and sell order flow], and other forms of market organization (such as single-price auctions) should be examined" (1990, 1016). Some recent institutional developments are consistent with the authors' recommendations. Toronto's Computer Assisted Trading System displays limit orders to system users, and Wunsch's after-hours single-price auctions help concentrate market liquidity.

The King and Wadhwani and Gennotte and Leland models explain how trading itself can generate intermarket volatility. Joseph E. Stiglitz (1989) and Lawrence H. Summers and Victoria P. Summers (1989), go further by asserting that financial markets are excessively volatile because of irrational traders' speculative activity. Decreasing transactions costs owing to technological innovation and derivative markets promotes this speculation. These authors recommend a transactions tax to "throw sand into the gears" of financial markets (Tobin 1984, cited in Summers and Summers 1989, 263). Each securities purchase or sale would be subject to a "small" tax—for example, 0.5 percent of the stock price. In fact, many governments around the world impose stock transaction taxes, although the trend abroad is toward eliminating such taxes (see Roll 1989, table 4).

The gradual unification of world financial markets and continuing improvement in information flows will probably reduce the information asymmetry that produces contagion effects. However, in the view of those advocating transactions taxes these developments would just exacerbate irrational trading. At the core of their argument is the belief that financial markets are inefficient—that is, asset prices do not reflect "fundamentals." A growing list of so-called market anomalies seems to contradict efficient-markets theory. The apparent excess volatility analyzed by Robert J. Shiller (1989) stands as a challenge to efficient-markets proponents. Nevertheless, the theory is only being challenged, not overturned. Transactions taxes and other remedies for supposed excess trading and excess volatility have been proposed and sometimes implemented with little regard for their efficacy or possible adverse consequences.

Trading halts or circuit breakers, margin requirements, and price limits are also suggested as means of controlling trading. Of all these devices, margin requirements have been the most extensively studied and debated. In essence this work concludes that adjustments to margin requirements have no significant impact on stock market volatility (see David A. Hsieh and Miller 1990). Using data from twenty-three stock markets, Roll (1989) undertook a cross-market study of the effects of transactions taxes, margin requirements, and price limits on market volatility and found that none effectively reduce volatility.

Circuit breakers shut down an entire market temporarily to give participants a "time-out," mainly to avoid a panic selling spree. Both the New York Stock Exchange and Chicago Mercantile Exchange have instituted such circuit breakers (see Franklin R. Edwards 1988, 1989), although evidence is lacking concerning their usefulness. As Gennotte and Leland (1990) point out, the weekend of October 17-18, 1987, was an extended trading halt for the market declines of the previous week, but participants were not inclined to stage a market reversal the following Monday. It is not at all obvious that circuit breakers stabilize prices. To the contrary, they could induce traders to sell earlier and in larger quantities, fearing that a trading-halt price limit will soon be reached. This movement could destabilize prices. Sanford J. Grossman (1990) has argued persuasively that market equilibrium would be restored more quickly without halting trading. Rather than attempting to suppress mispricings, Grossman concludes that the market would be better served by being informed of them, whether they arise from panic or any other source, because better-informed traders would recognize such occurrences as profit opportunities and thus reverse the price movements.

Conclusion

The globalization of financial markets simultaneously fragments traditional financial transactions marketplaces and integrates them via electronic means. Physical marketplaces (the trading floors) are becoming obsolete, while "virtual" marketplaces—networks of computers and computer terminals—are emerging as the "site" for transactions. The new technology is diminishing the role for human participants in the market mechanism. Stock-exchange specialists are being displaced by the new systems, which by and large are designed to handle the demands of institutional investors, who increasingly dominate transactions. Futures and options floor traders also face having their jobs coded into computer algorithms, which automatically match orders and clear trades or emulate open-outcry trading itself.

International capital flows and the trading volume associated with them have been expanding over time. The internationalization of financial markets implies that investment portfolios are becoming more homogenized and creates a demand for worldwide twenty-four-hour trading. Derivative markets also benefit from this trend as multinational corporations need financial services around the clock for hedging and other reasons.

The competitive forces propelling changes in financial markets also compel changes in regulatory oversight of these markets.[24] Technology helps minimize some problems—for example, by making it possible to establish accurate audit trails of trades and thereby discouraging certain kinds of trading abuses—while it creates others, such as business being drawn to markets with the most lenient regulatory standards. Nevertheless, financial marketplaces are perhaps closest to the textbook paradigm of voluntary exchanges for mutual benefit of transacting parties. Competition among the world's financial exchanges as well as among their regulators is likely to be the most efficient way to elicit the best mechanisms for conducting and regulating transactions.

More problematic is the nature of trading and volatility associated with it. Does trading itself generate volatility that interferes with consumption, investment, and other economic decisions, in turn lowering social welfare? This article has given an overview of new automated trading systems and communications networks that are integrating markets. The technology discussed improves market mechanisms and information flows, but it may have the negative side effect of promoting "excess" trading. If markets are efficient, volatility per se is generally regarded as a neutral characteristic of markets. Derivative markets will continue developing to allow any desired degree of hedging against volatility. Only if markets are inefficient can a case can be made for curtailing volatility, but the evidence is ambiguous regarding market inefficiency. Even less clear is the efficacy of measures proposed to safeguard markets against volatility.

Notes

1. See Summers and Summers (1989) and the discussion of their proposal below.
2. Frequent trading will be necessary when the number of securities available to "complete markets" is smaller than the number of future "states." See Huang and Litzenberger (1988, chapter 7). This situation will be all the more likely if financial markets are incomplete. However, theory does not give an indication of how much trading is appropriate to allocate wealth over time efficiently.
3. The difference between purchases and sales represents the net capital flow, which is less relevant in considering the growth of securities trading and market liquidity.
4. $321\% = [(75.28/17.85) - 1] * 100$ and $43\% = [(361.37/253.38) - 1] * 100$.
5. See Smith (1991). Ginnie Mae stands for Government National Mortgage Association, a government-chartered agency that makes a secondary market in home mortgages and enhances the liquidity of that market by securitizing individual mortgages into "pass-through" certificates. The futures was on this underlying security.
6. The NYSE is in the process of instituting "A Look at the Book" program that permits public subscribers to the service to view the limit orders for 50 of the 2,370 NYSE-listed stocks. This service will be available through vendors and will show the limit-order book at three fixed times during the trading day. Currently, only the specialists and other NYSE members, such as floor brokers, on the exchange floor have access to the specialists' books.
7. Market orders specify quantity for trade at the current price. Limit orders specify price and quantity.
8. The meanings of the acronyms are given in Table 5.
9. The bid price is the price for which a dealer is willing to buy a stock, and the offer is the price for which he or she is willing to sell the stock.
10. See Bodie, Kane, and Marcus (1989) or Francis (1991) for further institutional details about organized exchanges and OTC markets and such details as listing requirements.
11. This account of SOES is based on Domowitz (1990).
12. See U.S. Securities and Exchange Commission (1991, 69); another NASDAQ system described in this source is POR-TAL (Private Offerings, Resales, and Trading through Automated Linkages), which is used in the secondary market for privately placed equity and debt. See note 24 below for further description.
13. See NASDAQ (1991, 14-15). Because of differences in accounting conventions, the NASDAQ figures are inflated compared with the NYSE figures.
14. See Hansell (1989, 102). The amount of institutional participation in NASDAQ stocks as measured by the volume of block trading has been about 43 percent in recent years. See NASDAQ (1991).
15. Instinet-sponsored section in *Institutional Investor* (January 1991).
16. See Kolb (1991, 17-18) for a general discussion of EFP transactions and Miller (1990) for EFPs in connection with the CME's S&P 500 stock-index futures contract.
17. The futures exchange, however, would collect an additional fee for allowing the off-exchange or ex-pit EFP. The Commodity Exchange Act prohibits noncompetitive and prearranged transactions in futures, with the exception of EFPs. See Behof (1990, 2).
18. See Roll (1988, 29). Roll notes that the Spanish market trades groups of stocks continuously for ten minutes at a time. This article contains much interesting information about foreign stock markets.
19. See Kolb (1991, 59-61) for a succinct account of the FBI undercover sting operation at the CME and CBOT, which began in early 1987 and resulted in indictments against forty-seven traders in January 1989.
20. Information on Globex came from 1991 CME promotional literature. Domowitz (1990) provides a detailed description and analysis of the Globex trading algorithm as well as those for two other trading systems.
21. The Brady Commission's basic recommendations were: (1) to have one agency be the overarching regulator of U.S. financial markets; (2) to have a unification of clearing systems of financial exchanges and OTC markets; (3) to have "consistent" margin requirements across different exchanges; (4) to institute coordinated "circuit breakers" across exchanges; and (5) to improve information systems to monitor trading activity in related markets.
22. The Securities and Exchange Act of 1934 authorized the Federal Reserve Board to established initial and maintenance margins to prevent excessive leveraging of securities purchases on securities exchanges. (In practice, the Board has set only minimum initial margin levels.) Part of the rationale for control over margins was to limit massive selling off of leveraged positions during market downturns.
23. See Brady et al. (1988, especially 51-52). Despite the potential dangers, no defaults occurred in the clearinghouse system during October 1987.
24. The SEC's April 1990 approval of Rule 144A is an instance of a change in regulatory standards that reflect changes in the nature of financial transactions. This rule simplifies the SEC's disclosure requirements for private placement issuers (see Chu 1991). Foreign corporations are now able to raise capital in U.S. markets without having to meet the SEC's stringent financial disclosure requirements as long as transactions are limited to large institutional investors. British financial authorities have instituted a similar relaxation of regulations for institutional investors (see Grundfest 1990).

    NASDAQ's new PORTAL system is used for communicating bids and offers on privately placed securities traded under the provisions of Rule 144A.

References

Angrist, Stanley W. "Futures Trade on Screens—Except in U.S." *Wall Street Journal*, May 21, 1991, C1, C14.

Behof, John P. "Globex: A Global Automated Transaction System for Futures and Options." Study by the Federal Reserve Bank of Chicago, June 1990.

Bodie, Zvi, Alex Kane, and Alan J. Marcus. *Investments*. Homewood, Ill.: Irwin, 1989.

Brady, Nicholas F., James C. Cotting, Robert G. Kirby, John R. Opel, and Howard M. Stein. *Report of the Presidential Task Force on Market Mechanisms*. Submitted to the President of the United States, the Secretary of the Treasury, and the Chairman of the Federal Reserve Board, January 1988.

Brodsky, William J. "Futures in the Nineties: Confronting Globalization." In *Proceedings from a Conference on Bank Structure and Competition*, 615-23. Federal Reserve Bank of Chicago, 1990.

_____. "The Future Is Now." *Institutional Investor* 25 (January 1991): 7.

Chicago Board of Trade. *Commodity Trading Manual*. CBOT, 1985.

Chu, Franklin J. "The U.S. Private Market for Foreign Securities." *The Bankers Magazine* 174 (January/February 1991): 55-60.

Domowitz, Ian. "The Mechanics of Automated Trade Execution Systems." *Journal of Financial Intermediation* 1 (1990): 167-94.

_____. "Equally Open and Competitive: Regulatory Approval of Automated Trade Execution in the Futures Markets." Center for the Study of Futures Markets Working Paper #214, forthcoming 1991.

Edwards, Franklin R. "Studies of the 1987 Stock Market Crash: Review and Appraisal." *Journal of Financial Services Research* 1 (1988): 231-51.

_____. "Regulatory Reform of Securities and Futures Markets: Two Years after the Crash." Center for the Study of Futures Markets Working Paper #189, June 1989.

Francis, Jack Clark. *Investments: Analysis and Management*. 5th ed. New York: McGraw-Hill, Inc., 1991.

"Futures Markets Will Let Their Fingers Do the Dealing." *The Economist*, March 19, 1988, 77-78.

Gennotte, Gerard, and Hayne Leland. "Market Liquidity, Hedging, and Crashes." *American Economic Review* 80 (1990): 999-1021.

Grossman, Sanford J. "Institutional Investing and New Trading Technologies." In *Market Volatility and Investor Confidence: Report to the Board of Directors of the New York Stock Exchange, Inc.*, G2-1-17. June 7, 1990.

Grundfest, Joseph A. "Internationalization of the World's Securities Markets: Economic Causes and Regulatory Consequences." *Journal of Financial Services Research* 4 (1990): 349-78.

Guy, Paul. "IOSCO Moves Ahead." *FIA Review* (May/June 1990): 8-10.

Hamao, Yasushi, Ronald W. Masulis, and Victor Ng. "Correlations in Price Changes and Volatility across International Stock Markets." *Review of Financial Studies* 3 (1990): 281-307.

Hansell, Saul. "The Wild, Wired World of Electronic Exchanges." *Institutional Investor* (September 1989): 91ff.

Harvey, Campbell R. "The World Price of Covariance Risk." *Journal of Finance* 46 (1991): 111-57.

Heimann, John G. *Globalization of the Securities Markets*. Statement in hearings before the Senate Subcommittee on Securities of the Committee on Banking, Housing, and Urban Affairs. June 14, 1989, 76.

Howard, Barbara. "The Trade: Technology Aims to Take the Final Step." *Institutional Investor* 25 (January 1991): 15-16.

Hsieh, David A., and Merton H. Miller. "Margin Regulation and Stock Market Volatility." *Journal of Finance* 45 (1990): 3-29.

Huang, Chi-fu, and Robert H. Litzenberger. *Foundations for Financial Economics*. New York: North-Holland, 1988.

Kang, Jane C., and John C. Lawton. "Automated Futures Trading Systems." *FIA Review* (May/June 1990): 6-7.

King, Mervyn A., and Sushil Wadhwani. "Transmission of Volatility between Stock Markets." *Review of Financial Studies* 3 (1990): 5-33.

Kolb, Robert W. *Understanding Futures Markets*. 3d ed. Miami: Kolb Publishing Company, 1991.

Lewis, Janet. "The Euro-Futures War." *Institutional Investor* 24 (March 1990): 129ff.

London International Financial Futures Exchange. *APT Information Package*. 1991.

Miller, Merton H. "International Competitiveness of U.S. Futures Exchanges." *Journal of Financial Services Research* 4 (1990): 387-408.

NASDAQ. *Fact Book 1991*. 1991.

Neumark, David, P.A. Tinsley, and Suzanne Tosini. "After-Hours Stock Prices and Post-Crash Hangovers." *Journal of Finance* 46 (1991): 159-78.

New York Stock Exchange. *Fact Book 1991*. 1991a.

New York Stock Exchange. *Off-Hours Trading*. Brochure. 1991b.

Roll, Richard. "The International Crash of October 1987." *Financial Analysts Journal* 44 (September/October 1988): 19-35.

_____. "Price Volatility, International Market Links, and Their Implications for Regulatory Policies." *Journal of Financial Services Research* 3 (1989): 211-46.

Rosenbaum, Amy. "Scouting Automation: What's the Competition Like?" *Futures* 19 (April 1990): 52-54.

Salwen, Kevin G., and Craig Torres. "Big Board After-Hours Trading May Lead to a Two-Tiered Market." *Wall Street Journal*, June 13, 1991, C1, C17.

Sheeline, William E. "Who Needs the Stock Exchange?" *Fortune*, November 19, 1990, 119ff.

Shiller, Robert J. *Market Volatility*. Cambridge, Mass.: MIT Press, 1989.

Smith, Stephen D. "Analyzing Risk and Return for Mortgage-Backed Securities." Federal Reserve Bank of Atlanta *Economic Review* 76 (January/February 1991): 2-11.

Stiglitz, Joseph E. "Using Tax Policy to Curb Speculative Short-Term Trading." *Journal of Financial Services Research* 3 (1989): 101-15.

Summers, Lawrence H., and Victoria P. Summers. "When Financial Markets Work Too Well: A Cautious Case for a Securities Transactions Tax." *Journal of Financial Services Research* 3 (1989): 261-86.

Szala, Ginger, and Amy Rosenbaum. "Deregulation in Japan May Have Different Meaning." *Futures* 19 (February 1990): 42-44.

Tobin, James. "On the Efficiency of the Financial System." *Lloyds Bank Review*, no. 153 (July 1984): 1-15.

U.S. Congress. Office of Technology Assessment. *Trading Around the Clock: Global Securities Markets and Information Technology—Background Paper*. OTA-BP-CIT-66. Washington, D.C.: U.S. Government Printing Office, July 1990a.

_____. *Electronic Bulls and Bears: U.S. Securities Markets and Information Technology*. OTA-CIT-469. Washington, D.C.: U.S. Government Printing Office, September 1990b.

U.S. Securities and Exchange Commission. *Questionnaire of the Working Party on Regulation of Secondary Markets*. May 29, 1991.

Wunsch, R. Steven. "Single-Price Auctions." *Institutional Investor* 25 (January 1991): 20.

*T*he Effect of the "Triple Witching Hour" on Stock Market Volatility

Steven P. Feinstein and William N. Goetzmann

*T*he term "triple witching hour" can conjure up images of broomsticks and brew, perhaps the scene from Shakespeare's *Macbeth* in which a trio of witches recite incantations around a boiling cauldron. For stock traders, through, the term represents something far more frightening. To them the "triple witching hour" refers to the four times each year when stock index futures, stock index options, and options on individual stocks expire simultaneously. Typically on triple witching hour days, large blocks of stock change hands as hedgers, arbitrageurs, and speculators seek to maximize returns or minimize losses as they settle the contracts entered into previously.

Analysts have alleged that the triple witching hour is a time of great volatility and wide price swings in the stock market. In mid-1987 the Chicago Mercantile Exchange and the New York Futures Exchange were so moved by the concern over triple witching hour volatility that they changed the rules governing the expiration of index futures and options. Trading in most index futures contracts and some index options now ends one day earlier, with expiration effectively taking place at the open of trading on the expiration day instead of at the close. The impact of triple witching hours and expiration days in general, though, extends far beyond the matter of whether the pattern of stock trading is atypical on certain days of the year. Of interest also is the fact that many of the new features that distinguish modern financial markets from markets of the past are integral to the triple witching hour phenomenon. These new features include futures and options trading, computerized trading, program trading of large blocks of stocks, and index arbitrage. Examination of triple witching hour days offers the opportunity to explore the impact of these innovations.

This article was originally published in the Atlanta Fed's September/October 1988 Economic Review. *At the time the article was written, Feinstein was an economist in the financial section of the Atlanta Fed's research department and Goetzmann was a doctoral candidate at the Yale School of Organization and Management.*

By looking at triple witching hour days in general, some insight can also be gained into fundamental questions about financial markets. To what extent does the mechanism of exchange—the market itself—affect asset prices? Are stocks rendered riskier merely by the existence of option contracts that are, in effect, "side bets" on stock performance? Why should the popularity of financial instruments that simply reallocate claims on firms' earnings change the inherent risk profile of the market itself?

Information about triple witching hour days can also be used to test widely held views about financial asset prices. For example, the efficient market hypothesis holds that stock prices continuously reflect all available information and that prices change only when new information becomes available. Thus, when stock prices swing sharply, analysts must wonder if certain information is driving the movement or whether the mechanism of trade itself is precipitating the price swing.

Yet another branch of theory—option and futures pricing—hinges on the notion that these derivative instruments are "redundant." That is, an investment in options or futures can be perfectly mimicked with investment strategies involving only stocks and bonds. If in fact futures and options are redundant investment vehicles and markets had previously been efficient, the price behavior of stocks should be the same now as before the advent of the new markets. Consequently, price behavior across triple witching hour days should not be unusual since triple witching hours did not exist before the new instruments were created. If, on the other hand, prices do behave differently on triple witching hour days than on other days, either the new assets are not truly redundant, markets previously were not efficient, or markets currently are not efficient.

This article reviews the current research into the triple witching hour phenomenon and investigates whether the market really is more volatile on triple witching hour days. This research also presents preliminary results of the effect of the new settlement procedures on market volatility.

The New Financial Instruments

Stock Index Futures and Index Arbitrage. In order to understand triple witching hour day activity, one should understand the mechanics of stock index futures and options. Stock index futures first traded in 1982. They originated on the same midwestern exchanges that traditionally traded commodity futures and options, and in many ways are similar to their agricultural precursors (see box on page 27).[1] Like a futures contract on coffee or corn, a stock index futures contract will return profits when the price of the underlying asset rises and create losses when the asset price falls.

A stock index futures contract is an instrument that allows an investor to participate in the stock market without ever actually purchasing stocks. Moreover, stock index futures enable investment in large diversified portfolios through a single transaction rather than the numerous transactions that are required to form a diversified stock portfolio. In this way, the investor can save substantially in commission expenses. Although stock index futures are derivative instruments, that is, instruments whose prices are contingent on the values of other assets, the daily transaction volume measured in dollars for stock index futures now exceeds that of actual stocks.[2]

The market for stock index futures created the opportunity for a new type of investment strategy, index arbitrage, which involves exploiting the difference between the value of an underlying stock index portfolio and the price of the corresponding stock index future. Theoretically that difference should never become very large. If, however, a gap opens up between the two, the opportunity for a nearly riskless profit results. To execute the strategy, one would buy the less expensive instrument—either the portfolio or the index future—and sell the more expensive one. If the future is less expensive, one should buy ("take a long position in") the future and sell ("short") the portfolio of actual stocks. If the stock portfolio is less expensive, arbitrage calls for a purchase of the stock portfolio and a short position in the future. (Commissions and the cost of borrowing the necessary funds must also be considered.) Either action ensures a certain profit because the two prices must converge by the time of expiration.

For example, suppose the Standard and Poor's (S&P) 500 index futures price were $300, but the actual Standard and Poor's 500 stock portfolio could be purchased for $250. Seeing this discrepancy, an arbitrageur would calculate whether the gap between the future and the spot prices were enough to cover commissions and the costs of borrowing necessary funds. If indeed the gap were large enough, the arbitrageur could buy the actual stocks and take a short position in the futures. If the price of the actual stocks fell by the expiration date, a loss would be incurred on the

A Comparison of Commodity Futures and Stock Index Futures

A commodity future is a contract that obligates an agent either to buy or sell a given quantity of a commodity at a prespecified price on a certain date. For example, taking a "long" position in a coffee futures contract obligates the agent to buy a certain large quantity of coffee (37,500 pounds) when the contract expires. The party taking the "short" position is obligated to sell the commodity. The price is determined via bidding at the time the contract is initiated and is referred to as the *futures price*. Taking a long position in a coffee futures contract is very similar to buying coffee outright, except delivery and payment are postponed until the contract's expiration. Since the contract conveys ownership of coffee, albeit deferred, coffee futures prices should be strongly related to the current price of coffee (also known as the *spot price* or cash price of coffee). Moreover, as the expiration date approaches, owning coffee and "owning" a coffee futures contract become nearly the same thing, and so the spot price of coffee and the coffee futures price converge. At expiration, buying a coffee futures contract is the same as buying actual coffee; the futures price must equal the spot price at the time.

One might think of a stock index futures contract as a contract that obligates an agent either to buy or sell a large portfolio of stocks at a prespecified price upon expiration of the contract. This simplification helps one to understand what determines stock index futures prices and what causes those prices to change. If this simplification were accurate, a stock index future would be just like a coffee futures contract, with the exception that stocks would be bought and sold instead of coffee. In re-

ality, though, stock futures differ from commodity futures in that a stock portfolio is never actually delivered. When the contract expires, the agents exchange money—that is, the contract "cash settles." If the spot price has risen on net during the life of the contract so that the spot price upon expiration is greater than the original futures price, the "short" party pays the "long" party the difference in cash.

For example, suppose you took a long position in a stock index futures contract when the futures price was $100. If, by expiration, the value of the underlying stock portfolio had risen to $120 you would receive cash payments totaling $20—the difference between $100 and $120—over the life of the contract. You would have made money because the stock index value rose above the level the futures price had been when you entered into the futures contract. The cash settlement is not made all at once at expiration, however. Rather, it is made in part at the end of each trading day on the basis of the change that transpired that day in the futures price. On the expiration day you receive or pay only the difference between the futures price from the previous day and the spot price at expiration. Thus, in the example in which the original futures price was $100 and the expiration spot price was $120, the long party would receive payments each day as the futures price rose and perhaps have to make payments to the short party on those days when the futures price fell. Over the life of the contract, though, the net transfer would total $20 paid by the short party to the long party.

actual stock investment, but the profit on the futures investment would more than offset that loss. Suppose, on the other hand, stock prices rose. In that case money would be lost on the short futures position, but even more would be realized from the change in the price of the actual stocks. Again the investor would reap a guaranteed profit. No matter what happens to the price of stocks, the arbitrageur benefits.[3]

Eventually, the arbitrageur must "unwind" his position, that is, sell the stock portfolio and exit the futures contract. In order to retain the arbitrage revenue and clear a profit, unwinding must take place when the two prices are the same or closer together than when the arbitrage strategy was initiated. Convergence may occur before the contract expiration but must certainly occur at expiration—at the witching hour.

Unwinding must be done quickly so that the arbitrageur is not left holding only one risky part of the

arbitrage portfolio without the offsetting half. To accomplish the speedy dispensing of their stock holdings, arbitrageurs often employ the Designated Order Turnaround system of the New York Stock Exchange, a computerized stock order routing system. Alternatively, arbitrageurs may place orders with exchange specialists to execute the orders at the moment the futures contract expires. In either case, index arbitrage requires large volumes of stock to be bought and sold quickly, with many of these transactions occurring on triple witching hour days.

Stock Options. If the unwinding of index arbitrage positions were the only unusual activity taking place on certain days, those days might be called witching hour days, not *triple* witching hour days. Yet stock options and stock index options expire on those days as well, which may generate additional volume. The owner of a stock option has the right, but not the obligation, to buy or sell a certain stock by a specified

Options Demystified

An option is a contract that affords the buyer the right, but not the obligation, to buy or sell an asset for a pre-specified price on or before some selected date. The pre-specified price, which is written into the option contract, is called the *strike price* or *exercise price*. The selected date is the *expiration date*, the last date on which the option owner can choose to buy or sell the underlying asset. The option owner can choose not to exercise the option and thus forfeit the right to buy or sell the underlying asset. In that case the option expires unexercised.

The two types of options are call options and put options. *Call options* confer the right to buy assets; *put options* confer the right to sell. One can think of a call option as a deposit. Suppose a college fraternity is planning a party for the next homecoming. To assure an ample supply of root beer for its party, the fraternity members may wish to place a deposit at the local grocery store reserving the right to buy a crate of root beer for a given price on the day of the party. Here, the fraternity is buying an option, and the grocery store is writing the option. The underlying asset is the crate of root beer, and the cash amount to be paid upon delivery of the root beer is the strike price. The amount of money paid in advance to the grocery store is the option price. Should the fraternity members decide they do not want the root beer, they may wish to surrender the deposit, not buy the root beer, and let the option expire unexercised.

Suppose on the other hand that the price of root beer increases dramatically before the day of the party. Maybe an explosion disables the local bottling plant or a root beer tasters' convention is scheduled for the same day as the party. The agreement with the grocery store would thus become more valuable. The grocery store is bound to sell the root beer to the fraternity for the previously agreed-upon price even though the spot price of root beer has risen in the interim. The fraternity members may exercise the option, buy the root beer at the strike price, and thus enjoy their assets at a bargain price. Alternatively, they may choose to exercise the option, buy the root beer at the strike price, then sell the root beer on the open market for the new higher spot price and retain the profit.

Stock call options are very much like the root beer deposit in this example. The call option buyer has the right but not the obligation to buy a certain stock for the strike price before or on the expiration date. If the market price of the underlying stock rises above the strike price, the option owner can exercise the option, buying the stock for the strike price, and then sell the stock for the higher current market price. The seller of the option must have the necessary shares of stocks to sell to the option buyer. If he does not, he must first buy those shares.

---

time and at a particular price. (See box above for a brief explanation of options.) The following possible scenario illustrates how option expirations can lead to increased stock trading activity.

A call option owner (someone who has bought the right to purchase a certain stock) exercises the option and demands that the option "writer" (the party who sold the option) sell a share of stock. The writer first buys the stock at the stock exchange and then, to fulfill the contractual agreement, sells it to the option owner at the strike price. The option owner then resells the stock to capture profit from the difference between the price stated in the option contract and the current market price. The option's expiration date is the deadline for these maneuvers. Consequently, the existence of stock call options may generate increased trading activity on those days.

A scenario involving stock put options may yield similar activity. The owner of a put option has the right to sell shares of stock at a previously agreed-upon price. If the stock price falls below the strike price, exercise of the option is profitable. If the put owner wishes to exercise the option on an expiration

day but does not already own the necessary shares of stock, he must first buy the shares at the market price. He then can sell them for the higher strike price to the party that sold the put and pocket the profit. The put writer might then wish to close out his position and sell the newly acquired stock. Again, one earlier option transaction might, upon expiration, generate three separate stock transactions.

Options on individual stocks have been traded on U.S. exchanges since 1973. Stock options may follow different quarterly schedules, but in general they expire on the third Friday of the month. Four times a year this day coincides with the expiration of index futures and index options.

Stock Index Options. The third aspect of the triple witching hour involves the expiration of stock index options. Since their introduction in 1983, stock index options have made it possible to buy or sell options on entire stock indexes in addition to options on individual stocks. Stock index put options have proved attractive to hedgers who own large portfolios that are likely to rise and fall in value in concert with the market as a whole. By purchasing a stock index put option, investors can protect against losses caused by a market-wide decline.[4] Index options are also popular among speculators who wish to profit from the vicissitudes of the stock market as a whole. By investing in stock index options rather than individual stock options, speculators and hedgers need not be concerned with the idiosyncratic risks associated with individual stocks since the value of a stock index option is based on the value of a large, diversified portfolio.

Unlike options on individual stocks, stock index options settle in cash. No stocks change hands when stock index options are exercised. The exercising party simply receives a cash payment from the option writer equal to the difference between the strike price and the current market value of the underlying index. Although exercisers of index options need not actually sell or buy stocks, such exercise might provoke the option writer, instead, to execute a stock transaction. An option writer is responsible for the difference between the current stock index value and the option strike price. If the stock market has gained or lost much value since the writing of the option, payment by the option writer can be substantial.

Call option writers often hold the underlying stocks in their portfolios so that, should the option be exercised, they can sell the stocks on the exchange in order to raise the funds needed to pay the call option owner.[5] At expiration one can expect any in-the-money options (options for which immediate exercise is profitable) to be exercised, sending some option writers scrambling to cover their positions, thereby promoting heavy stock trading on expiration days.

Stock Volatility Effect

The previous section of this article reviewed how stock index futures, stock options, and stock index options might bring about frenetic equity trading on days when each of these instruments expires. This increased trading activity could in turn exacerbate price volatility. A temporary mismatch between buy and sell orders will either send the price up or down as the price equilibrates supply and demand pressures. Only a small price change is necessary to close a slight gap between buy and sell orders, but a large price change may be necessary when the gap is wide. When trade orders suddenly flood the exchange, large gaps are more likely, and thus large price swings are more likely to occur. On triple witching hour days the full

expiration effects of stock options, stock index options, and stock index futures bear on the markets at the same time. This simultaneity provides one reason to expect higher volatility on those days. Of course, even if triple witching hour days are more volatile than other days, other reasons for the phenomenon could exist.

Reviewing the Evidence. Notwithstanding the theoretical reasons for triple witching hour day volatility and the belief by market participants and business journalists that this volatility exists, the phenomenon is ultimately an empirical question and one that warrants close scrutiny of the facts. Several academic studies have addressed the volatility of the triple witching hour days. Some researchers have investigated component parts of the triple witching hour phenomenon, such as the effects of large transactions on prices, while others have probed the impact that the stock index futures market has had on underlying stock price movements.[6]

Among the recent research directly investigating triple witching hour days, the paper by Hans Stoll and Robert E. Whaley (1986a) is the most comprehensive. They looked for evidence of unusual volume and price effects on and around expiration days. Testing the period from May 1982 through December 1985, the researchers failed to find that stock index future expiration days exhibited higher volatility than nonexpiration days.[7] They did conclude, however, that from July 1983 through December 1985, the last hour of trading on triple witching hour days was a frenetic one, exhibiting far greater volume and volatility than the last hour of trading on nonexpiration days.

Stoll and Whaley's results were corroborated in a study by Franklin R. Edwards (1988). Edwards compared hour-by-hour price fluctuations on triple witching hour days with hour-by-hour fluctuations from nonexpiration days during the period from July 1983 through October 1986. Edwards too found that price volatility was significantly greater in the last hour of triple witching days than on ordinary days.

Stoll and Whaley, as well as Edwards, arrived at their conclusions based on the statistical procedure known as an F-test, which compares stock prices in one sample with those from another sample. Based on assumptions of certain properties regarding the distribution of stock returns in both samples, the test determines the likelihood that stock prices were equally volatile in the two samples. One troubling feature of the F-test, however, is that it assumes that stock returns are normally distributed; that is, when plotted on a graph, the distribution would resemble a bell curve. However, an abundance of evidence shows that stock returns are not normally distributed but instead are characterized by sporadic extreme observations, either occasional huge losses or huge gains.[8] The recent stock market crash of October 1987 is a graphic reminder that the distribution of stock returns does not conform to a normal distribution. Consequently, the F-test, whose results are easily distorted by extreme occurrences, is not reliable for drawing inferences about underlying stock return distributions and thus for identifying trends that are likely to persist in the future.[9]

Market Volatility and the Triple Witching Hour: A New Perspective

The primary objective of the research presented in this article is to determine if the triple witching hour days in the period before 1987 were, in fact, characterized by unusually high volatility. Unlike past research, this effort uses a statistical procedure that does not require the assumption of normally distributed stock returns. Furthermore, the research presented here benefited from several more triple witching hour days than were available for earlier studies.

This article also includes an examination of the first five triple witching hour days since the 1987 rule change. A study of this data can help determine whether the new expiration procedures succeeded in reducing triple witching hour day volatility.

The tests used are distribution-free statistical tests, that is, they do not rely on the assumption of normally distributed stock returns. The test works as follows: if triple witching hour days are not unusual with regard to volatility, then any given triple witching hour day will just as likely fall in the top half as in the lower half of all days ranked according to volatility. This implication of the hypothesis is tested by ranking all days in the sample by volatility and simply counting how many triple witching hour days ranked in the top 50 percent and how many ranked in the bottom 50 percent. From the results of this tabulation, one can determine whether the hypothesis about equal volatility and the triple witching hour effect is reasonable.

The Data. This research examines the daily returns of the S&P 500 index from January 1983 through June 1988, the period over which stock index futures and index options have been traded. The returns are calculated as daily percent changes in closing prices. The volatility measure used was the absolute value of the daily stock return, which reflects the magnitude of each day's price swing.[10]

Prior to June 1984, stock index futures and stock index options expired on the third Thursday of the final month of the quarter. Consequently, the first five expiration days in the sample used here are Thursdays. Since that time all triple witching hour days have been the third Friday of the final month of the quarter.

Before June 1987, the close of trading on the expiration day marked the end of trading in and expiration of stock index futures and stock index options. Since then, with the change in rules, trading in most index futures contracts and some index options ends on the Thursday before the third Friday, but settlement and expiration take place on the next day.[11] The settlement price for the index futures and options is a composite of the opening prices of the individual stocks in the index. In effect, the contracts governed by the new rule now expire at the opening of trading on Friday rather than at the close.

According to the Chicago Mercantile Exchange, the rationale for changing the expiration of stock index futures and options on stock index futures from the close of trading on Friday to the open was as follows: whereas arbitrageurs would previously unwind positions using market-on-close order—to time their stock transactions exactly with the expiration of the futures or options—now they must place market-on-open orders. Although a specialist cannot delay the close of trading, he may delay the opening of trading in a particular stock if he observes a large imbalance between buy and sell market-on-open orders. With this extra time he can find parties willing to absorb some of the surplus orders. Thus, large price swings might no longer be necessary to equilibrate temporary surges in supply or demand.

Also, because trading in options and futures now stops on the Thursday prior to expiration, some market participants may choose to unwind their positions on a day when they can still buy and sell futures or options. Therefore, the new expiration rules might have the effect of spreading both volume and volatility over two days, whereas they used to be concentrated on one.

Design of the Tests. This study tests first for higher-than-usual volatility of the S&P 500 on the expiration days between January 1983 and May 1987. The test is based on a comparison of the price swings on those days with the median price swing from all other days in the January 1983 to May 1987 sample.[12] Most of the expiration days in this sample, however, occurred on Fridays, and, as documented in Kenneth R.

French's (1980) research, the day of the week bears on stock price behavior. Therefore, these expiration days were then compared specifically to the other Fridays in the sample. These two tests yield similar results.

Even the second test, though, does not completely control for the day-of-the-week effect, since some of the expirations in the sample were on Thursdays. Therefore, the two tests were repeated using only the subsample in which all expirations occurred on Fridays—the May 1984 to May 1987 subsample. The results are the same, as will be shown later in this article.

To test whether the results in the sample period were associated with the introduction of options on index futures, all of these tests were repeated using data from the four years immediately prior to their introduction, 1979-82.[13] Third Fridays in March, June, September, and December were designated as "pseudo-expiration" days, following the same rule in force throughout most of our 1983-87 test period. If indeed the patterns in the 1983-87 sample resulted from the introduction of index options, then one would expect to find no similar pattern in the 1979-82 period.

In the period since the 1987 rule change, the triple witching hour is in effect spread out over two days, a Thursday and the following Friday. If a volatility effect is present, it may be on one day or the other, or perhaps spread out over the two days. Consequently, for this recent sample, expiration Fridays were compared to all other Fridays, expiration Thursdays were compared to all other Thursdays, and the two-day price swings that transpired over expiration Thursday-Friday clusters were compared to those price swings that transpired over all other Thursday-Friday clusters.

Results. The two tests run on the 1983-87 data set clearly rejected the hypothesis that expiration days were equally likely to have above- as below-median price swings. These results are presented in Table 1. Chart 1 shows the price swings for each of the 17 expiration days during those years; the median price swing for all other days and the median price swing for all other Fridays are represented by the top and bottom horizontal lines, respectively. Thirteen of the 17 expiration days had price swings above the median of all other days. If above-median and below-median price swings were equally likely on expiration days, the probability of 13 or more above-median price swings, as occurred in the sample, would be only 2.5 percent. Comparing expiration days to nonexpiration Fridays produced a slightly stronger result, 14 above the median and 3 below. Outcomes with this many or

more above-median observations have a probability of only 0.6 percent under the hypothesis that triple witching hour days were just like other Fridays. The test suggests that the hypothesis is unlikely; one can conclude that unusual volatility typified triple witching hour days.

Restricting the sample to the post-March 1984 period when all expirations were on Fridays yields the same results, which are presented in Table 2 and illustrated in Chart 2. Triple witching hour days appeared unusual compared to all other trading days, as well as to other Fridays. Of the 12 expiration days in this subperiod, 10 exhibited volatility above the median of all other days. Outcomes with 10 or more above-median price swings out of a possible 12 would have just a 1.9 percent chance of occurring under the hypothesis of no unusual volatility on triple witching hour days. The second test produced an even stronger result: 11 of the 12 days fell above the median for other Fridays. The probability of this result occurring under the hypothesis of no unusual volatility on triple witching hour days is only 0.3 percent. One can thus conclude that triple witching hour days were more volatile than ordinary Fridays and more volatile compared to all other trading days as well.

These results showed a marked contrast to similar tests run on the 1979-82 data. "Pseudo-triple witching hour" days were created for this presample by examining the third Friday of the final month of the quarter. If something were unusual about these days of the year, apart from being triple witching hour days after 1982, similar patterns of volatility would also be expected in this earlier period. As shown in Table 3 and Chart 3, these expectations were not fulfilled. Exactly half of the pseudo-triple witching hour days, eight of the sixteen, fell above the median of all other days' volatility, and, similarly, eight fell above the median of other Fridays. This result is likely when nothing is unusual about the 16 pseudo-triple witching hour days. Thus, the study of the 1979-82 data suggests that nothing peculiar about third Fridays in quarter-ending months was evident in the period prior to the introduction of index options.

The Period since the Rule Change. Table 4 and Charts 4, 5, and 6 present the results from the tests conducted on the period since the expiration rule change. Of the five expiration Fridays since the rule change, four fell below the median of all other Fridays and one fell above. The probability of this few or fewer above-median observations would be 18.8 percent if it were in fact the case that expiration Fridays were no different from all other Fridays. With

Chart 1
S&P 500 Daily Percentage Price Swings
(Triple Witching Hour Days vs. Medians, January 1983-May 1987)

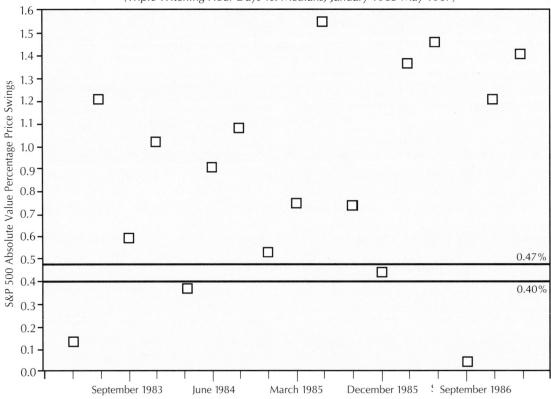

The horizontal lines represent median price swings for the period January 1983-May 1987. The top line shows the median for all days during this period; the bottom line shows the median for Fridays. A box above the median represents a greater-than-usual price swing for that triple witching hour day. A box below the median indicates a lower-than-usual price swing for that day. A box between the medians for the different samples represents a lower-than-usual price swing relative to all days in the sample but a greater-than-usual price swing for Fridays during the sample period. Thus, this chart shows that on triple witching hour days between March 1983 and March 1987, price swings in the S&P 500 Index were typically greater than on Fridays and on all days in general.

Table 1
Test of S&P 500 Index Volatility on Triple Witching Hour Days
(January 1983-May 1987)

Test	Sample Size	Below-Median Price Swings	Above-Median Price Swings	Probability* (Percent)
Expiration days vs. all other days	17	4	13	2.5
Expiration days vs. nonexpiration Fridays	17	3	14	0.6

*Probability of the occurrence of at least the indicated number of above-median price swings under the assumption that expiration days are as likely to exhibit above- as below-median price swings.

Source: Figures in all tables and charts were calculated at the Federal Reserve Bank of Atlanta from data obtained from Data Resources, Inc., Lexington, Mass.

Chart 2
S&P 500 Daily Percentage Price Swings
(Triple Witching Hour Days vs. Medians, May 1984-May 1987)

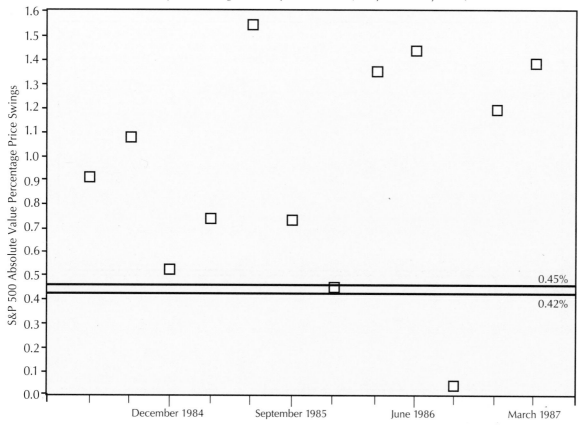

The horizontal lines represent median price swings for the period May 1984-May 1987. The top line shows the median for all days during this period; the bottom line shows the median for Fridays. This chart demonstrates that even after controlling for a "day-of-the-week" effect, the daily percentage price swings on triple witching hour days were greater than usual for other days in the period May 1984-May 1987.

Table 2
Test of S&P 500 Index Volatility on Triple Witching Hour Days
(May 1984-May 1987)

Test	Sample Size	Below-Median Price Swings	Above-Median Price Swings	Probability* (Percent)
Expiration days vs. all other days	12	2	10	1.9
Expiration days vs. nonexpiration Fridays	12	1	11	0.3

Probability of the occurrence of at least the indicated number of above-median price swings under the assumption that expiration days are as likely to exhibit above- as below-median price swings.

Chart 3
S&P 500 Daily Percentage Price Swings
(Pseudo-expiration Days vs. Medians, January 1979-December 1982)

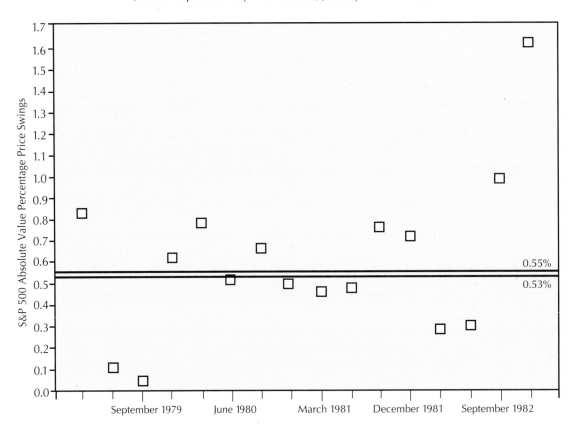

The horizontal lines represent median price swings for the period January 1979-December 1982. The top line shows the median for all days during this period; the bottom line shows the median for all Fridays. Since the boxes representing triple witching hour day price swings are distributed fairly evenly above and below the lines, this chart indicates that before the introduction of options on index futures, pseudo-expiration days were not likely to be more volatile than typical days.

Table 3
Test of S&P 500 Index Volatility on Pseudo-expiration Days
(January 1979-December 1982)

Test	Sample Size	Below-Median Price Swings	Above-Median Price Swings	Probability* (Percent)
Pseudo-expiration days vs. all other days	16	8	8	59.8
Pseudo-expiration days vs. other Fridays	16	8	8	59.8

*Probability of the occurrence of at least the indicated number of above-median price swings under the assumption that expiration days are equally likely to exhibit above- as below-median price swings.

Chart 4
S&P 500 Daily Percentage Price Swings
(Expiration Fridays vs. Medians, May 1987-July 1988)

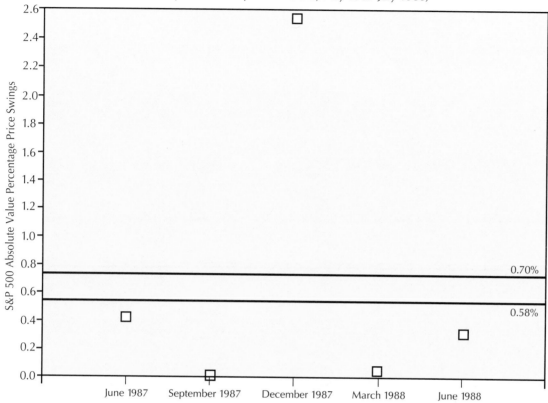

The horizontal lines represent median price swings for the period May 1987-July 1988. The top line represents the median for all days during this period; the bottom line represents the median for Fridays. The chart shows that since the rule change which moved the end of trading on most index futures contracts and some index options to one day earlier, the propensity for expiration Fridays to exhibit greater-than-usual price swings may have been reduced.

Table 4
Test of S&P 500 Index Volatility on Expiration Days
since the 1987 Rule Change

Test	Sample Size	Below-Median Price Swings	Above-Median Price Swings	Probability* (Percent)
Expiration Fridays vs. all other Fridays	5	4	1	18.7
Expiration Thursdays vs. all other Thursdays	5	2	3	50.0
Expiration Thursday-Friday clusters vs. all other Thursday-Friday clusters	5	5	0	3.1

*Probabilities listed for the first and third tests are the probability of the occurrence of at least the indicated number of below-median price swings under the assumption that expiration days are as likely to exhibit above- as below-median price swings. The probability listed for the second test is the probability of the occurrence of at least the indicated number of above-median price swings under the assumption that expiration days are as likely to exhibit above- as below-median price swings.

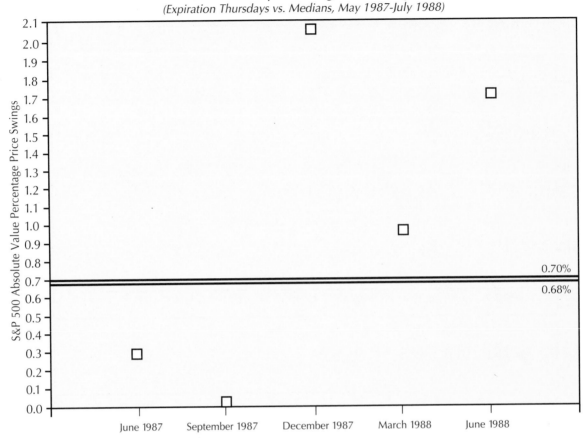

Chart 5
S&P 500 Daily Percentage Price Swings
(Expiration Thursdays vs. Medians, May 1987-July 1988)

The horizontal lines represent median percentage price swings for the period May 1987-July 1988 after the rule change. The top line represents the median for all days during this period; the bottom line represents the median for all Thursdays. Since the boxes in this chart show no distinct pattern, and since the sample on which the chart is based is such a small one, these results are not conclusive regarding price swings on expiration Thursdays since the rule change.

such a small sample, definitive conclusions cannot be drawn, but it appears that the rule change may have reduced the propensity for expiration Fridays to exhibit unusually high volatility. Prior to the rule change, ten Fridays fell above the median and only two below, whereas since the rule change only one has fallen above the median and four have fallen below.

The purpose of examining Thursdays and Thursday-Friday clusters is to test the possibility that the rule change simply shifted volatility to the Thursday preceding expiration or perhaps spread the excess volatility across two days. The test of Thursday volatility, however, could not confirm or reject this possibility. Of the five Thursdays preceding expiration Fridays, three fell above the median for all other Thursdays, and two fell below. No con-

clusions can be drawn from this result, and more observations are needed in order to determine whether these Thursdays are now more or less volatile than ordinary Thursdays.

On the other hand, the test of Thursday-Friday clusters does provide evidence against the notion that the excessive volatility is still generated by the expirations but is now simply spread out over two days. All five of the expiration Thursday-Friday cluster two-day price swings fell below the median of all other Thursday-Friday clusters, which indicates that expiration Thursday-Friday clusters are not likely to display higher-than-usual volatility; if anything, they are likely to display lower-than-usual volatility. Again, though, one must exercise caution when interpreting these results.

Chart 6
S&P 500 Percentage Price Swings over Thursday-Friday Clusters
(Expiration Thursday-Friday Clusters vs. Medians, May 1987-July 1988)

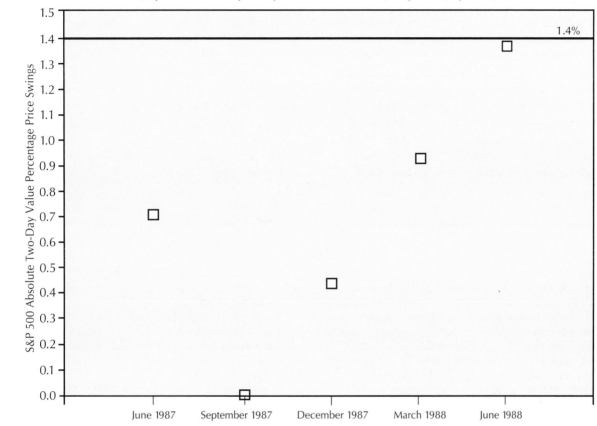

The horizontal line represents median price swing for Thursday-Friday clusters during the May 1987-July 1988 period. Since all the boxes fall below the line indicating typical price swings for Thursday-Friday clusters, the results of this test appear to indicate that expiration Thursday-Friday clusters are not likely to display greater-than-usual price swings. If anything, they are likely to exhibit lower-than-usual price swings. The sample to this date is small, though, and another pattern may emerge over time.

The sample size of five observations is small, and a different pattern quite possibly will emerge with time. Moreover, traders may have practiced extra caution and restraint in this early period under the new rule while waiting to see its effects. Also, curbs placed on computerized trading in the aftermath of the October 1987 stock market crash could have contributed to the apparent reduction in volatility on triple witching hour days.

Conclusion

This study of the volatility on triple witching hour days finds that before the rule change, volatility on those days was likely to be greater than the volatility of ordinary trading days. In other words, the change in stock market prices over the course of a triple witching hour day was likely to be greater than the price changes experienced over most ordinary days.

This result is significant to investors. If the witching hour effect systematically influences stock price volatility, this effect should also influence the pricing of stocks and derivative instruments. The value of index options, for instance, depends directly upon expected market volatility. Thus, the witching hour effect, or its possible disappearance, must be taken into account by those who wish to price financial assets.

In a theoretical perspective, the greater volatility suggests something curious: the structure of the market for derivative assets may actually influence the valuation of the primary securities. The possibility that this influence exists runs counter to the theory that stock prices continuously reflect only that information relating to the risk-adjusted expectation of the future cash flows of a company.

This article described a possible explanation for higher-than-usual volatility on expiration days before the rule change, that is, large mismatches between buy and sell orders brought on by the flood of orders submitted by agents covering or settling positions. Another possibility is that with higher volume on expiration days, more new information was brought to the market—information that could have pushed prices one way or the other. Yet, these explanations are only possibilities. Though this research sheds lit-tle light on the true cause of the volatility, the study does clarify just what the empirical effect of the triple witching hour was before the rule change.

Finally, the early evidence suggests that since the rule change, expiration Fridays are no longer likely to exhibit higher-than-usual volatility, and expiration Thursday-Friday clusters are likely to exhibit less volatility than other Thursday-Friday clusters. Nonetheless, because of the limited amount of information available since the rule change and other potentially influential events during this period, this result is tentative; the newly emerging evidence could still contradict this result. For now observers must wait to see whether the triple witching effect is still a reality or a thing of the past.

Notes

1. The U.S. Commodity Futures Trading Commission (CFTC), which oversees agricultural commodity trading, also oversees trading in stock index futures and options on stock index futures.
2. Galberson (1987).
3. Stock index arbitrage is not practical for the small or even moderately sized investor. Execution of the strategy with the S&P 500 stocks requires a $25 million position in stocks (Stoll and Whaley, 1986b).
4. Suppose a pension fund includes a stock portfolio similar in composition to the S&P 500, and the fund manager must ensure that the fund maintains a value above a certain level, $10,000 for example. One way to achieve this security is through the purchase of S&P 500 put options with combined strike prices totaling $10,000. Should the value of the stock portfolio fall below $10,000, the puts can be exercised, earning for the fund a cash payment equal to the shortfall between the current market value of the stocks and the $10,000.
5. A position in a stock index future can serve the same purpose.
6. See, for example, Kraus and Stoll (1972); Kawaller, Koch, and Koch (1988); Edwards (1988); Finnerty and Park (1987); or U.S. Congress (1985).
7. Their sample of nonexpiration days included only Thursdays from the years when stock index futures expired on Thursdays, and Fridays from the years when expirations were on Fridays. In this way, they controlled for possible day-of-the-week effects.
8. See Fama (1965), Mandelbrot (1963), and Blattberg (1974).
9. The F-test is still a useful device, however, primarily for summarizing comparisons of stock return volatilities from different samples.
10. In a nonparametric test like the one employed in this study, using absolute value of returns gives the same result as squared returns. Note also that the expectation of the squared return equals the stock return variance, should that variance exist.
11. The instruments that are now governed by the new procedures are S&P 500 futures, options on S&P 500 futures, some S&P 500 index options, New York Stock Exchange (NYSE) Composite Index futures, and options on NYSE Composite Index futures. The old rules still govern some S&P 500 index options, S&P 100 index options, Major Market Index futures and options, and Value Line Index futures and options.
12. May 5, 1987, was chosen as the terminal date for the pre-rule change period since it is halfway between the expiration of the March 1987 contract, the last to expire under the old rules, and the June 1987 contract, the first to expire under the new rules.
13. A four-year sample is roughly the same size as the previously described test samples.

References

Blattberg, Robert C., and Nicholas J. Gonedes. "A Comparison of the Stable and Student Distributions as Statistical Models for Stock Prices." *Journal of Business* 47 (1974): 244-80.

Edwards, Franklin R. "Does Futures Trading Increase Stock Market Volatility?" *Financial Analysts Journal* 44 (January/February 1988): 63-69.

Fama, Eugene F. "The Behavior of Stock Market Prices." *Journal of Business* 38 (January 1965): 34-109.

Finnerty, Joseph E., and Hun Y. Park. "Stock Index Futures: Does the Tail Wag the Dog?" *Financial Analysts Journal* 43 (March/April 1987): 57-61.

French, Kenneth R. "Stock Return and the Weekend Effect." *Journal of Financial Economics* 8 (March 1980): 55-69.

Galberson, William. "Futures and Options: How Risk Rattled Wall Street." *New York Times*, November 1, 1987.

Kawaller, Ira G., Paul D. Koch, and Timothy W. Koch. "The Relationship between the S&P 500 Index and S&P 500 Index Futures Prices." Federal Reserve Bank of Atlanta *Economic Review* 73 (May/June 1988): 2-10.

Kraus, A., and H.R. Stoll. "Price Impact of Block Trading in the NYSE." *Journal of Finance* 27 (June 1972): 569-88.

Mandelbrot, Benoit. "The Variation of Certain Speculative Prices." *Journal of Business* 36 (October 1963): 399-419.

McMurray, Scott, and Beatrice A. Garcia. "Wary Traders Brace for Problems at Double Triple-Witching Time." *Wall Street Journal*, June 12, 1987.

"SEC Staff Considering a Move to Lessen Stock Swings Tied to Triple Expirations." *Wall Street Journal*, May 12, 1986.

Stoll, Hans R., and Robert E. Whaley. "Expiration Day Effects of Index Options and Futures." Monograph Series in Finance and Economics, Monograph 1986-3. Salomon Brothers Center for the Study of Financial Institutions, Graduate School of Business Administration, New York University, 1986a.

_____ . "Program Trading and Expiration Day Effects." Ownes Graduate School of Management, Vanderbilt University Working Paper 86-31, 1986b.

_____ . "Program Trading and Expiration Day Effects." *Financial Analysts Journal* 43 (March-April 1987): 16-28.

U.S. Congress. House. Committee on Agriculture. *A Study of the Effects on the Economy of Trading in Futures and Options*. 98th Cong. 2nd sess., 1985.

The Relationship between the S&P 500 Index and S&P 500 Index Futures Prices

Ira G. Kawaller, Paul D. Koch, and Timothy W. Koch

*T*he advent of markets for stock index futures and options has profoundly changed the nature of trading on stock exchanges. These markets offer investors flexibility in altering the composition of their portfolios and in timing their transactions. Futures and options markets also provide opportunities to hedge the risks involved with holding diversified equity portfolios. As a consequence, significant portions of cash market equity transactions are now tied to futures and options market activity.

The effect of the stock index futures and options markets on traditional stock trading has aroused both the ire of critics and the acclaim of supporters. Critics allege that futures trading unduly influences the underlying equity markets, especially on days when futures contracts expire. For example, on various expiration days from 1984 to 1985, the stock markets closed with equity prices either rising or falling dramatically during the final hour of trading.[1] The phenomenon of sharp price swings and the seeming relation to futures market activity has, especially in the wake of the October 19, 1987, stock market crash, prompted various suggestions for modifying the design of the contracts to lessen their impact on the market.[2]

Proponents of futures markets, on the other hand, do not view the final-day price swings as a problem, since the swings are generally temporary and nonsystematic. In fact, proponents argue that such markets provide an important *price discovery function* and offer an alternative marketplace for adjusting equity exposure. The term price discovery function refers to the ability to use a certain market indicator—in this case, stock index futures—to forecast upcoming changes in the prices of securities. For the price discovery function to be most helpful, though, an investor must be

This article was originally published in the Atlanta Fed's May/June 1988 Economic Review. *At the time the article was written, Kawaller was the director of the New York office of the Chicago Mercantile Exchange, Paul Koch was a visiting scholar at the Atlanta Fed, and Timothy Koch held the Chair of Banking at the University of South Carolina.*

able to determine when a change in the futures market will be reflected in the underlying market.

This article addresses some basic questions that have a fundamental bearing on the debate between the critics and advocates of futures markets. Do intraday movements in the index futures price provide predictive information about subsequent movements in the index, or do movements in the index presage futures price changes? Is the price relationship different on expiration days and the days leading up to expiration?

Analysis of the Standard and Poor's (S&P) 500 futures and the S&P 500 index can help answer these questions. This article shows that lags exist not only between movements in index futures prices and subsequent movements in the index, but also between the index and subsequent index futures prices, though these lags are not symmetrical. The index lags behind the index futures price by up to 45 minutes, but the index futures price tends to trail the index only briefly. Examination of the lagged relationships on expiration days and the days prior to them indicates that the relationships are remarkably stable, implying that neither expiration day volatility nor the climate preceding these days interferes with the price discovery function that index futures seem to offer.[3]

An Overview of the S&P 500 Index and Index Futures

The S&P 500 stock index represents the market value of all outstanding common shares of 500 firms selected by Standard and Poor's. Prior to April 6, 1988, this group always consisted of 400 industrials, 40 financial institutions, 40 utilities, and 20 transportation firms.[4] Though all of the shares are not traded on the New York Stock Exchange (NYSE), the cumulative market value equals approximately 80 percent of the aggregate value of NYSE-listed stocks. The index changes whenever the price and thus the cumulative market value of any underlying stock changes.

An S&P 500 futures contract represents the purchase or sale of a hypothetical basket of the 500 stocks underlying the S&P 500 index, set in a proportion consistent with the weights set by the index, with a market value equal to the futures price times a multiplier of 500. The futures price should be tied to the cost of investing in and carrying an S&P 500 look-alike basket of stocks until the expiration of the index

future. The cost of carry incorporates transactions fees, taxes, and the expense of financing the investment, minus the dividends derived from the basket of stocks and any additional reinvestment income.

As a requirement for gaining access to the market, traders must post an initial margin deposit or collateral equal to a fraction of the futures contract market value (price x 500). Futures prices change intermittently throughout each trading day, and at day's end traders must cover any losses when prices move against them. Alternatively, they may withdraw any profit in excess of their initial margin requirement should prices move favorably. During the period from which data for this study were drawn, contracts expired on the third Fridays of March, June, September, and December, with the futures contracts marked to the closing index value at 4:15 p.m., Eastern time.[5]

Basic Functions of Stock Index Futures

Stock index futures typically serve three functions: trading, hedging, and arbitrage. First, traders can take speculative positions in futures to take advantage of anticipated broad market price movements. Second, hedging, which involves the purchase or sale of index futures in anticipation of an intended cash market trade, compensates for adverse price moves in the cash market, and thus reduces aggregate risk. Simple hedges typically involve the purchase (sale) of an asset in the cash market and sale (purchase) of futures contracts on the same asset. As long as the cash-futures spread remains the same and the costs of effecting and financing the transaction are covered, gains (losses) on the cash market purchase are countered by losses (gains) on the future. The investor thus may mitigate the risk of loss and the possibility of gain on the cash market purchase.

Arbitrage is a third strategy served by stock index futures. It involves the simultaneous purchase and sale of stocks and futures and subsequently enables an investor to capture profits from realignments of relative prices following an apparent inconsistency in the index and the index futures price. When the index futures price moves outside the range determined by the cost of the look-alike basket and the cost of carry, arbitrage will tend to drive the futures price and the index toward their cost-of-carry relationship. If the actual futures price is higher than the cost of the look-alike basket and the cost of carry, the futures contract is overvalued, justifying the purchase of the look-alike basket of stocks and the simultaneous sale of the futures contract. If the futures price falls below the price of the look-alike portfolio plus the cost of carry, the futures contract is undervalued, and the reverse trade would be profitable. In both cases, the arbitrage transactions realign the futures price and the index.

Because physical delivery does not take place, the futures contract is said to be "settled in cash." Cash settlement is an important feature of stock index futures. An arbitrageur who has sold futures and bought the underlying basket of stocks does not deliver the basket of stocks to the investor who bought futures. Instead the arbitrageur must sell the basket of stocks. Any open futures positions are marked to the final settlement index calculation when the futures expire. Once the arbitrageur pays or receives the value of the price change from the prior day, the position is closed. A common practice for arbitrageurs, however, is to trade large blocks of stocks or whole portfolios at prices tied to closing prices on the futures expiration days. As a result, these large volumes of orders late in the day have tended, on some occasions, to create at least temporary imbalances in the cash equity markets.

Movements in Futures Prices. Numerous studies have explained the price relationship between stock index futures and the underlying stocks in terms of arbitrage behavior. Futures prices normally vary relative to stock prices within ranges that are not sufficient to trigger arbitrage. In fact, arbitrage opportunities are often not available. A number of scholars have attempted to identify and measure arbitrage trading boundaries.[6] Their results indicate that the futures to cash price differential, referred to as the *basis*, should fall within boundaries determined by the cost of carry. Because market interest rates have historically exceeded the dividend rate on common stocks, the "fair value" or theoretical stock index futures price normally exceeds the stock index.[7]

Conventional wisdom among professional traders dictates that movements in the S&P 500 futures price affect market expectations of subsequent movements in cash prices. The futures price presumably embodies all available information regarding events that will affect cash prices. Purchase or sale of index futures requires one transaction, while purchase or sale of a look-alike portfolio generally involves 200 or more stocks and a minimum $5 million investment. Consequently, the index futures price is likely to respond to new information more quickly than cash market prices in general and, thus, more quickly than

---

Table 1
Possible Effects of Movements in the S&P 500 Index and S&P 500 Index Futures

Movement in the S&P 500 Index	
may be affected by	**may affect**
• prior index levels	• upcoming index levels
• current futures prices	• upcoming futures prices
• prior futures prices	
• other market information	

Movement in the S&P 500 Index Futures Prices	
may be affected by	**may affect**
• prior futures prices	• upcoming futures prices
• current index levels	• upcoming index levels
• prior index levels	
• other market information	

---

the S&P 500 index. This lag of the index behind the futures price results because the underlying stocks must be traded in order for the index to reflect a change in value. Since most index stocks do not trade each minute, the cash market responds to the new information with a lag.[8] S&P 500 index movements may similarly convey information about subsequent price variation in the futures contract; however, the lag of the futures price behind the index is likely to be much shorter than the lag of the index behind the futures price.

If new information on the health of the economy is bullish, a trader has the choice of buying either S&P 500 futures or the underlying stocks. While the futures trade can be effected immediately with little up-front cash, actual stock purchases require a greater initial investment and may take longer to implement since they require a subsequent stock selection. This preference for index futures as a vehicle for speculative transactions explains why changes in futures prices may lead changes in stock prices and the S&P 500 index. Futures prices may thus provide an indicator of forthcoming cash prices, which follow when investors who are unwilling or unable to use futures incorporate the same information that led to changes in futures prices into their own cash market transactions.

Changes in the S&P 500 index can also lead changes in the futures price, if the value of the index conveys information that affects futures prices. Futures traders are likely to incorporate recent changes in the index in their pricing decisions. For example, if the index declines because investors are selling stocks connected with options trading, the decline may induce a change in sentiment that is reflected in subsequent futures prices.[9]

Potential lead and lag patterns between index futures and the index are complicated by two more possible relationships: the futures and the index may move together as new information affects both index futures and cash market trades. Each measure may lead the other as market participants find clues about impending values of index futures and broad market movements in previous futures prices and broad cash market movements, respectively. Technical analysts, or chartists, rely heavily on patterns of relationships between past and future values of series such as the S&P 500. A summary of possible relationships between the S&P 500 index and S&P 500 futures prices is shown in Table 1.

Tests of the Intraday Relationship between S&P 500 Futures and the S&P 500 Index

A complex set of potential relationships could exist between S&P 500 futures and the S&P 500 index prices. Movements in each are thought to be influenced by the past and current movements of both as well as by other market information. The study reported on in this article tried to gauge the magnitude and variability of the relationships between the index and the futures by estimating distributed lags between the two prices. Distributed lags employ a method of weighting past data to determine their effects on the data under study.

The pattern of lags between index futures and the index may not be constant over time. While shifting patterns are conceivable throughout the life of the futures contract, the focus of interest on expiration day effects begs the question of whether these temporal relationships show any differentiation on those days. On expiration days, the traders' need to close positions may generate market imbalances that could conceivably overwhelm the mechanism by which new information influences index futures and cash market prices. An expiration-day breakdown in this mechanism would diminish the benefits of the index futures market—at least on expiration day—as a medium for discovery.

The data are minute-by-minute prices of index futures contracts and the S&P 500 index on all trading days in 1984 and 1985. The Chicago Mercantile Exchange provided the data.[10] Pairing the reported index with the last index futures price quoted during the minute that the index appeared yielded 360 pairs of index and futures observations each day (six-hour trading day x 60 observations per hour). To judge whether the index futures-index relationship changes as the expiration day approaches, lags were estimated for six trading days in each quarter beginning in the second quarter of 1984 and ending with the last quarter of 1985.[11] The days are 88, 60, 30, and 14 days prior to expiration, 1 day prior to expiration, and expiration day. These days were chosen to represent the approach of expiration and the effect of this approach on the index futures-index relationship.

The nature and extent of the lead/lag relationships between index futures prices and the index were measured using a number of analyses. First, a time series analysis was performed to study the movements of futures prices relative to prior futures prices. Next, the same method of analysis gauged movement of the S&P 500 index based on past index performance. These time series analyses studied the minute-to-minute changes in both the index and the futures prices. The next step in the analysis was to construct a model to describe the dynamic intraday price relationships between the index and the futures prices. In this model, index movements depend on their own past movements, current and past movements in the futures price, and other relevant market information (see Table 1). Likewise, futures price movements are modeled to depend on their own past movements, current and past movements in the index, and other relevant market information.[12]

Consistent evidence on both the form of the lag relationships and their stability over time emerges from these tests: first, the contemporaneous relationship between futures prices and the index is quite strong—dwarfing the lagged relationships. In fact, the futures and index move almost in lock step. Second, lags between index futures prices and the index are not symmetrical. The index lags behind the index futures price by up to 45 minutes, while the futures price lags behind the index only briefly if at all. This result supports the contention that index futures do, in fact, serve a price discovery function. Third, the lagged relationships do not appreciably change as expiration day approaches or on expiration day itself.

Different patterns of lagged relationships between S&P 500 futures and the S&P 500 index are given in Chart 1. It shows the distributed lag coefficients for two days in the fourth quarter of 1984; results for other days in this contract period, as well as days in other contract periods, are quite similar. Typically, the first coefficient, which describes the contemporaneous relationship, is the greatest, or one of the greatest, on each day. In the panels showing lags from futures to the index, relatively large and statistically significant coefficients show up with lags as long as 45 minutes. Panels showing lags from the index to futures typically show the one-minute lag as the largest coefficient and the only one that is significant. These results parallel evidence garnered from earlier time-series analyses.[13]

Chart 1 also shows quite similar patterns in the distributed lag coefficients 88 days prior to expiration day and on expiration day. Coefficients showing the lead from futures to the index continue to be mostly positive even on expiration day. They are significant or nearly significant through 20 to 30 minutes on each day, though the lag appears somewhat less on expiration day. Other quarters record quite similar patterns.

Implications

Evidence uncovered in the tests of lagged relationships between S&P 500 index futures prices and the S&P 500 index points to the usefulness of the futures as a predictor of broad equity market movements measured by the index. The S&P 500 futures price and underlying index evidently respond to market information simultaneously, and the index shows lags of up to 45 minutes behind the futures. Importantly, the magnitudes of the contemporaneous effects on different days are consistently much larger than the lagged effects. Thus, though the price discovery function has been demonstrated, the indications of forthcoming cash market changes provided by past futures prices are not sufficient to provide an exploitable trading strategy.

Consistency in the lagged relationships over the days approaching expiration day and on expiration day also indicates that the pattern of lags between futures and the index is not disturbed by the closing out of arbitrage positions. This consistency implies that index futures trading continues to make its contribution to price discovery, even on expiration days that transpired without market activity restrictions.

Chart 1
Sample Distributed Lags for the
S&P 500 Index and S&P 500 Index Futures Prices

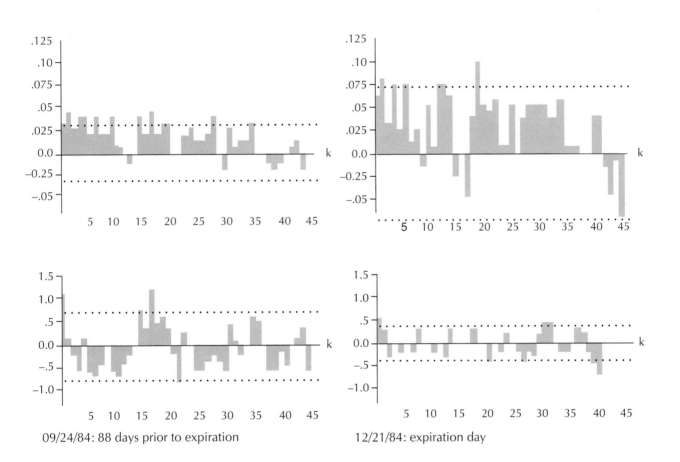

09/24/84: 88 days prior to expiration   12/21/84: expiration day

Chart 1 shows the relationship between minute-to-minute movements in the S&P 500 futures price and the S&P 500 index. The top graph in each set shows how past minute-to-minute movements in the futures price affect current movements in the index, and the bottom figure shows how past movements in the index affect current movements in the futures price.

The vertical axis in each figure represents the magnitude of the minute-to-minute impacts of each value on the other. The horizontal axis charts the number of minute-to-minute lags incorporated into the model. For example, for k=1 minute lag, the value plotted in the top graph shows the impact of the futures price change one minute earlier on the current index value. At the number '20' on the horizontal axis, the effect on the current index value of the futures price 20 minutes earlier is plotted.

When the vertical lines within the graph fall between the two dotted horizontal lines, the magnitude of the distributed lag coefficient is less than twice its standard error, and thus is not statistically significant. When the vertical lines within the graph fall outside the dotted lines, the magnitude of the distributed lag coefficient is more than twice its standard error, and, thus, is statistically significant.

When the vertical lines are concentrated in the positive portion of the figure (above 0.0), most of the lagged impacts of one price on the other are positive, that is, increases in one price are then followed by increases in the other price.

When the vertical lines are concentrated in the negative portion of the figure (below 0.0), most of the lagged impacts of one price on the other are negative, that is, increases in one price are then followed by decreases in the other.

Notes

1. The term "triple witching hour" was used to describe this trading period because the Chicago Mercantile Exchange's (CME) S&P 500 futures, the Chicago Board of Trade Options Exchange's (CBOE) S&P 100 options, and contracts on individual stock options all expired on the third Fridays of March, June, September, and December. After March 1987, the final day of trading for S&P 500 futures was moved to the day prior.

2. The U.S. Securities and Exchange Commission, the Government Accounting Office, and the executive branch (the Brady Commission), as well as various exchange and private research groups, are currently studying the relation of price swings to futures market activity.

3. These results do not explain expiration day swings, nor do they suggest that such swings are desirable.

4. Standard and Poor's has recently announced that the composition of the S&P 500 will now be flexible.

5. Since this study, the final settlement procedures for S&P 500 futures have changed. Contracts currently expire one business day prior to the third Friday of the contract month, with the final settlement price based on a special calculation of the Friday opening prices for each of the 500 stocks. Upon expiration, one final cash adjustment is made to reflect the last day's gains or losses.

6. Cornell and French (1983a, b); Figlewski (1984a, b); Modest and Sundaresan (1983); and Stoll and Whaley (1986).

7. The theoretical upper and lower bounds are discussed extensively in the literature. For example, see Stoll and Whaley (1986): 8-10, or Kawaller (1987): 447-49.

8. New information could affect a subset of index stocks disproportionately relative to the entire stock market. In such cases, not all index stocks must be traded each minute for the index to adjust completely and quickly to new information.

9. In options trading, an investor purchases the right to buy or sell a given security at a fixed strike price before a specific date in the future. If the investor does not exercise this right before the date in the contract, the option expires and the option buyer forfeits the money.

10. At the time of this study, the index was available only each minute. Since then, index quotations have been calculated and disseminated at about 15-second intervals.

11. Prior to the June 1984 contract, S&P 500 futures expired on Thursdays. This article's sample is restricted to the last three contracts in 1984 and all contracts that expired in 1985. Also note that futures trade for 15 minutes after the stock markets close. Quotes from these 15 minutes are not considered in this analysis. Finally, since September 30, 1985, quotes are available beginning at 8:30 a.m., but the analysis is restricted to the six hours (360 observations) from 9:01 a.m. and 3:00 p.m. so that the results can be compared across quarters.

12. In the context of this model, zero restrictions are tested on the distributed lag coefficients, allowing, alternately, the contemporaneous coefficient and the coefficient at lag one minute to remain unconstrained. See Kawaller, Koch, and Koch (1987) for details.

13. The tests with no restrictions on the contemporaneous and first coefficients also confirm the longer lags from the futures to the index and the very short lag from the index to the futures.

Bibliography

Cornell, Bradford, and Kenneth French. "The Pricing of Stock Index Futures." *Journal of Futures Markets* 3 (Summer 1983a): 1-14.

_____ . "Taxes and the Pricing of Stock Index Futures." *Journal of Finance* 38 (June 1983b): 675-94.

Elton, Edwin J., Martin J. Gruber, and Joel Rentzler. "Intraday Tests of the Efficiency of the Treasury Bill Futures Market." *Review of Economics and Statistics* 66 (February 1984): 129-37.

Figlewski, Stephen. "Explaining the Early Discounts on Stock Index Futures: The Case of Disequilibrium." *Financial Analysts Journal* 40 (July-August 1984a): 43-47.

_____ . "Hedging Performance and Basis Risk in Stock Index Futures." *Journal of Finance* 39 (July 1984b): 657-69.

_____ . "Hedging with Stock Index Futures: Theory and Application in a New Market." *Journal of Futures Markets* 5 (Summer 1985): 183-99.

Gastineau, Gary, and Albert Madansky. "S&P 500 Stock Index Futures Evaluation Tables." *Financial Analysts Journal* 39 (November-December 1983): 68-76.

Geweke, John. "Testing the Exogeneity Specification in the Complete Dynamic Simultaneous Equations Model." *Journal of Econometrics* 6 (April 1978): 163-85.

Granger, Clive W. "Investigating Causal Relations by Econometric Models and Cross-Spectral Methods." *Econometrics* 37 (July 1969): 423-38.

Haugh, Larry D. "Checking the Independence of Two Covariance-Stationary Time Series: A Univariate Residual Cross-Correlation Approach." *Journal of the American Statistical Association* 71 (June 1976): 378-85.

Kawaller, Ira G. "A Comment on Figlewski's 'Hedging with Stock Index Futures: Theory and Application in a New Market.'" *Journal of Futures Markets* 5 (Fall 1985): 447-49.

_____ . "A Note: Debunking the Myth of the Risk-Free Return." *Journal of Futures Markets* 7 (June 1987): 327-31.

Kawaller, Ira G., Paul D. Koch, and Timothy W. Koch. "The Temporal Price Relationship between S&P 500 Futures Prices and the S&P 500 Index." *Journal of Finance* 5 (December 1987): 1309-29.

Koch, Paul D., and James F. Ragan, Jr. "Investigating the Causal Relationship Between Wages and Quits: An Exercise in Comparative Dynamics." *Economic Inquiry* 24 (January 1986): 61-83.

Koch, Paul D., and Shie-Shien Yang. "A Method for Testing the Independence of Two Time Series that Accounts for a Potential Pattern in the Cross-Correlation Function." *Journal of the American Statistical Association* 81 (June 1986): 533-44.

Modest, David, and Mahadeaum Sundaresan. "The Relationship between Spot and Futures Prices in Stock Index Futures Markets: Some Preliminary Evidence." *Journal of Futures Markets* 3 (Summer 1983): 15-41.

Stoll, Hans R., and Robert E. Whaley. "Expiration Day Effects of Index Options and Futures." Vanderbilt University, March 1986.

U.S. Securities and Exchange Commission. Letter to the Honorable John D. Dingell, June 13, 1986a.

_____. Letter to Mr. Kenneth J. Leiber and others, June 13, 1986b.

_____. *Roundtable on Index Arbitrage*, July 9, 1986c.

*B*eyond Plain Vanilla: A Taxonomy of Swaps

Peter A. Abken

*S*wap contracts of various kinds have become a mainstay of financial risk management since their introduction in the late 1970s. In the most general terms, a swap is an exchange of cash flows between two parties, referred to as counterparties in the parlance of swap transactions. Swaps, which transform the cash flows of the underlying assets or liabilities to which they are related into a preferred form, have been used in conjunction with positions in debt, currencies, commodities, and equity. Most swap agreements extend from one to ten years, although many have been arranged for much longer periods.[1]

The key players responsible for originating and propelling the swaps market are money center banks and investment banks. These institutions benefit from the fee income generated by swaps, which are off-balance-sheet items, and by the spreads that arise in pricing swaps. Innovations in the swaps market, as in other financial services areas, may be characterized as a Darwinian struggle, in which competition heats up and margins narrow as a particular kind of swap becomes accepted and widely used. Such swaps are disparagingly said to be traded "like commodities." That is, little value is added by the dealer in structuring a swap and bringing counterparties together; consequently, little return is realized for the service of intermediation or position taking.

Perhaps the most basic, and most popular, swap involves the conversion of interest payments based on a floating rate of interest into payments based on a fixed rate (or vice versa). Because many variants of interest rate and other swaps have emerged over the years, this most basic type has become known as the "plain vanilla" swap.[2] As swap forms take on plain vanilla status, the firms that originated them are compelled to develop new

This article was originally published in the Atlanta Fed's March/April 1991 Economic Review. *The author is a senior economist in the financial section of the Atlanta Fed's research department.*

types of swaps to regain their margins, amounting to monopoly rents, on new products. Some swap variations succeed, while others languish or fail.

In this article the plain vanilla swap is a starting point for a detailed taxonomy of the various species and subspecies of swaps. Swap variants are classified along cladistic principles, categorized and compared in terms of their features and applications. Examples illustrate many of the important types of swaps.

The Market

A Brief History. Before taking a detailed look at swaps, an overview of the market will help put their proliferation into perspective. Although some swaps had been arranged in the late 1970s, the first major transaction was a 1981 currency swap between IBM and the World Bank. This deal received widespread attention and stimulated others.

The currency swap actually evolved from a transaction popular in the 1970s, the parallel loan agreement, that produced cash flows identical to a swap's. For example, in one of these agreements a firm in the United States borrows a million dollars by selling a coupon bond and exchanges (swaps) this amount for an equivalent amount of deutsche marks with a German firm, which borrows those deutsche marks in its domestic market. This is the initial exchange of principal. Thereafter, the U.S. firm makes mark-denominated coupon payments and the German firm makes dollar-denominated coupon payments. Upon maturity of the underlying debt, the firms swap principal payments. These firms have effectively borrowed in one another's capital markets, although for a variety of reasons (such as foreign exchange controls or lack of credit standing in foreign markets) they could not borrow directly. As Clifford W. Smith, Charles W. Smithson, and Lee Macdonald Wakeman (1990a) point out, the problems with such an agreement were that default by one firm does not relieve the other of its contractual obligation to make payments and that the initial loans remain on-balance-sheet items during the life of the agreement for accounting and regulatory purposes. The currency swap, on the other hand, stipulates that a default terminates the agreement for both counterparties and, in general, limits credit-risk exposure to the net cash flows between the counterparties, not the gross amounts. This type of currency swap is essentially a sequence of forward foreign exchange contracts.[3]

Following the 1981 currency swap, the first interest rate swap, in mid-1982, involved the Student Loan Marketing Association (Sallie Mae). With an investment bank acting as intermediary, Sallie Mae issued intermediate-term fixed rate debt, which was privately placed, and swapped the coupon payments for floating rate payments indexed to the three-month Treasury bill yield. Through the swap, Sallie Mae achieved a better match of cash flows with its shorter-term floating rate assets.[4] At the end of 1982, the combined notional principal outstanding for interest rate and currency swaps stood at $5 billion. Notional principal is the face value of the underlying debt upon which swap cash flows are based.

The commodity swap made its appearance in 1987, when it was approved by a number of U.S. banking regulators (see Schuyler K. Henderson 1990 and Krystyna Krzyzak 1989b, c). Banks had been prohibited from direct transactions in commodities or related futures and forward contracts. In 1987 the Office of the Comptroller of the Currency permitted Chase Manhattan Bank to act as a broker in commodity swaps between an Asian airline and oil producers. Shortly afterward Citicorp also obtained approval for engaging in commodity swaps through its export-trading subsidiary. Regulations were further relaxed in February 1990 to allow national banks to use exchange-traded futures and options to hedge commodity swap positions. However, much commodity swap activity took place offshore because of uncertainties about the Commodity Futures Trading Commission's (CFTC) view of commodity swaps. The CFTC undertook a study of off-exchange transactions in February 1987 to determine whether they came under the CFTC's regulatory jurisdiction. In July 1989 the CFTC established criteria that would exempt commodity swaps from its regulatory oversight.[5] Since the CFTC's decision commodity swap activity has been increasing in the United States. As of early 1990, commodity swaps outstanding totaled about $10 billion in terms of the value of the underlying commodities (Julian Lewis 1990, 87).

Equity swaps are the newest variety, first introduced in 1989 by Bankers Trust. Based on both domestic and foreign stock indexes, these instruments may take complex forms, such as paying off the greater of two stock indexes against a floating rate of interest. The mechanics of such instruments and their advantages will be discussed below.

The Size of the Market. As of year-end 1989, the size of the worldwide swaps market, as measured by the dollar value of the notional principal, stood at

Table 1
U. S. Dollar Interest Rate Swaps
1985-89*

Survey Period	End User			ISDA User			Total		
	Contracts	Notional Principal	Average Contract	Contracts	Notional Principal	Average Contract	Contracts	Notional Principal	Average Contract
1985	5,918	$141,834	$23.97	1,061	$28,348	$26.72	6,979	$170,182	$24.38
1986	10,752	$235,829	$21.93	3,330	$76,921	$23.10	14,082	$312,750	$22.21
1987	16,871	$379,880	$22.52	7,472	$161,637	$21.63	24,343	$541,517	$22.25
1988	20,381	$484,272	$23.76	8,968	$243,894	$27.20	29,349	$728,166	$24.81
1989	23,324	$622,602	$26.69	13,303	$371,144	$27.90	36,627	$993,746	$27.13
Total Interest Rate Swaps 1987-89									
1987	23,768	$476,247	$20.04	10,359	$206,641	$19.95	34,127	$682,888	$20.01
1988	35,031	$668,857	$19.09	14,529	$341,345	$23.49	49,560	$1,010,203	$20.38
1989	50,193	$955,492	$19.04	23,635	$547,108	$23.15	73,828	$1,502,600	$20.35

* All dollar amounts are in millions of dollars in U.S. dollar equivalents.

Source: International Swap Dealers Association Market Survey.

$2.37 trillion. This figure does not include commodity or equity swaps, but these new types of swap have relatively small amounts outstanding compared with interest rate and currency swaps. The International Swap Dealers Association (ISDA), a trade organization, periodically surveys its members, who include most of the major swap dealers. Table 1 displays the survey results for swaps in various categories. The interest rate swap market, involving swaps denominated in one currency, composed roughly two-thirds of the market, or $1.5 trillion as of year-end 1989. Of that amount, two-thirds consisted of U.S. dollar swaps, the most prevalent kind of swap. The average contract size was $20.35 million and $27.13 million for total and total dollar interest rate swaps, respectively. Currency swap market data are given in Table 2. The U.S. dollar is less dominant among currency swaps, for which it represents 41 percent of the total, compared with its 66 percent share of interest rate swaps. For the years during which the survey has been conducted, swaps of every type have grown rapidly.[6]

In all categories the position of the end users has been a multiple of those of the swap dealers. Inter-dealer swaps arise mainly in connection with hedging activities. A certain amount of double counting is therefore involved in the aggregate figures because one swap can set up a number of others as counterparties hedge their positions.

The latest ISDA survey reveals that the most active category for new swaps originated during the period January 1 to June 30, 1990, was non-U.S. dollar interest rate swaps, which grew by 26.4 percent. U.S. dollar swaps increased by 8.2 percent in this period. In contrast, total currency swaps rose by 2.9 percent, with U.S. dollar currency swaps contracted increasing by 4.6 percent. These semiannual growth rates show considerable variability over time and thus do not indicate trend movements. Further discussion of the ISDA survey results appears below in the section on currency swaps.

*I*nterest Rate Swaps

Interest rate swaps account for the most volume in the swaps market, as seen in the previous section. The explanation to follow covers many of the numerous features that can modify the plain vanilla swap. Though discussed in detail only in relation to interest rate swaps, these alternate forms actually or potentially apply to currency, commodity, and equity swaps as well; they can be combined in innumerable ways to alter any kinds of cash flows.

The basic fixed-for-floating interest rate swap involves a net exchange of a fixed rate, usually expressed as a spread over the Treasury bond rate corresponding to the swap maturity, for a floating rate of interest. That floating rate is tied or indexed to any of a number of short-term interest rates. The London Interbank Offered Rate (LIBOR) is the most common.[7] Other rates include the Treasury bill rate, the prime rate, the Commercial Paper Composite, the Certificate of Deposit Composite, the federal funds rate, the J.J. Kenney index, and the Federal Home Loan Bank System's Eleventh District cost-of-funds index. The Eleventh District index has been used mainly by thrift institutions in California.[8] The J.J. Kenney index is based on short-term tax-exempt municipal bond yields.

The fixed rate payer (and floating rate receiver) is said to have bought a swap or to have "gone long" a swap. Similarly, the floating rate payer (and fixed rate receiver) is said to have sold a swap or "gone short" a swap. Swaps are quoted by a dealer (or broker) usually in terms of the spread over the Treasury security of comparable maturity. For example, a swap with seven-year time to maturity, or tenor, might be quoted at 65-72. The dealer is offering to buy a swap (pay fixed) at a rate that is 65 basis points above the seven-year Treasury yield, and offering to sell a swap (receive fixed) at 72 basis points over that yield.[9] The dealer is therefore collecting a 7 basis point margin for standing between the counterparties.

Like floating rate notes, the floating rate payments on a swap do not necessarily match the timetable of the floating rate index.[10] The payment may be based on the average of the underlying index during some specified interval. The point at which the floating rate is established, based on the floating rate at that time or over some previous period, is termed the reset date. This date is not necessarily the same as the settlement date, when payment on the swap is made to the other counterparty. If reset and settlement dates do not coincide, the swap is said to be paid in arrears, which is also a common convention for floating rate notes. The floating rate may be reset daily, weekly, monthly, quarterly, or semiannually, while typically the settlement dates fall monthly, quarterly, semiannually, or annually (Anand K. Bhattacharya and John Breit 1991, 1158).

As over-the-counter instruments, interest rate swap terms are open to negotiation. The conventional way

Table 2
U. S. Dollar Currency Swaps
1987-89*

Survey Period	End User			ISDA User			Total		
	Contracts	Notional Principal	Average Contract	Contracts	Notional Principal	Average Contract	Contracts	Notional Principal	Average Contract
1987	4,665	$129,181	$27.69	1,366	$33,425	$24.48	6,031	$162,606	$26.96
1988	6,777	$201,374	$29.71	2,297	$68,103	$29.66	9,074	$269,477	$29.70
1989	9,078	$257,748	$28.39	3,414	$96,418	$28.24	12,492	$354,166	$28.35

Total Currency Swaps
1987-89

Survey Period	End User			ISDA User			Total		
	Contracts	Notional Principal	Average Contract	Contracts	Notional Principal	Average Contract	Contracts	Notional Principal	Average Contract
1987	5,173	$294,608	$28.47	1,439	$71,006	$24.67	6,612	$365,614	$27.65
1988	7,724	$469,092	$30.37	2,547	$164,550	$32.30	10,271	$633,642	$30.85
1989	11,270	$647,516	$28.73	4,015	$222,182	$27.67	15,285	$869,698	$28.45

* All dollar amounts are in millions of dollars in U.S. dollar equivalents.

Source: International Swap Dealers Association Market Survey.

to quote a swap rate is relative to the floating rate index "flat." That is, a swap counterparty would pay the fixed rate and receive LIBOR. Swaps can also be arranged to include a spread above or below the floating rate—for example, LIBOR + 10 basis points. In addition, fixed rate payers and floating rate payers can agree to making payments at different periods—quarterly floating rate payments versus semiannual fixed rate payments.[11] However, swap counterparties usually prefer net transactions so that only a difference check passes between them, thereby limiting credit exposure. In the section below the first alteration of the basic plain vanilla structure that is considered encompasses different treatments of a swap's notional principal. The second general variation outlined allows for specially tailored coupon structures, and the discussion includes consideration of option-like features. Third, different types of underlying instruments—in particular, asset swaps and their uses in creating synthetic assets—are examined. Finally, option structures are discussed, including options on swaps, known as swaptions.

Variations on Notional Principal. The plain vanilla swap is nonamortizing. Nonamortizing swaps, known as "bullet" swaps, have a constant underlying notional principal upon which interest payments are made. This structure is easily modified to accommodate any kind of predictable changes in the underlying principal. Uncertainty about the future amount of the principal, which frequently arises with mortgage-backed securities, is usually better handled using option features, which will be discussed shortly.

Amortizing, Annuity, and Mortgage Swaps. Amortizing swaps are typically used in conjunction with mortgage loans, mortgage-backed securities, and automobile- and credit-card-backed securities. All of these tend to involve repayment of principal over time. In general it is difficult to match the amortization schedule of a swap, which usually cannot be changed after its initiation, against the amortization rate on these assets or liabilities; thus, the swapholder runs the risk of being over- or underhedged. A particular example of an amortizing swap is discussed in more detail in the section below on asset swaps. One specific kind is the mortgage swap, which is simply an amortizing swap on mortgages or mortgage-backed securities. The extreme form of an amortizing swap, in which the notional principal diminishes to zero as the principal of a fixed rate mortgage does, is an annuity swap.

Accreting Swaps. The flip side of an amortizing swap is an accreting swap, which, as its name sug-

gests, allows the notional principal to accumulate during the life of the swap. Both amortizing and accreting swaps are sometimes also called sawtooth swaps. The accreting swap arises commonly with construction finance, in which a construction company or developer has a floating rate drawdown facility with a bank. That is, a line of credit may be tapped that would lead to increasing amounts of floating rate borrowing. An accreting swap would convert those floating rate payments into fixed rate payments, although again there is a risk of not exactly matching notional principal amounts at each settlement date. It is possible to create amortizing or accreting swaps from bullet swaps of varying tenor instead of arranging a swap specifically with the desired characteristics.

Seasonal Swaps and Roller Coasters. Finally, amortizing and accreting notional principals can be combined to form a seasonal swap, which allows the notional principal to vary according to a counterparty's seasonal borrowing needs such as those retailers typically experience. A swap that allows for periodic or arbitrary but predictable swings in notional principal is called a roller coaster.

Variations on Coupon Payments. Altering cash flows of underlying securities is one of the primary functions of swaps. In the following section a number of important types of swaps that accomplish this end are discussed, including those with option-like features.

Off-Market Swaps. The plain vanilla swap is also characterized as a par value swap. That is, the fixed rate for the swap is established such that no cash payment changes hands when the swap is initiated. The term *par value* derives from the swap's being viewed as a hypothetical exchange of fixed for floating rate bonds. When arranged at market interest rates, both bonds are equal to their face values (par value). Nonpar, or off-market, swaps involve fixed or floating rates that are different from the par value swap rates. Differences in the fixed rate above or below the par value swap rate entail a cash payment to the fixed rate payer from the floating rate payer if the fixed rate coupon is above the par value swap rate, and vice versa if it is below. The payment's amount is the present value of the difference between the nonpar and par value swap fixed rate payments. Swap counterparties commonly perform this kind of calculation in the process of marking an existing swap to market. An existing swap may be terminated (if permitted in the swap agreement) by such a marking to market of the remaining swap payments. High or low coupon swaps, as off-market swaps are alternatively called, are created simply by doing the calculation at the outset and making or receiving the appropriate payment. One reason for engaging in this type of swap is to change the tax exposure of underlying cash flows. Another is that spreads above or below the floating rate index can be introduced. John Macfarlane, Janet Showers, and Daniel Ross (1991) explain the mechanics of this variation.

Basis Swaps. A basis swap is an exchange of one floating rate interest payment for another based on a different index. Consider an example in which a bank, First SmartBucks, has invested in two-year floating rate notes that pay the bank one-month LIBOR plus 100 basis points. First SmartBucks has funded this purchase by issuing one-month certificates of deposit. The problem is that LIBOR and the CD rate will not track each other perfectly, exposing First SmartBucks to a so-called basis risk; it may pay more on its CDs than it receives from its floating rate notes. The problem is solved by entering into a basis swap with a swap dealer, who will pay the one-month CD rate in exchange for LIBOR. Chart 1 illustrates the transaction. Aside from the initial fee for the swap, the cost of this hedging transaction manifests itself as a 10 basis point spread under the CD rate received from the dealer. This hedge may also be less than perfect, however, because the dealer probably would use the Certificate of Deposit Composite, which may not track

First SmartBucks's CD rate perfectly, to index his payments. Nevertheless, the swap is likely to mitigate the original basis risk.

Yield Curve Swaps. The yield curve swap, a variant of the basis swap, typically is an exchange of interest payments indexed to a short-term rate for ones tied to a long-term rate. For example, a counterparty could contract to make semiannual floating rate payments based on six-month LIBOR and receive floating rate payments indexed to the prevailing thirty-year Treasury bond yield, less a spread to the swap dealer.[12] The ten-year Treasury bond yield has also been used for yield curve swaps on the long end, as well as three-month LIBOR on the short end.

Yield curve swaps gained popularity in early 1988 when the yield curve began to flatten—that is, when long rates fell relative to short rates (Krzyzak 1988, 29). Savings and loan institutions were major users of this new swap because they found it useful for adjusting the interest rate exposures of their portfolios (see asset swaps below). These swaps were also well suited to speculating on shifts in the yield curve while hedging against changes in its level. Finally, these instruments were combined with a new kind of floating rate debt, called FROGs (floating rate on governments), to transform the FROG's coupon into LIBOR. The coupon was reset semiannually and tied to the yield on newly issued Treasury bonds.[13] This strategy

Chart 1
A Basis Swap

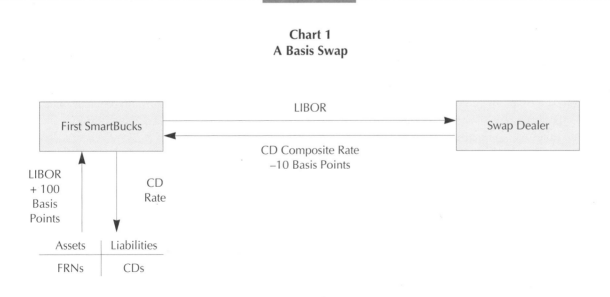

First SmartBucks transforms LIBOR interest coupons into CD composite rate payments via a basis swap.

reportedly achieved a lower cost of funding than a standard LIBOR floating rate issue.

Caps, Floors, and Collars. A floating rate payer can combine option contracts with a swap to tailor the maximum size of potential swap payments. Interest rate caps, floors, and collars are instruments closely related to swaps that can alter swap cash flows.[14] As an example, consider a plain vanilla swap with a fixed rate of 8 percent (the swap rate). At a reset date, a rise in the floating rate above 8 percent would obligate the floating rate payer to pay the counterparty the net amount of the notional principal outstanding times the difference between the actual floating rate—say, 10 percent—and the swap rate. By buying a 9 percent cap of the same maturity as the swap the user would never pay more than one percentage point above the swap rate. The cap could be obtained from another counterparty, or it could be bundled with the swap in one transaction. However, buying a cap from another counterparty introduces an additional credit risk.

A counterparty who sells (or writes) a cap is obligated to pay the excess over the cap's strike rate (9 percent in this example). The purchaser in return pays a cap "premium" up front. In fact, caps are sequences of interest rate options with maturities that match the schedule of floating rate payments. Analogous to caps, interest rate floors pay off whenever the floating interest rate falls below the prespecified floor level. To defray some or all of the cost of buying a cap, the floating rate payer could sell a floor with a strike rate less than the swap rate. Such a sale would create an interest rate collar. Thus, rather than paying for the protection of the cap outright, the floating rate payer could give up part of the payments from the swap resulting from large declines in the floating rate below the swap rate. That is, the maximum possible payment from the other swap counterparty would effectively be the difference of the swap rate and the floor strike rate times the notional principal.

Synthetic Swaps. The "collaring" of a swap suggests that a floating rate payer could completely offset a swap by buying a cap and selling a floor that both have strike rates equal to the swap rate. Similarly, a fixed rate payer could nullify a swap by selling a cap and buying a floor with strike rates equal to the swap rate. In these cases the floating rate payer would, in effect, be buying a "synthetic" swap and the fixed rate payer would be selling one. However, swaps are not usually unwound in this way because it is generally cheaper simply to buy or sell the corresponding swap; caps and floors may not be sufficiently liquid at the desired strike rates to execute these transactions at

reasonable prices. (That is, an illiquid—infrequently traded—cap or floor would be quoted with large spreads.) Nevertheless, arbitrage between the swap and cap/floor markets is possible and does occur if rates for these instruments get too far out of line.

Participating Swaps. A hybrid version of the fixed rate swap and interest rate cap allows a counterparty to benefit partially from declining rates while not requiring any up-front payment as with a cap. Consider an example using LIBOR. The counterparty would receive LIBOR to pay its floating rate debt. In turn, instead of paying a fixed interest rate as for a plain vanilla swap, a higher fixed rate is established (above the swap rate), which is the maximum rate the counterparty would pay if LIBOR rises above that level. However, if LIBOR falls below this maximum rate, the counterparty's payment would decline less than one-for-one with LIBOR. For example, the swap terms could stipulate that a one percentage point drop in LIBOR would reduce the swap payment by one-half percentage point. The so-called participation rate in this case is 50 percent. In other words, the counterparty would participate in 50 percent of any decline in LIBOR below the maximum rate. The maximum rate and the participation rate are set to price the swap at zero cost upon initiation. The price of this swap's option feature is paid by giving up part of the gains from falling rates.

The participating swap can also be structured to have the counterparty pay LIBOR and receive payments indexed to a fixed schedule. That is, a minimum rate would be specified in the swap, with payments above that minimum determined by the product of the prevailing LIBOR multiplied by the participation rate. A counterparty might want to use such a swap in conjunction with its floating rate assets. Participating swaps can be structured for any interest rates and are also used for currencies and commodities.

Reversible Swaps and Roller Coasters. Reversible swaps and roller coasters are a couple of exotic variants on swap structures. A reversible swap allows a counterparty to change status from floating rate payer to fixed rate payer or vice versa at some point during the life of the instrument. The roller coaster takes this concept a step further by having the counterparties reverse roles at each settlement date. Distinct from the earlier type of roller coaster involving variations in notional principal, this one has been used in only a limited number of transactions.

Zero Coupon Swaps. As its name implies, all payments on one side of the swap come at the end in one "balloon" payment, while the other side makes periodic fixed or floating rate payments. One use of zero coupon swaps is to transform the cash flows from zero coupon bonds into those of fixed coupon bonds or floating rate bonds, or vice versa.

Asset Swaps. Asset swaps are precisely what their name suggests. They effectively transform an asset into some other type of asset, such as the conversion of a fixed rate bond into a floating rate bond. The conversion results in synthetic securities because of the swap's effects. The analysis of asset swaps actually contains nothing new. The earlier example of First SmartBucks's use of a basis swap, exchanging LIBOR for the CD Composite rate, was a type of asset swap. Asset swaps are usually considered in connection with portfolio management and are low-cost tools for changing the characteristics of individual securities or portfolios.

Bhattacharya (1990) discusses an interesting application of asset swaps to a particular kind of mortgage-backed security. The collateral behind mortgage-backed securities is subject to prepayment. For example, homeowners may pay off their mortgage principals early in the event they move or mortgage rates drop sufficiently. Collateralized Mortgage Obligations (CMOs) repackage mortgage cash flows into a variety of securities that carry different prepayment risks. Planned Amortization Class (PAC) bonds are structured to have amortization schedules more predictable than those of other CMO classes. However, the risks are nevertheless sufficient to make PAC bonds trade at fairly wide spreads over corresponding Treasury securities. PAC bonds have been popular candidates for amortizing asset swaps that convert the bonds' fixed coupons into floating rate payments tied to any index. These asset swaps have the potential to make PAC bonds attractive to a broader class of investors and consequently channel more funds to the mortgage market. Such swaps may be a more cost-effective means of altering the characteristics of mortgage-backed securities than having an even broader array of such securities being issued.

As a tool for bond portfolio management, asset swaps can change a portfolio's exposure to interest rate risk. The value of a portfolio, and of any bonds within it, fluctuates with shifts in interest rates, tending to fall as market rates rise and vice versa. The sensitivity to interest rate risk is measured by a portfolio's duration, which is based on the future timing and size of its cash flows.[15] A portfolio manager can extend a portfolio's duration, increasing its volatility with respect to interest rate movements, by entering into asset swaps to receive fixed rate cash flows and to pay float-

ing rate cash flows. Conversely, a portfolio can be protected or "immunized" against interest rate movements by contracting to make fixed rate cash flows and receive floating rate. The intuition here is that the more a portfolio's (or security's) cash flows move with current market rates, the closer its value will stay to face value. Money market funds, for example, experience little change in asset value because they have very short duration. In contrast, a fund consisting of long-term zero coupon bonds, which have durations equal to their maturities, would have extremely volatile asset values.

Asset swaps are particularly useful for adjusting a portfolio when securities sales would result in capital losses. For example, a portfolio manager would be reluctant to change the portfolio's duration by selling off bonds that are "under water" (currently valued below par). As just discussed, an asset swap is ideal for this kind of adjustment.[16] As another example, some bonds cannot be traded because they were purchased from an underwriter through a private placement to avoid registration and other costs associated with public issues. Using an asset swap obviates the need to trade the underlying security to alter interest rate exposure.

Forward and Extension Swaps. Forward swaps are analogous to forward or futures contracts as hedging instruments. The difference is that forward or futures contracts hedge cash flows at a single point in the future whereas forward swaps (and swaps generally) hedge streams of cash flows. Extension swaps are an application of forward swaps.

Forward Swaps. Financial managers, such as corporate treasurers, often want to hedge themselves against rising interest rates when considering a future debt issue. For example, selling a new issue of bonds may be necessary to refund outstanding corporate bonds that mature in one year. The yield on that issue is unknown today but could be locked in using a forward or deferred swap. If rates have risen when the outstanding bonds mature, the firm sells the swap, realizing a gain equal to the present value of the difference between the cash flows based on the current swap rate and those based on the lower fixed rate of the forward swap. This gain would offset the higher coupon payments on the newly issued fixed rate bond; the effective rate paid would be the same as the forward swap rate.

However, a fall in rates would translate into a loss on the forward swap upon sale, although the newly issued fixed rate bond would itself carry a lower rate. The effective rate on the fixed rate issue would again be the forward swap rate, neglecting differences in transactions costs. The forward swap in this example is used as a hedging tool, establishing a certain fixed rate today instead of an unknown fixed rate at the future date for debt issuance.

Extension Swaps. An extension swap is merely a forward swap appended to an existing swap before its term ends to extend it by some additional period (Jeffry Brown 1991, 127). If the forward swap is arranged based on current forward interest rates, the extension swap would be obtained at no cost. However, if a counterparty wants the forward swap rate to match an outstanding swap's rate, an up-front cash payment (or receipt) might be necessary to compensate for the change in market rates since the outstanding swap's origination. The extension swap in this case would be a type of off-market swap.

Swaptions. The earlier discussion of amortizing swaps and the example of an asset swap involving a PAC bond emphasized the risk inherent in mismatches of principal with notional principal. The amount of principal is not always perfectly predictable, especially for many new types of asset-backed securities. Option contracts are designed to handle contingencies of this kind, and, not surprisingly, a market has developed for options on swaps, known as swaptions. (There is also a market for options on caps and floors, which, as one might guess, are called captions and floortions.)

Like any option, swaptions entail a right and not an obligation on the part of the buyer. Unfortunately, the nomenclature for swaptions is confusing, so the details are often simply spelled out in talking about them. A call swaption (a call option on a swap or payer swaption) is the right to buy a swap—pay a fixed rate of interest and receive floating. A put swaption (put option on a swap or receiver swaption) is the right to sell a swap—pay floating and receive fixed. The swaption on the plain vanilla swap is the most common, although swaptions can be written on more complicated swaps. Both the maturity of the swaption and the tenor of the underlying swap, which commences at a stipulated future date, must be specified. Also like options, swaptions come in both American and European varieties. The European swaption, which accounts for about 90 percent of the market, may be exercised only upon its maturity date, whereas the American swaption may be exercised at any time before maturity (Robert Tompkins 1989, 19). Only European swaptions will be considered in this discussion, unless otherwise noted.

A call swaption would be exercised at maturity if the swaption strike rate—the fixed rate specified in the contract—is lower than the prevailing market fixed rate for swaps of the same tenor. The swaption could be closed out by selling the low fixed rate swap obtained through the swaption for a gain, rather than entering into that swap. Similar reasoning applies to the decision to exercise a put swaption.

Swaptions are quite different from caps and floors, although these instruments are frequently used in similar situations. A swaption involves one option on a swap, while a cap (or floor) represents a series of options expiring at different dates on a floating interest rate. In addition, cap prices depend partly on the volatility of near-term forward rates, whereas swaption prices reflect the volatility of future swap rates, which in turn are averages of more distant, less volatile forward rates. Consequently, swaptions are much cheaper than caps or floors. Like options, swaptions require up-front payments, but these have recently fallen in the range of 20-40 basis points as compared with 200-300 basis points for caps or floors (Krzyzak 1989a, 13). American swaptions would be slightly more costly than European swaptions because of the additional right to exercise the instrument before maturity.

Callable, Puttable, and Reversible Swaps. For hedging applications, perhaps the swaption's most basic use is to give a swap counterparty the option to cancel a swap, at no further cost beyond the initial swaption premium. A fixed-for-floating swap bundled together with a put swaption is known as a callable swap. The swap can be canceled upon the maturity of the embedded swaption if, for example, interest rates have fallen. Exercising the swaption creates an offsetting floating-for-fixed swap. A floating-for-fixed swap combined with a call swaption is called a puttable swap. The swap can be terminated if interest rates have risen—that is, if a higher fixed rate could be received from a new swap.

Another example of a swaption application involves the PAC bond considered earlier. The amortizing swap to pay fixed and receive floating could be hedged against the possibility that the rate of amortization is faster than that structured in the swap. A put swaption purchased along with the original fixed-for-floating swap would (partially) hedge this risk. The purchaser would buy a swaption(s) in the amount necessary to partially offset the underlying swap in order to cover the potential additional amortization of principal. An American swaption would be appropriate for this application.

The reversible swap described earlier can be synthesized by a fixed-for-floating plain vanilla swap combined with put swaptions for twice the notional principal of the underlying swap. Assuming a swaption has the same notional principal amount as the swap, the first swaption cancels the existing swap and the second creates a floating-for-fixed swap upon maturity, running for the remaining term of the original swap.

Extendable Swaps. As the name suggests, an extendable swap contains the option to lengthen its term at the original swap rate. Such a swap simply amounts to an ordinary swap with a swaption expiring at the end of the swap's tenor. Note the difference between an extendable swap and an extension swap. The former gives the holder the option to extend a swap; the latter is a commitment. The same distinction applies to swaptions and forward swaps.

Leveraged Buyout Hedging. Another application of swaptions has been in leveraged buyouts, in which a firm's management takes on large amounts of debt to "take a firm private." Lenders, such as commercial banks, often require the firm to hedge its debt, which typically is floating rate. A call swaption with a strike rate at a level the firm could safely meet would accomplish this end. Should the floating rate rise sharply, the swaption would be exercised, converting the remaining floating rate payments to manageable fixed rate payments. However, lenders involved in leveraged buyout financing often prefer to sell caps because a swaption, if exercised, makes its writer a counterparty to a highly leveraged (and often low-rated) firm. A cap writer faces no credit risk from the cap buyer.

Synthetic Straight Debt. A final example of swaption usage is in stripping callable debt. This strategy has been popular in the swaption market's brief history. Corporate bonds are frequently issued with options allowing the issuer to refinance the debt issue at a lower coupon if interest rates fall before the bonds mature. The issuer usually cannot exercise the embedded call until after some prespecified date. The callable debt's buyer has effectively written a call option on the price of the bond to the issuer, the firm. If bond prices rise above the strike price of the calls (implying that interest rates have fallen sufficiently), the issuer has the right to call the bonds away after paying the strike price.

Because many participants in these markets have believed that the calls attached to these bonds are undervalued, the following arbitrage strategy developed. Firms wanting fixed rate debt issued callable bonds and "stripped" the embedded call options by selling call swaptions, with the net result of creating synthetic noncallable or "straight" bonds at a lower yield than that prevailing on comparable fixed rate bonds. The yield reduction stemmed from selling the undervalued bond market calls at a profit in the swap market.[17]

As an illustration of the basic strategy, assume the bond is callable at par. That is, if at the call date the relevant interest rate is at or below the original coupon rate, the bond will be called. To strip the call option, the issuer writes a put swaption, which, if exercised, obligates the firm to pay fixed and receive floating on a swap commencing on the bond's first call date and ending at the bond's maturity date. In this example the swaption strike would be set to the bond's coupon rate. If interest rates fall, the put swaption is exercised. In turn, the firm would call its debt and simultaneously issue floating rate debt, whose coupon payments would be met by the floating rate payments coming from the swap counterparty. On balance, the firm would continue to make fixed rate payments, though to the swap counterparty instead of to the bondholders. There are many variations on this strategy. Also, embedded put options can be stripped from bonds in a similar way.[18]

The Size of the Swaption Market. As of year-end 1989, $79.7 billion in U.S. dollar and non-U.S. dollar swaptions was outstanding, as measured by the value of the underlying notional principal.[19] The market grew 118 percent compared with the figure for year-end 1988, the first year the survey included swaptions. The size of the caps, collars, and floors market was considerably larger. For year-end 1989, the total U.S. dollar and non-U.S. dollar value of the notional principal for caps, collars, and floors was $457.6 billion, representing a 57 percent increase over the previous year's figure.

Non-U.S. Dollar Denominated Interest Rate Swaps. The interest rate swap market is active worldwide. About one-third of interest rate swaps outstanding involved currencies other than the U.S. dollar. Table 3 reports the latest International Swap Dealers Association survey results for year-end 1989 reflecting swaps involving a single currency. The dollar equivalent of the notional principal outstanding is shown, ranked by currency. The Japanese yen is a distant number two to the U.S. dollar, accounting for 8.5 percent of the market. The British pound and deutsche mark are next in order, with the New Zealand dollar ranking last.

Currency Swaps

Basic currency swaps were described earlier in connection with their evolution from parallel loan agreements. The fixed-for-fixed currency swap is the

Table 3
Interest Rate Swaps
as of December 31, 1989*

Currency	U.S. Dollar Equivalent	End-User Counterparty (percent)	ISDA Counterparty (percent)	Currency as Percentage of Total ($1,502.6 billion)
U.S. Dollar	$993,746	62.65	37.35	66.14
Yen	$128,022	52.25	47.75	8.52
Sterling	$100,417	60.13	39.87	6.68
Deutsche Mark	$84,620	61.46	38.54	5.63
Australian Dollar	$67,599	84.35	15.65	4.50
French Franc	$42,016	89.92	10.08	2.80
Canadian Dollar	$29,169	87.66	12.34	1.94
Swiss Franc	$28,605	55.65	44.35	1.90
European Currency Unit	$18,988	58.51	41.49	1.26
Dutch Guilder	$5,979	65.14	34.86	.40
Hong Kong Dollar	$2,149	60.12	39.88	.14
Belgian Franc	$835	79.16	20.84	.06
New Zealand Dollar	$444	82.66	17.57	.03

* All dollar amounts are in millions of dollars in U.S. dollar equivalents.

Source: International Swap Dealers Association Market Survey.

most rudimentary type of swap and is roughly equivalent to a series of forward foreign exchange contracts. For example, a firm could borrow yen at a fixed interest rate and swap its yen-dominated debt for fixed rate dollar-denominated debt. The exchange rate for converting cash flows throughout the life of the swap would be established at the outset. Forward foreign exchange contracts, if they were available in long-dated maturities, could also lock in the exchange rate for future cash flows.

All of the features enumerated for interest rate swaps can be applied singly or in combination to swaps involving different currencies. A number of applications of currency swaps are discussed below.

Currency Coupon Swaps. One of the currency swap's early variants is the currency coupon swap, otherwise known as the cross-coupon swap. This swap is like a plain vanilla swap in which the fixed interest rate is paid in one currency while the floating rate is paid in another. However, the principal involved in the transaction is usually exchanged as well.

An Example. Consider a hypothetical transaction between a U.S. firm, USTech, and a British bank, Brit-

Bank. A U.S. swap dealer intermediates the transaction, in part because this institution has the relevant credit information about the swap counterparties that they lack individually. USTech is setting up a British subsidiary and issuing dollar-denominated floating rate bonds tied to LIBOR to finance this operation. USTech wants to hedge itself on two counts, though: first, it wants protection against foreign exchange rate fluctuations because the subsidiary's sales revenue will be in sterling but will be needed to service the dollar-denominated floating rate debt; second, USTech prefers to make fixed rate payments. A currency coupon swap would enable the firm to make sterling-denominated fixed rate payments while receiving dollar-denominated LIBOR, which it would pass to its floating rate bondholders. On the other hand, BritBank would like sterling-denominated fixed rate cash flows instead of dollar-denominated LIBOR payments from floating rate notes that it holds in a portfolio within its trust department. The bank wants the fixed rate sterling cash flows to extend the duration of its portfolio.

As is typical of currency swaps, this one involves exchanges of principal at the beginning and end of the swap. The dealer collects his margin on the fixed rate side of the swap. Like the fixed rate currency swap, the exchange rate for the currency coupon swap is established at the outset and prevails at each of the subsequent settlement dates. Payments at those dates are for the gross amounts of the cash flows, not the net amount as with interest rate swaps, although some swaps stipulate that net amounts be exchanged.

European Currency Unit Swaps. The European Currency Unit (ECU) has become an increasingly important "currency" in the Eurobond market. If progress is made toward monetary union of the European Community (EC), the ECU may become European markets' official unit of account. It currently is valued as a weighted average of twelve EC currencies. Although growing rapidly, the number of outstanding ECU-denominated bonds constitutes only about 4 percent of the outstanding amount of publicly issued Eurobonds (Graham Bishop 1991, 72.) Cross-coupon ECU swaps have been used to transform both principal and coupon payments denominated in the ECU into other currencies and vice versa.

Terry Shanahan and Jim Durrant (1990) discuss an example in which a U.S. multinational firm needed to finance subsidiaries in France, Belgium, and the Netherlands. The firm borrowed in the Eurobond market by floating ECU-denominated fixed rate debt and converted the issue via a cross-coupon swap into floating rate debt with payments in French francs, Belgian francs, and Dutch guilders. The firm exchanged the principal, consisting of a basket of currencies in proportion to each currency's share in the ECU, raised from the bond buyers. In return, the firm received an equivalent value of the three currencies from the swap counterparty. During the life of this five-year swap, the firm received annual ECU coupon payments from the counterparty, which the firm passed on to the bondholders, and it made annual floating rate payments in guilders and Belgian francs and semiannual floating rate payments in French francs to the counterparty. Upon maturity of the swap, the initial transfer of principal was reversed. The counterparty exchanged ECU principal for repayment in the three currencies from the U.S. firm. In turn, the firm redeemed its bonds with the ECU payment from the counterparty.

Swapping Illiquid Bonds and Private Placements. A major impetus for the growth of currency swaps has been and continues to be the portfolio management of illiquid securities. The earlier discussion of portfolio duration adjustment showed a basic rationale for using swaps, which holds particularly true in the Eurobond market, where many bonds lack the liquidity to be traded readily. In addition, for internationally diversified portfolios, bond trading may be desired to change portfolios' exposures to exchange rate fluctuations. Currency swaps fulfill portfolio managers' needs for such risk management.

Currency (and interest rate) swaps have been especially useful in managing portfolios of privately placed bonds. In terms of a number of costs to the issuer, these bonds are significantly cheaper than publicly placed bonds. Use of privately placed bonds avoids the public disclosure and registration requirements as well as compliance with U.S. accounting regulations; it also minimizes legal costs, reduces underwriting costs, and speeds placement. Yet such securities appeal to a much narrower class of investors because of their illiquidity.

In April 1990 the Security and Exchange Commission approved Rule 144A, which greatly simplifies disclosure requirements for private placement issuers (Franklin Chu 1991, 55). Non-U.S. corporations that need to fund their U.S. subsidiaries will find it much easier to raise capital through private placements. The disadvantages of holding these relatively illiquid securities is expected to be lessened both by the use of swaps in portfolio management and by the growth of a secondary market for private placements (Brady 1990, 86).

The Size of the Market. The U.S. dollar is the preeminent currency in the currency swaps market. Table 4 shows that the dollar has a 41 percent share in the currency swaps market, followed by the Japanese yen with a 23 percent share. The Swiss franc, Australian dollar, and German mark occupy the next ranks, with the Hong Kong dollar taking the smallest share of the market for the surveyed currencies.

Commodity Swaps

Commodity swaps are straightforward extensions of financial swaps, though a number of institutional factors make commodity swapping much riskier than the financial variety. As mentioned earlier, only about $10 billion in notional value has been transacted in this relatively new market. However, commodity prices historically have been much more volatile than financial asset prices, and volatility tends to promote the development and use of hedging instruments. Commodity swaps' volume has reportedly doubled in the past year and is expected to do so again in 1991 (Janet Lewis 1990, 207). Another impetus is likely to

Table 4
Currency Swaps
as of December 31, 1989*

Currency	U.S. Dollar Equivalent	End-User Counterparty (percent)	ISDA Counterparty (percent)	Currency as Percentage of Total ($869.7 billion)
U.S. Dollar	$354,166	72.78	27.22	40.72
Yen	$201,145	71.83	28.17	23.13
Swiss Franc	$64,823	77.42	22.58	7.45
Australian Dollar	$61,768	70.77	29.23	7.10
Deutsche Mark	$53,839	79.93	20.07	6.19
European Currency Unit	$39,948	83.06	16.94	4.59
Sterling	$33,466	74.11	25.89	3.85
Canadian Dollar	$32,580	81.72	18.28	3.75
Dutch Guilder	$10,132	82.53	17.47	1.17
French Franc	$8,435	88.74	11.26	.97
New Zealand Dollar	$5,818	81.90	18.10	.67
Belgian Franc	$2,997	86.89	13.11	.34
Hong Kong Dollar	$583	90.39	9.61	.07

* All dollar amounts are in millions of dollars in U.S. dollar equivalents.

Source: International Swap Dealers Association Market Survey.

be the resolution of some regulatory uncertainties, as discussed above. Energy-related commodities hedged via swaps to date include crude oil, heating oil, gasoline, naphtha, natural gas, jet fuel, maritime diesel fuel, and coal. Swap maturities have ranged from one month to five years. A relatively smaller number of swaps have been arranged for gold and for base metals, mainly copper and aluminum, as well as a few in nickel and zinc (Brady 1990, 87).

The most popular commodity swap has been the plain vanilla fixed-for-floating swap, very much akin to the plain vanilla interest rate swap. End users turn to swaps for hedging for essentially the same reasons that they take positions in commodity futures contracts. Their pricing decisions can be based on a known future cost of inputs or revenue from outputs, allowing the appropriate margins to be built in. The end users avail themselves of hedging instruments to transfer the risk to others who specialize in managing that risk.[20] Exchange-traded futures and options contracts tend to be liquid for contracts with time to maturity of only a few months. Hedging large positions farther out in time would cause the futures prices to move against the hedger, raising the cost of the hedge.

In contrast, over-the-counter oil swaps are well suited to hedging intermediate-term risks that cannot be handled by simple positions in futures having relatively short maturity. At the same time, the implication is that swap intermediaries face greater risks because of difficulties they encounter in hedging their swap positions (see Janet Lewis 1990). Oil trading firms have an advantage in acting as dealers because they also carry out transactions in the underlying commodities, giving them additional flexibility in hedging.

A commodity swap may be important as a hedge for a firm that is considering financing a project using debt.[21] The same is true for interest rate and currency swaps as well, but commodity prices are notoriously volatile, giving lenders ample reason to require a commodity swap hedge.[22] In other words, swaps can increase a firm's ability to borrow.

An Example. A U.S. producer of oil, TexOil, Inc., sells oil at the spot price but wants to hedge against any large drops in the price of oil that would make production uneconomical. Another counterparty, a charter luxury liner company, LuvBoats Ltd., wants to hedge the proceeds from advanced ticket sales for the coming year. Maritime diesel fuel, purchased at the spot price, is a major operating cost for LuvBoats's ships. Chart 2 depicts a pair of plain vanilla swaps with a swap dealer intermediating the transaction.

As with any kind of swap transaction, a dealer does not necessarily need an offsetting counterparty to enter into a swap with another counterparty. The swap involving LuvBoats Ltd. is actually tied to the price of No. 2 heating oil, which is a more actively traded commodity than maritime diesel. The spread to the counterparty is lower because the swap dealer can better hedge its position, for example by using No. 2 heating oil futures contracts. LuvBoats is willing to bear some basis risk—the risk that maritime diesel and heating oil price movements will be less than perfectly correlated—to avoid paying the dealer a larger spread to index a swap to the price of maritime diesel. TexOil receives a fixed price of $25 per barrel of crude from the swap dealer, while LuvBoats pays a fixed amount of 74 cents per gallon of heating oil. Since the swap's origination, oil and refined product prices have declined, resulting in a $4.52 per barrel net payment to TexOil and a 9 cent per gallon net payment from LuvBoats at the current payment date.

Oil swaps can assume more complex forms. For example, they can be combined with currency and in-terest rate swaps to convert uncertain, dollar-denominated spot market purchases of oil into fixed deutsche mark payments. To meet regulatory guidelines, commodity swaps require the inclusion of caps and floors, although these are usually set at prices far from the prevailing commodity price and thus are unlikely to be reached. Caps, collars, floors, participating swaps, swaptions, and many other instruments have been adapted to the commodity markets. Also, oil and other commodity swaps typically reset based on daily averages of spot market prices for the underlying commodity. Averaging tends to make the floating side of a swap have a better correspondence with actual spot market purchases by the counterparties. A swap reset based on a single day's price would be less likely to be representative of such purchases.

Equity Swaps

Equity swaps are the newest type of swap and are a subset of a new class of instruments known as synthetic equity.[23] Equity swaps generally function as an asset swap that converts the interest flows on a bond portfo-

Chart 2
Commodity Swaps

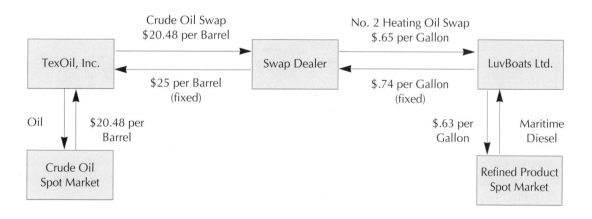

TexOil receives $25 per barrel and pays the spot price for crude oil. LuvBoats receives the spot price for No. 2 heating oil and pays a fixed price for heating oil. LuvBoats in turn buys maritime diesel at the spot price for diesel. There are 42 gallons in a barrel.

lio into cash flows linked to a stock index. The stock indexes that have been used include the Standard and Poor's (S&P) 500, the Tokyo Stock Price Index (TOP-IX) and Nikkei 225 (Japan), the Chambre des Agents de Change (CAC) 240 (France), the Financial Times Stock Exchange (FTSE) 100 (United Kingdom), the Toronto Stock Exchange (TSE) 300 (Canada), as well as others (see Salomon Brothers, Inc. 1990; Saul Hansell 1990; and Richard Metcalfe 1990, 40). Linking portfolio performance to an index means that dividends are not received as with actual equity ownership; the portfolio tracks only the capital gain component of the underlying stocks.

One of the advantages of using a synthetic swap is that transactions costs are mitigated, especially in dealing with less liquid foreign stock markets (Hansell 1990, 56). On the other hand, such swaps are also illiquid, which implies that their use be predicated on a buy-and-hold strategy for an investment portfolio. Equity swaps have been structured to have one- to five-year tenors and usually have quarterly or semiannual reset dates.

The mechanics of an equity swap are similar to the workings of other kinds of swaps. Typically, an investor will swap either fixed or floating rate interest payments for payments indexed to the performance of a stock index such as the S&P 500. If the index appreciates during the interval between settlement dates, the investor receives a payment from the counterparty equal to the rate of appreciation times the swap's notional principal. At the same time, the investor pays, for example, LIBOR less a spread representing the margin to the dealer. Actual settlement would involve only the difference between these bases. In the event the S&P 500 falls, the investor would pay the rate of depreciation times notional principal and LIBOR less a spread. Of course, the investor is receiving LIBOR or another floating rate from his or her investment portfolio. The net result of the swap is that the portfolio's income behaves like that of an index equity portfolio.

A variation of the basic equity swap—the asset allocation swap—links the equity side of the swap to the maximum of two indexes. For example, the swap agreement could stipulate that the counterparty receive the maximum of the rate of appreciation (or pay the maximum rate of depreciation) on the S&P 500 or Nikkei 225 at each settlement date. This kind of swap effectively swaps a portfolio into a foreign stock portfolio or domestic stock portfolio instantly, without transactions costs (apart from those associated with the swap). There are many other possibilities for asset allocation swaps. As another example, the swap could be indexed to the maximum of the S&P 500 or a bond index. Index options could be embedded in the swaps to trade away upside exposure in exchange for downside protection from index moves.

Conclusion

Swaps are but one kind of instrument that has been spawned in the profusion of financial innovation during the last two decades.[24] In the most general terms, swaps are contracts that transform cash flows from underlying assets or liabilities. They have been designed to incorporate great flexibility in that task and hence are frequently described as instruments that tailor cash flows. This article encompasses the four basic types of swap: interest rate, currency, commodity, and equity. Each group in turn branches into a variety of forms that can accommodate virtually any application. However, novelty does not guarantee success. The most successful swaps have frequently been the simplest, plain vanilla variety.

Swaps integrate credit markets. By the nature of their function, swaps can link money markets (short-term financing) and capital markets (long-term financing). Swaps also play a significant role in the so-called globalization of financial markets because they obviate the need for many investors to carry out transactions in underlying foreign securities, thereby contributing to the international diversification of portfolios. International arbitrage of securities and swaps markets is left to those participants who have the lowest transactions costs, increasing global market efficiency.

Swaps are an important tool for simplifying financial transactions that cross national borders. At the same time, they pose potential risks to the stability of financial markets. Recent concern about the strength of both banks and investment banks has focused the attention of swap market participants on counterparties' creditworthiness, upon which the financial obligations contracted through a swap agreement depend.[25]

However, part of the reason that swaps evolved was to reduce the credit exposure of counterparties involved in similar financial arrangements. Swaps generally confine credit risk to exposure to the net difference in cash flows, not the gross amounts or exposure of underlying principal, and defaults have been rare occurrences.[26] The implementation of the

Basle Agreement in 1992 will establish more uniform capital standards for the world's commercial banks and should help to further reduce credit risks in the swap market.[27]

Notes

1. Shirreff (1989) reports that swaps with thirty-year maturities or "tenors" have been arranged. Such long-lived swaps typically involved counterparties with top credit ratings or relied on third-party credit enhancements.
2. Wall and Pringle (1988) discuss the plain vanilla swap in detail and consider the reasons for using swaps.
3. A forward contract commits the buyer to purchase the underlying asset at a prespecified price (the forward price) upon maturity of the contract. A call option gives the buyer the right, but not the obligation, to purchase an underlying asset at a prespecified price on or sometime before the maturity date of the option. The put gives the corresponding right to sell at a prespecified price. These instruments will be described further at appropriate places in the exposition.
4. See McNulty and Stieber (1991) for a more detailed account.
5. See Henderson (1990) for details about the CFTC's criteria.
6. The growth may be exaggerated by these figures because the number of survey respondents, not reported in the tables, has also been increasing. However, the ISDA points out that the major swap dealers have consistently participated in their surveys.
7. See Kuprianov (1986) for a background discussion of Eurodollar futures and LIBOR.
8. See McNulty and Stieber (1991, 100-101) for information about the Eleventh District cost-of-funds rate.
9. A basis point is a hundredth of a percentage point.
10. Ramaswamy and Sundaresan (1986) analyze floating rate securities and discuss the characteristics of such securities.
11. See Macfarlane, Showers, and Ross (1991) for a discussion of nonstandard swap terms. This article gives a detailed account of swap terminology and conventions.
12. Ordinarily, comparisons of yields along the yield curve are made using instruments of comparable default risk. Yield curve swaps exchange floating payments on debt bearing different default risks. Because the underlying three-month Eurodollar time deposit is default risky, LIBOR is greater than the riskless three-month Treasury bill yield. The swap therefore exchanges credit spreads as well as yield curve spreads.
13. See Goodman (1991, 160-61) for details about this strategy.
14. See Abken (1989) for an introduction to these instruments.
15. See Bodie, Kane, and Marcus (1989) for an introduction to duration analysis.
16. This example is cited by Bhattacharya (1990, 56).
17. Goodman (1991) and Brown and Smith (1990) discuss call monetization using several strategies. Forward swaps may also be used for this purpose. Brown and Smith discuss many subtleties of these strategies.

18. Krzyzak (1988, 29; 1989a, 9) reports that the embedded calls were overvalued and that call monetization was used to undo the expensive call. In this case, call monetization would not be an arbitrage.
19. Chew (1991) discusses recent activity in the non-U.S. dollar swaptions markets, particularly deutsche mark instruments.
20. This point of view is not universal or uncontroversial. Williams (1986) argues that risk aversion has nothing to do with the use of futures. Rather, futures contracts reduce transactions costs in dealing with underlying commodities. His model assumes that all futures market participants are risk-neutral.
21. Also, Smith, Smithson, and Wilford (1990) discuss a conflict between stockholders and bondholders of a corporation, known as the underinvestment problem, that swaps can mitigate.
22. See Spraos (1990) for a case study of a complex copper swap required in part for this reason.
23. Other examples of synthetic equity include over-the-counter equity options, public warrant issues, and bonds containing equity options. See Hansell (1990). Index-linked certificates of deposit were a retail form of synthetic equity offered by a number of commercial banks and savings and loans in 1987.
24. See Finnerty (1990) for a comprehensive survey of financial innovations since the 1970s.
25. Krzyzak (1990) and Brady (1991) describe the concerns and difficulties experienced by low-rated swap dealers in dealing with higher-rated counterparties. See Abken (1991) for a model of swap valuation in which swaps are subject to default by the participating counterparties.
26. Aggarwal (1991) reports several sources giving a figure of $35 million in write-offs resulting from swap defaults as of year-end 1988. The collapse of Drexel, Burnham, Lambert in 1989 brought with it potential defaults on its swap book. Most of these swaps were closed out or rearranged with other swap dealers, avoiding defaults that would have shaken the swaps market. See Perry (1990) for an account of the Drexel collapse and its aftermath on the swaps market. Evans (1991) reports that U.S. and foreign banks face potential defaults of up to $1 billion because of to a British court ruling that nullifies swap contracts with about 80 British municipalities.
27. See Wall, Pringle, and McNulty (1990) for a discussion of the Basle Agreement and its treatment of swaps under the new capital standards. Levis and Suchar (1990) give further discussion and detailed examples.

References

Abken, Peter A. "Interest-Rate Caps, Collars, and Floors." Federal Reserve Bank of Atlanta *Economic Review* 74 (November/December 1989): 2-24.

_____. "Valuation of Default-Risky Interest-Rate Swaps." Federal Reserve Bank of Atlanta working paper, forthcoming, 1991.

Aggarwal, Raj. "Assessing Default Risk in Interest Rate Swaps." In *Interest Rate Swaps*, edited by Carl R. Beidleman, 430-48. Homewood, Ill.: Business One Irwin, 1991.

Bhattacharya, Anand K. "Synthetic Asset Swaps." *Journal of Portfolio Management* 17 (Fall 1990): 56-64.

_____, and John Breit. "Customized Interest-Rate Risk Agreements and Their Applications." In *The Handbook of Fixed Income Securities*, 3d ed., edited by Frank J. Fabozzi, 1157-89. Homewood, Ill.: Business One Irwin, 1991.

Bishop, Graham. "ECU Bonds: Pioneer of Currency Union." *Euromoney* (January 1991): 71ff.

Bodie, Zvi, Alex Kane, and Alan J. Marcus. *Investments*. Homewood, Ill.: Richard D. Irwin, Inc., 1989.

Brady, Simon. "How to Tailor Your Assets." *Euromoney* (April 1990): 83-89.

_____. "Time Runs Out for Low-Rated Swappers." *Euromoney* (February 1991): 9-10.

Brown, Jeffry P. "Variations to Basic Swaps." In *Interest Rate Swaps*, edited by Carl R. Beidleman, 114-29. Homewood, Ill.: Business One Irwin, 1991.

Brown, Keith, and Donald J. Smith. "Forward Swaps, Swap Options, and the Management of Callable Debt." *Journal of Applied Corporate Finance* 2 (Winter 1990): 59-71.

Chew, Lillian. "Strip Mining." *Risk* 4 (February 1991): 20ff.

Chu, Franklin J. "The U.S. Private Market for Foreign Securities." *Bankers Magazine* (January/February 1991): 55-60.

Evans, John. "British Court Rules Swaps by Municipalities Illegal." *American Banker*, January 25, 1991, 13.

Finnerty, John D. "Financial Engineering in Corporate Finance: An Overview." In *The Handbook of Financial Engineering*, edited by Clifford W. Smith and Charles W. Smithson, 69-108. Grand Rapids, Mich.: Harper Business, 1990.

Goodman, Laurie S. "Capital Market Applications of Interest Rate Swaps." In *Interest Rate Swaps*, edited by Carl R. Beidleman, 147-74. Homewood, Ill.: Business One Irwin, 1991.

Hansell, Saul. "Is the World Ready for Synthetic Equity?" *Institutional Investor* (August 1990): 54-61.

Henderson, Schuyler K. "A Legal Eye on Hedging's Newest Club." *Euromoney* (May 1990): 95-96.

Krzyzak, Krystyna. "Don't Take Swaps at Face Value." *Risk* 1 (November 1988): 26-31.

_____. "Swaptions Deciphered." *Risk* 2 (February 1989a): 9-17.

_____. "From Basis Points to Barrels." *Risk* 2 (May 1989b): 8-12.

_____. "Copper-Bottomed Hedge." *Risk* 2 (September 1989c): 35-39.

_____. "Swaps Survey: Around the Houses." *Risk* 3 (September 1990): 51-57.

Kuprianov, Anatoli. "Short-Term Interest Rate Futures." Federal Reserve Bank of Richmond *Economic Review* (September/October 1986): 12-26.

Levis, Mario, and Victor Suchar. "Basle Basics." *Risk* 3 (April 1990): 38-39.

Lewis, Janet. "Oil Price Jitters? Try Energy Swaps." *Institutional Investor* (December 1990): 206-8.

Lewis, Julian. "The Bandwagon Starts to Roll." *Euromoney* (May 1990): 87-94.

Macfarlane, John, Janet Showers, and Daniel Ross. "The Interest-Rate Swap Market: Yield Mathematics, Terminology, and Conventions." In *Interest Rate Swaps*, edited by Carl R. Beidleman, 233-65. Homewood, Ill.: Business One Irwin, 1991.

McNulty, James E., and Sharon L. Stieber. "The Development and Standardization of the Swap Market." In *Interest Rate Swaps*, edited by Carl R. Beidleman, 97-113. Homewood, Ill.: Business One Irwin, 1991.

Metcalfe, Richard. "Out of the Shadows." *Risk* 3 (October 1990): 40-42.

Perry, Phillip M. "Drexel Redux? Credit Quality Is a Hot Topic." *Corporate Risk Management* (May/June 1990): 27-29.

Ramaswamy, Krishna, and Suresh M. Sundaresan. "The Valuation of Floating-Rate Instruments: Theory and Evidence." *Journal of Financial Economics* 17 (December 1986): 251-72.

Salomon Brothers, Inc. "Equity-Linked Index Swaps." Sales brochure, 1990.

Shanahan, Terry, and Jim Durrant. "Driving Factors." *Risk* 10 (November 1990): 14ff.

Shirreff, David. "Where Others Fear to Tread." *Risk* 8 (September 1989): 11-16.

Smith, Clifford W., Charles W. Smithson, and Lee Macdonald Wakeman. "The Evolving Market for Swaps." In *The Handbook of Financial Engineering*, edited by Clifford W. Smith and Charles W. Smithson, 191-211. Grand Rapids, Mich.: Harper Business, 1990.

Smith, Clifford W., Charles W. Smithson, and D. Sykes Wilford. "Financial Engineering: Why Hedge?" In *The Handbook of Financial Engineering*, edited by Clifford W. Smith and Charles W. Smithson, 126-37. Grand Rapids, Mich.: Harper Business, 1990.

Spraos, Paul B. "The Anatomy of a Copper Swap." *Corporate Risk Management* 2 (January/February 1990): 8, 10.

Tompkins, Robert. "Behind the Mirror." *Risk* 2 (February 1989): 17-23.

Wall, Larry D., and John J. Pringle. "Interest Rate Swaps: A Review of the Issues." Federal Reserve Bank of Atlanta *Economic Review* 73 (November/December 1988): 22-37.

Wall, Larry D., John J. Pringle, and James E. McNulty. "Capital Requirements for Interest-Rate and Foreign-Exchange

Hedges." Federal Reserve Bank of Atlanta *Economic Review* 75 (May/June 1990): 14-27.

Williams, Jeffrey. *The Economic Function of Futures Markets.* New York: Cambridge University Press, 1986.

Interest Rate Swaps: A Review of the Issues

Larry D. Wall and John J. Pringle

*I*n the last two decades a myriad of new instruments and transactions have brought about significant changes in financial markets. Some of these innovations have attracted considerable publicity; stock index futures and options, for example, were an important element in the studies of the October 19, 1987, stock market crash.[1] However, not all of these new developments are well-known to the public. One recent innovation that is quietly transforming credit markets is interest rate swaps—an agreement between two parties to exchange interest payments for a predetermined period of time.

The interest rate swap market began in 1982. By 1988 the outstanding portfolios of 49 leading swap dealers totaled $889.5 billion in principal, of which $473.6 billion represented new business in 1987.[2] Reflecting their rapid growth, swaps have gained considerable importance in the capital markets. Thomas Jasper, the head of Salomon Brothers' swap department, has estimated that 30 to 40 percent of all capital market transactions involve an interest rate, foreign-exchange, or some other type of swap.[3]

Their rapid growth is one reason swaps have generated considerable interest among academics, regulators, accountants, and market participants alike. Paramount among the questions surrounding swaps are the reasons for their use and the basis of their pricing. Regulators are also keenly concerned with the risks swaps pose to financial firms, while accountants are debating appropriate reporting. This article reviews the current literature and presents some new research on interest rate swaps. Among the issues addressed are the workings of interest rate swaps, the reasons that firms use such swaps, the risks associated with interest rate swaps, the pricing of these swaps, the regulation of participants in the

This article was originally published in the Atlanta Fed's November/December 1988 Economic Review. *Wall is a research officer in charge of the financial section of the Atlanta Fed's research department, and Pringle holds the C. Knox Massey Professor of Business Administration chair at the University of North Carolina at Chapel Hill.*

swap market, and the disclosure of swaps on firms' financial statements.

What Is an Interest Rate Swap?

Interest rate swaps serve to transform the effective maturity (or, more accurately, the repricing interval) of two firms' assets or liabilities. This type of swap enables firms to choose from a wider variety of asset and liability markets without having to incur additional interest rate risk, that is, risk that arises because of changes in market interest rates. For instance, a firm that traditionally invests in short-term assets, whose returns naturally fluctuate as the yield on each new issue changes, may instead invest in a long-term, fixed-rate instrument and then use an interest rate swap to obtain floating-rate receipts. In this situation, one firm agrees to pay a fixed interest rate to another in return for receiving a floating rate.

Interest rate swaps have fixed termination dates and typically provide for semiannual payments. Either interest rate in a swap may be fixed or floating.[4] The amount of interest paid is based on some agreed-upon principal amount, which is called the "notional" principal because it never actually changes hands. Moreover, the two parties do not exchange the full amounts of the interest payments. Rather, at each payment a single amount is transferred to cover the net difference in the promised interest payments.

An example of an interest rate swap is provided in Chart 1. Atlanta HiTech agrees to pay Heartland Manufacturing a floating rate of interest equal to the London Interbank Offered Rate (LIBOR), which is commonly used in international loan agreements.[5] In return, Heartland Manufacturing promises to pay Atlanta HiTech a fixed 9.18 percent rate of interest. The swap transaction is ordinarily arranged at current market rates in order for the net present value of payments to equal zero. That is, the fixed rate on a typical interest rate swap is set so that the market value of the net floating-rate payments exactly equals the market value of the net fixed-rate payments. If the swap is not arranged as a zero-net-present-value exchange, one party pays to the other an amount equal to the difference in the payments' net present value when the swap is arranged.

Chart 2 demonstrates three aspects of the swaps market: converting floating-rate debt to fixed-rate debt, converting a floating-rate asset to a fixed-rate asset, and using an intermediary in the swap transaction. In Chart 2, Widgets Unlimited can issue short-term debt but is averse to the risk that market interest rates will increase. To avoid this risk, Widgets enters into a swap in which it agrees to pay the counterparty a fixed rate of interest and receive a floating rate. This arrangement resembles long-term, fixed-rate debt in that Widgets' promised payments are independent of market interest rate changes. If market interest rates rise, Widgets will receive payments under the swap that will offset the higher cost of its short-term debt. Should market rates fall, though, under the terms of the swap Widgets will have to pay its counterparty money.

The combination of short-term debt and swaps is not identical to the use of long-term debt. One difference is that Widgets' interest payments are not truly fixed. The company is protected from an increase in market rates but not from changes in its own risk premium. The swap would not compensate Widgets if its own cost of short-term debt increased from LIBOR-plus-0.5 percent to LIBOR-plus-0.75 percent. If the cost of short-term debt to Widgets decreased to LIBOR-plus-0.30 percent, however, the cost of the debt issue would fall by 0.20 percent. In addition, the counterparty to the combination generally does not provide the corporation with the interest rate option implicit in many bonds issued in the United States, whereby they can be called in at a fixed price regardless of current market rates. Call options allow issuers to exploit large changes in market interest rates.[6] In contrast, standard interest rate swap contracts may be unwound or canceled only at prevailing market interest rates.

The other swap user in this example illustrates a swap's potential to convert a floating rate asset to one in which the rate is fixed. OneState Insurance, a small life insurance company, has long-term, fixed-rate obligations but would like to invest part of its portfolio in short-term debt securities. OneState Insurance can invest in short-term securities without incurring interest rate risk by agreeing to a swap in which the insurer pays a floating rate of interest and receives a fixed rate of interest. This combination provides the insurance company with a stream of income that does not fluctuate with changes in short-term market interest rates.

This example also demonstrates the usefulness of an intermediary in a swap. Although Widgets and OneState Insurance could have entered into a swap agreement with each other, in this example (see Chart 2), both Widgets Unlimited and OneState Insurance actually have a swap agreement with DomBank. Numerous large commercial and investment banks as

Chart 1
An Interest Rate Swap without a Dealer

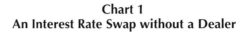

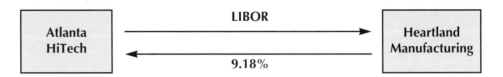

In this example, Atlanta HiTech agrees to pay Heartland Manufacturing a floating rate of interest equal to the London Interbank Offered Rate. In return, Heartland agrees to pay Atlanta HiTech a fixed 9.18% rate of interest. These two companies do not actually exchange the full amounts of the interest payments, but at each payment, a single amount is transferred to cover the net difference in the promised interest payments.

well as insurance companies have entered into the swap market as intermediaries. DomBank is compensated in an amount equal to the difference between what is received on one swap and what is paid under the other one. In this example, the fee is equal to 10 basis points.

Using DomBank is advantageous to Widgets and OneState Insurance for two reasons. First, the use of an intermediary reduces search time in establishing a swap agreement. DomBank is willing to enter into a swap at any time, whereas Widgets and OneState Insurance might take several days to discover each other, even with a broker's help. Second, an intermediary can reduce the costs of credit evaluation. Either of the participants in an interest rate swap may become bankrupt and unable to fulfill their side of the contract. Thus, each swap participant should understand the credit quality of the other party. In this example, Widgets and OneState are not familiar with each other, and each would need to undertake costly credit analysis on the other before agreeing to deal directly. However, total credit analysis costs are significantly reduced since both parties know the quality of DomBank and DomBank knows their respective credit standings.

Reasons for Interest Rate Swaps

Why do two firms agree to swap interest payments? They could either acquire assets or issue liabilities with their desired repricing interval (or maturity) and eliminate the need to undertake a swap. An early explanation for swaps was that they reduce corporations' funding costs by allowing firms to ex-

ploit market inefficiencies.[7] Although this explanation remains popular with some market participants, academic analysis has questioned the ability of market inefficiencies to explain the existence and growth of the swap market. Several other explanations for the swap market's popularity that do not rely on market inefficiency have also been provided. The next section of this article presents both original research and a review of recent literature to determine alternative reasons for the surge in use of interest rate swaps.

Quality Spread Differential. The cost savings explanation of swaps claims that swaps allow corporations to arbitrage quality spread differentials. A *quality spread* is the difference between the interest rate paid for funds of a given maturity by a high-quality firm—that is, one with low credit risk—and that required of a lower-quality firm. The quality spread *differential* is the difference in quality spreads at two different maturities. Table 1 provides the calculation of the quality spread differential based on the example provided in Chart 1. Atlanta HiTech, which has a AAA rating, can obtain short-term financing at six-month LIBOR-plus-0.20 percent or fixed-rate financing at 9.00 percent. Heartland Manufacturing can obtain floating-rate funding at six-month LIBOR-plus-0.70 or fixed-rate funds at 10.20 percent. For floating-rate funding, the quality spread, or difference in rates, between the two firms is 50 basis points, but it widens to 120 basis points for fixed-rate funding. The difference in quality spread, or the quality spread differential, in this example is 70 basis points.

The quality spread differential may be exploitable if Atlanta HiTech desires floating-rate funds and Heartland Manufacturing seeks a fixed rate. Table 2 shows how the quality spread differential is exploited through an interest rate swap. Atlanta HiTech is-

Chart 2
An Interest Rate Swap with a Dealer

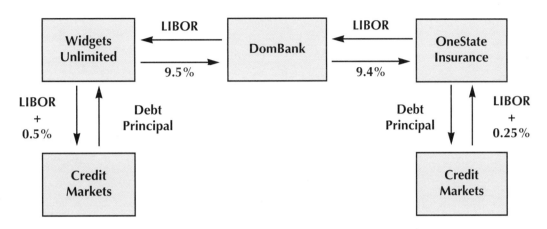

This chart demonstrates three aspects of the swaps market:

(1) Converting floating-rate debt to fixed-rate debt (Widgets Unlimited)
(2) Converting floating-rate assets to fixed-rate assets (OneState Insurance)
(3) Using an intermediary (DomBank) to facilitate the swap

sues fixed-rate debt, and Heartland issues floating-rate debt. Then the two firms enter into an interest rate swap. The net result is that Atlanta HiTech obtains funds at LIBOR minus 18 basis points and Heartland obtains fixed-rate funds at 9.88 percent. Compared with their cost of funds had they not used the interest rate swap strategy, this result represents a 38 basis point savings for Atlanta HiTech and a 32 basis point savings for Heartland. Note that the division of the gain in this example is arbitrary and that the two parties could split the gains differently. However, the total gains to the swapping parties will always equal the quality spread differential—70 basis points in this example.

Table 2 clearly demonstrates the ability of swaps to help exploit apparent arbitrage opportunities. However, some observers question whether arbitrage opportunities actually exist. Stuart Turnbull (1987) argues that swaps are zero-sum games in the absence of market imperfections and swap externalities. He also suggests that quality spread differentials may arise for reasons that are not subject to arbitrage. Clifford W. Smith, Charles W. Smithson, and Lee Macdonald Wakeman (1986) note that, even if quality spread differential arbitrage were possible, such activity by itself would not explain swap market growth. In fact, the annual volume of new swaps

should be declining as arbitrage becomes more effective.

If the quality spread differential is not entirely the result of market inefficiencies, why does it exist? In a 1987 research paper, the authors of this article point out that quality spread differentials could arise for a number of reasons, including differences in expected bankruptcy costs. Because the expected discounted value of bankruptcy-related losses increases at a faster pace for lower-rated corporations than for higher-rated ones, quality spreads increase with maturity. In this case, the lower initial cost of swap financing is offset by higher costs later.

Alternatively, Jan G. Loeys (1985) suggests that quality spread differentials could arise as risk is shifted from creditors to shareholders. Creditors have the option of refusing to roll over their debt if the firm appears to be riskier than when the debt was incurred, and short-term creditors have more opportunities to exercise this option. Thus, the creditors of a firm that issues short-term debt bear less risk than the creditors of a firm that issues long-term debt. If the creditors of firms that issue short-term debt bear less risk, the equity holders and long-term creditors necessarily bear more risk.

A third possible explanation for the quality spread differential involves differences in short- and long-

Table 1
Numerical Example of a Quality Spread Differential

	Atlanta HiTech	Heartland Manufacturing	Quality Spread
Credit rating	AAA	BBB	
Cost of Raising Fixed-Rate Funding	9.00%	10.20%	1.20%
Cost of Raising Floating-Rate Funding	6-month LIBOR plus 0.20%	6-month LIBOR plus 0.70%	0.50%
Quality Spread Differential			0.70%

term debt contracts. Long-term contracts frequently include a variety of restrictive covenants and may incorporate a call option that is typically not present in short-term debt contracts. The differences in these contract provisions may be reflected in the interest rates charged on various debt contracts. For example, Smith, Smithson, and Wakeman point out that the long-term corporate debt contracts issued by U.S. firms in domestic markets typically have a call provision that is not adjusted for changes in market interest rates. However, long-term debt contracts issued in the Eurobond markets frequently have call provisions that adjust call prices for market rate changes. Thus, quality spread differentials will reflect differences in contract terms if they are calculated using domestic U.S. market rates for lower-quality firms and Eurobond rates for higher-quality firms.

In a forthcoming paper, one of the authors of this article suggests that the quality spread differential may reflect differences in the agency costs associated with short- and long-term debt. Agency costs arise because managers, owners, and creditors have different interests, and managers or owners may take actions that benefit themselves at the expense of the other parties and at the expense of total firm value. In particular, Larry D. Wall notes that the owners of firms that issue long-term, noncallable debt create an incentive to underinvest and to shift investments from low-risk to high-risk projects.[8] A firm may underinvest in new projects because most of the benefit of some projects is received by creditors in the form of a reduced probability that the firm will default. Owners will prefer a high-risk project to a low-risk project because they receive the gains on successful high-risk projects while creditors may suffer most of the losses

if the projects fail. Creditors recognize the incentives created by long-term debt and demand a higher risk premium in compensation. The problems created by long-term debt may be reduced or eliminated by short-term debt, that is, debt which matures shortly after the investment decision.[9] An interest rate swap allows lower-quality firms to issue short-term debt while avoiding exposure to changes in market interest rates. Thus, the combination of short-term debt and swaps may be less costly than long-term debt.

In their 1987 paper, the authors also point to another agency cost—that of liquidating insolvent firms—which may be reduced by using short-term debt. Insolvent firms have an incentive to underinvest because, according to David Mayers and Clifford W. Smith (1987), creditors receive almost all of the benefit. Creditors of these firms can reduce the costs associated with underinvestment by taking control of the firm as soon as possible after the firm becomes insolvent. However, creditors may not gain control of a firm until it fails to make a promised debt payment. Short-term debt may hasten creditors' gaining control when a firm has adequate funds to pay interest but lacks the resources to pay interest on its debt and repay the principal.

According to Wall and John J. Pringle, the quality spread differential is not exploitable to the extent that it arises from differences in the expected costs of bankruptcy, shifts in risk from creditors to equityholders, or actual differences in contract terms. However, the quality spread differential can be exploited to the extent that it arises from agency costs. Moreover, arbitrage may eliminate differentials that arise from market inefficiencies, whereas one firm's swap does not reduce the potential agency cost savings to anoth-

Table 2
Numerical Example of a Swap's Ability to Reduce a Firm's Cost of Funding

	Atlanta HiTech	Heartland Manufacturing
Direct Funding Cost		
Fixed-rate funds raised directly by Atlanta HiTech	(9.00%)	
Floating-Rate funds raised directly by Heartland		(6-month LIBOR + 0.70%)
Swap Payments		
Atlanta HiTech pays Heartland floating rate	(LIBOR)	LIBOR
Heartland pays Atlanta HiTech fixed rate	9.18%	(9.18%)
All-in cost of funding	LIBOR – 0.18%	9.88%
Comparable cost of equivalent direct funding	LIBOR + 0.20%	10.20%
Savings	38 basis points	32 basis points

er firm. Thus, agency cost explanations could provide at lease a partial explanation for the continuing growth of the swap market.

An important question facing the quality spread differential-based explanations is the extent to which the differential reflects exploitable factors. The authors note that the various explanations of the quality spread differential are not mutually exclusive. For example, if the differential is 70 basis points, then perhaps only 30 basis points may be exploitable.

One empirical study that has some bearing on the quality spread differential is by Robert E. Chatfield and R. Charles Moyer (1986). This study examines the risk premium on 90 long-term puttable bonds issued between July 24, 1974, and August 2, 1984, and a control sample of 174 nonputtable bonds. The put option on long-term, floating-rate debt gives creditors the option to force the firm to repay its debt if the firm becomes riskier.[10] The study finds that the put feature reduces the rate that the market requires on long-term debt by 89 basis points for the bonds in the sample. Chatfield and Moyer provide strong evidence that at least part of the quality spread differential does not arise due to inefficiencies in the markets for short- and long-term debt. However, the observed savings arising from the put feature may be attributable to some of the factors discussed earlier, including bankruptcy costs, risk shifting from creditors to equityholders, and agency costs. Thus, the Chatfield and

Moyer results cannot be used to determine the magnitude of agency-cost savings available through interest rate swaps.

Other Explanations. Several explanations for the increased use of the interest rate swap market which do not depend on exploiting the quality spread differential are available. One is that swaps may be used to adjust the repricing interval (or maturity) of a firm's assets or liabilities in order to reduce interest rate risk. For example, a firm may start a period with an acceptable degree of exposure to changes in market interest rates. Subsequently, though, it desires a change in its exposure because of shifts in its product environment or in the volatility of interest rates. Swaps provide a low-cost method of making immediate changes in exposure to market interest rates. For example, suppose that a firm is initially fully hedged with respect to interest rate changes but that a subsequent change in its product markets increases its revenues' sensitivity to interest rates. This company may be able to offset the increased sensitivity by entering into a swap whereby it agrees to pay a floating rate of interest, which better matches revenues, and receives a fixed rate of interest to cover payments on its outstanding debt.[11]

Smith, Smithson, and Wakeman (1987a) suggest that swaps may allow firms greater flexibility in choosing the amount of their outstanding debt obligations. In particular, reducing debt levels may be a problem if swaps are not used. To reduce its outstanding long-term debt, a firm may need to pay a premium (that is, the call price may exceed the current market value of the debt). On the other hand, if it issues short-term debt without a swap, it may be exposed to adverse changes in market interest rates. However, by issuing a combination of short-term debt and swaps, the firm avoids the need to pay a premium to retire debt and simultaneously eliminates its exposure to changes in market interest rates.

Marcelle Arak and others (1988) present a general model in which firms will choose the combination of short-term debt and interest rate swaps over short-term debt; long-term, fixed-rate debt; and long-term, variable-rate debt. The model suggests that the combination will be preferred if the firm expects higher risk-free interest rates than does the market, the firm is more risk-averse than the market with respect to changes in risk-free rates, the firm expects it own credit spread to be lower than that expected by the market, and the borrower is less risk-averse to changes in its credit spread than is the market. The researchers also note that not all four conditions need to be met at the same time.

Arak and her colleagues' model is very broad and could include the agency cost models as subsets. An additional implication of their model is that firms may use swaps to exploit information asymmetries. Suppose that a company desires fixed-rate financing to fund a project. It could issue long-term debt, but, if management thought that the company would soon receive a better credit rating, issuing long-term debt would force the firm to pay an excessive risk premium. By issuing short-term debt, the firm could obtain a lower cost of long-term funds in the future when its credit rating improved. However, this strategy would expose the firm to interest rate risk. By instead issuing a combination of short-term debt and interest rate swaps the firm's managers can exploit their information about the true credit risk of the firm without exposing the organization to changes in market interest rates.[12] When the good news comes, the firm's floating rate payments to outside creditors fall while its payments under the swap remain the same, thus reducing the firm's total financing costs. One important limitation of this explanation is that it applies only to firms that expect improved credit ratings in the near future.

In yet another alternative to the quality spread differential explanation, Loeys points out that swaps may allow firms to exploit differences in regulation. He notes that Securities and Exchange Commission (SEC) registration requirements raise the cost of issuing bonds in the United States by approximately 80 basis points above the cost of issuing bonds in the Eurobond market. Thus, the costs of obtaining fixed-rate funding may be reduced by having companies with access to the Eurobond market issue long-term debt and then enter into a swap with firms that lack access to but prefer fixed-rate funding. Smith, Smithson, and Wakeman, observing that a variety of regulations differ across countries in ways that can be exploited, refer to this explanation as tax and regulatory arbitrage.

A Review of the Explanations. The various explanations of interest rate swaps discussed above are not mutually exclusive, since different firms may use swaps for different reasons. One of the most popular explanations of interest rate swaps—that they allow arbitrage of the quality spread differential—is also the explanation with the weakest theoretical support. The other explanations are all theoretically plausible. Unfortunately, published empirical evidence on the reasons for using swaps is almost nonexistent. Linda T. Rudnick (1987) provides anecdotal evidence that reductions in financing costs are one of the primary reasons that firms enter into interest rate swaps. In research currently in progress, the authors of this article are examining the financial characteristics of firms that reported the use of swaps in the notes to their 1986 financial statements.

One limitation of the nonarbitrage explanations of swaps is that they provide only one reason for floating-rate payers to enter into swaps, namely, the ability to change the maturity structure of the firm's assets and liabilities. Moreover, this single explanation fails to provide a sound reason for a firm to issue long-term, fixed-rate debt and then enter into a swap agreement. If a company does issue long-term debt and then enters into a swap agreement as a floating-rate payer, either fixed-rate payers are sharing part of their gains with the floating-rate payer or floating-rate payers obtain some as yet undiscovered benefit from swaps.

*R*isks Associated with Swaps

Interest rate swap contracts are subject to several types of risk. Among the more important are interest rate, or position, risk and credit risk. Interest rate risk arises because changes in market interest rates cause a change in a swap's value. Credit risk occurs because either party may default on a swap contract. Both participants in a swap are subject to each type of risk.

Interest Rate Risk. As market interest rates change, interest rate swaps generate gains or losses that are equal to the change in the replacement cost of the swap. These gains and losses allow swaps to serve as a hedge which a company can use to reduce its risk or to serve as a speculative tool that increases the firm's total risk. A swap represents a hedge if gains or losses generated by the swap offset changes in the market values of a company's assets, liabilities, and off-balance sheet activities such as interest rate futures and options. However, a swap is speculative to the extent that the firm deliberately increases its risk position to profit from predicted changes in interest rates.

The determination of whether and how to use a swap is straightforward for a firm that is a user, one which enters into a swap agreement solely to adjust its own financial position.[13] First, the company evaluates it own exposure to future changes in interest rates, including any planned investments and new financings. Then, its views on the future levels and volatility of interest rates are ascertained. Firms wishing greater exposure to market rate changes enter into swaps as speculators. Alternatively, if less exposure is desired, the company enters into a swap as a hedge.

The problem facing a dealer—a firm that enters into a swap to earn fee income—is more complicated. A dealer may enter into a swap to hedge changes in market rates or to speculate in a manner similar to users. However, a dealer may also enter a swap to satisfy a customer's request even when the dealer wants no change in its interest rate exposure.[14] In this case, the dealer must find some way of hedging the swap transaction.

The simplest hedge for one swap transaction by a dealer is another swap transaction whose terms mirror the first swap. An example of this arrangement is given in Chart 2, in which the dealer's promised floating-rate payments of LIBOR to Widgets Unlimited is exactly offset by OneState's promise to pay LIBOR. Similarly, the fixed payments to OneState Insurance are covered by Widgets' promised fixed payments, and DomBank is left with a small spread. This combination of swaps is referred to as a *matched pair*. One problem with relying on matched pairs to eliminate interest rate risk is that the dealer is exposed to interest rate changes during the time needed to find another party interested in a matching swap. Another problem is that the dealer may be relatively better at arranging swaps with fixed-rate payers and, thus, have problems finding floating-rate payers to execute the matching swap (or vice versa).

An alternative to hedging one swap with another swap is to rely on debt securities, or on futures or options on debt securities, to provide a hedge. Steven T. Felgran (1987) gives an example whereby a dealer agrees to pay a fixed rate and receive a floating rate from a customer. The dealer uses the floating-rate receipts to support a bank loan, which is then used to purchase a Treasury security of the same maturity and value as the swap. Any gains or losses on the swap are subsequently offset by losses or gains on the Treasury security. Felgran does note one problem with using Treasury securities to hedge a swap: the spread between them and interest rate swaps may vary over time.[15] According to Felgran, dealers are unable to hedge floating-rate payments perfectly. Sources of risk include differences in payment dates and floating-rate reset days, disparities in maturity and principal, and "basis risk," that is, the risk associated with hedging floating payments based on one index with floating payments from another index.

Using the futures market to hedge swaps also entails certain drawbacks. Wakeman points to the "additional risk created by the cash/futures basis volatility." He also notes that matching the fixed-rate payments from a swap with the Treasury security of the closest maturity may not be optimal when the Treasury security is thinly traded. As an alternative he suggests that "on-the-run" (highly liquid) Treasury issues be used for hedging. The investment amount and type of issues to be used may be determined applying a duration matching strategy. Still, this approach is unlikely to eliminate interest rate risk for the swap dealer since duration matching provides a perfect hedge only under very restrictive assumptions.

Credit Risk. Aside from interest rate and basis risk, both interest rate swap participants are subject to the risk that the other party will default, causing credit losses. The maximum amount of the loss associated with this credit risk is measured by the swap's replacement cost, which is essentially the cost of entering into a new swap under current market conditions with rates equal to those on the swap being replaced.

A simple example can demonstrate the credit risk of swaps. Suppose Widgets Unlimited agrees to pay a fixed rate of 9.5 percent to DomBank, and in return Widgets will receive LIBOR on a semiannual basis through January 1994. If the market rate on new swaps maturing in January 1994 falls to 8 percent, the swap has positive value to DomBank—that is, DomBank would have to pay an up-front fee to entice a third party to enter into a swap whereby DomBank receives a fixed rate of 9.5 percent. DomBank will suffer a credit loss if Widgets becomes bankrupt while the rate is 8 percent and pays only a fraction of its obligations to creditors. On the other hand, if the rate on swaps maturing January 1994 rises to 10.5 percent and DomBank defaults, Widgets may suffer a credit loss.

This example demonstrates that both of the parties to an interest rate swap may be subject to credit risk at some time during the life of a swap contract. However, only one party at a time may be subject to credit risk. If rates in the above example fall to 8 percent, DomBank can suffer credit losses, but Widgets is not exposed to credit risk. That is, the swap has negative value to Widgets when the market rate is 8 percent; Widgets would be happy to drop the swap agreement if DomBank were to go bankrupt. In practice, though, Widgets is unlikely to receive a windfall from Dom-Bank's failure. The swap contracts may provide for Widgets to continue making payments to DomBank or, if the contract is canceled, provide for Widgets to pay DomBank the replacement cost of the swap.[16]

One way of reducing the credit risk associated with swaps is for the party to whom the swap has negative value to post collateral equal to the swap's replacement cost. Some swaps provide for collateral but most do not. According to Felgran, swap collateralization is of uncertain value because such documentation has yet to be adequately tested in court. Moreover, some parties that would be happy to receive collateral are themselves reluctant to post it when swap rates move against them. Certain commercial banks in particular have a strong incentive to avoid collateralization. Such institutions take credit risks in the ordinary course of business and are comfortable with assuming credit risk on interest rate swaps. Investment bankers, on the other hand, are typically at risk for only short periods of time with their nonswap transactions and are not as experienced in evaluating credit risk. Thus, the continued presence of credit risk in the swap market strengthens the relative competitive position of commercial banks.

Several simulation studies have explored the magnitude of the credit risk associated with individual swaps or matched pairs of swaps. Arak, Laurie S. Goodman, and Arthur Rones (1986) examine the credit exposure—or maximum credit loss—of a single interest rate swap to determine the amount of a firm's credit line that is used by a swap.[17] They assume that short-term rates follow a random walk with no drift; in other words, the change in short-term rates does not depend on the current level of or on past changes in short-term rates. After the swap begins,

the floating-rate component of the swap is assumed to move one standard deviation each year in the direction of maximum credit exposure. The standard deviation of interest rates is calculated using 1985 data on Treasury issues. Their results suggest that until the swap matures, maximum annual credit loss on swaps is likely to be between 1 and 2 percent of notional principal.

J. Gregg Whittaker (1987b) investigates the credit exposure of interest rate swaps in order to develop a formula for swap pricing. Using an options pricing formula to value swaps and assuming that interest rates follow a log-normal distribution and volatility amounts to one standard deviation, Whittaker finds that the maximum exposure for a 10-year matched pair of swaps does not exceed 8 percent of the notional principal.

The Federal Reserve Board and the Bank of England studied the potential increase in credit exposure of a matched pair of swaps.[18] The study's purpose is to develop a measure of the credit exposure associated with a matched pair of swaps that is comparable to the credit exposure of on-balance sheet loans. The results are used to determine regulatory capital requirements for interest rate swaps. The joint central bank research assumes that for regulatory purposes the swaps' credit exposure should be equal to its current exposure, that is, the replacement cost plus some surcharge to capture potential increases in credit exposure. The investigation uses a Monte Carlo simulation technique to evaluate the probabilities associated with different potential increases in credit exposure.[19] Interest rates are assumed to follow a log-normal, random-walk distribution with the volatility measure equal to the 90th percentile value of changes in interest rates over six-month intervals from 1981 to mid-1986. The credit exposure of each matched pair is calculated every six months and the resulting exposures are averaged over the life of the swap. The study concludes with 70 percent confidence that the average potential increase in credit exposure will be no greater than 0.5 percent of the notional principal of the swap per complete year; at the 95 percent confidence level it finds the average credit risk exposure to be no greater than 1 percent of the notional principal.

Terrence M. Belton (1987) follows this line of research in analyzing the potential increase in swap credit exposure, but he uses a different method of simulating interest rates. Belton estimates a vector autoregressive model over the period from January 1970 to November 1986 to estimate seven different Treasury rates. (Vector autoregressive models estimate current values of some dependent variables, in this case interest rates at various maturities, as a function of current and past values of selected variables. Belton uses current and past interest rates as explanatory variables.) Changes in the term structure are then simulated by drawing a set of random errors from the joint distribution of rates and solving for future values at each maturity. In effect, Belton's procedure allows the historical shape in the yield curve and historical changes in its level and shape to determine the value of various interest rates in his simulations. Belton's analysis differs from prior studies in that he uses stochastic, or random, default rates rather than focusing exclusively on maximum credit exposure. His results imply that the potential increase in credit exposure of swaps caused by rate changes can be covered by adding a surcharge of 1 percent to 5 percent of the notional principal to the current exposure for swaps with a maturity of 2 to 12 years.

While the foregoing analyses suggest several ways of estimating the increased credit exposure associated with matched pairs of swaps, these approaches might not be applicable to swap portfolios. Starting with the assumption that dealers use matched pairs of swaps and that the swaps are entered into at market interest rates, Wall and Kwun-Wing C. Fung (1987) note that the fixed rate on the matched pairs will change over time as interest rates move up and down. Wall and Fung point out that if rates have fluctuated over a certain range, a bank may have credit exposure on some swaps in which it pays a fixed rate and on others in which it pays a floating rate. In this case, an increase in rates generates an increase in the credit exposure of swaps in which the dealer pays a fixed rate but also causes a decrease in the exposure of swaps in which the dealer pays a floating rate. Similarly, a decrease in rates will increase the exposure on the swaps in which the dealer pays a floating rate and decrease exposure on those in which the dealer pays a fixed rate.[20]

In a more empirical vein, Kathleen Neal and Katerina Simons (1988) simulate the total credit exposure of a portfolio of 20 matched pairs of interest rate swaps. The initial portfolio is generated by originating one pair of five-year swaps per quarter from the fourth quarter of 1981 through the fourth quarter of 1986 at the prevailing interest rate. For the period 1987 through 1991, the interest rates are generated randomly based on the volatility observed in historical rates.[21] The maturing matched pair is dropped each quarter from the sample and a new five-year swap is added to the portfolio at the simulated interest rates. After running "several thousand" simulations

and assuming a portfolio of interest rate swaps with a notional principal of $10 million, Neal and Simons find the average maximum credit loss to be $185,000 and the 90th percentile exposure, $289,000.

No single correct approach is available to determine the expected credit exposure on an interest rate swap. The results may be influenced by the assumptions that are made about the distribution of future interest rates. However, several studies using different methodologies have reached the conclusion that the maximum exposure on a matched pair of swaps is unlikely to exceed a small fraction of the swap's notional principal. Moreover, the analysis of a single matched pair may overstate the expected exposure of a swap portfolio. Therefore, additional simulations of portfolio analysis risk may be appropriate to determine the risk exposure of swap dealers. Dominique Jackson (1988) reports that a survey of 71 dealers showed that 11 firms had experienced losses with "total write-offs accounting for $33 million on portfolios which totaled a notional (principal) of $283 billion."

How Should Swaps Be Priced?

In addition to considering the reasons for engaging in swaps and the attendant risks, the literature on interest rate swaps addresses two important pricing questions: (1) how should the overall value of a swap be established, and (2) what spread between higher-rated and lower-rated firms is appropriate to cover swap credit risk? James Bicksler and Andrew H. Chen (1986) provide an analysis of a swap's overall value. They suggest than an interest rate swap be treated as an exchange of a fixed-rate bond for a floating-rate bond. According to this approach, the fixed-rate payer has in effect sold a fixed-rate bond and purchased a floating-rate bond. Bicksler and Chen suggest that pricing an interest rate swap is essentially the same as pricing a floating-rate bond.

Insight into the appropriate spreads between high- and lower-rated firms can be obtained by comparing the quality spreads on bonds versus those on swaps. Patrick de Saint-Aignan, the chairman of the International Swap Dealers Association and a managing director at Morgan Stanley, remarks that "there's a credit spread of 150 basis points in the loan market but of only 5 to 10 basis points in swaps."[22] However, Smith, Smithson, and Wakeman (1987a) note that the risk exposure, as a proportion of notional principal for swaps, is far less than the exposure on loans. Lenders have credit exposure for all principal and interest payments promised on the loan, whereas a swap participant's credit exposure is limited to the difference between two interest rates. Thus, the credit risk borne by swap dealers is a far smaller proportion of the (notional) principal than that assumed by lenders.

Belton also addresses the question of appropriate spreads to compensate for swaps' credit risk by considering the default premium required to compensate one party for the expected value of the default losses from the other. For low-risk firms—companies with a 0.5 percent probability of default in one year and zero payment on default—the required premium is 0.70 basis points for a two-year swap and 3.02 basis points for a ten-year swap. For below-investment-grade firms—with a 2 percent probability of default per year and zero payment on default—the required premium ranges from 2.83 basis points for a two-year swap to 14.24 basis points for a ten-year swap. The differences in default premium of 2 to 14 basis points found by Belton for swaps is approximately in the 5 to 10 basis point range of the credit spread charged in swaps markets.

Whittaker (1987b) applies his options pricing method for calculating swaps' credit risk to the issue of swap pricing. He views a swap as a set of options to buy and sell a fixed-rate bond and a floating-rate bond. In his model default by the fixed-rate payer is analogous to a decision to exercise jointly a call option to purchase the fixed-rate bond and a put option to sell a floating-rate security. From this perspective, the decision to exercise one option is not independent of the decision to exercise another. Thus, one option may be exercised even though it is unprofitable to do so, provided that it is sufficiently profitable to exercise the other option. He then estimates the value of these options and suggests that "the market does not adequately take account of the exposure and pricing differentials across varying maturities." However, Whittaker claims that his results may not necessarily imply that the market is on average under-pricing swap credit risk.

One limitation of the above studies is that they fail to combine into an integrated framework the distribution of interest rates and the credit risk associated with swaps. A conceptually superior approach to interest rate swap valuation begins by separating the payments. The result looks like a series of forward contracts in which the floating-rate payer agrees to buy a zero-coupon Treasury security from the fixed-rate payer. This forward contract may then be decomposed into two options, one in which the floating-rate payer buys a call from the fixed-rate payer on the zero-coupon Treasury security and one in which the floating-rate payer sells a put on the security to the fixed-rate payer.

Unfortunately, the options derived from this analysis cannot be valued using standard options pricing formulas because both options are subject to credit risk. Herb Johnson and René Stulz (1987) analyze the problem of pricing a single option subject to default risk. However, swaps are a series of linked options whose payments in one period are contingent on the terms of the swap contract being fulfilled in prior periods. Thus, as Smith, Smithson, and Wakeman (1987b) suggest, to derive an optimal default strategy for swaps requires analysis of compound option issues similar to those discussed by Robert Geske (1977) for corporate coupon bonds.

The theoretical and pedagogical advantages of splitting a swap into a series of default-risky options are that the decomposition clearly illustrates the primary determinants of swap value: the distribution of the price of default-risk free bonds (interest rates), the possibility of default by either participant, and the linked nature of the options through time. The practical problem with the decomposition is that developing a pricing formula is not straightforward.

Requirements Imposed on Swaps

Regulation. In contrast to most other financial markets in the United States, the interest rate swap market is subject to remarkably little regulation and does not have a central exchange or even a central clearing mechanism. The terms of a swap agreement are determined by the parties to the contract and need not be disclosed. Nor does the existence of a swap need to be disclosed at the time the agreement is executed. (The financial statements' disclosure requirements for individual firms are discussed later in this article.) While certain regulators have a general responsibility for the financial soundness of some participants in the swap market, no public or private organization has overall responsibility for its regulation.

In general, this lack of regulation has not resulted in any major problems. Legislatures could make one potentially valuable contribution, though, by providing specific statutory language on the treatment of swap contracts when one party defaults. Market participants are currently waiting for the courts to determine if default procedures will follow the language of the swap contract or if the courts will impose some other settlement procedure. For example, many swaps are arranged under a master contract between two parties that provides for the netting of payments across swaps. This clause is desirable because it reduces the credit risk borne by both parties. However, the risk exists that a bankruptcy court will ignore this clause and treat each swap separately.

Even though the swap market is not subject to regulation, individual participants are. In particular, federal banking regulators in the United States are including interest rate swaps in the recently adopted risk-based capital standards. These standards are designed to preserve and enhance the safety and soundness of commercial banks by requiring them to maintain capital commensurate with the levels of credit risk they incur.[23]

Banks' capital standards first translate credit exposure on swaps into an amount comparable to on-balance sheet loans. The loan equivalent amount for swaps is equal to the replacement cost of the swap plus 0.5 percent of the notional principal. This loan equivalent amount is then multiplied by 50 percent to determine a risk-adjusted asset equivalent. Banks are required to maintain tier-one (or core) capital equal to 4 percent of risk-adjusted assets and total capital equal to 8 percent by 1992.[24]

The central banks of 12 major industrial powers have agreed to apply similar risk-based capital requirements to their countries' financial firms.[25] However, these standards do not apply to U.S. investment banks or insurance companies. Thus, capital requirements are not being applied to all swap dealers. Some market participants are concerned that the standards will place dealers that are subject to capital regulation at a competitive disadvantage.[26]

Accounting. Like regulatory requirements, accounting standards for swaps are minimal at best, owing largely to their rapid development. Existing accounting standards provide a general requirement that a firm disclose all material matters but do not require a company to disclose its participation in the interest rate swap market. Different firms appear to be following many of the same rules in accounting for the gains and losses under swap contracts, but some important discrepancies exist in practice.

Keith Wishon and Lorin S. Chevalier (1985) note that swap market participants generally do not recognize the existence of swaps on their balance sheets, a practice which is consistent with the treatment of futures agreements. However, they aver that the notes to the firm's financial statements should disclose the existence of material swap agreements and discuss the swap's impact on the repricing interval of the firm's debt obligations. Harold Bierman, Jr. (1987) recommends that firms also disclose the transaction's effects on their risk position.

Another issue at the inception of some swap contracts is accounting for up-front payments. Wishon and Chevalier believe that any up-front payments that reflect yield adjustments should be deferred and amortized over the life of the swap. While acknowledging that payers appear to be following this policy, the researchers note that some recipients have taken the position that all up-front fees are arrangement fees and may be immediately recognized in income. Bierman argues that yield-adjusting fees cannot be distinguished from others. Thus, all fees should be treated in the same manner. He further maintains that the most appropriate treatment is to defer recognition and amortize the payments over the life of the contract.

According to Wishon and Chevalier, regular payments and receipts under a swap agreement are frequently recorded as an adjustment to interest income when the swap is related to a particular debt issue. Though the receipts and payments are technically not interest, this approach is informative, especially if footnote disclosure is adequate. They report, nonetheless, that changes in the market value of the swap are generally not recognized in the income statement if gains and losses are not recognized on the security hedged by the swap. This treatment parallels that of futures, which meets the hedge criteria in the Financial Accounting Standards Board's Statement Number 80, "Accounting for Futures Contracts."

Another issue arising during the life of an interest rate swap is the presentation of the credit risk. For a nondealer, credit risk may not be material and, therefore, need not be reported. However, Wishon and Chevalier argue that the credit risk taken by a dealer is likely to be material and should be disclosed.

Some firms may enter into swaps as a speculative investment. Wishon and Chevalier contend that speculative swaps should be accounted for in the same manner as other speculative investments. Among the alternatives they discuss are using either the lower of cost or market method of valuation, with writedowns only for losses that are not "temporary," and the lower of cost or market in all cases. Both approaches are flawed. The treatment of some swap losses as "temporary" is inappropriate because objective and verifiable predictions of changes in interest rates are impossible.[27] Yet using the lower-of-cost-or-market method of valuation in all cases will always result in a swap's being valued at its historical low, an excessively conservative position. Probably the best approach is to report the swap's replacement cost and to recognize any gains or losses in the current period.

Bierman suggests that, when a speculative swap is terminated prior to maturity, the gain or loss should be recognized immediately. However, no consensus exists on the treatment if the swap is a hedge. Wishon and Chevalier report widespread disagreement on the appropriate treatment of a swap's termination. One common approach would defer and amortize any gains or losses on the swap over the life of the underlying financial instrument. The other calls for immediate recognition of any gains or losses. The treatment of gains or losses on futures hedges suggests that the deferral and amortization of early swaps termination is appropriate.

Eugene E. Comiskey, Charles W. Mulford, and Deborah H. Turner (1987-88), surveying the financial statements of the 100 largest domestic banks in 1986, discovered that some banks are deferring gains or losses in accordance with hedge accounting treatment even though hedge accounting would not be permitted in similar circumstances for futures.[28] They also found that five banks disclosed their maximum potential credit loss in the extremely unlikely event that every counterparty defaulted on all swaps that were favorable to the bank.

The Financial Accounting Standards Board issued an Exposure Draft of a proposed Statement of Financial Accounting Standards titled "Disclosures about Financial Instruments." The statement proposes disclosing a variety of new information about financial instruments, including the maximum credit risk; the reasonably possible credit loss; probable credit loss; the amount subject to repricing within one year, one to five years, and over five years; and the market value of each class of financial instrument. This statement specifically includes interest rate swaps in its definition of financial instruments. If, when, and in what form this proposal will be adopted is unclear.

Commercial banks in the United States are currently required to disclose the notional principal on their outstanding interest rate swap portfolio to the federal bank regulators.[29] It would seem that regulators should also consider requiring disclosure of the replacement cost of outstanding swaps given that replacement cost is an element of the risk-based capital standards.

Conclusion

This article surveys the literature and some research in progress on interest rate swaps. The extremely rapid growth of the market has left academics trying to explain the existence of the market and the pricing of these instruments, regulators attempting to determine what risks these instruments pose to financial firms, and accountants endeavoring to determine how institutions should report their use of swaps. Evidence is beginning to accumulate to dispel some of the early misconceptions about this market, but far more analysis remains before interest rate swaps can be fully understood.

Notes

1. See Abken (1988) for a review of the studies of the stock market crash.
2. The size of the interest rate swap market is typically stated in terms of the notional principal of the outstanding swaps. See the explanation of interest rate swap transactions for a discussion of the role of the notional principal. Refer to Jackson (1988) for a discussion of the size of the interest rate and currency swap markets.
3. See Celarier (1987): 17. This estimating appears to encompass the effect of both interest rate swaps and a related instrument called a currency swap. A currency swap is an arrangement between two organizations to exchange principal and interest payments in two different currencies at pre-arranged exchange rates. For example, one corporation agrees to pay a fixed amount of dollars in return for receiving a fixed number of Japanese yen from another corporation. This article focuses on interest rate swaps, and hereafter the term *swaps* will be used as a synonym for interest rate swaps. Beckstrom (1986) offers a discussion of different types of swaps.
4. Both fixed-rate interest payment to floating-rate payment swaps and floating-rate to floating-rate swaps whereby, for example, one party pays the London Interbank Offered Rate (LIBOR) while the other party pays the commercial paper rate, are observed in the market.
5. LIBOR is the most common floating rate in interest rate swap agreements, according to Hammond (1987).
6. However, the call option is not a free gift provided by the bond market to corporations. Corporations pay for this call option by paying a higher rate of interest on their bonds.
7. See Bicksler and Chen (1986) as well as Whittaker (1987a) and Hammond (1987) for further discussion.

8. See Myers (1977); Bodie and Taggart (1978); and Barnea, Haugen, and Senbet (1980).

9. Long-term, callable debt may also reduce the agency problems of underinvestment and risk shifting problems. However, Barnea, Haugen, and Senbet point out that callable debt does not eliminate the underinvestment problem. Wall (forthcoming) suggests that callable bonds may not solve the risk shifting problem in all cases and also notes that short-term debt will solve both problems if it matures shortly after the firm makes its investment decision.

10. Investors may also have an incentive to exercise the put option on fixed-rate bonds when interest rates increase. An easy way to control for this feature is to focus exclusively on floating-rate bonds. However, Chatfield and Moyer's study contained fixed-rate, puttable bonds. Their research controlled for the interest rate feature of the put option on these bonds by including a variable for the number of times per year the coupon rate on a bond adjusts and a measure of interest rate uncertainty.

11. Bennett, Cohen, and McNulty (1984) discuss the use of swaps for controlling interest rate exposure by savings institutions.

12. Robbins and Schatzberg (1986) suggest that callable bonds are superior to short-term debt in that they permit firms to signal their lower risk and to reduce the risk borne by equityholders. However, their results depend on a specific example. Wall (1988) demonstrates that the callable bonds may fail to provide a separating equilibrium if seemingly small changes are made to their example.

13. This analysis does not consider the use of the futures, forward, and options markets. See Smithson (1987) for a discussion of the various financial instruments that may be used to control interest rate risk.

14. The dealer may enter into a swap for a customer even though the dealer desires a change in exposure in a direction opposite to the swap.

15. Indeed, some variation in the spread should be expected since the Treasury yield curve incorporates coupon interest payments and principal repayments at the maturity of the swap whereas the swap contract provides only for periodic interest payments.

16. Widgets would probably prefer to cancel the contract and enter into a new swap contract with a different party. Otherwise, market rates could increase above 9.5 percent and then DomBank might be unable to make the promised payments. See Henderson and Cates (1986) for a discussion of terminating a swap under the insolvency laws of the United States and the United Kingdom.

17. One way the banks typically limit their risk to individual borrowers is to establish a maximum amount that the organization is willing to lend to the borrower, called the borrower's credit line. The amount of a credit line used by a loan is the principal of the loan; however, the amount of the line used by a swap is less clear since a swap's maximum credit loss is a function of market interest rates.

18. See also Muffet (1987).

19. The Monte Carlo technique involves repeated simulations wherein a key value, in this case an interest rate, is drawn from a random sample.

20. Consider two matched pairs of swaps. For the first matched pair the bank agrees to two swaps: 1) the bank pays a fixed rate of 11 percent and receives LIBOR on the first swap, and 2) the bank pays LIBOR and receives 11 percent. For the second matched pair the bank pays and receives a 9 percent fixed rate for LIBOR. Assume that the notional principal, maturity, and repricing interval of all swaps are equal. If the current market rate for swaps of the same maturity is 10 percent, the bank has credit exposure on the 9 percent fixed-rate swap in which it pays a fixed rate of interest and has credit exposure on the 11 percent fixed-rate swap in which it pays a floating rate of interest. If the market rate on comparable swaps increases to 10.5 percent, credit exposure increases on the 9 percent swap in which the dealer pays a fixed rate and decreases on the 11 percent swap in which the dealer pays a floating rate. Given the assumptions of this example, the change in exposure is almost zero when the market rate moves from 10 percent to 10.5 percent.

21. The paper does not explain how swap replacement values and interest rate volatility were calculated.

22. David Shirreff (1985): 253.

23. The standards do not include any framework for evaluating the overall interest rate risk being taken by banking organizations.

24. The standards effective in 1992 define core (tier-one) capital as common stockholders' equity, minority interest in the common stockholders' equity accounts of consolidated subsidiaries, and perpetual, noncumulative preferred stock. (The Federal Reserve will also allow bank holding companies to count perpetual, cumulative preferred stock.) Total capital consists of core capital plus supplementary (tier-two) capital. Supplementary capital includes the allowance for loan and lease losses; perpetual, cumulative preferred stock: long-term preferred stock, hybrid capital instruments including perpetual debt, and mandatory convertible securities; and subordinated debt and intermediate-term preferred stock.

25. The framework for risk-based capital standards has been approved by the Group of Ten countries (Belgium, Canada, France, the Federal Republic of Germany, Italy, Japan, the Netherlands, Sweden, the United Kingdom, and the United States) together with Switzerland and Luxembourg.

26. Pitman (1988) discusses the capital standards' implications for various swap market participants.

27. If the predicted changes in interest rates were subject to objective verification, that would suggest that arbitrage opportunities exist. That is, investors may be able to earn a profit with no net investment (financing the purchase of one debt security with the sale of another) and without assuming any risk (since objective verification proved that interest rates will move in the predicted direction). However, efficient markets theory implies that the market will immediately compete away any arbitrage opportunities.

28. Deferral of gains or losses on futures is permitted only if the future is designated as a hedge for an "existing asset, liability, firm commitment or anticipated transactions," according to Comiskey, Mulford, and Turner, 4, 9.

29. See Felgran (1987) for a listing of the top 25 U.S. banks by notional principal of swaps outstanding.

References

Abken, Peter A. "Stock Market Activity in October 1987: The Brady, CFTC, and SEC Reports." Federal Reserve Bank of Atlanta *Economic Review* 73 (May/June 1988): 36-43.

Arak, Marcelle, Arturo Estrella, Laurie Goodman, and Andrew Silver. "Interest Rate Swaps: An Alternative Explanation." *Financial Management* 17 (Summer 1988): 12-18.

Arak, Marcelle, Laurie S. Goodman, and Arthur Rones. "Credit Lines for New Instruments: Swaps, Over-the-Counter Options, Forwards and Floor-Ceiling Agreements." Federal Reserve Bank of Chicago, *Conference on Bank Structure and Competition*, 1986, 437-56.

Barnea, Amir, Robert A. Haugen, and Lemma W. Senbet. "A Rationale for Debt Maturity Structure and Call Provisions in the Agency Theoretic Framework." *Journal of Finance* 35 (December 1980): 1223-34.

Beckstrom, Rod. "The Development of the Swap Market." In *Swap Finance*, Vol. 1, edited by Boris Antl, 31-51. London: Euromoney Publications Limited, 1986.

Belton, Terrence M. "Credit-Risk in Interest Rate Swaps." Board of Governors of the Federal Reserve System unpublished working paper, April 1987.

Bennett, Dennis E., Deborah L. Cohen, and James E. McNulty. "Interest Rate Swaps and the Management of Interest Rate Risk." Paper presented at the Financial Management Association meetings, Toronto, October 1984.

Bicksler, James, and Andrew H. Chen. "An Economic Analysis of Interest Rate Swaps." *Journal of Finance* 41 (July 1986): 645-55.

Bierman, Harold, Jr. "Accounting for Interest Rate Swaps." *Journal of Accounting, Auditing, and Finance* 2 (Fall 1987): 396-408.

Black, Fischer, and Myron Scholes. "The Pricing of Options and Corporate Liabilities." *Journal of Political Economy* 81 (1973): 637-59.

Bodie, Zvi, and Robert A. Taggart. "Future Investment Opportunities and the Value of the Call Provision on a Bond." *Journal of Finance* 33 (September 1978): 1187-1200.

Celarier, Michelle. "Swaps' Judgement Day." *United States Banker* (July 1987): 16-20.

Chatfield, Robert E., and R. Charles Moyer. "'Putting' Away Bond Risk: An Empirical Examination of the Value of the Put Option on Bonds." *Financial Management* 15 (Summer 1986): 26-33.

Comiskey, Eugene E., Charles W. Mulford, and Deborah H. Turner. "Bank Accounting and Reporting Practices for Interest Rate Swaps." *Bank Accounting and Finance* 1 (Winter 1987-88): 3-14.

Federal Reserve Board and Bank of England. "Potential Exposure on Interest Rate and Exchange Rate Related Instruments." Unpublished staff paper, 1987.

Felgran, Steven D. "Interest Rate Swaps: Use, Risk and Prices." *New England Economic Review* (November/December 1987): 22-32.

Geske, Robert. "The Valuation of Corporate Liabilities as Compound Options." *Journal of Financial and Quantitative Analysis* 12 (1977): 541-52.

Hammond, G.M.S. "Recent Developments in the Swap Market." *Bank of England Quarterly Review* 27 (February 1987): 66-79.

Henderson, Schuyler K., and Armel C. Cates. "Termination Provisions of Swap Agreements under U.S. and English Insolvency Laws." In *Swap Finance*, vol. 2, edited by Boris Antl., 91-102. London: Euromoney Publications Limited, 1986.

Jackson, Dominique. "Swaps Keep in Step with the Regulators." *Financial Times,* August 10, 1988, 22.

Johnson, Herb, and René Stulz. "The Pricing of Options with Default Risk." *Journal of Finance* 42 (June 1987): 267-80.

Loeys, Jan G. "Interest Rate Swaps: A New Tool For Managing Risk." Federal Reserve Bank of Philadelphia *Business Review* (May/June 1985): 17-25.

Mayers, David, and Clifford W. Smith. "Corporate Insurance and the Underinvestment Problem." *Journal of Risk and Insurance* 54 (March 1987): 45-54.

Muffet, Mark. "Modeling Credit Exposure on Swaps." Federal Reserve Bank of Chicago, *Conference on Bank Structure and Competition*, 1987, 473-96.

Myers, Stewart C. "Determinants of Corporate Borrowing." *Journal of Financial Economics* 5 (November 1977): 147-76.

Neal, Kathleen, and Katerina Simons. "Interest Rate Swaps, Currency Swaps, and Credit Risk." *Issues in Bank Regulation* (Spring 1988): 26-29.

Pitman, Joanna. "Swooping on Swaps." *Euromoney* (January 1988): 68-80.

Robbins, Edward Henry, and John D. Schatzberg. "Callable Bonds: A Risk Reducing, Signaling Mechanism." *Journal of Finance* 41 (September 1986): 935-49.

Rudnick, Linda T. "Discussion of Practical Aspects of Interest Rate Swaps." Federal Reserve Bank of Chicago, *Conference on Bank Structure and Competition*, 1987, 206-13.

Shirreff, David. "The Fearsome Growth of Swaps." *Euromoney* (October 1985): 247-61.

Smith, Clifford W., Charles W. Smithson, and Lee Macdonald Wakeman. "The Evolving Market for Swaps." *Midland Corporate Finance Journal* 3 (1986): 20-32.

_____ . "The Market for Interest Rate Swaps." University of Rochester Working Paper Series No. MERC 87-02 (May 1987a).

_____ . "Credit Risk and the Scope of Regulation of Swaps." Federal Reserve Bank of Chicago. *Conference on Bank Structure and Competition*, 1987b, 166-85.

Smithson, Charles W. "A LEGO® Approach to Financial Engineering: An Introduction to Forwards, Futures, Swaps, and Options." *Midland Corporate Finance Review* 4 (Winter 1987): 16-28.

Stulz, René M., and Herb Johnson. "An Analysis of Secured Debt." *Journal of Financial Economics* 14 (December 1985): 501-21.

Turnbull, Stuart M. "Swaps: A Zero Sum Game?" *Financial Management* 16 (Spring 1987): 15-21.

Wakeman, Lee Macdonald. "The Portfolio Approach To Swaps Management." Chemical Bank Capital Markets Group unpublished working paper, May 1986.

Wall, Larry D. "Interest Rate Swaps in an Agency Theoretic Model with Uncertain Interest Rates." *Journal of Banking and Finance* (forthcoming).

_____ . "Alternative Financing Strategies: Notes Versus Callable Bonds." *Journal of Finance* 43 (September 1988): 1057-65.

Wall, Larry D., and Kwun-Wing C. Fung. "Evaluating the Credit Exposure of Interest Rate Swap Portfolios." Federal Reserve Bank of Atlanta Working Paper 87-8 (December 1987).

Wall, Larry D., and John J. Pringle. "Alternative Explanations of Interest Rate Swaps," Federal Reserve Bank of Chicago, *Conference on Bank Structure and Competition*, 1987, 186-205.

Weiner, Lisabeth. "Dollar Dominates Swaps, Survey Shows: Deals in U.S. Currency Outstrip Yen, Deutsche Mark by Far." *American Banker*, February 26, 1988, 2.

Whittaker, J. Gregg, "Interest Rate Swaps: Risk and Regulation." Federal Reserve Bank of Kansas City *Economic Review* (March 1987a): 3-13.

_____ . "Pricing Interest Rate Swaps in an Options Pricing Framework." Federal Reserve Bank of Kansas City unpublished working paper RWP 87-02. Presented to the Financial Management Association Meetings, Las Vegas, October 1987b.

Wishon, Keith, and Lorin S. Chevalier. "Interest Rate Swaps—Your Rate or Mine?" *Journal of Accountancy* (September 1985): 63-84.

Interest Rate Caps, Collars, and Floors

Peter A. Abken

*S*ince the late 1970s interest rates on all types of fixed income securities have become more volatile, spawning a variety of methods to mitigate the costs associated with interest-rate fluctuations. Managing interest-rate risk has become big business and an exceedingly complicated activity. One facet of this type of risk management involves buying and selling "derivative" assets, which can be used to offset or hedge changes in asset or liability values caused by interest-rate movements. As its name implies, the value of a derivative asset depends on the value of another asset or assets.

Two types of derivative assets widely discussed in the financial press are options and futures contracts.[1] Another derivative asset that has become extremely popular is the interest-rate swap.[2] This article examines a group of instruments known as interest-rate caps, collars, and floors, which are medium- to long-term agreements that have proven to be highly useful for hedging against interest-rate uncertainties. In this regard, caps, collars, and floors can be thought of as insurance policies against adverse movements in interest rates.

Like interest-rate swaps, to which these instruments are closely related, caps, collars, and floors are designed to hedge cash flows over time rather than on a single date. The discussion below will show how caps, collars, and floors are related to each other, as well as how they may be constructed from the most basic derivative asset, the option. The article also shows the ways in which caps, collars, and floors are created in practice, along with the different kinds of intermediaries involved in the cap market.[3] The rationale for hedging is reviewed, as are examples of how caps, collars, and floors are used by different financial institutions. The last section of

An earlier version of this article originally appeared in the Atlanta Fed's November/December 1989 Economic Review. *This revised version is reprinted from The* CME Financial Strategy Paper *1991 series published by the Chicago Mercantile Exchange. The author is a senior economist in the financial section of the Atlanta Fed's research department.*

the article considers the credit risk associated with buying caps, collars, or floors and presents a new approach for determining the expected cost of default on these instruments.

What Is an Interest-Rate Cap?

An interest-rate cap, sometimes called a ceiling, is a financial instrument that effectively places a maximum amount on the interest payment made on floating-rate debt. Many businesses borrow funds through loans or bonds on which the periodic interest payment varies according to a prespecified short-term interest rate. The most widely used rate in both the caps and swaps markets is the London Interbank Offered Rate (LIBOR), which is the rate offered on Eurodollar deposits of one international bank held at another.[4] A typical example of floating-rate borrowing might be a firm taking out a $20 million bank loan on which the interest would be paid every three months at 50 basis points (hundredths of a percent) over LIBOR prevailing at each payment date. Other short-term rates that are used in conjunction with caps include commercial bank certificate of deposit (CD) rates, the prime interest rate, and certain tax-exempt interest rates.

Data on the size of the cap market are sketchy. The International Swap Dealers Association (ISDA) conducted a survey of its members in March 1989, and 44 of the association's 97 members responded. Almost 90 percent of the respondents reported participating in the markets for caps, collars, floors, and options on swaps. As of year-end 1988, these members alone held 7,521 caps, collars, and floors, with a total notional principal of $290 billion. The volume conducted through 1988 was reported as having notional principal of $172 billion. These figures inflate the size of the market considerably because they are not adjusted for transactions among the dealers themselves, such as the purchase or sale of caps or floors to hedge existing positions in these instruments. On the other hand, the survey did not cover the entire market. Nonetheless, the figures probably still greatly overstate the size of the market, net of interdealer transactions or positions.[5] The interest-rate swaps market is vastly larger at over $1 trillion.

Most studies of caps concern agreements offered by commercial or investment banks to borrowers seeking interest-rate protection. These instruments are often tailored to a client's needs, and, particularly in the case of caps, may be marketable or negotiable. Caps, collars, and floors can also be manufactured out of basic derivative assets: options or futures contracts, or a combination of the two. The following discussion will define caps, collars, and floors in terms of option contracts, which are the simplest type of derivative asset.

Call and Put Options. An option is a financial contract with a fixed expiration date that offers either a positive return (payoff) or nothing at maturity, depending on the value of the asset underlying the option. At expiration, a call option gives the purchaser the right, but not the obligation, to buy a fixed number of units of the underlying asset if that asset's price exceeds a level specified in the option contract. The seller or "writer" of a call has the obligation to sell the underlying asset at the specified exercise or strike price if the call expires "in the money." The payoff on a call need not actually involve delivery of the underlying asset to the call buyer but rather can be settled by a cash settlement. If the asset price finishes below the exercise price, the call is said to expire "out of the money."

Put options are analogous to calls. In this case, though, the purchaser has the right to sell, rather than buy, a fixed number of units of the underlying asset if the asset price is below the exercise price. The options discussed in this article will all be "European" options, which can only be exercised on the expiration date, as opposed to "American" options, which can be exercised any time before or at expiration. As will be seen, caps, floors, and collars are European-style option-based instruments, and the European interest-rate call option is the basic building block for the interest-rate cap.

Options on debt instruments can be confusing if it is unclear just what the option "price" represents. For debt instruments, the strike price is referred to as the strike level, reflecting an interest rate. Recall that the price of a debt instrument, such as a Treasury bill or CD, moves inversely with its corresponding interest rate; as the interest rate of a Treasury bill rises, its price falls. Thus, a call on a Treasury bill rate is effectively a put on its price. (To keep the exposition clear, all discussion will be in terms of options on interest rates. The strike price will be referred to as the strike level.) A call with a strike level of 8 percent (on an annual basis) on some notional amount of principal is effectively a cap on a floating-rate loan payment coinciding with the expiration of this option. (The notional amount of principal is a sum used as the basis for the option payoff computation. Cap, collar, and floor agreements do not involve any exchange of principal.)

Assume the call's payment date, known as the reset date, falls semiannually. If the interest rate is less than 8 percent on the reset date, the call expires worthless. If the interest rate exceeds 8 percent, the call pays off the difference between the actual interest rate and the strike level times the notional principal, in turn multiplied by the fraction of a year that has elapsed since purchase of the option. For example, if the actual rate of interest six months later were 10 percent and if the notional principal were $1 million, the payment received from the call writer would be 2 percent (the 10 percent actual rate minus the 8 percent strike level) x $1,000,000 x 180/360 = $10,000.

A put option on an interest payment works in a similar way and is the foundation for the interest-rate floor. The holder of a floating-rate loan could protect against a loss in interest income from the loan by buying an interest-rate put. A fall in the interest rate below the strike level of the put would result in a payoff from the option, offsetting the interest income lost because of a lower interest payment on the loan.

An option writer is basically an insurer who receives a premium payment from the option buyer when an option is created (sold). In fact, the option price is alternatively called the option premium. The same party can simultaneously write and buy options, thus creating an interest-rate collar. Before exploring this strategy further, option pricing must be reviewed briefly.

Option Pricing. An option's price before expiration depends on several variables, including the value of the underlying asset on which the option is written, the risk-free rate of interest (usually a Treasury bill that matures at the same time as the option), the time remaining before expiration, the strike price or level, and the volatility of the underlying asset price.[6] For later reference, readers should know how an option price changes in response to a change in an underlying variable, all other variables remaining constant. A call price rises (falls) when the underlying asset price, volatility, or time to expiration increases (decreases). It falls (rises) with an increase (decrease) in the exercise price. A put price rises (falls) with an increase (decrease) in the strike price or volatility. It falls (rises) with an increase (decrease) in the underlying asset price or interest rate. Unlike a call price, a put price is not unambiguously affected by an increase in the time to expiration, but the put price depends at any time on how far in or out of the money the put is.[7]

For an interest-rate call option, the higher the strike level compared to the current interest rate, the lower the option value. Choosing a high strike level

(out-of-the-money) call is less expensive than buying an at-the-money or in-the-money call. Similarly, a low strike (out-of-the-money) put is cheaper than one with a higher strike level.

This relationship between an option's strike level and its price (the amount the option is out of the money) is analogous to a large deductible on an insurance policy. Such a policy is less likely to pay off and is therefore less expensive. Likewise, the cost of interest-rate "insurance" can be reduced by taking a large deductible—that is, buying an out-of-the-money option—and thereby protecting only against large, adverse interest-rate movements.

Creating an interest-rate collar is another method for reducing the cost of interest-rate insurance. The call-option premium for an interest-rate cap may be partially or completely offset by selling a put option that sets an interest-rate floor. For a floating-rate debt holder, the effect of this dual purchase is to protect against rate movements above the cap level while simultaneously giving up potential interest savings if the rate drops below the floor level.

If the cap and floor levels of a collar are narrowed to the extent that they coincide at the current floating interest rate—that is, both put and call options are at the money—the resulting collar is so tight that it is similar to a forward contract on an interest rate, which is a derivative asset that locks in the current forward rate. When the contract expires, the change in the contract's value that has occurred since the inception of the contract exactly offsets the change in the interest payment due. A rise in the floating-rate payment is matched by an equal gain in the interest paid to the contract holder; a fall in the floating-rate payment is balanced by an equal loss on the forward contract. In effect, a forward contract converts a floating-rate payment to a fixed-rate payment.

The discussion thus far has been about a single payment, yet, as mentioned earlier, actual cap, collar, or floor agreements are designed to hedge a series of cash flows, not just one. A cap can thus be perceived as a series of interest-rate call options for successively more distant reset dates; a floor is a similarly constructed series of put options. Assume that an interest payment on floating-rate debt falls due in three months, at the next reset date. If the interest rate on the reset date exceeds the strike level, the cap writer would make a payment to the cap buyer on a date to coincide with the cap buyer's own payment date on the underlying floating-rate debt.

A collar that consists of a series of at-the-money call and put options is equivalent to an interest-rate swap. Buying the cap and selling the floor transforms floating-rate debt to fixed-rate debt, whereas selling the cap and buying the floor switches fixed-rate debt into floating-rate debt. A swap that is constructed out of cap and floor agreements is called a synthetic swap. Caps brokers and dealers will sometimes determine rates on floors by deriving the rate from swap and cap rates, which come from instruments that are more actively traded than floors and therefore more accurately reflect current market values.

In practice, swaps are not usually put together from cap and floor agreements. Caps and floors are more readily tradable than swaps because credit risk is one-sided; swaps carry a credit risk that is two-sided in nature. Matching buyers and sellers for swaps is therefore more involved than for caps or floors.[8]

Examples of some caps, collars, and floors should help the reader understand their operation. As the foregoing single-payment-date discussion illustrates, creating these instruments amounts to an exercise in option pricing. One widely used option-pricing model, known as the Black futures option model, is used in the following examples.[9] Robert Tompkins (1989) explains caps pricing in terms of Black's model, and the examples that follow are loosely patterned on Tompkins' approach.

The chief virtue of the Black model is its simplicity and ease of use, even though it has a serious internal inconsistency when used to value debt options: the assumption that the short-term interest rate (that is, the Treasury bill rate) is constant. Options on short-term interest rates have value, though, only if those rates are less than perfectly predictable. In the last section of this paper, a more complex model that does not suffer from this shortcoming is used to price options.[10]

Eurodollar Futures and Forward LIBOR. In order to give realistic yet simple examples of caps, collars, and floors, this article assumes that the reset dates coincide with the expiration dates of Eurodollar futures contracts, which are traded at the Chicago Mercantile Exchange (CME) and the London International Financial Futures Exchange (LIFFE). Purchase of a Eurodollar futures contract locks in the interest payment on a $1 million three-month time deposit to be made upon expiration of the futures contract. The interest rate on the deposit is three-month LIBOR. On the other hand, the seller of a Eurodollar futures contract is obligated to pay the specified LIBOR-based interest payment at expiration.[11]

Eurodollar futures expire in a quarterly cycle two London business days prior to the third Wednesday of March, June, September, and December. The Chicago Mercantile Exchange currently offers contract expiration months extending four years.[12] The interest rate implied by a Eurodollar futures price may be regarded as a forward interest rate, that is, the three-month LIBOR expected by the market to prevail at the expiration date for each contract.[13]

The Black model uses the futures price for a particular contract expiration month as an input to determine the value of a European call and put option on that contract. In the case of Eurodollar futures contract, the add-on yield (100 minus the futures price) is plugged into Black's formula. Another crucial variable is the volatility, which is either estimated from the historical volatility of the Eurodollar futures yield or obtained as an implied volatility from traded Eurodollar futures options.[14] Again, higher volatility results in higher-cost call and put options and hence more expensive caps and floors.

Table 1 (page 91) gives two-year cap, floor, and collar prices on three-month LIBOR for two arbitrarily chosen dates, June 19, 1989, and December 14, 1987, that give reset dates which coincide with Eurodollar futures expiration dates. The first date illustrates pricing during a relatively low volatility period when the term structure of LIBOR rates, as given by the "strip" of prices on successively more distant contracts, was just about flat. The market was predicting virtually no change in short-term interest rates over this two-year horizon. In panel A of Table 1, the contract expiration months are given along with the forward rates or add-on yields for each futures contract. The row labeled time to expiration shows the number of days from the creation of the cap, floor, or collar to the expiration date for each contract. Another input into Black's formula, the risk-free rate, is taken to be the Treasury bill or zero-coupon bond yield for which the expiration falls nearest to the futures expiration date.

The first example prices a two-year 10 percent cap, which consists of the sum of seven call options. At 10 percent, this cap is clearly out of the money. The computed call option price is expressed in basis points. The calls become progressively more expensive as the time to expiration increases, reflecting the rising time value of the calls. The shorter-maturity calls have little value because they are out of the money and, given the volatility, only a slight chance exists that they might finish in the money. Although the more distant calls are also out of the money, there is more time (and more uncertainty) about what LIBOR will do. Thus, their value is greater because of the higher probability that they might expire in the money. The sum of these calls is the cap rate, which is 147 basis points (rounded from 147.1).[15] For a three-month contract with a nominal face value of $1 million, a one-basis-point move is worth $25 ($1 million x .01% x 90/360). Translated into dollars, 147.1 basis points is $3,677.60 (147.1 x $25), which represents the dollar cost of placing a cap for two years on a $1 million loan. This example was computed ignoring the risk of default on the cap. It also assumes that payments at reset dates, if owed, are made at the time of the reset date.

Next, a slightly out-of-the-money 7.5 percent floor is shown. The total cost is 96 basis points, or $2,396.61. As mentioned above, the cost of interest-rate protection can be reduced by creating a collar, which is sometimes referred to as a ceiling-floor agreement. In this example, selling a 7.5 percent floor would substantially reduce the cost of a 10 percent cap. The combination would cost about 51 basis points, or $1,281. However, by judiciously selecting the floor level—in this case, 7.85 percent—the price of the cap can be driven to zero.[16] Marketing people delight in explaining that downside interest-rate protection (the cap) can be obtained at no cost: just sell a floor.[17] Of course, though, this strategy carries a cost. The holder of an interest-rate collar has traded away potential savings on interest-rate declines below the floor. This caveat notwithstanding, a collar for which the floor exactly matches the cap will be referred to as a zero-cost collar.

Panel B illustrates how the cost of caps and floors falls by selecting more out-of-the-money levels. Increasing the cap by one percentage point to 11 percent reduces the cap rate substantially to 63 basis points, or $1,575.84. Decreasing the floor by half a percentage point to 7 percent more than halves the cost to 48 basis points, or $1,198.08. A zero-cost collar with an 11 percent cap effectively lowers the floor to 7.19 percent.

The final example, reflected in panel C of Table 1, shows prices for caps, collars, and floors during the relatively high volatility period after the October 1987 stock market break. As depicted in Chart 1, Eurodollar futures' volatility surged during and after the October 21 crash; the degree of fluctuation had abated greatly by late January, although it had not returned completely to precrash levels. The implied volatility was 25 percent on December 14, 1987, as compared to 18 percent on June 19, 1989, in the earlier examples. The 10 percent cap priced in panel C is substantially more costly than the one in panel A. The cost is 321 basis points, or $8,025.53. Another important factor contributing to the higher cost is the rising structure of LIBOR forward rates. Although the futures nearest to expiration indicate a forward rate of 8.09 percent as compared to 9.02 percent in the June 19, 1989, example, the distant futures for December 14, 1987, have forward rates that are well above those for June 19. The upward sloping term structure of interest rates for December 14 reinforces the effect of higher volatility on raising cap and floor rates. The floor is more expensive as well at 193 basis points, or $4,829.68. Interestingly, the zero-cost collar with a 10 percent cap is only slightly more constraining with a floor of 8.05 percent as compared to 7.85 percent in the previous example, which exhibited low volatility and flat term structure.[18]

Caps, Collars, and Floors in Practice

At first sight, creating caps, collars, and floors would appear to be a simple matter because options are traded on the Eurodollar futures contract. Selecting the appropriate strike levels and expiration dates would appear to be all one needs to manufacture a cap, collar, or floor. However, as mentioned above, Eurodollar contracts extend into the future for at most four years (which nevertheless is an unusually large number of months for a futures contract). Eurodollar futures options traded at the Chicago Mercantile Exchange currently have expiration dates ranging out only two years, in a quarterly cycle that matches that of the Eurodollar futures contracts.[19] The options also are limited to strike levels in increments of 25 basis points, whereas the futures have increments of one basis point. Unlike Eurodollar futures and options, caps, collars, and floors have been created with maturities extending as much as 10 years. Furthermore, actual caps, collars, and floors can be created on any day, not just on futures and options expiration dates. The actual use of futures and options to fashion caps, collars, and floors is neither a straightforward nor a riskless matter.

The solution to this problem is the use of existing futures and options contracts to create the desired positions synthetically. Synthesizing an options position using options or futures contracts—or a combination of the two—requires not only taking appropriate positions in the existing liquid contracts but also altering

Table 1
Examples of Two-Year Cap, Floor, and Collar Prices on Three-Month LIBOR

Panel A: June 19, 1989; Volatility, 18 percent						
	September 1988	December 1988	March 1989	June 1989	September 1989	December 1989	March 1990
Time to expiration (days)	91	182	273	364	455	546	637
Forward rate	9.02	8.84	8.64	8.71	8.77	8.87	8.86
Risk-free rate	8.46	8.47	8.54	8.56	8.59	8.59	8.56
Call prices (10.0 percent strike)	5.3	10.3	12.9	19.9	26.5	34.1	38.1
Put prices (7.5 percent strike)	.6	4.7	11..8	15.4	18.6	20.6	24.2

10 percent cap	7.5 percent floor	Zero-cost collar
Cost in basis points: 147	Cost in basis points: 96	10 percent cap implies
Cost in dollars: $3,677.60	Cost in dollars: $2,396.61	7.85 percent floor

Panel B: June 19, 1989; Volatility, 18 percent						
	September 1988	December 1988	March 1989	June 1989	September 1989	December 1989	March 1990
Call prices (11 percent strike)	.4	2.2	3.8	7.6	11.8	16.9	20.3
Put prices (7 percent strike)	.1	1.3	4.7	7.2	9.5	11.2	13.9

11 percent cap	7 percent floor	Zero-cost collar
Cost in basis points: 63	Cost in basis points: 48	11 percent cap implies
Cost in dollars: $1,575.84	Cost in dollars: $1,198.08	7.19 percent floor

Panel C: December 14, 1987; Volatility, 25 percent						
	March 1988	June 1988	September 1988	December 1988	March 1989	June 1989	September 1989
Time to expiration (days)	91	182	280	371	455	553	644
Forward rate	8.09	8.34	8.62	8.88	9.11	9.31	9.48
Risk-free rate	6.09	6.79	7.11	7.51	7.66	7.79	7.92
Call prices (10 percent strike)	2.1	12.5	28.9	45.9	62.0	78.0	91.6
Put prices (7.5 percent strike)	16.2	23.0	26.8	29.0	30.5	32.9	34.8

10 percent cap	7.5 percent floor	Zero-cost collar
Cost in basis points: 321	Cost in basis points: 193	10 percent cap implies
Cost in dollars: $8,025.53	Cost in dollars: $4,829.88	8.05 percent floor

Note: Dollar amount is for $1,000,000 in notional principal.

Chart 1
Implied and Historical Volatilities for Eurodollar Futures Prices
(Daily data, December 1985-July 1989)

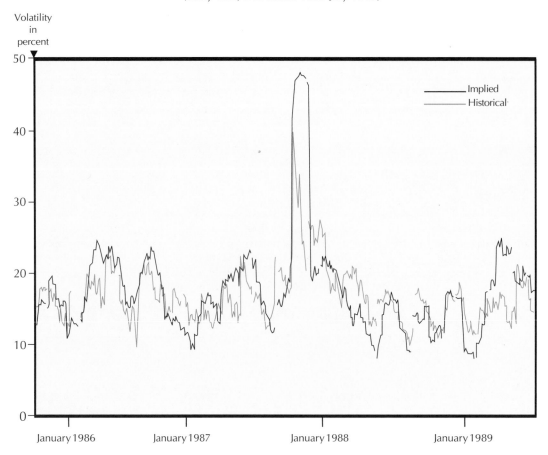

Higher volatility, such as that exhibited around the time of the October 1987 stock-market break, results in more expensive caps, shown in Charts 2, 3, and 4.

Note: Gaps in Chart 1 result from missing observations.

Source: Chicago Mercantile Exchange.

that position over time so that the value of the actual position tracks or "replicates" the desired position. This process is known as dynamic hedging. Theoretically, the replicating portfolio of actual futures and options contracts can exactly match the value of, say, a cap sold to a counterparty.[20] In reality, managing a replicating portfolio is a risky and costly activity.[21] Tracking errors cumulate since costly trading cannot be conducted continuously as is theoretically required and because mismatches can occur with the expiration dates and possibly also with the interest rates involved. Using Eurodollar futures to hedge a cap based on the commercial paper rate exemplifies the latter.[22]

The Over-the-Counter Market

In view of the complexities and risks of dynamic-hedging strategies, most cap, collar, and floor users prefer over-the-counter instruments. Commercial and investment banks create these instruments themselves, possibly by manufacturing them through dynamic hedging. Nonfinancial users tend to rely on the expertise of these financial institutions and are willing to pay for the convenience of interest-rate risk management products issued through an intermediary. The intermediaries may also be more willing to bear the risks associated with hedging because of the scale of their operations. In fact, Keith C. Brown and Donald J. Smith (1988) describe the increasing involvement of banks in offering interest-rate risk management instruments as the reintermediation of commercial banking. Since the 1970s, commercial banks have played less of a role in channeling funds from lenders to borrowers. With the growth of interest-rate risk management, though, their intermediary role is being restored, albeit in a different form.

Commercial banks, particularly the largest money-center banks, are better able to absorb and control the hedging risks associated with managing a caps, collars, and floors portfolio, and these institutions are better able to evaluate the credit risks inherent in instruments bought from other parties. Credit risk arises because any counterparty selling a cap, for example, is obligated to make payments if the cap moves in the money on a reset date. That counterparty could go bankrupt at some point during the course of the cap agreement and would default on its obligation. (This issue is examined in detail in the last section of this article.) By taking positions in caps, collars, and floors, commercial banks—and to a lesser extent, investment banks—act as dealers by buying and selling to any counterparties. Within their portfolio or "book" of caps and floors, individual instruments partially net out, leaving a residual exposed position that the banks then hedge in the options and futures markets. Much trading of caps, collars, and floors consists of positions and risk exposures, so much of the caps market's volume is generated by inter-dealers transactions. In addition to the dozen or so commercial and investment banks in New York and London that dominate the caps market, there are about half a dozen caps brokers, who do not take positions themselves but instead match buyer and seller.[23] Caps, collars and floors are usually sold in multiples of $5 million, but because of the customized nature of the over-the-counter market other amounts can be arranged. Most caps have terms that range from one to five years and have reset dates or frequencies that are usually monthly, quarterly, or semiannual. Caps based on three-month LIBOR are the most common and the most liquid or tradable. From the purchaser's point of view, buying a cap that matches the characteristics of the liability being hedged might seem best. Even strike levels and notional principal amounts can be chosen to vary over the term of an agreement in a predetermined way, but good fit comes at a price. Transactions costs are higher for such tailored products, as reflected by the larger difference between bid and offer rates on uncommon

caps. This wider spread also increases the cost of removing caps by selling them before their term expires. Many users opt for a liquid cap and are willing to absorb the basis risk—the risk from a mismatch of interest basis or other characteristics—in order to avoid the higher cost of a less liquid instrument.

Caps and floors are usually available at strike levels within several percentage points of the current interest-rate basis and are most commonly written out of the money. Settlement dates typically occur after reset dates, upon maturity of the underlying instrument. For example, interest on a three-month Eurodollar deposit is credited upon maturity of the deposit. A cap on three-month LIBOR would have a three-month lag between a reset date and actual settlement. Most payments for caps are made up front, although they can also be amortized. When a cap and a floating-rate loan come from the same institution, the two are usually treated as a single instrument; thus, when the floating rate exceeds the strike level, payment is limited to the strike level and the cap does not pay off directly.[24]

Long-Term Caps. During the mid-1980s, early in the development of the caps market, longer-term caps were created directly from floating-rate securities rather than synthetically. Two kinds of floating-rate instruments were used: floating-rate CDs and floating-rate notes.[25] Floating-rate notes are debt obligations usually indexed to LIBOR, and floating-rate CDs are medium-term deposit instruments that are also typically indexed to LIBOR. The innovation that sparked much activity in the caps market was the issuance of capped floating-rate notes and CDs that in turn had their caps stripped off and sold as separate instruments sometimes known as "free-standing" caps.

As an illustration, consider the floating-rate CD. Banks use ordinary CDs as well as variable-rate CDs to acquire funds for the purpose of making loans and funding other balance-sheet assets. The capped floating-rate CD was promoted as a method of raising funds below LIBOR, the rate on an uncapped CD with a variable rate of interest. The reason is that, after issuing a capped floating-rate CD to a depositor, a bank could then sell the corresponding cap into the caps market and collect premium income. Because CDs of this type typically fund floating-rate loans, the bank would be fully hedged after selling the cap. Funding costs would be lowered if the premium for the cap on the floating-rate CD were less than the premium that the bank collected upon selling the cap into the market.[26] This method of creating or "sourcing" caps, floors, and collars—through capped floating-rate CDs and floating-rate notes—became extremely popular but was short-lived. Reportedly, the longer-term caps were gradually perceived to be undervalued, such that cap writers were not being compensated for the risks of having to make payments to cap holders if interest rates rose above strike levels.[27] Also contributing to the demise of this method of sourcing was a flattening of the yield curve that made floating-rate borrowing less attractive and reduced cap prices. Today, few caps, collars, or floors are created beyond the five-year maturity.

Charts 2-4 give actual cap bid and offer rates, in basis points, quoted by one major caps broker in New York. The bid rate is the rate at which the broker is willing to buy a cap; the offer rate is the rate at which the broker sells a cap. The spread between the two represents the transactions costs of matching buyer with seller. Charts 2,3, and 4, respectively, give the rates on two-year 8 percent, three-year 10 percent, and five-year 10 percent caps. These rates are just a sample; many other strike levels are available. The strike levels quoted change over time as interest rates change. Cap strike levels that move too far in the money or out of the money are discontinued and replaced by caps with strike levels that are in greater demand. All of these series are highly correlated. They are also correlated with the volatilities shown in Chart 1, which are a major determinant of cap values.[28]

The Motivation for Hedging and Some Hypothetical Examples

With some background on the caps, collars, and floors market, the use of interest-rate risk management instruments can now be put into perspective by briefly considering the nature of hedging. Caps, collars, and floors are often talked about in terms of an insurance analogy. They are instruments that can be used to hedge assets or liabilities and protect against loss resulting from interest-rate risk. In practice, though, distinguishing between hedging and speculating in interest-rate risk management is sometimes difficult, especially with option-based instruments. Discretion is required in selecting the timing of the hedge, the strike level, and the maturity of the instrument, all of which are usually predicated on some opinion of what interest rates and other variables are expected to do. Selling a cap or floor, for example, is a way to generate income on a fixed-income portfolio by collecting the premiums. The decision to sell often reflects a difference of opinion regarding the volatili-

ty implied by the cap or floor. If a money manager thinks a cap is overvalued because the market's expectation of volatility is higher than his or her own, then selling an out-of-the-money cap might be a good move. If the money manager's judgment about volatility is correct, even small upward moves in the interest rate may not wipe out all of the premium income. At the same time, the sale provides a limited hedge against small downward moves in rates, again because of the premium receipt.

Even determining the effect of hedging can be problematic, since a firm's purchase of a cap, for example, to hedge the interest-rate risk of a particular liability could increase the variability of the firm's net worth. The financial claim being hedged may itself help offset the variability of another financial claim on the balance sheet. The net result of a specific hedge could be to increase the interest-rate risk exposure of the firm.

A more fundamental issue is why firms hedge in the first place. A basic insight derived from the economics of uncertainty is that risk aversion leads individuals to prefer stable income and consumption streams to highly variable ones. Given an assumption of risk aversion on the part of decision makers, one can show that their welfare or utility (that is, their economic well-being) is greater over time if they enjoy smooth income or consumption opportunities rather than erratic ones.[29] Hedging is a way of improving economic well-being by trading off income or consumption in good times for greater income or consumption in bad times. Thus, a hedging strategy serves a well-defined purpose for risk-averse economic agents, such as farmers or a firm's owner-manager. The issue is less clear-cut for widely held corporations, which actually are the typical users of interest-rate risk-management tools. A corporation owned by a large number of stockholders need not operate like a risk-averse decision maker because each stockholder can insulate his or her wealth and consumption opportunities from risk, specific to the corporation's activities, by holding a diversified portfolio of assets.

Clifford W. Smith and René M. Stulz (1985) surveyed managers of widely held, value-maximizing corporations to determine the motivations behind hedging behavior. According to the researchers, managers engage in hedging of a firm's value for three basic reasons. The first explanation is tax-related; Smith and Stulz argue that, on average, a less variable pretax firm value implies a higher after-tax firm value than does a more variable pretax value. The reasoning

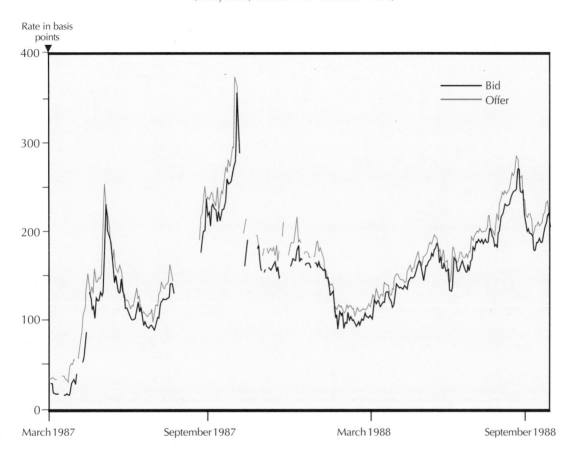

The spread between the bid and offer rates represents the transactions costs of matching buyer and seller.

Note: Gaps in Charts 2, 3, and 4 reflect days for which rates were not available.

Source: Noonan, Astley, and Pearce, Inc.

turns on their assumption that the level of corporate tax liabilities grows at an increasing rate with rising pretax firm value because of the progressive structure of the tax code. Hedging helps reduce the variability of pretax firm value and therefore raises after-tax value. Second, Smith and Stulz maintain that hedging lowers the probability that the firm will go bankrupt and thus incur bankruptcy costs. Hedging firm value would benefit stockholders by reducing the expected future costs of bankruptcy that lower current firm value. A related point is that a firm's debt may often contain covenants that force the company to alter investment policies that the shareholders would like to see undertaken. Hedging reduces the likelihood of

financial distress and the limitations on managers' discretion that bond covenants may impose. A third reason for hedging is that when managerial compensation is tied to the firm's value, managers may become more risk-averse in order to maintain that value.

Participants in the Caps, Collars, and Floors Market. While the precise social value of interest-rate risk management products is not fully understood in the case of widely held corporations, such products are clearly becoming increasingly popular among corporate treasurers and other financial managers. End users of caps, collars, and floors typically include firms seeking to limit exposure to adverse movements in short-term interest rates, such as a firm that sells

Chart 3
Three-Year 10 Percent Cap Bid and Offer Rates
(Daily data, March 1987-June 1989)

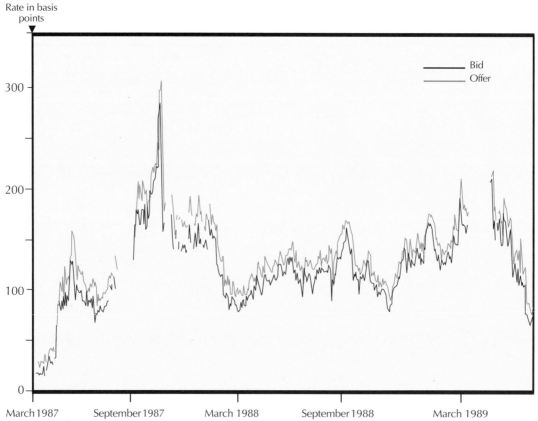

The rates depicted in Chart 3 are highly correlated with those in Charts 2 and 4, as well as with the volatilities in Chart 1.

Source: Noonan, Astley, and Pearce, Inc.

commercial paper to fund its purchases of inventory. Specific market participants are depository institutions, particularly savings and loan associations (S&Ls); corporations going through leveraged buyouts (LBOs) or taking on debt to fend off hostile takeovers; and real estate developers, who are often highly leveraged with floating-rate debt. Unfortunately, the only information about these applications is anecdotal. Also, compared to the potential market, the actual market is very small. Many potential users are unaware of or cautious about interest-rate risk management instruments.

Any user of interest-rate swaps is potentially also a user of caps, collars, and floors. Larry D. Wall and John J. Pringle (1988) conducted a systematic search of annual reports for 4,000 firms that used interest-rate swaps in 1986. The stocks of these firms were traded on the New York Stock Exchange, the Ameri-

can Stock Exchange, or the over-the-counter market. Of this sample, 250 firms were identified as swaps market participants. Over 50 percent of this group were banks, savings and loans, and other financial services firms; commercial banks alone accounted for half of these. In addition, Wall and Pringle report that "the overwhelming majority of thrifts (59 percent), manufacturing firms (69 percent), and nonfinancial, nonmanufacturing firms (77 percent) are exclusively fixed-rate payers."[30] As a conjecture, the profile of caps, collars, and floor users may be quite similar to that for swaps users. The fact that credit risks for caps and floors are one-sided, however, suggests that firms with weaker credit ratings probably use caps and floors because they cannot gain access to the swaps market on favorable terms.

Anecdotal accounts from various sources illustrate how different end users employ caps, collars, or floors in their management of interest-rate risk. Many savings and loans, for instance, have been active users of these option-based instruments. The interest-rate risk confronting S&Ls, and depository institutions generally, may be considered in terms of their net interest margins, that is, the difference between the rates at which an institution lends and borrows. S&Ls are particularly vulnerable to changes in interest rates because maturities (or alternatively, the durations) of these institutions' assets, predominantly long-term mortgages, greatly exceed the maturities of their liabilities, most often short-term time and savings deposits. Thus, a rise in rates raises the interest expense on an S&L's short-term liabilities with possibly little increase in interest earnings on its mortgages. The net interest margin narrows and could very well become negative. One solution is to convert the floating-rate interest expense on the liabilities into fixed-rate payments via an interest-rate swap. The net interest margin would then become much more stable. However, a weak credit standing could make such a swap too expensive or unobtainable. A cap on the floating-rate liabilities could be an effective alternative. An S&L's credit rating would be irrelevant to a cap writer, who bears no credit exposure.[31]

As another example, consider a commercial bank's portfolio manager who is responsible for overseeing a portfolio of floating-rate notes. Suppose this manager believes that a large drop in short-term interest rates, currently at about 8 percent, is about to occur. He wants to protect the portfolio's earning and therefore buys an out-of-the-money 7 percent interest-rate floor. Concerned about the cost of this protection and reasonably convinced that rates will not rise substantially, he also decides to sell a 9 percent interest-rate cap to create a collar on the portfolio. This example highlights the discretion involved in selecting a hedge. A floor could have been in place all along, but maintaining a floor reduces a portfolio's return by the amount of the premium expense. Only when the manager has strong concerns about a drop in rates is the floor purchased.

As a final example, the corporate treasurer of a consumer products firm is worried about the prospects of a rise in interest rates because her company has recently undergone a leveraged buyout. The financing strategy for the LBO included heavy reliance on floating-rate debt secured from a syndicate of commercial banks. The firm's debt-to-equity ratio has soared, and even a modest rise in rates could bankrupt the company. After the LBO the firm's credit standing was downgraded by the rating services;

consequently, access to the swap market is effectively foreclosed. Buying a two-year interest-rate cap to cover the firm's floating-rate exposure seems to be a prudent action.[32] The treasurer expects earnings will be more robust after a two-year interval. Also, the protection gained for a relatively short-term horizon makes sense because during this period the firm would be downsizing and reorganizing its operations.

Credit Risk

The earlier discussion of the over-the-counter market for caps, collars, and floors alluded to the risk of default inherent in these instruments. That risk is present because the seller of a cap or floor is agreeing to fulfill a contract in the event the cap or floor moves in the money on a payment date. Since the seller is a firm, whether a commercial bank, investment bank, or non-financial institution, its assets are limited, and thus the company is exposed to the possibility of bankruptcy. The probability of default is rather small for the typical caps, collar, or floor writer who also typically issues investment-grade bonds into the market. Moody's Investors Service, one of the major bond rating firms, recently released a study indicating that from 1970 to 1988 the average annual rate of default by issuers of investment-grade bonds was 0.06 percent, as compared to an average annual default rate of 3.3 percent for junk bond issuers.[33] Because the consequences of default can be financially damaging, default risk receives careful analysis, particularly by counterparties entering into caps and swaps agreements. This section of the article takes a detailed look at how default risk is evaluated and how it affects the pricing of caps, collars, and floors.

Caps as Default-Risky Options. Almost all of the option pricing models used to value caps ignore default risk. An exception is the model proposed by Herb Johnson and René Stulz (1987), in which they derive formulas for default-risky or "vulnerable" puts and calls. Unfortunately, their formulas cannot be straightforwardly applied to caps, collars, or floors because of the time dimension involved in these options-based instruments. As has been emphasized, caps are a sequence of options—default-risky options. Fulfilling a given option contained in a cap depends on the absence of bankruptcy at earlier reset dates. If bankruptcy occurred earlier, the current option would not be honored by the cap writer. The sequential time dimension involved in valuing caps makes the mathematics

Chart 4
Five-Year 10 Percent Cap Bid and Offer Rates
(Daily data, March 1987–June 1989)

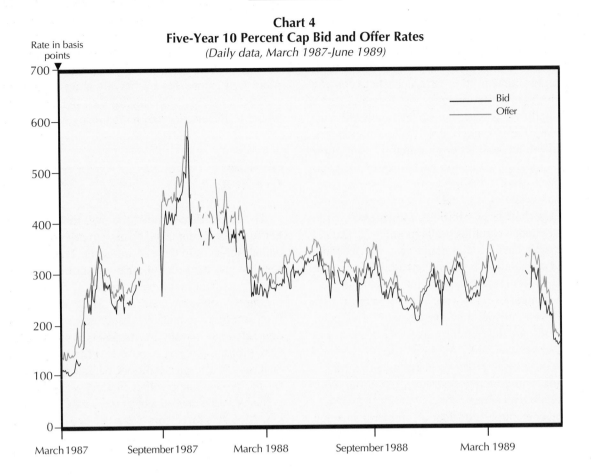

The longer expiration date on a five-year cap results in prices that are relatively higher than those on shorter-term caps.

Source: Noonan, Astley, and Pearce, Inc.

formidably complex.[34] This author has tackled the complexity of cap valuation by using computer-intensive methods to handle the intricate contingencies implied in cap, collar, floor, and swap agreements (Peter A. Abken, 1990 and 1991). His computer model avoids the contradictory assumption inherent in the Black model used for short-term debt options—that short-term interest rates are constant—but at the cost of trading off a simple analytical formula for a complicated computer algorithm. Nevertheless, the intuition behind the new model is simple and easily explained.

The value of a European option can be thought of as the average or expected value of its payoffs at expiration, discounted back to the present. Options are difficult to value because the payoff upon expiration is a "kinked," or discontinuous, function of the underlying asset price. A call option is worth zero if the underlying asset price at expiration is less than the strike

price, and positive in value if the underlying asset price exceeds the strike price, increasing dollar for dollar with the amount above the strike. The Black-Scholes and Black formulas compute the value of a call as the expected value of the future payoffs.[35] Some payoffs are more likely to occur than others, and the formulas account for the probabilities associated with the payoffs.

Monte Carlo Simulation. One method for valuing options relies on extensive computations to determine the expected payoffs. Known as Monte Carlo simulation, this process was first applied to option pricing problems by Phelim P. Boyle (1977). The standard application involves stock option pricing. A stock price, on which an option is valued, is assumed to rise and fall randomly over time, although its value at any point can be described in terms of its statistical distribution, which is known or assumed. In standard problems the distribution for stock price changes is assumed to be fully characterized by its mean and variance. Using this information, artificial future stock-price paths, also known as realizations, can be created numerically by computer. By randomly generating a large enough number of price paths (tens of thousands, at a minimum) and evaluating the payoff on an option with a given strike price at a particular point in time—the option's expiration date—an average over these randomly generated payoffs can be made. The option price is given by appropriately discounting the expected future payoff into current dollars. Of course, the Black-Scholes formula accomplishes the same thing mathematically and is conceptually equivalent. To the penny, both methods will give the same price using identical assumptions regarding the statistical characteristics of stock price movements. The Monte Carlo method, though cumbersome, pays off in cases where the asset price moves in unusual ways, such as in random jumps—for example, due to a stock market crash. The Black-Scholes model rules out such movements by assumption. Cap valuation is another area where Monte Carlo methods offer a simplification over approaches that may not otherwise be mathematically tractable.

Three factors taken together contribute to the complexity of default-risky cap valuation. The first is that debt prices on instruments like Treasury bills or Eurodollar deposits vary with interest rates. Second, each constituent option in a cap is subject to default and must be valued as a default-risky option. Third, the payoff on a given option depends on the nonoccurrence of default on options from earlier periods.

The payoff of a vulnerable call option is the lesser of the firm's value or the default-free option payoff. The value of the firm is the market value of its equity (before including the value of its cap). If the value of the firm that sold the option is greater than the payoff, no default occurs. If the payoff exceeds the firm's value, the company defaults and the option holder receives the value of the firm—or some share of it, as determined by the bankruptcy courts—when the company is liquidated. In view of the fact that a vulnerable call may pay off less, but never more, than a default-free call, the value of a vulnerable call must be less than the value of an otherwise comparable default-free call.

The Elements of the Caps Model. To convey the basic ideas behind the construction of the caps model, this section of the article sketches out the model, the technical details of which can be found in Abken (1990). Two so-called state variables are computer

generated to implement the simulation. The options making up a cap are valued based on the underlying interest rate, as discussed earlier. The entire path of the term structure of interest rates is generated using the model developed by Cox, Ingersoll, and Ross (1985). A single state variable, the instantaneous spot rate of interest (that is, the rate on the bond maturing in the next instant), drives all movements in the term structure. Bond prices across the maturity spectrum are assumed to depend only on the spot rate and time to maturity. The second state variable represents the value of the firm, which also fluctuates randomly over time, reflecting unpredictable changes in interest rates, earnings, and other variables that determine firm value.

The example to be considered is parallel to the one discussed earlier in Table 1, but the focus is now on credit risk. The cap model will value two-year caps on a three-month interest rate. The cap consists of seven reset dates, at each of which the firm's value is compared to the call option payoff. Default-free and default-risky caps are valued. The difference in the price or rate for these otherwise identical caps is the credit spread for default risk. The example developed below illustrates how default risk is particularly sensitive to the correlation over time between firm value and interest-rate movements.

More Examples. Table 2 gives the results of the simulations. The parameter values for the CIR model used in the simulations were obtained from Chen and Scott (1990), based on a sample period that ran from January 1980 to December 1988. Default-risky cap rates were computed as a function of the correlation between the spot interest rate process and firm value process. Intuitively, a cap writer whose firm value is negatively correlated with interest-rate movements poses a greater credit risk than one that is positively correlated. A negative correlation means that high interest rates are associated with low firm value; hence, default is more probable than it would be for a zero or positive correlation.

The default rate in the row for zero correlation between spot rate and firm value was calibrated to be .20 percent per year. This choice is intended to reflect the experience of a cap dealer who carried a BBB bond rating.[36] The default rate was set by adjusting the parameters of the firm value equation until the selected default rate was achieved in the simulation. The same firm value parameters were then used for all other simulation runs involving different correlation coefficients. Default rates therefore varied in response to changes in the spot rate/firm value correlation.

The default-free cap rate for this example is 281.49 basis points. As the spot rate/firm value correlation becomes smaller and then negative, the default-risky cap rates fall, reaching a maximum credit spread of 16.31 basis points. At zero correlation the spread is 1.55 basis points and drops to very small amounts for positive correlations. The default rates also rise inversely with the correlation coefficient, but proportionately less than the credit spreads.

The cap rates and credit spreads are estimates and have an error associated with them. As Boyle (1977) notes, for crude Monte Carlo simulation the standard error diminishes by a factor that is inversely proportional to the square root of the number of simulation trials. Each simulation trial generated monthly values for each state variable over the two-year life of the cap. The simulations in the table used the method of antithetic variates described by Boyle (1977) and by Hull and White (1987). Antithetic variates were employed for the spot rate and firm value processes. The estimates in each row were generated from 40,000 independent sets of realizations of the state variables.

The antithetic variate combinations increased the total number of realizations to 160,000. The standard error of each estimate appears in parentheses.

No data on actual credit spreads are published. In conversations with the author, cap market participants place the credit spreads that have occurred in the range of 5 to 10 basis points for two- to three-year caps. The estimated spreads using the cap model are roughly in that range. Further research into actual credit spreads and refinements of the cap model should sharpen the estimation results and make the model more useful. The model has other applications as well. Abken (1991) values default-risky interest-rate swaps by decomposing swaps into default-risky cap and floor components.

Conclusion

Interest-rate caps, collars, and floors are among the newest interest-rate risk management instruments.

Table 2
Default-Free and Default-Risky Cap Rates Estimated by Monte Carlo Simulation, 10 Percent Two-Year Cap

Initial spot rate: 8 percent; Default-free cap rate: 281.49 (1.16)			
Correlation	Default-Risky rate	Credit spread	Default Rate
−.8	265.18 (.97)	16.31 (.42)	1.23
−.6	270.70 (1.03)	10.79 (.30)	.89
−.4	274.89 (1.08)	6.60 (.21)	.61
−.2	277.94 (1.12)	3.55 (.14)	.38
.0	279.94 (1.15)	1.55 (.09)	.20
.2	280.98 (1.16)	.51 (.05)	.08
.4	281.37 (1.16)	.11 (.02)	.02
.6	281.48 (1.16)	.01 (.01)	.00

Note: The correlation is between the spot rate and firm value processes. Cap rates and credit spreads are expressed in basis points. Default rates are annualized percentage rates. Standard errors are given in parentheses.

This article has given an exposition of these closely related instruments, which are options-based and designed to limit exposure to fluctuations in short-term interest rates on floating-rate assets or debt. Their applications are not limited to hedging. Like options, they are also convenient for speculating on interest-rate movements. In practice, however, the distinction between these two applications is rarely clear-cut. Several examples served to illustrate how financial managers use caps, collars, and floors

The article also discussed the credit risks associated with caps, collars, and floors, which for the most part are over-the-counter contracts offered by one firm to another. Default risk is inherent in this kind of arrangement and can be priced. A new cap valuation model produced credit spreads that are not much different from those observed in the cap market between stronger and weaker credit risks among cap writers. Interest-rate risk management has been growing in importance for financial managers. This article may improve their understanding of the credit risk of caps, collars, and floors and help determine the cost of interest-rate protection.

Notes

1. Recent Federal Reserve Bank of Atlanta *Economic Review* articles include Abken (1987), Feinstein and Goetzmann (1988), Kawaller, Koch, and Koch (1988), and Feinstein (1989).
2. See Wall and Pringle (1988) for an introduction to interest-rate swaps.
3. For brevity, the market for caps, collars, and floors will be referred to as the *cap market*.
4. See Kuprianov (1986): 16-20, for a discussion of Eurodollar deposits and Eurodollar futures.
5. The information on the ISDA survey was reported in *Risk* 2 (April 1989): 11.
6. A detailed discussion of option pricing is beyond the scope of this article. A basic overview can be found in Abken (1987). See Cox and Rubinstein (1985) or Jarrow and Rudd (1983) for more thorough introductions to option pricing.
7. See Abken (1987): 6, for more detail.
8. See Henderson (1986) for further discussion.
9. See Black (1976).
10. To the author's knowledge, no published studies have compared the accuracy of different option-pricing models for pricing caps and related instruments. One reason may be that there are no publicly available data on these rates, and another is that these instruments are relatively new. Little empirical research exists on the adequacy of different interest-rate option-pricing models. Boyle and Turnbull (1989) use the Courtadon option-pricing model in evaluating collar rates, but they do not compare their rates with those from other models nor with actual market rates.
11. Because the CME and most LIFFE Eurodollar futures are "cash-settled," a $1 million deposit is rarely made, but instead only the difference between the current, or spot, LIBOR and the contracted LIBOR times the notional principal actually changes hands.
12. Prior to June 1989 contract months extended three years.
13. A Eurodollar futures price is actually an index value that equals 100 minus the "add-on" yield (three-month LIBOR). Thus, the futures price and add-on yield move inversely with each other. See Kuprianov (1986): 16, for more detail on Eurodollar futures and short-term interest-rate futures generally. Both the add-on yield and the futures price are usually quoted in the financial press.
14. See Feinstein (1989) for details on the estimation, interpretation, and uses of implied volatilities. The Eurodollar futures options are actually American options, but the early exercise feature has negligible value for the slightly out-of-the-money options usually used in estimating the implied volatilities with a European futures option formula.
15. Sums in Table 1 may not add up due to rounding error. Cap rates are usually rounded to whole basis points. The dollar amounts are the exact amounts computed in constructing Table 1.
16. Another way to create a zero-cost collar is to set the floor first and then determine the appropriate cap. The method discussed in the text is more common.
17. Collars have also been offered that give the buyer a payment for taking the collar, that is, the value of the floor sold exceeds the cost of the cap purchased. See "NatWest Uses Incentives to Push Rate Collars," *American Banker*, August 2, 1989.
18. These examples are consistent with the recent findings of Boyle and Turnbull (1989) in their examination of collars. Using a different option-pricing model than the Black model, they found that a 100 percent increase in the volatility causes the floor level to change by less than one basis point. If their findings are also valid for the Black model, most of the difference observed in the examples in the text is attributable to the difference in yield curves.
19. Before March 1989, contract expiration dates had a maximum maturity of one year. See Chicago Mercantile Exchange (February/March 1989):7.
20. The term *counterparty* is standard terminology for the other party in a swap, cap, floor, or collar agreement.
21. Another complication in using futures in a replicating portfolio is that futures contracts are marked to market daily.

This situation may create cash flow problems since futures positions that lose value may be subject to frequent margin calls. Even though the replicating portfolio is used to hedge a cap, which matches it in value, the cash flows from the cap come only when it is sold and on interest payment dates.

22. See Abken (1987) for more on the synthetic creation of options. Mattu (1986) gives examples of replicating portfolios for caps and floors.

23. Shirreff (1986) gives an interesting though somewhat dated overview of the caps market and the various players in it.

24. LeGrand and Fertakis (1986): 134.

25. Floating-rate CDs are also called variable-rate CDs.

26. See *Intermarket* (October 1986): 14, for an account of the first such sale of a cap from a capped floating-rate note (FRN). By selling a cap off an issue of $100 million in 12-year capped FRNs, Banque Indosuez of Paris lowered its interest rate by one-eighth of a point below LIBOR. Uncapped, the notes would have sold at LIBOR. The capped FRNs were issued at LIBOR plus three-eighths. On an annual basis, Indosuez therefore collected the equivalent of 50 basis points on the sale of its cap.

27. Shirreff (1986): 29.

28. The volatilities shown in Chart 1 are probably not the same as those used to generate the cap rates. The volatilities were obtained from a different source than the cap rates, but they should be highly correlated with the actual volatilities used to price the caps.

29. Newbery and Stiglitz (1981) give a comprehensive discussion of risk aversion and the rationale for hedging.

30. Wall and Pringle (1988): 22.

31. The example given was described in terms of a "flow concept" of interest-rate risk, that is, the impact of a change in interest rates on the net interest margin. Another way to view interest-rate risk is in terms of a "stock concept," the change in net worth of the firm. A parallel shift in the term structure of interest rates would reduce the value of an S&L's long-term mortgages more than it would reduce the value of its short-term liabilities. Net worth would be reduced or possibly turn negative. Purchasing a cap—an asset on the balance sheet—would offset loss of net worth to some extent because it would gain value as interest rates rise. See Spahr, Luytjes, and Edwards (1988) for a good exposition of this application of caps and how they hedge interest-rate risk.

32. Commercial banks underwriting debt for highly leveraged financings often require their floating-rate borrowers to buy caps for a portion of the debt. This hedging requirement may be stipulated in the loan covenant. See Richardson (1989): 12.

33. See *Moody's Special Report* (1989).

34. Cap valuation can be formulated as a kind of compound option problem. See Geske (1977) to appreciate the complexities involved in valuing securities that are composed of sequences of options.

35. In a discrete time model the expected value is a weighted average of all possible payoffs, each payoff multiplied by the probability of its occurring.

36. According to Moody's study, the lowest investment-grade bonds, rated Baa (or BBB by Standard and Poor's) had average annual default rates over two-year horizons of 0.25 percent. A Standard and Poor's BBB-rated investment bank was reportedly at a disadvantage in writing caps compared to stronger writers. See Shirreff (1986): 34.

The 0.13 default rate used in the example was chosen to reflect the lower risk of default on a cap relative to a bond.

References

Abken, Peter A. "An Introduction to Portfolio Insurance." Federal Reserve Bank of Atlanta *Economic Review* 72 (November/December 1987): 2-25.

____."Valuing Default-Risky Interest Rate Caps: A Monte Carlo Approach." Federal Reserve Bank of Atlanta Working Paper 90-5, 1990.

____. "Valuation of Default-Risky Interest-Rate Swaps." Federal Reserve Bank of Atlanta Working Paper, 1991, forthcoming.

Arak, Marcelle, Laurie S. Goodman, and Arthur Rones. "Credit Lines for New Instruments: Swaps, Over-the-Counter Options, Forwards and Floor-Ceiling Agreements." In *Proceedings of a Conference on Bank Structure and Competition*. Federal Reserve Bank of Chicago (May 1986): 437-56.

Black, Fisher. "The Pricing of Commodity Contracts." *Journal of Financial Economics* 3 (January/March 1976): 167-79.

Boyle, Phelim P. "Options: A Monte Carlo Approach." *Journal of Financial Economics* 4 (May 1977): 323-38.

Boyle, Phelim P., and Stuart M. Turnbull. "Pricing and Hedging Capped Options." *Journal of Futures Markets* 9 (February 1989): 41-54.

Brown, Keith C., and Donald J. Smith. "Recent Innovations in Interest Rate Risk Management and the Reintermediation of Commercial Banking." *Financial Management* 17 (Winter 1988): 45-58.

"Caps and Floors." *The Banker* (February 1989): 9.

Chen, Ren-Raw, and Louis Scott. "Maximum Likelihood Estimation for a Multi-Factor Equilibrium Model of the Term-Structure of Interest Rates." University of Georgia, Mimeo, 1990.

Chicago Mercantile Exchange. *Market Perspectives*. Various issues.

Commins, Kevin. "Managing Interest Rate Risk." *Intermarket* (May 1987): 28-34.

Cox, John C., Jonathan E. Ingersoll, and Stephen A. Ross. "A Theory of the Term Structure of Interest Rates." *Econometrica* 53 (1985): 385-408.

Cox, John C., and Mark Rubinstein. *Options Markets*. Englewood Cliffs, N.J.: Prentice-Hall, 1985.

Feinstein, Steven P. "Forecasting Stock-Market Volatility Using Options on Index Futures." Federal Reserve Bank of Atlanta *Economic Review* 74 (May/June 1989): 12-30.

Feinstein, Steven P., and William N. Goetzmann. "The Effect of the 'Triple Witching Hour' on Stock Market Volatility." Federal Reserve Bank of Atlanta *Economic Review* 73 (September/October 1988): 2-18.

Geske, Robert. "The Valuation of Corporate Liabilities as Compound Options." *Journal of Financial and Quantitative Analysis* 12 (1977): 541-52.

Henderson, Schuyler K. "Securitizing Swaps." *International Financial Law Review* (September 1986): 31-34.

Hull, John and Alan White. "The Pricing of Options on Assets with Stochastic Volatilities." *Journal of Finance* 42 (1987): 281-300.

Jarrow, Robert A., and Andrew Rudd. *Option Pricing*. Homewood, Ill.: Richard D. Irwin. Inc. 1983.

Johnson, Herb, and René Stulz. "The Pricing of Options with Default Risk." *Journal of Finance* 42 (June 1987): 267-80.

Kawaller, Ira G., Paul D. Koch, and Timothy W. Koch. "The Relationship between the S&P 500 Index and S&P 500 Index Futures Prices." Federal Reserve Bank of Atlanta *Economic Review* 73 (May/June 1988): 2-10.

Kuprianov, Anatoli. "Short-Term Interest Rate Futures." Federal Reserve Bank of Richmond *Economic Review* (September/October 1986): 12-26.

LeGrand, Jean E., and John P. Fertakis. "Interest Rate Caps: Keeping the Lid on Future Rate Hikes." *Journal of Accountancy* (May 1986): 130-36.

Mattu, Ravi. "Hedging Floating Rate Liabilities: Locks, Caps and Floors." Chicago Mercantile Exchange Strategy Paper, 1986.

Moody's Special Report. "Historical Default Rates of Corporate Bond Issuers, 1970-1988." July 1989.

Newbery, David M.G., and Joseph E. Stiglitz. *The Theory of Commodity Price Stabilization: A Study in the Economics of Risk*. New York: Oxford University Press, 1981.

Richardson, Portia. "Put on Your Thinking Cap." *Intermarket* (March 1989): 10-13.

Shirreff, David. "Caps and Options: The Dangerous New Protection Racket." *Euromoney* (March 1986): 26-40.

Smith, Clifford W., and René M. Stulz. "The Determinants of Firms' Hedging Policies." *Journal of Financial and Quantitative Analysis* 20 (December 1985): 391-405.

Spahr, Ronald W., Jan E. Luytjes, and Donald G. Edwards. "The Impact of the Uses of Caps as Deposit Hedges for Financial Institutions." *Issues in Bank Regulation* (Summer 1988): 17-23.

Sutherland, L. Frederick. "Squeezing Cash: How to Make an LBO Work." *Corporate Cashflow* (June 1988): 47-50.

Tompkins, Robert. "The A-Z of Caps." *Risk 2* (March 1989): 21-23, 41.

Wall, Larry D. "Alternative Explanations of Interest Rate Swaps: A Theoretical and Empirical Analysis." *Financial Management* (forthcoming, 1989).

Wall, Larry D., and John J. Pringle. "Interest Rate Swaps: A Review of the Issues." Federal Reserve Bank of Atlanta *Economic Review* 73 (November/December 1988): 22-37.

Interest Rate Instruments

Innovations in Modeling the Term Structure of Interest Rates

Peter A. Abken

This article was originally published in the Atlanta Fed's July/August 1990 Economic Review. *The author is a senior economist in the financial section of the Atlanta Fed's research department.*

*T*he phrase *term structure of interest rates* refers to the relationship between interest rates on bonds of different maturities. It is no doubt familiar to most who peruse the newspaper's financial pages. A precise understanding of what determines the relationships among these interest rates is still lacking, however, despite a voluminous amount of research. The reason for this open-endedness is not hard to grasp: current interest rates to a large extent reflect expectations of future interest rates, as well as all relevant factors that impinge on them.

Financial economists have long sought to characterize, and more importantly to predict, interest-rate movements using mathematical models. These models tend to shape thinking about the term structure even if a formal model is not a conscious part of this process. Policymakers, money managers, and other investors often look to the term structure for clues about the market's expectation regarding future interest rates. To make sense of the array of interest rates determined in financial markets, any such divination usually implicitly or explicitly uses a theory of the term structure. The interest-rate forecasts embedded in the term structure may help to form individual forecasts, upon which all kinds of economic decisions are based. Differences between individual and market outlooks on interest rates may also spur investors and speculators to bet against the market through their trading of bonds. This trading moves bond prices and thus leads to a melding of private information with the public information embodied in the term structure.

Since about the mid-1980s the most important application of term-structure models has been in valuing various kinds of interest-rate options. The most basic of these are bond options, which can be used to hedge the value of bond portfolios against capital losses. Interest-rate caps and swaps are examples of more complex interest-rate contingent claims that can hedge interest payments on debt whose interest rate fluctuates periodically with market rates.[1] Caps and swaps can be viewed as portfolios of bond options and may be valued using term-structure models. Much current financial research centers on refining existing term-structure models and on developing new ones that are easier to use and more accurate in their predictions.

This article begins with a review of the elementary theories of the term structure. These theories—the expectations hypothesis, the liquidity premium hypothesis, and the preferred habitat hypothesis—have been standards in economics since the 1960s and still constitute the core of contemporary textbooks. These theories are no longer "state of the art," however. This article attempts to bridge the gap between the traditional hypotheses of the term structure and more recent, less accessible work stimulated by innovations in options pricing theory since the early 1970s. Additionally, the discussion of the term-structure models explores the connection between the new modeling "technology" that produced the path-breaking Black-Scholes option-pricing formula published in 1973 and its applicability to pricing bonds, which, like options, are another kind of so-called contingent claim.

Intended as a nonmathematical exposition of both the traditional and recent models of the term structure, this article introduces the term structure by briefly reviewing the three traditional hypotheses as well as the newer models, which are essentially elaborations of the same concepts. Two recent-vintage term-structure models, developed in the mid-1980s, are examined in detail—the Cox-Ingersoll-Ross (1985b) and Ho and Lee (1986) models, which have been highly influential and represent different directions that modeling efforts have taken. To provide a context for these models, related models are also discussed. A brief survey of very recent research shows how these newer models have been extended or applied, and an option pricing example using the Ho and Lee model illustrates an important application of these models.

Whether pricing bonds or contingent claims, all models considered in this article share certain basic principles. The new models explicitly build in uncertainty about the course of future interest rates; they are models of random interest rates. Knowledge of constraints on the behavior of interest-rate movements allows for construction of models that value

bonds or interest-rate contingent claims. This article explains how this valuation is accomplished.

*T*he Term Structure under Uncertainty

The term structure of interest rates refers to yields on bonds that are alike in all respects except their time to maturity. Default risk, for example, should be the same across all bonds to allow meaningful comparisons of bond yields spanning the maturity spectrum. Not only because credit risk is absent but also because government bonds offer the broadest range of maturities of all bonds, most analyses of the term structure are conducted using default-free government bonds. The box on page 113 gives some elementary definitions concerning zero-coupon bonds as well as the arithmetic for relating zero-coupon bond prices and yields to maturity. The box on page 116 considers the basic building blocks for the expectations hypothesis and explains how arbitrage forces equality in the holding-period returns on bonds of different maturities. The analysis shown has been conducted in a theoretical world of perfect certainty about future interest rates.

Expectations Hypothesis. Once the future becomes uncertain, investors face interest-rate risk.[2] This risk is irrelevant for investors whose future cash needs exactly match their bonds' maturity dates. The bonds mature at par, and no capital gains or losses are possible. Such a coincidence is the exception rather than the rule, though. If investors need cash sooner, they are necessarily exposed to the possibility of capital loss; that is, newly issued bonds for the same maturity date may bear higher yields, forcing existing bond holders to sell at a discount to match the higher yield. Conversely, if their bonds mature sooner than the time of their cash need, the investors risk reinvesting at a lower yield in a new bond that matures on the desired date. If they had bought a longer-term bond at the outset, no such risk would have been incurred.

In economics the existence of risk implies that the outcome of a decision is not known precisely; however, a range of possible outcomes is known, each of which has some chance—some probability—of occurring. Thus, investors are assumed to know the range of outcomes and, more specifically, the probability distribution for the likelihood that any particular outcome will occur. These and other statistical concepts are fundamental to theories of the term structure because they quantify investors' expectations.

In the expectations hypothesis of the term structure, risk has no effect on investors' choices. All that matters is their expectation of future interest rates at all maturities. Here the term *expectation* is used in its narrow statistical sense to mean average or mean value for a particular future interest rate. The range of outcomes for an interest rate may be quite wide or quite narrow, but that issue is irrelevant to investors. Investors are said to be "risk neutral."

The expectations theory posits that, regardless of the holding period considered, any possible combination of bonds must offer the same rate of return. This idea, illustrated in the box on page 116 for one- and two-year bonds, works exactly the same way for any other maturity combinations. Any long-term bond yield is the average of the current short-term yield and future expected short-term yields. The essential assumption is that investors care only about holding-period returns and consider all bonds of different maturities as perfect substitutes. All interest rates along the yield curve are therefore linked by arbitrage.

Liquidity Premium Hypothesis. Rather than "risk neutral," investors may be "risk averse," in which case their average sensitivity to bearing risk will be reflected in bond prices. The usual presumption is that longer-term bonds are riskier in the sense that their principal is more exposed to interest-rate fluctuations over time. Specifically, this exposure makes them less liquid (less readily converted to cash by selling them) because they bear a greater potential for capital loss before maturity. Risk-averse investors therefore are believed to require a "liquidity premium" to induce them to hold longer-term bonds willingly. The liquidity premium manifests itself as an increase in the forward rate above the future spot rate, which results in a shifting of the yield curve above the one predicted by the expectations hypothesis. Known as the liquidity premium hypothesis, this concept is a refinement of the expectations hypothesis. The liquidity premium is alternatively known as a *risk premium*, which will be the term used hereafter. To distinguish it, the expectations hypothesis is sometimes called the pure (or risk-neutral) expectations hypothesis.

The liquidity premium hypothesis is rather vague about what determines the risk premium, other than supposing that such a premium is the investor's reward for bearing interest-rate risk. The new models incorporating this hypothesis give more structure to the underlying determinants of the risk premium.

Once risk aversion is assumed to affect interest rates, interpretation of the term structure becomes problematic. Without knowing the size of the risk premium, the expectations hypothesis cannot be used to infer future short-term interest rates. Any forward rate now consists of a risk premium and the expected short-term interest rate. Consider the simple example of deciding between an investment in a sequence of consecutive one-year bonds or an investment in a two-year bond, like that used in the box on page 116. Assume that the one-year yield is 5 percent and the future one-year yield is known to be 7 percent. If the true risk premium were known to be 0.5 percent (or 50 basis points), the two-year yield would be:

$$[5\% + (7\% + 0.5\%)]/2 = 6.25\%,$$

that is, the average of the short rate and the forward rate (which is the sum of the future short rate and the risk premium). The two-year yield is 6.25 percent instead of 6 percent as in the risk-neutral case (where the risk premium is zero). If the risk premium is unknown, all that can be inferred from the current term structure (one- and two-year bond yields) is that the implied forward rate is 7.5 percent. More information is required to disentangle the risk premium from the expected short rate.

For a hypothetical continuum of interest rates along the yield curve, Chart 1 shows the relationship among yield curve, expected short-term interest rates, and forward rates. If the term structure slopes downward—that is, short-term bond yields are above long-term bond yields—one may safely infer that expected short-term rates are lower than the current rate, even if there are risk premia in the forward rates. However, upward-sloping yield curves do not imply that expected short-term rates are rising, since flat or declining expected short-term rates may be sufficiently augmented by rising risk premia to produce rising forward rates. Chart 2 illustrates this phenomenon.[3] These interpretations will be discussed again in the review of recent theoretical models of the term structure.

Preferred Habitat Hypothesis. A third traditional theory is the preferred habitat hypothesis, which posits that interest rates along the yield curve result from market forces in different maturity segments. Sufficiently large risk premia or discrepancies between investors' and market expectations of interest rates may lure investors away from their preferred habitat. Thus, as Franco Modigliani and Richard Sutch (1966) have observed, "risk aversion should not lead investors to prefer to stay short but, instead, should lead them to hedge by staying in their maturity habitat, unless other maturities (longer or shorter) offer an expected premium sufficient to compensate for the risk and cost of moving out of one's habitat" (184).[4]

Life insurance companies' and pension funds' typical preference for investments in longer-term bonds exemplifies preferred habitats, as does depository institutions' likely penchant for short-term bonds. Life insurance companies and pension funds have relatively predictable long-term liabilities, which they match against investments in long-term bonds and other long-term assets. Similarly, depository institutions tend to fund relatively short-term loans with short-term liabilities. Their bond holdings, therefore, also tend to have short-term maturities.

The supply and demand for bonds within each habitat is assumed to have an impact on interest rates; bonds of different maturities are not considered perfect substitutes. In short, institutional characteristics, not just interest-rate expectations, play a role in determining the term structure. An earlier version of this theory, the market segmentation hypothesis, assumed a rigid segmentation of markets, which is now generally regarded as implausible. The preferred habitat hypothesis synthesizes the expectations and market segmentation hypotheses.

Innovations in Modeling the Term Structure

In 1973 Fischer Black and Myron Scholes published their pathbreaking article, "The Pricing of Options and Corporate Liabilities," which transformed not only academic financial research but also actual financial practice. Their celebrated formula allowed academics and practitioners alike to price all kinds of contingent claims.[5] The theory proved to have very broad applications. John C. Cox, Stephen A. Ross, and Mark Rubinstein (1979) have noted that option-pricing theory "applies to a very general class of economic problems—the valuation of contracts where the outcome to each party depends on a quantifiable uncertain future event" (230). Term structure modeling is one area of financial research that has benefited from the advent of modern option-pricing theory. A detailed review of two general approaches, using two specific models, will develop the connection between option-pricing theory and term-structure modeling. The two models highlight the basic directions of recent research.

The Ho and Lee Model. Proposed by Thomas S.Y. Ho and Sang-Bin Lee in 1986, the Ho and Lee

Chart 1
Liquidity Premium Theory

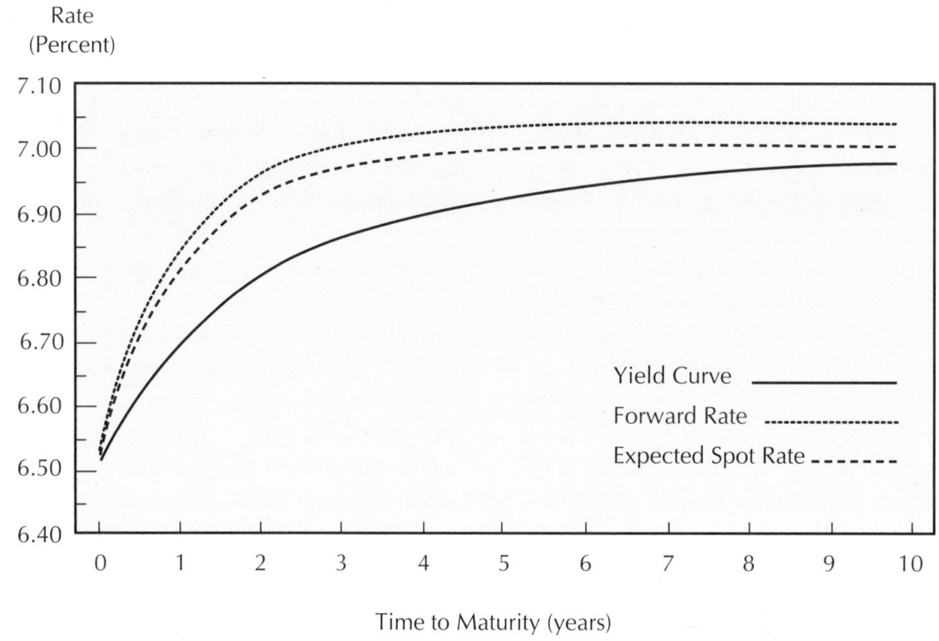

model is a useful starting point in the exposition of term-structure models because it uses what is called a lattice approach. The lattice approach to option pricing explicitly conveys what is meant by a "quantifiable uncertain future event." The basic problem to model is how the price of a zero-coupon bond changes from the present to its future maturity date. Only at the present moment and at the future maturity date is the bond price known with certainty. The Ho and Lee model is one attempt to quantify the evolution of bond prices over time. As will be illustrated below, this quantification is essential to pricing contingent claims on bonds.

Ho and Lee abstract from the complexities of actual bond price movements by assuming (1) that a bond price moves only at fixed intervals over time (for example, every day or every minute) and (2) that they move either up or down when they change. The up or down price changes have an associated probability of occurring, of, say, 20 percent and 80 percent, respectively. Thus, starting from some known price at the current date, future price changes are restricted to evolve by successive up or down movements, which trace out a tree or lattice pattern.

Chart 3 illustrates the branching process that begins with the initial discount bond price. The initial bond in the example has fifteen months (five quarters) to go before maturity, when it will pay $1. The yield to maturity is assumed to be 9 percent, and the current price is $0.894. The annualized yield to maturity appears in parentheses. Successively shorter-term bond prices and yields appear above the 9 percent, fifteen-month bond. Thus, the entire term structure is given in the far left-hand column (five quarters to maturity), starting at the top of the list with a 7 percent, three-month bond that matures (and disappears) in the next column and extending to the longest maturity bond, the 9 percent bond at the bottom of the list. The illustration is therefore given for an upward-sloping term structure.

The tree fans out from the initial price as up and down possibilities proliferate at each future point in time. Each path through the branches to any particular vertex or node in the tree diagram represents a particular succession of up and down price movements. These movements correspond to the realizations of particular "states," which are the possible random outcomes schematically depicted in the tree diagram. After one period elapses from the initial date, two states are possible; after two periods, three states; and so forth. In other words, time is measured horizontally, although states are indicated vertically in the tree

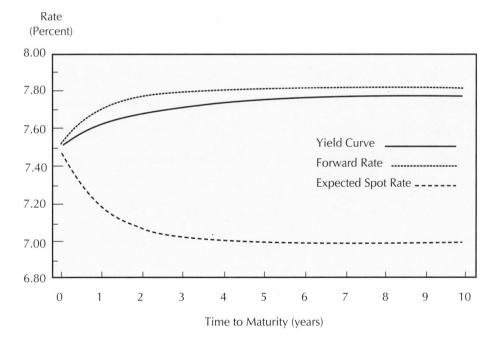

Chart 2
Liquidity Premium Theory

diagram. The tree therefore depicts the value of a particular bond in all states as it approaches maturity. In this example, the bond initially has five periods to mature, then four, then three, and so forth. The final branches in the diagram end with $1 in all states, since the bond's value at maturity is known with certainty. The branches link the path of the initial five-quarter bond as it approaches maturity. The shorter-term bonds could also be joined in this fashion to show their progression.

The essential idea behind the evolution of the bond price tree is that the forward rates implied by the initial term structure would actually be the future short-term rates to prevail in the absence of disturbances or shocks causing changes in interest rates. In the Ho and Lee model, bond prices throughout the tree result from perturbations of the initial implied forward rates. Any state price at a given time represents the initial implied forward rate altered by an accumulation of up and down shocks, resulting in a particular position in the tree diagram. Moreover, the size of the price changes, governed by the perturbation function, is restricted in such a way that no arbitrage profits can be realized; that is, the internal consistency of the model requires that no arbitrary portfolio of discount bonds of different maturities can be formed that earns more than the risk-free rate when the portfolio is perfectly hedged (risk free).

To see how prices are related in the tree diagram, consider any two adjacent state prices. The node marked "A" in Chart 3 is derived as the discounted value of the two certain $1 payoffs at the maturity date, each of which has an equal chance of occurring in this example (that is, the probability is 0.5). The discount factor of 0.967 at node A is in fact the price of a one-period discount bond. This discount factor was computed using Ho and Lee's formula for the perturbation function evaluated at this particular node.[6] All state prices for time 1 are one-period prices. For all earlier periods the bond prices are computed using the same recursive procedure. At node B the price is again the weighted average of two future bond prices times the one-period bond price:

$$(0.5 \times 0.940 + 0.5 \times 0.945) \times 0.975 = 0.919 .$$

This calculation represents a discounted expected value since at node B there are two possible future

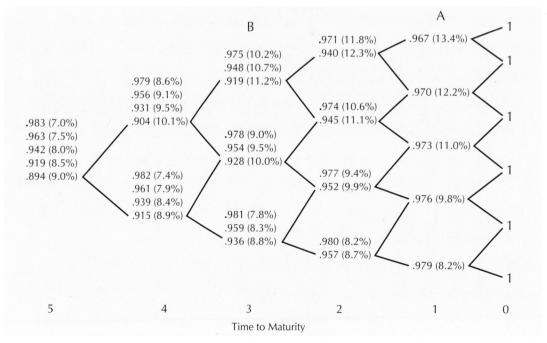

Chart 3
Evolution of Bond Prices in the Ho and Lee Model
(yields in parentheses)

Note: *The one-period bond appears at the top of each column; time to maturity increases by one period with each successive row.*

Basic Terminology

The basic financial instrument of interest is a zero-coupon bond that promises a fixed payment, which will be assumed to be $1, at a future date.[1] The bond makes no interim payments, that is, it has no coupons. While zeros—Treasury bills and zero-coupon Treasury bonds—trade in the bond markets, many bonds make periodic coupon payments. Because any coupon bond can be decomposed into a zero coupon bond by treating each future coupon payment as well as the repayment of principal as a separate zero coupon, modeling in terms of zeros is not unrealistic.[2] The models to be considered also abstract from credit (or default) risk so that the uncertainty stems only from unknown future interest rates.

A zero-coupon bond is alternatively known as a discount bond because its price is less than its $1 face or par value. Its return is derived strictly from the appreciation in price at the time of maturity. For the sake of simplicity, bonds are assumed to be issued at yearly intervals with maturities in multiples of a year, making the shortest maturity bond a one-year bond. The current date will be time 0.

The bond price, B, is the price at time t, when the bond is purchased, for principal repayment upon maturity at later date T. The difference between t and T is called the bond's time to maturity. Consider a bond with one year to maturity (a one-year bond) issued today at time 0. The bond's yield to maturity, $R(1)$, is determined from the following equation involving the bond's price:

$$1/B(1) = 1 + R(1), \text{ or}$$
$$B(1) = 1/[1 + R(1)].$$

The time to maturity is enclosed in parentheses. If the time to maturity is one year and the yield $R(1)$ is 8 percent, then $B(1)$ is approximately 0.926. The term $R(1)$ is expressed as a simple interest rate. Clearly, yield and bond price are inversely related: as one goes up the other goes down.[3]

Consideration of multiple periods entails compounding of interest. The yield to maturity, $R(n)$, of an n period zero-coupon bond is

$$1/B(n) = [1 + R(n)]^n, \text{ or}$$
$$B(n) = 1/[1 + R(n)]^n.$$

The term $R(n)$ is also expressed as a simple annual interest rate. Plotting the yield to maturity against time to maturity gives the so-called yield curve. The reasons for its shape or structure are the subject of the various hypotheses discussed in the main text.

Notes

1. Of course, any par value can be used simply by multiplying the bond price by the face amount. For example, a bond promising $10,000 upon maturity would be worth 10,000 times the purchase price of the $1 par value discount bond.
2. See Bodie, Kane, and Marcus (1989, 420) for a procedure used to infer zero-coupon bond prices from the prices, coupons, and principal payments of coupon bonds.
3. For a fuller discussion of this terminology as well as the basics concerning the traditional hypotheses of the term structure, the reader is referred to Bodie, Kane, and Marcus (1989). Almost any undergraduate investments or money-and-banking textbook contains some discussion of these topics.

outcomes. Either the bond price rises to 0.945 or falls to 0.940. The average of these is discounted to time 3 using the one-period bond price for time 3. Again, the discount factor is the one-period bond price, 0.975, determined one period earlier (at the top of the bond price list for node B). In summary, the tree diagram represents an expected value calculation, for which the known initial bond price of 0.894 is the final outcome.

At first glance the tree diagram may not seem very useful since the final computation is a bond price that was already known at the outset. However, the important aspect of this exercise is that the various price paths (possible branching patterns) are fully described in the tree. This quantification of a bond's future state prices is essential for contingent claims pricing.

A characteristic of this type of lattice model is that the order of up and down movements does not matter; instead, the cumulative number of up (or down) moves from the initial node determines the price at any future time-state node. Inspection of the tree reveals that, from any interior node, moving rightward first up and then down is identical to moving down, then up. This restriction plays an important role in valuing bonds in this model. Also, the initial upward-sloping term structure retains its slope regardless of its location in future periods, but the levels change. In fact, all interest-rate movements are perfectly correlated in the Ho and Lee model. More complex models that will be considered below avoid this unrealistic feature.

Another drawback of the model is the fact that, depending on the model's parameter values, some bond prices may exceed face value before maturity. This outcome along a price path implies that the bond's interest rate is negative. Peter Ritchken and Kiekie Boenawan (1990) prove that such an occurrence represents an internal inconsistency of the model and show how to modify the model to preclude negative interest rates. Charts 3 and 4 were produced using the Ritchken-Boenawan modification.

Despite its limitations, the Ho and Lee model has the virtue of clearly and simply illustrating how the current term structure is derived as the discounted expectation of the future bond payoffs. More recent models of this type rectify some of these limitations and consequently are transforming this modeling ap-

proach into a more useful tool for applications as well as theory.

A Shift in Risk Aversion. The term-structure movements depicted in Chart 3 are assumed to be generated in a world in which investors do not need to be compensated for bearing interest-rate risk. If investors' preferences shifted to become risk averse with respect to interest-rate risk, what effect would that have on the evolution of bond prices? In general, the expected rate of return for an asset would have to increase for the investor to continue holding that asset willingly. For illustrative purposes, the probability of an upward move was assumed to be the same as the probability of a downward move in Chart 3. The increase in risk aversion is quantified as an increase in the probability of an upward move from 50 percent to 60 percent. These probabilities are arbitrarily chosen to show the change in the evolution of bond prices. Any increase in the up-move probability would accomplish the same end.[7]

The Ho and Lee model takes the initial term structure as given in the course of valuing future bond prices and contingent claims. Consequently, a shift in preferences is considered to occur after the initial pe-

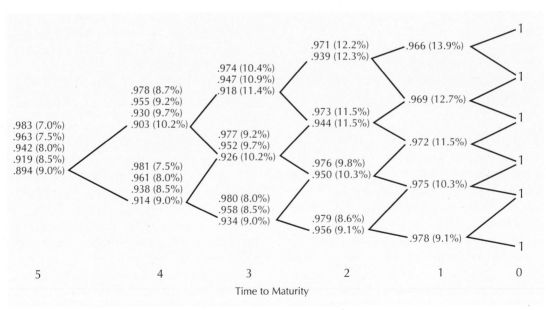

Chart 4
Ho and Lee Model
Shift in Risk Aversion
(bond prices yields in parentheses)

Time to Maturity

Note: The one-period bond appears at the top of each column; time to maturity increases by one period with each successive row.

riod. Chart 4 gives the new tree diagram, starting with the same initial term structure as Chart 3 and also ending with bond prices equal to par upon maturity in period 5. However, the rate of price appreciation in Chart 4 is always greater (or bond prices are everywhere lower), regardless of the path taken through the tree diagram. The terminal payoff of $1 is the same in both diagrams. The downward shift in prices across all states and times occurs because the discount rates have increased because of the rise in risk aversion. In other words, interest rates are always greater in Chart 4, which reflects the risk premium now included in rates.

The Cox-Ingersoll-Ross Model. The Cox-Ingersoll-Ross model takes an approach to valuing fixed-income securities and their contingent claims that is fundamentally different from Ho and Lee's. The basic difference is that the former is a general equilibrium model, whereas the latter is a partial equilibrium model. Essentially, the Cox-Ingersoll-Ross approach has a deeper theoretical foundation and hence more ambitious goals in terms of economic modeling. The practical distinction is not as sharp at the level of using these models to value bond options.

The Ho and Lee model is a partial equilibrium model in the sense that the initial term structure and the process generating shifts in that structure are assumed to be given outside of the model—that is, they are determined *exogenously*. On the other hand, as will be discussed below, the Cox-Ingersoll-Ross model takes investor preferences and unforecastable shocks to physical investment opportunities as given. That is, term-structure movements themselves are explained within the context of the model; they are explained *endogenously*. The importance of this general equilibrium formulation will become apparent after some preliminary discussion.

The Cox-Ingersoll-Ross model can be stripped of its underlying general equilibrium structure, rendering it a partial equilibrium model. This simplification is a useful starting point for understanding this type of model. In fact, a number of similar models originated at about the same time as the Cox-Ingersoll-Ross model, but these were conceived as partial equilibrium models.[8]

Another difference between the Cox-Ingersoll-Ross and Ho and Lee models is that the former uses continuous-time mathematics, which demands considerably greater technical sophistication than does the discrete-time mathematics of the Ho and Lee model. The use of continuous-time mathematics requires assumptions that all bonds and other financial instruments trade at every moment in time—that is, continuously—and, furthermore, that bonds mature at every moment in time. While highly artificial, this kind of model allows the tools of continuous-time mathematics to deliver pricing formulas for bonds and other financial instruments. In fact, the original Black-Scholes formula was derived using continuous-time mathematics.[9]

The simplest version of the Cox-Ingersoll-Ross model assumes that the term structure can be expressed as a function of one variable, the instantaneous risk-free rate or spot interest rate, that is, the interest rate on a bond that matures at the next "instant" in time. The continuum of bond prices along the term structure is expressed solely as a function of the spot rate and time (or, equivalently, time to maturity). All shocks to the term structure therefore emanate from the spot interest rate, which in fact is a proxy variable for the fundamental uncertainty in the economy. To give more content to this formulation requires appending the full general equilibrium structure of the economy to the model. In contrast, the partial equilibrium model simply posits the instantaneous rate as the source of random fluctuations in the term structure. The spot interest rate is referred to as a "state variable," a variable that summarizes information about uncertainty in the economy. More complex models can be constructed by including more state variables, each of which conveys independent bits of information about shocks to the term structure. A fuller interpretation of state variables will be possible once general equilibrium models are considered.

The Cox-Ingersoll-Ross model restricts the behavior of the spot rate by supposing that, although random in its movements from one instant in time to another, the spot rate tends to "revert" to a long-term level and never becomes negative. It is prevented from becoming negative because negative real interest rates are not economically meaningful in the context of their model. This restriction alone is not sufficient for a realistic model since the spot rate would exhibit too much variability over time. Thus the assumption of mean reversion was incorporated. Note that the original Ho and Lee model, cast in terms of nominal bond prices and interest rates, does allow negative interest rates and does not have a mean-reversion property.[10]

Valuing a bond using the Cox-Ingersoll-Ross model, like the Ho and Lee or any other valuation model, entails computing the expected value of the discounted payoff. Instead of positing a discrete number of states upon expiration of a bond as in Ho and Lee, the

The Term Structure under Certainty

The question to be answered is, how is the yield on a one-year bond (the "short" rate) related to the yield on a two-year bond (the "long" rate)? Alternatively phrased, for a two-year investment horizon, what governs the decision to select a sequence of two consecutive one-year bonds or one two-year bond? Of course, the answer is that one chooses the alternative that offers the highest yield, but this response must include an important qualification. The choice hinges on what the investor expects the yield will be on the one-year bond to be issued one year hence. Given that expectation, the investor would choose the higher-yielding alternative. However, if there were uncertainty about the future one-year yield, the investor might choose the certain yield on the two-year bond instead. For now we assume that investors hold their expectations with certainty. Certainty means that the expectation will actually be realized in the future.

Investors obviously have strong incentive to seek out the highest return on investments of a given riskiness.[1] This behavior influences the term structure by bidding bond prices, and therefore yields, to a level that reflects the market sentiment about future interest rates. For example, suppose that an investor observes the one-year bond to be currently yielding 5 percent and the two-year bond, 6 percent annually and that the investor believes that the future one-year yield will be 8 percent. To make an investment decision, the investor must determine what the future short rate is implied by market interest rates. For the investor to be indifferent about the investment alternatives over the two-year horizon, the total holding-period rates of return must be equal, that is,

$$2 \times 6\% = 5\% + \text{future short rate};$$
$$\text{future short rate} = 7\%.[2]$$

In other words, the fixed annual yield on the two-year bond summed over two years must equal the sum of the short rate and the expected future short rate. Although the future short rate is not directly observed, it is implied by the one-year and two-year bond rates and is usually referred to as the implied forward rate. In this example assuming certainty about expectations, the forward rate is the same as the expected future short rate.

Given his or her expectation that the future short rate is 8 percent, the investor would rationally choose to buy the current one-year bond and roll over that investment into the future one-year bond. This sequence of bonds would be equivalent to a two-year bond currently offering about 6.5 percent, as compared with the actual yield of 6 percent. The reason that the two-year bond is currently mispriced at 6 percent could be, for example, that investors received news leading them to expect higher inflation a year from now (raising their expected short rate). Their investment choice bids down the price of the two-year bond and hence bids up its yield. Once that yield reaches 6.5 percent, the bond market is back in equilibrium—investors are again indifferent about the investment alternatives. On the other hand, if the expectation were, say, for a 5 percent future one-year bond yield, investors would choose the two-year bond and consequently bid down its yield.

In this example, investors are said to have exploited an arbitrage opportunity. They have profited from the temporarily mispriced two-year bond without taking any risk.[3] Admittedly, this example is highly artificial because expectations are held with certainty; hence, there is by definition no risk. However, this kind of analysis carries over into a more realistic world characterized by uncertainty.

Notes

1. All bonds are simply assumed to exist and hence no consideration is given to borrowers' behavior, that is, to the decision to issue bonds of particular maturities. Since the discussion applies to default-free bonds— namely, Treasury securities—ignoring the issuer does not detract from the analysis.
2. Allowing for compounding of interest, the calculation is as follows: $(1.06)2 = (1.05)(1 + \text{future short rate})$. The future short rate is therefore approximately 7.0095 percent. Thus, the arithmetic average used in the text is fairly accurate in this example.
3. For the above example, the arbitrage was indirect since it involved selecting the better investment. A standard arbitrage transaction for this case would entail buying the higher-yielding investment alternative by selling the lower-yielding one; that is, arbitrage profits would be earned with a zero net investment. Profits are ensured since the yields must eventually equilibrate.

   This version of the example assumes that borrowing and lending rates are equal and that the proceeds from selling the lower-yielding bond "short" are immediately and fully available to buy the higher-yielding bond. In general, arbitrage connotes risklessly profiting from buying a good at a lower price and selling it at a higher price in the same or another market.

Cox-Ingersoll-Ross model allows for a continuum of outcomes. Again, bond valuation means determining the expected value of the discount factors to be applied in the continuum of states, since the maturity value of a bond is always par. The chief obstacle to making this determination is that the discount factors are unknown for risk-averse investors. Fortunately, the option-pricing methodology that originated with Black and Scholes provides an ingenious solution.

Risk-Neutral Valuation. With certain assumptions, option valuation can be formulated in such a way that knowledge of investors' risk aversion (that is, their discount functions) becomes irrelevant. This approach applies to many kinds of option-pricing problems though, unfortunately, not directly to term-structure applications for reasons to be discussed shortly. Although step-by-step details pertaining to option valuation are beyond the scope of this article, some background on the manner in which risk aversion is treated in valuation will aid the understanding of term-structure models. If certain assumptions are imposed—continuous trading, continuous price dynamics, and the property of nonsatiation (that is, that investors always prefer to consume more rather than less)—valuation may proceed as if in a risk-neutral world, one in which the discount rates contain no risk premia and thus are observable.[11] Valuation is said to be preference free. This line of reasoning has become known as the Cox-Ross risk-neutrality argument, first expounded in Cox and Ross (1976), and is a useful starting point for considering valuation of interest-rate contingent claims.

The validity of the risk-neutrality argument depends on the construction of a so-called hedge portfolio consisting of the derivative asset (for example, options) and underlying assets (like stocks) that are traded in such a way that the portfolio is without risk. The hedge portfolio would be constructed so that, for instance, a rise in the value of the stock component would be exactly offset by a fall in the value of the option component and vice versa. Because the portfolio is riskless, any funds invested in it would have to earn the risk-free rate of interest; otherwise, arbitrage would be induced between the hedge portfolio and the risk-free asset. The value of the portfolio's components can be determined without regard for risk premia. No matter what the actual degree of risk aversion, the fact that the portfolio is riskless means that the expected rate of return on its components can be assumed to be the riskless rate as well. In other words, the same option price would be derived for any discount rates (if they were known). Thus option

pricing proceeds using the preference assumption that makes valuation easiest: risk neutrality.[12]

Allowing for random interest rates complicates the valuation process. The crucial aspect of the risk-neutrality argument is that the stock or underlying asset is itself the state variable and is a traded asset. However, the instantaneous interest rate is not a traded asset and therefore cannot be used directly in constructing a hedge portfolio. Unlike the hedge portfolio used in deriving the Black-Scholes option pricing equation, risk cannot be eliminated in such a way that valuation is preference free.

Nevertheless, the problem of valuing bonds of differing maturity, each of which may require a different and unobservable expected rate of price appreciation (in order to be held willingly by the investor), can be simplified. It is usually assumed that the bond price depends only on the state variables (in this case, the instantaneous interest rate) and time. A hedge portfolio can be formed, but doing so requires knowing something about risk preferences in the economy. In particular, for the Cox-Ingersoll-Ross model forming a riskless hedge portfolio implies that all bonds have the same return-to-risk ratio in equilibrium. That ratio reflects risk preferences. The basic idea is that any two bonds of arbitrary maturity can be traded in such a way (in a hedge portfolio) that they are a perfect substitute for any other bond of arbitrary maturity.

The excess return for a bond of one maturity (over the risk-free rate) relative to that bond's volatility (the standard deviation of its rate of return) must in equilibrium equal the excess return on another bond of different maturity relative to its volatility. This may be expressed mathematically as:

$$\frac{\mu_1 - r}{\sigma_1} = \frac{\mu_2 - r}{\sigma_2} = \lambda(r,t),$$

where μ_1 and μ_2 are the expected bond returns, σ_1 and σ_2 are the bond volatilities, r is the risk-free rate, and λ is the market price of instantaneous interest-rate risk.[13] The function λ can be a function of the state variable and time (though often it is assumed to be a constant), but it cannot be a function of any bond's maturity since all bonds are related to λ by the above equation. If this relationship did not hold for bonds of any maturity, arbitrage would be possible. Investors would always choose the bond with the highest excess return-to-risk ratio, thereby raising the bond's price and reducing its excess return until the bond's excess return-to-risk ratio equals λ.

Hence, the simplification used in the Cox-Ingersoll-Ross model and other continuous-time term-structure models is that, rather than needing to know the exogenous expected return for each bond, the only exogenous element that needs to be identified is the market price of interest-rate risk, which by hypothesis is shared in common by all bonds.[14] This parameter must be estimated from actual bond price data to use the Cox-Ingersoll-Ross or other similar model. Once the market price of interest-rate risk is estimated, valuation proceeds using risk-neutral pricing methods. The end result is a formula to price bonds of any maturity. In the context of the Cox-Ingersoll-Ross model, the bond price is solely a function of the spot rate of interest and the bond's time to maturity. In more general versions of the model, the bond price is a function of the underlying state variables and time to maturity. To summarize, interest-rate contingent claim pricing does involve making a risk adjustment in arriving at a pricing formula, but valuation is not preference free.

Speaking in terms of risk-neutral valuation in the context of term-structure models is something of a misnomer. Investors are not necessarily risk neutral when λ is zero. They may be risk averse, but, because of the uncertainty resulting from randomness in the spot interest rate (or, more generally, uncertainty stemming from the state variables), their risk aversion

is such that they do not require a risk premium. These risk-averse investors' "portfolio decisions are completely myopic being made with no regard for hedging against changes in the state variables [which affect future output and consumption]" (Cox, Ingersoll, and Ross 1981, 783). Consequently, all future payoffs are discounted using risk-free rates, just as in those cases where the Cox-Ross risk neutrality argument applies. In pointing out this subtlety, Cox, Ingersoll, and Ross (1981) chose to call the case in which the factor risk premia are zero the "local expectations hypothesis" rather than the risk-neutral expectations hypothesis.[15]

An Illustration of the Cox-Ingersoll-Ross Model

Charts 5 and 6 are examples of the single-factor Cox-Ingersoll-Ross model, the simplest of their models. Its key features are illustrated in the graphs. The spot interest rate reverts to a long-term rate of 7 percent. Since expected spot rates are above the observed yield curve, any initial spot rate below the long-term rate results in an upward-sloping term structure. Any

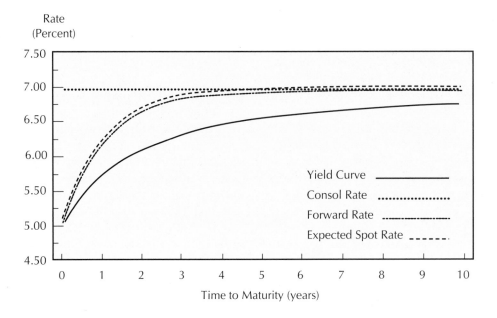

Chart 5
Cox-Ingersoll-Ross Model
(market price of risk = 0)

yield along the term structure can be expressed as a continuous-time average of the current spot rate and the expected spot rates. This relationship has a precise formula in the Cox-Ingersoll-Ross model. The expected spot rates were computed by formula in graphing their curves in Charts 5 and 6. Chart 6 shows a spot rate that is above its long-term rate, and consequently the term structure slopes downward. The rate at which the spot rate reverts to its long-term level is an important parameter that governs how the term structure moves over time. The other critical parameter affecting the term structure is the volatility of the spot rate.

Another feature of the single-factor Cox-Ingersoll-Ross model is that bonds of sufficiently long maturity have yields that are independent of the spot rate. This long-term yield, denoted as the consol rate (the yield on an infinite-maturity bond), appears as a heavy dotted line in all of the relevant charts. As maturity increases, the yield curve approaches this limiting yield "asymptotically," that is, very gradually. In contrast, multifactor models do not have the unrealistic characteristic that long-term bond yields are constant. The model developed by Michael J. Brennan and Eduardo S. Schwartz (1979) and another by Stephen M. Schaefer and Schwartz (1984) are two-factor models that include the consol rate as an instrumental variable. This kind of model allows randomness to affect the term structure from opposite ends of the maturity spectrum. In fact, Ren-Raw Chen and Louis Scott (1990) have found that allowing for two and three factors greatly improves the fit between term-structure model bond prices and actual market bond prices.

As discussed earlier, risk aversion drives a wedge between forward rates and expected future spot rates. Yet risk aversion is not the only factor that separates forward from expected future spot rates. Charts 5 and 6 show separate forward rates and expected future spot rate curves even though the market price of instantaneous interest-rate risk is zero. This type of discrepancy was first explicated by Stanley Fischer (1975) in considering the effect of inflation on nominal interest rates and then by Scott F. Richard (1978) in his two-factor term-structure model. Terence C. Langetieg (1980) observed that only in a world of certainty, not just risk neutrality, would risk premia be zero.

Cox, Ingersoll, and Ross (1981) gave a comprehensive analysis of the phenomenon, which arises from a mathematical condition known as Jensen's inequality.[16] A nontechnical explanation is that equality of forward and future expected spot rates implies a

Chart 6
Cox-Ingersoll-Ross Model
(market price of risk = 0)

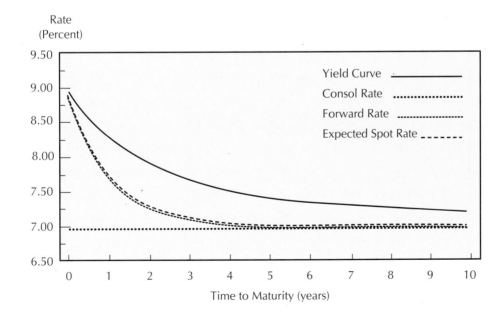

particular type of bond pricing equilibrium, one that is not generally compatible with other types. If, for example, the local expectations hypothesis is true and therefore a bond's current price is the expected discounted value of its face value, where the discount factor is a function of all the instantaneous spot rates expected to prevail up to the maturity date, then forward rates cannot equal expected spot rates in equilibrium. In fact, the bond yield implied by equality of forward and expected spot rates is greater than the yield implied by the local expectations hypothesis.

In other words, even for a zero market price of spread risk, forward rates are biased predictors of future expected spot rates for a reason that has nothing

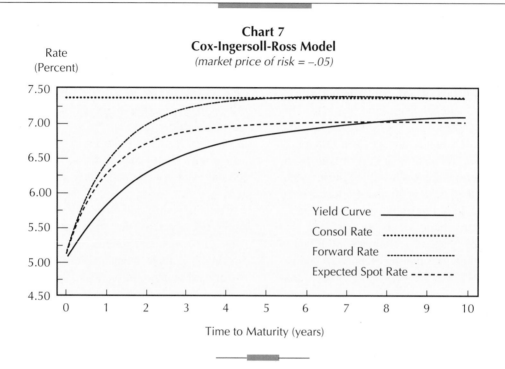

Chart 7
Cox-Ingersoll-Ross Model
(market price of risk = –.05)

Rate (Percent)

Yield Curve ————
Consol Rate ·············
Forward Rate ··········
Expected Spot Rate – – – –

Time to Maturity (years)

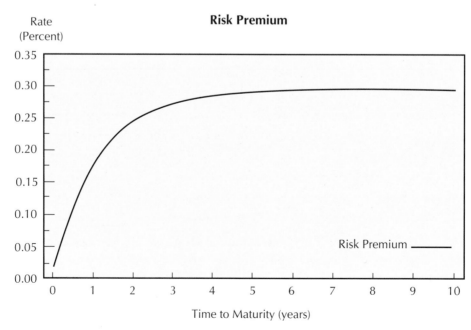

Risk Premium

Rate (Percent)

Risk Premium ————

Time to Maturity (years)

to do with risk premia. However, Charts 5 and 6 make it apparent that the discrepancy between forward and expected future spot rates is very small—only a few basis points (based on realistic parameter values for the Cox-Ingersoll-Ross model).[17]

Charts 7 and 8 are based on the same model generating Charts 5 and 6, but the market price of instanta- neous interest-rate risk is now negative, giving rise to positive risk premia. The expected spot-rate curve is the same as before; however, the forward-rate curve now rises above its level in the earlier charts because of the effect of risk premia. Consequently, the yield curve is higher everywhere in Charts 7 and 8 than it was in Charts 5 and 6.

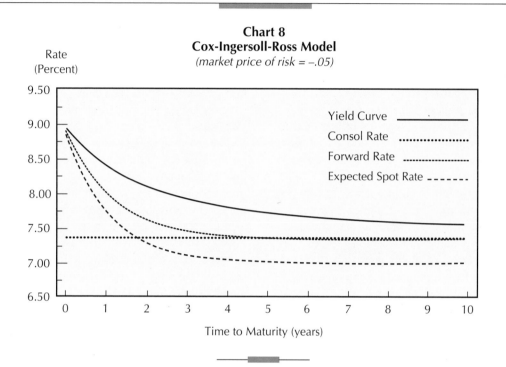

Chart 8
Cox-Ingersoll-Ross Model
(market price of risk = –.05)

Rate (Percent)

Yield Curve
Consol Rate
Forward Rate
Expected Spot Rate

Time to Maturity (years)

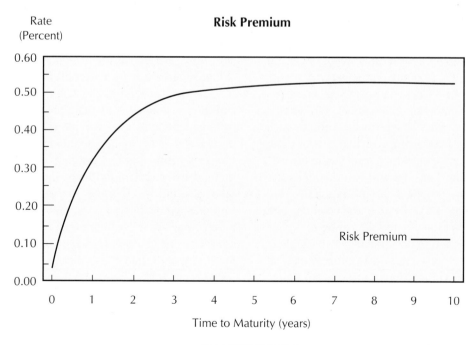

Risk Premium

Rate (Percent)

Risk Premium

Time to Maturity (years)

The risk premium graphed in the inset below the yield curves in Charts 7 and 8 represents the difference between the instantaneous expected rate of return on a bond of a given maturity and the expected rate of return on a bond that is an instant from maturing (the spot interest rate). This is the risk premium concept used by Cox, Ingersoll, and Ross, which they refer to as the term premium. For both upward- and downward-sloping yield curves, the risk premium curve increases with the maturity of the bond. In fact, for this model the risk premium is proportional to the interest elasticity of the bond price. That elasticity rises with the maturity of the bond. In other words, a 1 percent increase (or decrease) in interest rates depresses (or elevates) longer-term bond prices more than shorter-term bond prices. Thus, the Cox-Ingersoll-Ross model gives a risk premium structure similar to that predicted by the liquidity premium hypothesis. The actual interpretation is different, however, and will be discussed in the next section.

Other models give more complex risk premium behavior. For example, a one-factor model proposed by Francis A. Longstaff (1989), which in many respects is similar to the Cox-Ingersoll-Ross model, produces a risk premium that does not simply increase with maturity; that is, it can have a humped pattern as well that may lend greater realism to the model.

General Equilibrium. Up to this point, the risk premium has been simply a quantity that separates forward rates from expected spot rates. Neglecting the effect of Jensen's inequality, the risk premium's impact is the same in the liquidity premium and preferred habitat hypotheses. Cox, Ingersoll, and Ross (1985a, b) allowed a fuller interpretation of the risk premium by embedding their term-structure model in a larger model of the economy. Particularly since the 1970s, economic theory has placed greater emphasis on the rational maximizing behavior of individuals; Cox, Ingersoll, and Ross sought to incorporate such behavior explicitly into a term-structure model (and, more generally, in any model for valuing asset prices).

Individuals in the Cox-Ingersoll-Ross model's hypothetical economy are identical and rational in the sense that they know the structure of the economy and all relevant information for the decisions that they make. They seek continually to achieve the highest level of satisfaction possible, or, in more technical language, they maximize their "utility functions" through time. They are endowed initially with a certain amount of wealth, which they use to invest in the productive processes of the economy, purchase financial assets (which enable them to defer consumption today to a future date), and consume the economy's single output. Whatever output goes unconsumed is invested to produce more future output.

The individual's maximization problem is to decide on the *optimal* amount of each of these activities to undertake. The decisions will depend in part on their attitude toward risk, which is mathematically represented as an element of their utility function. Risk in this hypothetical economy derives partly from shocks to production that change wealth and comsumption over time. A big rise in the price of oil or the occurrence of drought are examples of such shocks. Production is also uncertain because of shocks to technology, which are modeled as the random evolution of a set of state variables. These state variables have no further interpretation, other than being the basic sources of uncertainty.

The optimizing decisions of the investor/consumer result in an economic equilibrium that includes equilibrium asset prices and interest rates. There are many implications of the Cox-Ingersoll-Ross general equilibrium model. The one to be emphasized here is the nature of the risk premium. Any security's rate of return in excess of the risk-free rate depends on its sensitivity to changes in wealth and to changes in each of the state variables. Cox, Ingersoll, and Ross (1985a) give the following interpretation of the risk premium: "Just as we would expect, individuals are willing to accept a lower expected rate of return on securities which tend to pay off more highly when marginal utility is higher. Hence, in equilibrium such securities will have a lower total risk premium" (376). What individuals ultimately care about is the flow of consumption they enjoy over time. Changing their securities portfolios is one way they achieve this goal. When times are lean and consumption is relatively low, the satisfaction from each additional increment to consumption—that is, its marginal utility—is high. (It is assumed that as consumption rises, marginal utility falls, which is to say that additional consumption carries less utility value.) Trading in securities is the method by which individuals smooth consumption (and raise utility). Because they have limited wealth, (in other words, budget constraints), individuals must prefer some securities more than others. In particular, securities that pay most when consumption is low are more valuable than those that pay most when consumption is high. Consequently, securities that yield most in lean times bear higher prices and hence lower risk premia. That is, their return in excess of the risk-free rate will be lower since risk-averse individuals prefer these kinds of securities. In other words, some securities are better at hedging certain kinds of risk than other securities, and the value of such securities will depend on investor preferences.

Risk-neutral consumers/investors do not care about fluctuations in their consumption flows or investment opportunities. As a result, they would not be willing to pay a premium for the hedging characteristics of any security; all securities would earn the risk-free rate in equilibrium. As mentioned above, however, individuals can be risk averse (specifically, by experiencing diminishing marginal utility with respect to consumption or, equivalently, wealth) but not require any risk premia. As Cox, Ingersoll, and Ross (1981) have pointed out, such a combination could occur if changes in the marginal utility of wealth were unaffected by changes in the state variables. Such conditions should be regarded as exceptional, though, and not realistically characteristic of the economy.

The general equilibrium structure provides a more detailed interpretation of a term-structure model. In particular, the one-factor Cox-Ingersoll-Ross model includes the specialized assumption that the risk premium does not depend on wealth but represents the "covariance of changes in the interest rate with percent changes in optimally invested wealth (the 'market portfolio')" (Cox, Ingersoll, and Ross 1985b, 393). In the one-factor model, a single state variable, which is unobservable, summarizes all underlying uncertainty. However, the spot interest rate depends on that state variable; it determines all movements in the spot rate. The state variable represents changes in physical investment opportunities, which in turn account for all variations in wealth. Thus, risk depends on how changes in bond prices determined by the spot rate vary with changes in wealth. Bonds that are better hedges against shifts in investment opportunities (and hence wealth) are more highly valued and carry lower risk premiums. For example, in the one-factor Cox-Ingersoll-Ross model if wealth tends to decline as the spot interest rate rises (the wealth-spot rate covariance is negative), then short-term bonds will carry lower risk premiums than longer-term bonds because they are subject to smaller capital losses. Because long-term bond prices decline more than short-term bond prices in response to a rise in the spot rate, long-term bonds are riskier to include in the wealth portfolio and require a greater risk premium as compensation. Similar reasoning applies to the interpretation of the risk premium arising in more complex multifactor models. This general equilibrium theory of the risk premium has considerably greater economic content than the comparatively vague no-tion that investors demand risk premia for illiquid bonds.

The general equilibrium approach of the Cox-Ingersoll-Ross model offers further insights into how underlying economic variables, such as shifts in investment opportunities, affect the term structure. Partial equilibrium models cannot reveal these linkages. In fact, Cox, Ingersoll, and Ross (1985b) make the point that partial equilibrium models can be internally inconsistent. First, there may not be any underlying equilibrium consistent with the assumptions concerning the choice of state variables, such as the spot interest rate, and the way they evolve randomly over time. In other words, the two assumptions may be incompatible. Second, arbitrarily selecting a functional form for the risk premium (for example, assuming that it is constant) may produce a model that implies arbitrage opportunities—a fatal modeling flaw.[18]

From a modeling standpoint, the general equilibrium approach is clearly preferable. In terms of actually implementing a bond pricing model, however, the difference between partial and general equilibrium may not be critical. Even if the general equilibrium model is internally consistent, it may misprice actual bonds as much as a partial equilibrium version. Poor predictions can stem from a misspecification of the actual underlying economy if, for instance, the details of the model are simply too far off. On the other hand, a more complex, realistic model might be impossible to use because essential parameters cannot be reliably estimated given limited data about the actual economy. Simpler models may perform better even if they are internally inconsistent.

Extensions and Variations on Term-Structure Models

Cox, Ingersoll, and Ross (1985b) explore some extensions of their basic model. They show how to incorporate more state variables. This addition results in general equilibrium multifactor models that are similar to the earlier multifactor models of Brennan and Schwartz (1979) and of Schaefer and Schwartz (1984). As more factors are added, the mathematical complexity increases considerably, making these models cumbersome. Simple formulas for pricing bonds are not available; rather, computer-intensive numerical methods must generally be used to obtain bond prices.

Longstaff (1989) attempts to get better performance out of a single-factor general equilibrium model by allowing for nonlinear behavior in the underlying state variable and consequently also in the observable spot interest rate. One impact of this nonlinearity is to make the spot rate revert to its long-term level more slowly from above than from below. Greater flexibility and realism are achieved because the possible theoretical shapes of the term structure are more varied. These attributes may model actual variations in the term structure better than the simple Cox-Ingersoll-Ross model.

Cox, Ingersoll, and Ross (1985b) also show how to adapt their approach to value nominal bonds. Their original model does not include the existence of money or inflation. They modify the model by incorporating the aggregate price level as another state variable and obtain a nominal bond-pricing formula. Alternatively, they recast the entire model in terms of nominal variables and derive interest-rate and bond-pricing equations similar in form to the real-variable model. In this revised model, the instantaneous nominal interest rate equals the sum of the instantaneous real interest, the expected instantaneous rate of inflation, and a group of terms that arise from the effects of Jensen's inequality. In other words, the so-called Fisher equation, which states that the nominal rate is the sum of the real rate and expected inflation, does not hold (for the same mathematical reason that forward rates do not equal expected future spot rates even when factor risk is zero). Richard's (1978) is an earlier partial equilibrium model that included expected inflation as one of two state variables.[19]

The Cox-Ingersoll-Ross model has been used in a number of recent applications involving the valuation of interest-rate contingent claims. Krishna Ramaswamy and Suresh M. Sundaresan (1986) value floating-rate instruments, which have interest payments that vary with current market rates, using the Cox-Ingersoll-Ross single-factor model. The Cox-Ingersoll-Ross model was adapted to valuing the cash flows from such instruments. Louis O. Scott (1989) prices default-free interest-rate caps using the Vasicek and Cox-Ingersoll-Ross single-factor models. John Hull and Alan White (forthcoming) apply modified versions of the Vasicek and Cox-Ingersoll-Ross models to price bond-options and interest-rate caps, which are derivative instruments designed to hedge floating-rate instruments. Peter A. Abken (1990) uses the Cox-Ingersoll-Ross single-factor model as a component of a model to price default-risky interest-rate caps. Sundaresan (1989) employs the Cox-Ingersoll-Ross model in his valuation model for interest-rate swaps, which are also hedging tools that have numerous

forms and applications. A basic use is to convert fixed-rate interest payments into floating-rate payments (or vice versa). Longstaff (forthcoming) extends the Cox-Ingersoll-Ross single-factor model to price options that have payoffs specified in terms of yields rather than prices. His preliminary empirical work demonstrates that the model predicts actual traded yield option prices with greater accuracy than other existing models. Abken (forthcoming) develops a swap valuation model that allows for default risk on the part of parties participating in a swap. The Longstaff yield option model is a component of his model.

The single-factor Ho and Lee model has been extended into both discrete- and continuous-time multifactor models by David Heath, Robert Jarrow, and Andrew Morton (1987, 1988). Like the Ho and Lee model, the Heath-Jarrow-Morton models use all the information in the current term structure, but they do so in a more sophisticated way, avoiding the deficiencies of the Ho and Lee model. In particular, the Heath-Jarrow-Morton models preclude negative interest rates and, since they are multifactor, do not imply perfectly correlated bond-price movements. The models are specified in terms of the evolution of the forward rate rather than the bond price as in Ho and Lee.

Unlike Ho and Lee's, these models are preference free, a characteristic that the authors cite as a major advantage of their method. Still, "fitting" the models to the actual forward-rate curve is problematic, and inaccuracies at this step become relayed into inaccurate bond-option prices. Heath, Jarrow, and Morton (1989) conducted an empirical test of the earlier Heath-Jarrow-Morton (1987) model and found that despite some problems, the test supports the model's validity.

In a similar vein, Philip H. Dybvig (1988) shows how to fuse the Ho and Lee model (or, more generally, models incorporating the information in the current term structure) with single- or multifactor state variable models. He finds that a relatively simple single-factor hybrid model fits the term structure very well over time.

Robert R. Bliss, Jr., and Ehud I. Ronn (1989a) have also extended and refined the Ho and Lee approach by including a set of state variables that affect movements in forward rates (that is, the perturbation function and the risk-neutral probabilities are functions of the state variables). Their modeling changes effectively prevent the occurrence of negative interest rates as in the Ho and Lee model and allow for a more flexible modeling of interest-rate movements. In Bliss and Ronn (1989b) the authors test their model by valuing actual options on Treasury-bond futures contracts.

The results indicate a systematic discrepancy between model predictions of option prices and actual option prices. A possible explanation for the bias (aside from actual options' being mispriced) is that their estimated perturbation functions, based on past observed forward-rate movements, do not sufficiently capture actual movements in forward rates.

Naoki Kishimoto (1989) extends the Ho and Lee model to enable valuation of assets such as stock options, convertible bonds, and junk bonds, for which risk stems not only from future interest-rate changes but also from other factors. The model combines the features of the Ho and Lee term-structure model with the Cox-Ross-Rubinstein method of modeling asset-price risk.

Black, Emanuel Derman, and William Toy (1990) have quite recently developed another variation on the Ho and Lee model. Their model posits a time-varying volatility for the spot interest-rate process and assumes that the spot rate is log-normally distributed, thereby preventing the realization of negative values. Like Ho and Lee's, this model does not give a simple formula for valuing either bonds or interest-rate contingent claims and consequently must be implemented as a computer algorithm.[20]

Contingent Claims Pricing

Having introduced the Ho and Lee model, it is now easy to illustrate how an option can be valued using this model and, by extension, any other term-structure model. Consider a European call option on a discount bond—a three-month Treasury bill. A call is usually specified in terms of a bond's price. The option gives the holder the right to buy the T-bill at a prespecified price upon expiration of the option. To make matters easy, the call is assumed to be European so that it may be exercised only upon expiration, unlike an American option, which can also be exercised earlier. The call in the illustration is assumed to have an 11 percent strike or, equivalently, a strike price of 0.973 (on a hypothetical T-bill with $1 face value). The underlying T-bill matures three months after the option. (Note that the option cannot meaningfully expire at the same time as the T-bill because the bill's price is known with certainty, that is, its price equals its face value.)

The object of this exercise is to determine the value of the call option when it has one year remaining before expiration. The earlier example from Chart 3 gives the state-price evolution for the T-bill that is rel-

evant for this problem. Chart 9 repeats the T-bill price tree but also includes the option prices at each node of the tree. Again, the valuation process starts from the expiration date at time 0. The call option has value only when the T-bill price is above the strike price of 0.973 (or equivalently the annualized bill rate is below 11 percent). Thus, the only positive option payoffs occur for the first two lower entries in the column on the far right. The rest of the computation proceeds exactly as it did in Chart 3, except that the call option payoff, not the bill price, is used in recursively working back to the initial date. The probability-weighted call option payoffs in the time 0 column are averaged pairwise and discounted using the three-month bill price corresponding to realized state price one period earlier. That bill price, shown in Chart 3, is derived from Ho and Lee's formula, which in turn is based on the initial term structure of interest rates. Repeating the procedure back to the present time at quarter 4 before expiration gives an option price of 0.00101 on a face value of $1. Multiplying by $1 million to be somewhat more realistic gives a call option price of $1,010. This figure can be converted into an interest rate, expressed in basis points (one-hundredths of a percent), by dividing by 25.[21] Therefore, for every $1 million face value of T-bills, the call option would cost 40.4 basis points.

More accurate valuation would be achieved by dividing the time interval to expiration more finely than into four quarters and thereby increasing the number of branches in the binomial tree. Still other models could be used to value the call option; however, the Ho and Lee model makes the mechanics of valuation fairly transparent.

Cox, Ingersoll, and Ross (1985b) give a closed-form solution for option prices based on their single-factor model.[22] It is similar in form to the Black-Scholes option-pricing formula although more complicated. Farshid Jamshidian (1989) has derived a closed-form solution for pricing bond options based on the single-factor Vasicek model. This formula is much easier to use than the formula of Cox, Ingersoll, and Ross. The choice of which to use is an empirical question that is the subject of current research.

Conclusion

This article has given an introduction to the new types of term-structure models that have appeared in the last fifteen years. These models have evolved not

Chart 9
Ho and Lee Model
Contingent Claim Valuation
Call Option on Three-Month T-Bill Price (Strike = .973 or 11%)
Value One Year before Option Expiration = $1,010 or 40.4 Basis Points

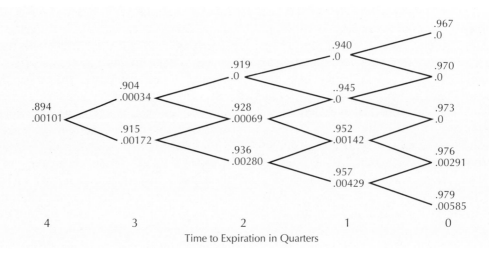

only because of the option-pricing revolution triggered by the Black-Scholes formula and its stimulation of financial research but also as a result of the rational expectations approach in economics and finance. Research in this field has also been motivated by the greater asset-price volatility that has characterized financial markets in recent years. In other words, market demand has been growing for term-structure models to help in the valuation of increasingly complex financial instruments such as interest-rate caps and swaps. It can be expected that financial theory and practice will continue to spur advances in one another.

Much research time and money are currently being devoted to building better term-structure and interest-rate contingent claims pricing models. The benefits of improved modeling have both academic and intellec-

tual significance to financial researchers as well as dollars and cents payoffs to market practitioners. Part of this research effort is devoted to refining existing models to give the best "fit" with actual market bond and option prices. A number of researchers have explored the performance and accuracy of some of the new term-structure models.[23] It is beyond the scope of this article to review their evaluations, but it is important to note that there tend to be trade-offs between ease of use and model accuracy. The type of application may also determine which model is appropriate: a simple single-factor model, for example, may be quite adequate for pricing short-term bond options, while more elaborate multifactor models may be needed for accurate pricing of longer-term options, which require greater precision in term-structure modeling.

Notes

1. See Abken (1989) for an introduction to interest-rate caps and Wall and Pringle (1988) or Smith, Smithson, and Wakeman (1988) for an introduction to interest-rate swaps.
2. Although uncertainty is sometimes regarded as connoting

risks that are not measurable, risk and uncertainty here are considered synonymous.
3. The Cox-Ingersoll-Ross term-structure model, which is discussed below, was used to generate these charts.

4. Modigliani and Sutch also note that similar considerations apply to bond issuers (that is, borrowers).

5. The Black-Scholes formula performs poorly for valuing options on bonds. The original model assumes (1) that the short-term interest rate is constant (implying that the term structure is always flat) and (2) that the volatility of the asset return on which the option is written is constant. However, the volatility of a bond's rate of return must diminish to zero, because the bond price must equal face value at maturity. The volatility cannot be reasonably assumed to be constant, unlike a stock's. Schaefer and Schwartz (1987) modify the Black-Scholes equation by making a bond's volatility proportional to its duration, which results in a decreasing volatility that reaches zero upon maturity. Hull and White (1989) extend the Schaefer-Schwartz model to relax the assumption of a constant short-term interest rate. These extensions of Black-Scholes are "preference-free" models, which are discussed later in this article. Ball and Torous's (1983) is another influential, though flawed, model in this vein that is a direct antecedent of the Schaefer-Schwartz and Hull-White models.

6. See Ho and Lee (1986) for the details about the perturbation function and its derivation.

7. Measuring such a shift in risk aversion would be very difficult, and, to the author's knowledge, has not yet been attempted empirically

8. These are by Vasicek (1977), Dothan (1978), Courtadon (1982), Richard (1978), Brennan and Schwartz (1979), and Langetieg (1980). The Cox-Ingersoll-Ross model first circulated in an unpublished manuscript dated July 1977.

9. See Black (1988) for Black's surprise and amusement at the continuing popularity of his original model with Scholes. He believes that the original model's highly restrictive assumptions limit its usefulness and suggests modifications to make the model perform better.

   The Black-Scholes formula can also be derived using discrete-time mathematics. See Cox, Ross, and Rubinstein (1979).

10. See Dybvig (1988) for an analysis and extension of the Ho and Lee model.

11. More precisely, "continuous price dynamics" means that the underlying asset price is assumed to follow an Ito process. See Jarrow and Rudd (1983) for an introduction to option pricing.

12. See Jarrow and Rudd (1983, chap. 7) for a more detailed exposition of the risk-neutrality argument.

13. The standard deviations in the denominators are actually negative quantities. The bond return standard deviation can be shown to be the product of the negative interest elasticity of the bond price times the positive standard deviation of the spot interest rate. Therefore positive excess return to volatility ratios (and positive risk premia in the term strucure) occur for negative values of $\lambda(r,t)$.

14. Ingersoll (1987, chaps. 17-18) gives a succinct, though technical, discussion of valuation methods when a model's state variables are not traded assets. See Cox, Ingersoll, and Ross (1981, 772) for the general method of forming a hedge portfolio for their multifactor term-structure model.

15. For risk-neutral investors, risk premia are zero only in special cases. Cox, Ingersoll, and Ross (1981) show that one case is the trivial one where interest rates are nonrandom (782-83). Another special case requires that the covariance of the bond's return with the marginal utility of wealth is zero. In general this covariance will not be zero and risk premia will exist. These authors also show that a sufficient condition for the local-expectations hypothesis to prevail for risk-averse investors is that they have logarithmic, state-independent utility (783).

16. In words, Jensen's inequality states that the mathematical expectation of a concave function of a random variable is less than the value of the concave function evaluated at the mean of the random variable. The inequality relationship is reversed for a convex function. See Cox, Ingersoll, and Ross (1981, 776-77) for an analysis of the effect of Jensen's inequality on different forms of the expectations hypothesis. See Fischer (1975, 513) for a simple example of Jensen's inequality that is also pertinent to the term-structure case.

17. Campbell (1986) argues that the discrepancy between forward and expected future spot rates is mathematically a second-order effect and can be ignored in doing empirical work. Using his linearized framework for analysis of the term structure, the differences among term structure theories studied by Cox, Ingersoll, and Ross (1981) disappear.

18. See Cox, Ingersoll, and Ross (1985b, 398) for a simple example of how an arbitrage opportunity could arise.

19. As a future research topic, it might be interesting to extend Richard's model to allow for the impact of monetary policy on the term structure. For example, anticipated inflation could be specified as a function of current or lagged short-term interest rates. This or some other type of reaction function could probably be incorporated as a first step in modeling the effects of monetary policy.

20. See Hull and White (forthcoming) for the continuous-time formulation of both the Ho and Lee model and the Black-Derman-Toy model. Dybvig (1988) also gives a continuous-time version of Ho and Lee.

21. The value of a basis point is derived first by dividing $1 million by 10,000 (the number of basis points in 100 percent) to give $100 per basis point per year. The underlying asset, the T-bill, has a three-month maturity; therefore, the value of a basis point per quarter is $25.

22. A closed-form solution is a formula that is "ready" to evaluate, given the model's parameters. In contrast, many models, such as Ho and Lee or Brennan and Schwartz, require numerical methods to arrive at bond or contingent claim prices.

References

Abken, Peter A. "Interest-Rate Caps, Collars, and Floors." Federal Reserve Bank of Atlanta *Economic Review* 6 (November/December 1989): 2-24.

_____. "Valuing Default-Risky Interest-Rate Caps: A Monte Carlo Approach." Federal Reserve Bank of Atlanta Working Paper 90-5, July 1990.

_____. "Valuation of Default-Risky Swaps and Options on Swaps." Federal Reserve Bank of Atlanta Working Paper, forthcoming.

Ball, Clifford A., and Walter N. Torous. "Bond Price Dynamics and Options." *Journal of Financial and Quantatative Analysis* 18 (December 1983): 517-31.

Black, Fischer. "The Holes in Black-Scholes." *Risk* 1 (March 1988): 30-33.

Black, Fischer, and Myron Scholes. "The Pricing of Options and Corporate Liabilities." *Journal of Political Economy* 81 (May/June 1973): 637-59.

Black, Fischer, Emanuel Derman, and William Toy. "A One-Factor Model of Interest Rates and Its Application to Treasury Bond Options." *Financial Analysts Journal* (January/February 1990): 33-39.

Bliss, Robert R., Jr., and Ehud I. Ronn. "Arbitrage-Based Estimation of Nonstationary Shifts in the Term Structure of Interest Rates." *Journal of Finance* 44 (July 1989a): 591-610.

_____. "A Non-Stationary Trinomial Model for the Valuation of Options on Treasury Bond Futures Contracts." University of Texas at Austin unpublished manuscript, November 1989b.

Bodie, Zvi, Alex Kane, and Alan J. Marcus. *Investments.* Homewood, Ill.: Richard D. Irwin, Inc., 1989.

Brennan, Michael J., and Eduardo S. Schwartz. "A Continuous Time Approach to the Pricing of Bonds." *Journal of Banking and Finance* 3 (July 1979): 133-55.

Brown, Stephen J., and Philip H. Dybvig. "The Empirical Implications of the Cox, Ingersoll, Ross Theory of the Term Structure of Interest Rates." *Journal of Finance* 41 (July 1986): 617-30.

Buser, Stephen A., Patric H. Hendershott, and Anthony B. Sanders. "Determinants of the Value of Call Options on Default-Free Bonds." *Journal of Business* 63 (January 1990): S33-S50.

Campbell, John Y. "A Defense of Traditional Hypotheses about the Term Structure of Interest Rates." *Journal of Finance* 41 (March 1986): 183-93.

Chen, Ren-Raw, and Louis Scott. "Maximum Likelihood Estimation for a Multi-Factor Equilibrium Model of the Term Structure of Interest Rates." University of Georgia unpublished manuscript, April 1990.

Courtadon, Georges. "The Pricing of Options on Default-Free Bonds." *Journal of Financial and Quantitative Analysis* 17 (March 1982): 75-100.

Cox, John C., Jonathan E. Ingersoll, Jr., and Stephen A. Ross. "A Re-Examination of Traditional Hypotheses about the Term Structure of Interest Rates." *Journal of Finance* 36 (September 1981): 769-99.

_____. "An Intertemporal General Equilibrium Model of Asset Prices." *Econometrica* 53 (March 1985a): 363-84.

_____. "A Theory of the Term Structure of Interest Rates." *Econometrica* 53 (March 1985b): 385-408.

Cox, John C., and Stephen A. Ross. "The Valuation of Options for Alternative Stochastic Processes." *Journal of Financial Economics* 3 (January 1976): 145-66.

Cox, John C., Stephen A. Ross, and Mark Rubinstein. "Option Pricing: A Simplified Approach." *Journal of Financial Economics* 7 (September 1979): 229-63.

Dietrich-Campbell, Bruce, and Eduardo Schwartz. "Valuing Debt Options." *Journal of Financial Economics* 16 (July 1986): 321-43.

Dothan, L. Uri. "On the Term Structure of Interest Rates." *Journal of Financial Economics* 6 (January 1978): 59-69.

Dothan, Michael U. *Prices in Financial Markets.* New York: Oxford University Press, 1990.

Dybvig, Philip H. "Bond and Bond Option Pricing Based on the Current Term Structure." Washington University in St. Louis Working Paper, September 1988.

Fischer, Stanley. "The Demand for Index Bonds." *Journal of Political Economy* 83 (June 1975): 509-34.

Heath, David, Robert Jarrow, and Andrew Morton. "Bond Pricing and the Term Structure of Interest Rates: A New Methodology for Contingent Claim Valuation." Cornell University Working Paper, October 1987.

_____. "Bond Pricing and the Term Structure of Interest Rates: A Discrete Time Approximation." Cornell University Working Paper, April 1988.

_____. "Contingent Claim Valuation with a Random Evolution of Interest Rates." Cornell University Working Paper, November 1989.

Ho, Thomas S.Y., and Sang-Bin Lee. "Term Structure Movements and Pricing Interest Rate Contingent Claims." *Journal of Finance* 41 (December 1986): 1011-29.

Hull, John, and Alan White. "An Extension to the Schaefer-Schwartz Bond Option Pricing Model." University of Toronto unpublished manuscript, February 1989.

_____. "Pricing Interest-Rate Derivative Securities." *Review of Financial Studies* 3 (forthcoming).

Ingersoll, Jonathan E., Jr. *Theory of Financial Decision Making.* Totowa, N.J.: Rowman and Littlefield, 1987.

Jamshidian, Farshid. "An Exact Bond Option Formula." *Journal of Finance* 44 (March 1989): 205-9.

Jarrow, Robert A., and Andrew Rudd. *Option Pricing.* Homewood, Ill.: Richard D. Irwin, Inc., 1983.

Kishimoto, Naoki. "Pricing Contingent Claims under Interest Rate and Asset Price Risk." *Journal of Finance* 44 (July 1989): 571-89.

Langetieg, Terence C. "A Multivariate Model of the Term Structure." *Journal of Finance* 35 (March 1980): 71-97.

Longstaff, Francis A. "A Nonlinear General Equilibrium Model of the Term Structure of Interest Rates." *Journal of Financial Economics* 23 (August 1989): 195-224.

_____. "The Valuation of Options on Yields." *Journal of Financial Economics* (forthcoming).

Marsh, Terry A., and Eric R. Rosenfeld. "Stochastic Processes for Interest Rates and Equilibrium Bond Prices." *Journal of Finance* 38 (May 1983): 635-45.

Modigliani, Franco, and Richard Sutch. "Innovations in Interest Rate Policy." *The American Economic Review* 56 (May 1966): 178-97.

Pearson, Neil D., and Tong-Sheng Sun. "A Test of the Cox, Ingersoll, Ross Model of the Term Structure of Interest Rates Using the Method of Maximum Likelihood." Unpublished manuscript, January 1989.

Ramaswamy, Krishna, and Suresh M. Sundaresan. "The Valuation of Floating-Rate Instruments: Theory and Evidence." *Journal of Financial Economics* 17 (December 1986): 251-72.

Richard, Scott F. "An Arbitrage Model of the Term Structure of Interest Rates." *Journal of Financial Economics* 6 (March 1978): 33-57.

Ritchken, Peter, and Kiekie Boenawan. "On Arbitrage-Free Pricing of Interest Rate Contingent Claims." *Journal of Finance* 45 (March 1990): 259-64.

Schaefer, Stephen M., and Eduardo S. Schwartz. "A Two-Factor Model of the Term Structure: An Approximate Solution." *Journal of Financial and Quantitative Analysis* 19 (December 1984): 413-24.

_____. "Time-Dependent Variance and the Pricing of Bond Options." *Journal of Finance* 42 (December 1987): 1113-28.

Scott, Louis O. "Pricing Floating Rate Debt and Related Interest Rate Options." University of Georgia unpublished paper, October 1989.

Smith, Clifford W., Charles W. Smithson, and Lee Macdonald Wakeman. "The Market for Interest Rate Swaps." *Financial Management* 17 (Winter 1988): 34-44.

Sundaresan, Suresh. "Valuation of Swaps." Columbia University Center for the Study of Futures Markets Working Paper 183, April 1989.

Vasicek, Oldrich A. "An Equilibrium Characterization of the Term Structure." *Journal of Financial Economics* 5 (November 1977): 177-88.

Wall, Larry D., and John J. Pringle. "Interest Rate Swaps: A Review of the Issues." Federal Reserve Bank of Atlanta *Economic Review* 73 (November/December 1988): 22-3.

Beyond Duration: Measuring Interest Rate Exposure

Hugh Cohen

While many factors contributed to the savings and loan industry's extensive losses in the 1980s, the biggest losses, those that brought on the savings and loan crisis, resulted primarily from interest rate fluctuations during the late 1970s and early 1980s (see George J. Benston and George G. Kaufman 1990). Those losses demonstrated the importance of calculating and avoiding interest rate risk for financial practitioners who fund and manage all sizes of portfolios. They also focused the attention of financial regulators, the public, and, ultimately, Congress on potential losses from interest rate risk. In the aftermath, hedging instruments and techniques have been applied more broadly.[1] Congress, in the Federal Deposit Insurance Corporation Improvement Act of 1991 (FDICIA), has also instructed federal bank regulators to account for interest rate risk in their risk-based capital requirements.

A simple and potentially inadequate approximation of interest rate risk exposure results from the use of a technique called "modified duration." This technique is used to gauge the changes in the value of an asset or portfolio of assets that occur in response to a parallel shift in interest rates. It thus measures the portfolio's sensitivity to interest rate fluctuations. Modified duration gauges interest sensitivity by making equal interest rate shifts at all maturities of the current term structure and revaluing a portfolio under the new (parallel) term structure.

Acceptance of modified duration as a measure of interest rate exposure can be seen in federal bank regulators' recent proposal of the method for the purpose of integrating interest rate risk exposure into risk-based capital

This article was originally published in the Atlanta Fed's March/April 1993 Economic Review. *The author is a senior economist in the financial section of the Atlanta Fed's research department.*

guidelines and in a modification of that proposal discussed by the Federal Reserve Board on March 31, 1993. The joint proposal seeks to approximate an institution's exposure to interest rate changes by measuring changes in its net economic value that would result from 100 basis point parallel shifts in interest rates over a three-month period. The change in net economic value would be measured as the change in the present value of its assets minus the change in the present value of its liabilities and off-balance-sheet positions. The more recent Federal Reserve proposal adds 200 basis point shifts and a nonparallel shift based on interest rate changes over the past five years to the proposed exposure measures.[2]

In addition, modified duration's simplicity has made it a common topic in textbooks. As useful as the method may be for teaching purposes, however, it is an insufficient measure for hedging interest rate exposure in the real world. This article identifies two major problems with using modified duration for this purpose. The discussion first presents the theory underlying modified duration and illustrates its benefits as a hedging model. For the analysis a simple mock portfolio was constructed and revalued using simulated term structures. The analysis points out some of the faults of modified duration, which failed to capture major elements of interest rate exposure, and suggests more accurate measures.

Understanding Duration

Duration is a term that is usually applied to bonds but can be used in reference to any cash-flow stream. The duration of a portfolio's cash flow may be thought of as the weighted average maturity of its securities' cash flows, where the weights are the proportion of the cash flows' present value in the current period over the total present value of the portfolio's future cash flows.

For example, consider the prices in Table 1 for $100.00 default-free securities to be paid off at a specified time in the future. The price of a zero-coupon, $100.00 face-value bond maturing in two years would be $89.96. The duration of the bond would be $(2 \cdot 89.96)/89.96 = 2$.

Next, consider a $100.00 face-value bond that pays 5 percent coupons semiannually. (The bond pays $5.00 [or .05 • $100.00] in six months, one year, and one and one-half years. Additionally, the bond pays $105.00 in two years, reflecting both interest and face-

value payments.) Assuming that the price of the bond is the sum of its individual payments, the price of this bond would be

$$Price = (.05 \cdot 97.89) + (.05 \cdot 95.56) + (.05 \cdot 92.77)$$
$$+ (1.05 \cdot 89.96)$$
$$= 4.8945 + 4.778 + 4.6385 + 94.458$$
$$= 108.769.$$

The duration of the bond would be

$$Duration = [(0.5 \cdot 4.8945) + (1.0 \cdot 4.778) + (1.5 \cdot 4.6385)$$
$$+ (2.0 \cdot 94.4586)]/108.769$$
$$= 1.87.$$

The duration of a two-year zero-coupon bond is two years, and the duration of a two-year 10 percent coupon bond (5 percent semiannually) is 1.87 years, illustrating that the duration of a zero-coupon bond is the maturity of the bond and that duration decreases as the coupon rate increases. (Duration declines as the proportion of the total income stream paid early increases.) The box on page 137 shows that a cash flow's duration is the sensitivity of its present value to a parallel shift in interest rates. The implication, therefore, is that the price of the zero-coupon bond is more sensitive to parallel shifts in interest rates than the price of the 10 percent bond is. This concept is important in hedging interest rate exposure. Moreover, if the cash flow's duration is zero, the cash flow will not change value in response to a small parallel change in interest rates. In other words, when the duration of a cash flow is zero, the present value of the cash flow is hedged against small parallel movements in the term structure. (See the box for a more complete discussion of duration.)

Table 1
Prices of $100.00 Default-Free Securities

Years until Maturity	Price of $100.00 Bond
0.5	$97.59
1.0	$95.56
1.5	$92.77
2.0	$89.96

*H*edging with Duration

A simple example will illustrate the process of hedging with duration. Consider a portfolio on July 1, 1992, that consisted of receiving $100.00 on July 1 of each year from 1993 through 1996 (face value: $400.00). According to the term structure constructed from the July 1, 1992, *Wall Street Journal*, this portfolio would have the price and duration depicted in Table 2.

The first column shows the date of payment, and the second column lists its present value. The sum of the second column is the portfolio's price. The third column is the time (years) remaining until the payment date. The fourth column weights the time into the future, multiplying it by the payment's price and dividing that figure by the total portfolio price. The sum of the weighted times is the duration of the portfolio. The fifth column is the new price of the payments if the term structure were shifted up by 1 basis point.[3]

Given that the portfolio's price changed with the shift in interest rates, is it possible to find a single cash flow that would hedge the portfolio's present value to this shift? One hedging instrument would be a single cash flow with a duration of 2.42 years (for simplicity approximated as 2.5 years) and a face value of $350.51. Because the duration of a single cash flow is the maturity of the cash flow, this security would be one that would mature on January 1, 1994. According to the term structure on July 1, 1992, a $398.81 face-value security maturing January 1, 1994, would be priced at $350.51. If the term structure were shifted 1 basis point higher, the new price of the cash flow would decrease to $350.43. The two asset prices change by the same amount with the shift in interest rates. Thus, the present value of the cash flow of the four-year portfolio can be hedged for small parallel movements of the term structure by shorting, or selling, the single cash-flow security that would mature in two and one-half years. Table 3 illustrates the benefits of using duration as a hedging tool.

A second example of hedging with duration involves a portfolio with a greater duration. In the interest of simplicity the example analyzes only default-free, fixed-income securities. A security is constructed to

Table 2
The Cash Flow Portfolio of a Four-Year Security[*]

Date of Payment	Price	Years until Payment	Weighted Time	Adjusted Price (+1 basis point)
July 1993	$96.03	1.0	0.27	$96.02
July 1994	$90.87	2.0	0.52	$90.85
July 1995	$84.94	3.0	0.73	$84.92
July 1996	$78.67	4.0	0.90	$78.64
Total	$350.51		2.42	$350.43

[*]*The portfolio receives $100.00 on each July 1 from 1993 through 1996. The term structure is constructed from the July 1, 1992,* Wall Street Journal.

Table 3
A Portfolio Hedged with a Single Cash Flow

Asset	Current Price	Adjusted Price	Difference
Long 4-Year Security	$350.51	$350.43	+$0.08
Short 2.5-Year Security	−$350.51	−$350.43	−$0.08
Combined Portfolio	0.0	0.0	0.0

resemble a thirty-year mortgage. However, again for simplicity, the prepayment option and default risk are not included and only biannual payments are considered. Specifically, at time July 1, 1992 (the beginning of the third quarter), a cash flow is considered that consists of $100.00 payments on January 1 and on July 1 in the years from 1993 through 2022 (a face value of $6,000.00). Using a term structure of interest rates constructed from the prices of stripped Treasury bonds as reported in the *Wall Street Journal* on July 1, 1992, this security had a market price of $2,316.38 and a duration of 9.54 years.

To hedge the price of this security, a bond with a single payment on January 1, 2002 (duration 9.5 years), was selected. Using the same term structure, a face value of $4,714.52 maturing on January 1, 2002, was calculated as having a market price of $2,316.38. Thus, this security was chosen as the hedging instrument. Imagine a portfolio that is long the thirty-year security and short the nine-and-one-half-year security.[4] Such a portfolio would have a face value of zero and a duration of approximately zero. To demonstrate the usefulness of matching duration, a 1 basis point parallel shift increase to the entire term structure was implemented, and the securities were repriced. After the shift, the thirty-year security has a market price of $2,314.17 and the nine-and-one-half-year security has a market price of $2,314.17. Thus, even though the securities' prices have changed by $2.21 (.1 percent), the price of the portfolio is unchanged. Table 4 illustrates how matching the duration of a portfolio can hedge the portfolio to small parallel shifts of the term structure.

Testing Parallel Shift Simulations

Users of duration-based models realize that the models are useful only for small movements in the term structure. However, interest rates in the United States may become very volatile in relatively short periods of time. To capture a more realistic measure of parallel movement interest rate exposure over three months, many practitioners simulate larger parallel shift movements. This study continues the previous example of a portfolio that is long the thirty-year security and short the nine-and-one-half-year security, altering the July 1 term structure by plus and minus 100 basis points throughout the curve (as in the interagency proposal cited earlier), and revaluing the securities with this new term structure. For a 100 basis point parallel shift increase in interest rates the portfolio price was +$4.99. For a 100 basis point decrease in rates the portfolio price was +$8.29. This analysis indicates that the portfolio faces little interest rate exposure. In fact, for any significant parallel shift in the term structure, the price of the portfolio increases. Thus, modified duration indicates that there should be no concern about losses from interest rate fluctuation.

As a test of this measure's accuracy, the portfolio price was recalculated using the actual term structure constructed from the stripped Treasury bond prices reported three months later, on October 1, 1992—and the difference in the price of the portfolio was −$54.75 (see Table 5). Modified duration would have grossly underestimated the actual interest rate exposure of the simplest portfolio during the third quarter of 1992. There are two important possible sources of such results: mismatched convexity and nonparallel term structure movements.

Adjusting for Convexity. While duration is the amount the price of a portfolio will change for small parallel movements in the term structure, convexity is how much duration will change for small parallel shifts in the term structure.[5] Thus, if durations are matched and convexities are not, the portfolio prices are hedged only to small changes in the term structure. After a small shift the durations would no longer be

---

Table 4
A Portfolio Hedged with Matching Durations

Asset	Current Price	Adjusted Price	Difference
Long 30-Year Security	$2,316.38	$2,314.17	+$2.21
Short 9.5-Year Security	−$2,316.38	−$2,314.17	−$2.21
Combined Portfolio	0.0	0.0	0.0

matched, and in the event of a larger parallel shift the portfolio prices would no longer be hedged.

The examples discussed demonstrate the results of unmatched convexity. Recall that the portfolios were perfectly hedged for a 1 basis point increase in the term structure but that their prices differed for a 100 basis point shift. Unmatched convexity is clearly evident in Table 6, in which the portfolio is priced for a 200 basis point shift. Compared with the price changes for a 100 basis point shift (+$4.99 to +$8.27), the price changes for a 200 basis point shift (+$19.21 to +$35.09) seem to indicate a nonlinear increase in the magnitude of the differences with the size of the parallel movement increases.

Eliminating convexity errors would be the first suggested improvement in simulating 100 basis point parallel shifts. This step is taken in the Federal Reserve's revised proposal, where simulations of 200 basis point shifts are included. Such shifts approximate two standard deviations of historical volatility. Because convexity errors can be large, at least two standard deviations should be simulated.[6]

Incorporating convexity clearly improves the accuracy of duration-based models. However, in the example above convexity was not a problem. Movements exceeding 100 basis points would have shown profits in the portfolio. Recall that the portfolio had a large positive price difference for both a 200 basis point increase and a 200 basis point decrease.

Nonparallel Shifts in the Term Structure. The biggest problem with using modified duration and parallel shift simulations is that term structure movements historically have rarely been parallel. Unfortunately, portfolios hedged for parallel movements of the term structure may have considerable exposure to nonparallel movements. A statistical technique called principal component analysis is a useful tool for illustrating this point. Principal component analysis breaks down a sequence of random motions into its most dominant independent components, with the first principal component being the most dominant, or most often occurring, component in the random sequence. The second principal component is the next dominant component after removing the first one. Chart 1 shows the two largest principal components of historical forward interest rate volatility.[7] In the chart the first principal component of forward interest rate fluctuation is similar to a parallel shift in that the entire curve moves in the same direction. Observe, however, that short-term rates are more volatile than long-term rates (a point missed by parallel shift simulation). This characteristic is similar to the nonparallel

Table 5
Simulating a Portfolio under a 100 Basis Point Shift

Simulation	Price of the 30-Year Security	Price of the 9.5-Year Security	Difference
+100 Basis Points	$2,111.24	$2,106.25	+$4.99
−100 Basis Points	$2,555.74	$2,547.47	+$8.27
Actual Outcome	$2,475.81	$2,530.56	−$54.75

Table 6
Simulating a Portfolio under a 200 Basis Point Shift

Simulation	Price of the 30-Year Security	Price of the 9.5-Year Security	Difference
+200 Basis Points	$1,934.39	$1,915.18	+$19.21
−200 Basis Points	$2,836.71	$2,801.62	+$35.09

shift that the revised proposal discussed by the Federal Reserve Board uses for monitoring interest rate risk. The second principal component of historical forward rate movement is fundamentally different from parallel shifts. It involves "twists" of the curve, or short-term and long-term rates moving in different directions. Combined, these two principal components account for more than 98 percent of the historical interest rate fluctuation (see Robert Litterman and Jose Scheinkman 1991).

Given that historically the most likely changes in the term structure are the independent movements of its principal components, a useful measure of interest rate exposure would be the change in the portfolio price in relation to the movements resulting from possible combinations of historical principal components of term structure fluctuation. Table 7 recalculates the market price of the portfolio for simulated term structures. The term structures are the result of 0, 1, 2, and 3 standard deviation movements of the historical principal components. The row number is the number of standard deviations of the first principal component. (For example, +1 in the row means that the term structure was raised by one standard deviation of the first principal component, and −2 means that the term structure was lowered by two standard deviations of

the first principal component.) The column number is the number of standard deviations of the second principal component (so that +1 in the column means that the term structure was steepened by one standard deviation of the second principal component and −2 means that it was flattened by two standard deviations of the second principal component, assuming the curve was initially steep). All standard deviations are for a three-month period. For every simulated term structure the profit/loss of the portfolio is calculated.

The greatest portfolio loss arising from the combinations of the first two historical principal components is −$59.18. This simulated loss is close to the actual loss of −$54.75 (see Table 5). Simulating more than parallel shifts indicates that the actual loss should not have been unexpected. Use of only parallel shift simulations was misleading as to the size of, and even the existence of, possible losses.[8] It is important to note that using historical interest rate fluctuations does not require any reporting information about the securities beyond what is required for modified duration; it simply requires the user to simulate more than parallel shift scenarios. Thus, better information is available at no additional cost.

In order to compare the different portfolios' exposure, the simulated portfolio values can be combined

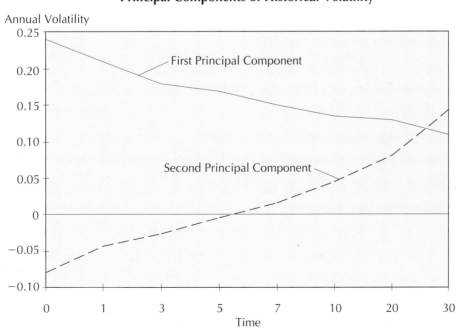

Chart 1
Principal Components of Historical Volatility

Table 7
Simulated Portfolio Values[*]

Standard Deviations Of First Principal Component	Standard Deviations of Second Principal Component						
	−3	−2	−1	0	1	2	3
−3	+53.99	+35.30	+16.79	−1.54	−19.70	−37.69	−55.53
−2	+46.73	+28.69	+10.82	−6.90	−24.47	−41.90	**−59.18**
−1	+45.59	+28.26	+11.07	−5.97	−22.89	−39.68	−56.35
0	+49.34	+32.77	+16.33	0.00	−16.22	−32.33	−48.35
1	+56.98	+41.20	+25.53	+9.95	−5.54	−20.94	−36.27
2	+67.63	+52.67	+37.79	+22.98	+8.25	−6.42	−21.03
3	+80.58	+66.44	+52.37	+38.35	+24.39	+10.47	−3.41

[*] *In dollars.*

into different test statistics. For example, the loss of −$59.18—the worst-case scenario—would be a useful statistic for determining margin (or capital) for the portfolios. However, this method may still yield errors. First, although primary principal components capture more than 98 percent of the historical movements, term structures do not move exactly as historical patterns predict. Thus, there is additional "noise" that does not get simulated. Second, it is possible (although unlikely) for interest rates to move more than three standard deviations during the three-month period. For this reason, some may argue that caution calls for more than three standard deviations to be included in the simulation. Third, any number of historical principal components can be used in the simulation. Clearly, including more components reduces the amount of unmonitored interest rate risk. Performing simulations with these dimensions in mind permits a more realistic assessment of the portfolio's actual interest rate exposure and results in a statistic with a greater degree of accuracy than modified duration.[9]

In the example discussed, one may question why the zero and one standard deviation movements were included in the simulations when the big gains and losses occurred in the two and three standard deviation movements. The smaller movements were included because, when options are part of a set of securities, portfolios may exist that make money for all large movements of the term structure but lose money when the term structure is relatively stable. It is, therefore, necessary to simulate more than just the extreme outcomes. For instance, consider a portfolio consisting of long positions in a far, out-of-the-money call and put options on Treasury bond futures contracts. If interest rates fluctuate by only small amounts, all options in this portfolio would expire out-of-the-money and the original cost of the options would be lost. However, if interest rates fluctuate by a large amount in either direction, the portfolio has options that will finish in-the-money.

Conclusion

Both Hugh Cohen (1991) and James H. Gilkeson and Stephen D. Smith (1992) show that the nature of cash flows is important in evaluating prices and risks. This article shows that the evolution of interest rate movements is also important in these evaluations. Modified duration and parallel shift simulations give useful rough approximations of interest rate exposure. However, because of the very simplicity that makes them attractive, these models have restrictions that affect their accuracy, especially over long or volatile periods of time.

This article illustrates that at the beginning of the third quarter of 1992, parallel shift simulations failed to detect the possibility of any losses to a simple portfolio, which in actuality sustained significant losses over the quarter. However, simulations based on historical term structure fluctuations, requiring no additional reporting information, would have warned the user that losses of the magnitude actually sustained were possible.

Using Duration to Hedge Interest Rate Exposure

Hedging with Constant Interest Rates

Consider at time 0 a default-free bond that pays $1.00 at time T in the future. Assuming a constant interest rate and continuous compounding, the result is the relationship

$$b(T) = \exp(-RT), \qquad (1)$$

where R is the constant interest rate per unit of time, T is the time in the future when the bond matures, and $b(T)$ is the price of the bond. For a coupon-paying bond,

$$Price\ of\ the\ bond = \sum_{i=1}^{i=n} CF_i \exp(-RT_i), \qquad (2)$$

where n is the total number of cash flows contained in the bond and CF_i is the ith cash flow at time T_i. Duration, a well-known function of a bond, is defined as

$$Duration = \frac{\sum_{i=1}^{i=n} T_i CF_i \exp(-RT_i)}{Price\ of\ the\ bond}. \qquad (3)$$

In words, duration is the weighted average maturity of the cash flow of the bond. Differentiating the price of a bond with respect to R finds that

$$\frac{d(Price\ of\ the\ bond)}{dR} = \sum_{i=1}^{i=n} - T_i CF_i \exp(-RT_i), \qquad (4)$$

which leads to the well-known relationship

$$\frac{\frac{d(Price\ of\ the\ bond)}{dR}}{Price\ of\ the\ bond} = -Duration. \qquad (5)$$

In words, the percent change in a bond's price in response to an infinitesimal positive change in the constant interest rate is minus the duration. Thus, under the assumption of a flat term structure, the duration of a bond is a single number that indicates the sensitivity of the bond price to a small change in interest rates. This result can be extended for more than constant interest rates.

Hedging with a Term Structure

Replace the assumption of a constant interest rate, R, with a forward interest rate curve denoted by $f(T)$. The forward interest rate is the interest rate agreed upon now at time 0 for an instantaneous default-free loan at time T.

For example, if $f(30) = 8\%$, it is implied that the annualized interest rate on a default-free loan agreed upon today that will mature thirty years in the future and will be instantaneously repaid is 8 percent. The forward interest rate curve is the forward rate, $f(T)$, for all $T \geq 0$. The forward interest rate curve can be used to price default-free cash flows. Again, let $b(T)$ be the time 0 price of a default-free bond that pays $1.00 at time T, and then

$$b(T) = \exp\left[-\int_0^T f(t)dt\right]. \qquad (6)$$

For a coupon-paying bond,

$$Price\ of\ the\ bond = \sum_{i=1}^{i=n} CF_i \exp\left[-\int_0^{T_i} f(t)dt\right]. \qquad (7)$$

Duration is similarly defined as the weighted average maturity of the cash flows:

$$Duration = \frac{\sum_{i=1}^{i=n} T_i CF_i \exp\left[-\int_0^{T_i} f(t)dt\right]}{Price\ of\ the\ bond}. \qquad (8)$$

If the price of the bond is differentiated with respect to a parallel shift in the forward rate curve [substitute $f(t) + R$ for $f(t)$ in equation 7 and differentiate with respect to R], the result as R approaches 0 is

$$\frac{d(Price\ of\ the\ bond)}{dR} = \sum_{i=1}^{i=n} -T_i CF_i \exp\left[-\int_0^{T_i} f(t)dt\right]. \qquad (9)$$

Substituting,

$$\frac{\frac{d(Price\ of\ the\ bond)}{dR}}{Price\ of\ the\ bond} = -Duration. \qquad (10)$$

This equation demonstrates the advantages of using duration as a measure of interest rate exposure. For any forward interest rate curve, the duration of a cash flow is the sensitivity of that cash flow to a small parallel shift in the term structure. The examples in the text illustrate the benefits and limitations of hedging with duration. For small parallel fluctuations in the term structure, the portfolios are well hedged. However, for larger parallel movements or nonparallel movements, the portfolios may sustain severe losses.

The fact that 100 and 200 basis point parallel shifts failed to detect that the mock portfolio could sustain any loss owing to interest rate exposure, or that a single-factor model detected only the possibility of small losses, should be alarming for those who depend solely upon these measures to determine their interest rate exposure. Furthermore, the mock portfolio constructed is the most straightforward sort of portfolio possible, consisting of only deterministic default-free cash flows. In contrast, the set of securities available to investors in interest rate contingent claims contains extremely complex securities. Even a "simple" fixed-rate mortgage contains a complicated prepayment option. In addition, caps, floors, swaps, futures, options on futures, and countless embedded options add to the complexity of the problem. The failure to capture the true interest rate exposure of this relatively simple mock portfolio illustrates that a large amount of interest rate exposure is undetected by these measures.

The findings reported here should serve as a warning to both investors and regulators interested in determining interest rate exposure. It is important to know that oversimplified approaches to measuring interest rate exposure can be misleading, even for simple securities. Given the complex nature of securities that are common within interest rate contingent claims, the results of parallel shift and single-factor simulations should not, by themselves, be viewed as accurately reflecting interest rate exposure.

Notes

1. One indication of this development has been the increase in the open interest of the Treasury bond futures contract. (Open interest is the number of futures contracts in existence.) Over the period from March 31, 1981, to March 31, 1993, the open interest of the nearest June futures contract increased from 51,847 to 317,804.
2. See Docket R-0764, an interagency proposal of the Federal Deposit Insurance Corporation, the Office of the Comptroller of the Currency, and the Board of Governors of the Federal Reserve System. The modified proposal presented to the Federal Reserve Board was reported in the *American Banker*, April 1, 1993, 1. It was not available in the *Federal Register* at the time of publication.
3. A basis point is 1/100 of 1 percent. If interest rates were 3 percent, a 1 basis point increase would raise them to 3.01 percent.
4. Selling a security short is equivalent to borrowing the security and selling it at its current market price with the intention of repurchasing the security at a future date and returning it to its original owner. A short seller profits when the price of the underlying security declines. Longing a security is equivalent to purchasing the security.
5. If duration is considered the first derivative of the portfolio price with respect to parallel interest rate movements, convexity would be the second derivative. For a discussion of the "convexity trap" in pricing mortgage portfolios see Gilkeson and Smith (1992).
6. The actual deviation of interest rates would lie within one standard deviation approximately 65 percent of the time. It would lie within two standard deviations approximately 95 percent of the time.
7. These components were supplied by a large financial institution in 1991.
8. Note that a one-factor historical model similar to the regulators' nonparallel shift would not have worked much better. The 0 column in Table 7 simulates only the first historical factor shifts, and the worst loss is −$6.90. Thus, two factors are the minimum number necessary for an adequate measure of this portfolio over this period.
9. If options were included in the portfolio, one would also want to simulate the effects of changes in the market's implied volatility of interest rates to the term structure simulation.

References

Benston, George J., and George G. Kaufman. "Understanding the Savings and Loan Debacle." *Public Interest* 99 (Spring 1990): 79-95.

Cohen, Hugh. "Evaluating Embedded Options." Federal Reserve Bank of Atlanta *Economic Review* 76 (November/December 1991): 9-16.

FDIC Improvement Act of December 19, 1991, Pub. Law 102-242, 105 Stat. 2236.

Gilkeson, James D., and Stephen D. Smith. "The Convexity Trap." Federal Reserve Bank of Atlanta *Economic Review* 77 (November/December 1992): 14-27.

Interagency proposal on revising risk-based capital standards as prescribed by Section 305 of FDICIA (Docket R-0764), Press release, *Federal Register*, July 31, 1992.

Litterman, Robert, and Jose Scheinkman. "Common Factors Affecting Bond Returns." *Journal of Fixed Income* (June 1991): 54-61.

Analyzing Risk and Return for Mortgage-Backed Securities

Stephen D. Smith

*T*he growth of an active secondary market for home mortgages was one of the many important innovations in financial markets over the past decade. Although organizations such as the Federal National Mortgage Association (FNMA or "Fannie Mae") have been buying securities backed by the Veterans Administration and the Federal Housing Administration for decades, only recently have mortgage-related securities become an integral component of financial statements for a number of banks and other intermediaries.[1] The growth of these securities has led to a dazzling array of derivative and hybrid products produced by repackaging the basic cash flows from a pool of fixed-rate mortgages.[2] Equally bewildering to potential investors in these products is the technology invented to calculate adjusted yields or, equivalently, adjusted spreads over Treasury yields.

Yield adjustments for mortgage-backed securities, or MBSs, are necessary primarily because of the law allowing homeowners to prepay the principal balance on their mortgages without penalty.[3] Since such prepayments occur primarily when market rates fall substantially below existing coupon rates (that is, contract rates) on the mortgages, investors in the mortgages face the risk that, after having paid a premium for a high coupon security, they will be saddled with money that must be reinvested at lower (current market) rates. Investment banks and other financial firms have developed methods for adjusting the yields on mortgage-related instruments to reflect this possibility of prepayments and the corresponding lower yields.

Regulators are becoming cognizant of these issues as they build a framework for analyzing the risk profiles of an increasingly large pool of securities with unconventional cash flow characteristics. Indeed, the Comptroller

This article was originally published in the Atlanta Fed's January/February 1991 Economic Review. *The author holds the H. Talmage Dobbs, Jr., Chair of Finance in the College of Business at Georgia State University and is a visiting scholar at the Atlanta Fed.*

of the Currency has recently provided some specific guidelines for the holdings of collateralized mortgage obligations (see William B. Hummer 1990).

The purpose of this article is to provide a nontechnical introduction to the methods used to analyze the risks and returns associated with investing in mortgage-related securities. This information should help potential investors better compare the cash flow and yield measures for mortgage-backed securities with those on alternative investments.

The Prepayment Problem

The problem of prepayment on a mortgage (an asset) is in some ways the reverse of the problem of early withdrawal of a fixed-rate certificate of deposit (CD; a liability). Imagine that a banker has issued a fixed-rate CD for some period of time, and suppose the depositor has the right to withdraw his or her funds at any time before maturity, without penalty. The depositor might withdraw early for two general reasons. If market rates on CDs rose substantially above the current rate on the CD, the CD holder might choose to withdraw early and reinvest the funds in a higher-yielding account. Whether funds are actually removed or simply rolled over into a new account at the current bank, the banker will be replacing this relatively low-cost CD with funds that will cost substantially more than the old deposit. The second reason for early withdrawal would fall into a "catch-all" category that includes noninterest factors like the depositor's moving or developing an unexpected need for funds. In either case, the bank suffers a cost if it imposes no early withdrawal penalty.

Prepayment on a mortgage is analogous to the CD example and may occur because rates fall substantially below the mortgage rate the homeowner is paying. Prepaying the mortgage for this reason is called "rational exercise" of the option. Exercising the prepayment option in other cases (such as moving for a new job) is called "irrational exercise" because such behavior is not tied directly to interest savings.[4]

Rational exercise of prepayment options forces mortgage holders to reinvest their funds at rates substantially below those they would have earned if prepayment had not occurred. Moreover, since mortgages typically have maturities much longer than those of most other assets or liabilities, the earnings loss is felt over a longer period of time. Uncertainty concerning repayment of principal makes convention-

al yield measures unreliable indicators of the return to be expected from holding mortgage-backed securities, as discussed below.

Shortcomings of Static Yield

Assuming that payments are guaranteed against default by a government agency such as the Government National Mortgage Association (GNMA or "Ginnie Mae"), a standard fixed-rate mortgage is, in the absence of the prepayment clause, nothing more than an annuity contract. Given a remaining life, a market price, and the promised payments per period, it is possible to find the contract's yield to maturity (YTM), or "static" yield. Static is used to denote the fact that an investor will earn the yield to maturity per period if all of the promised payments are made when due and are reinvested at the same rate (that is, rates do not change over the life of the loan). The latter condition is a well-known shortcoming of using the yield-to-maturity method to calculate the expected return on any security. It is the first condition that makes the yield-to-maturity approach particularly unattractive for analyzing mortgage-backed securities. In short, the static yield treats the payments from a mortgage-backed security as a sure thing over time, which they clearly are not.

The static yield approach will also distort calculations commonly used to measure the interest-rate risk of a security. Duration and convexity are two such measures. However defined, the duration of a fixed-income security is basically a measure of the percentage change in a security's price if interest rates change by a small amount.[5] Securities with shorter durations experience smaller price decreases, in percentage terms, for a small increase in rates than do securities with longer duration. Likewise, smaller increases occur for shorter duration securities when rates decrease.

However, duration is itself a function of the level of interest rates. In fact, duration declines as interest rates rise (and vice versa) for standard fixed-income securities. This relationship is simply a result of the fact that price changes are not symmetric. The percentage change in bond prices as rates increase is smaller than the price changes associated with equal rate decreases. Thus, the risk measure (duration) is inversely related to the interest-rate level. *Convexity* is the term usually applied to this "drift" in the duration. However, unlike fixed-income securities, mortgage-related securities' prepayment option makes cash flows a function of interest rates. Risk measures such as duration need to be adjusted to reflect this fact.

To summarize, the standard yield-to-maturity approach for calculating risk and return is inadequate when analyzing mortgage-related securities primarily because prepayment risk causes cash flows to be a function of interest rates and other factors. By treating the promised cash flows as certain, an investor is likely to overstate seriously the return from holding mortgage-backed securities. The option adjusted spread (OAS) approach discussed in the following section is an attempt to adjust the cash flows to reflect prepayment risk.[6]

The Logic of the Option Adjusted Spread Approach

The basic premise of the option adjusted spread approach is that prepayments, and therefore cash flows, will be a function of both the evolution of interest rates and other (for example, demographic) factors that could cause irrational prepayments on pools or portfolios of mortgages. A distribution of future cash flows (or prices) is generated by assigning probabilities to plausible alternative future interest-rate scenarios. Finally, in a step analogous to finding the discount rate (the static yield) that equates the present value of the promised cash flows to the current price, a yield measure can be found that equates the average present value of these option adjusted cash flows to the current price. The difference between this adjusted yield and that on a base security—a comparable duration Treasury bond, for example—is considered the option adjusted spread. Although this analogy is not exactly correct unless the yield curve is flat (see the appendix for general definitions of option adjusted spread), the general idea is that similar calculations result in a yield measure for mortgage-backed securities that has been adjusted for the expected level (and timing) of prepayments over the life of the mortgage pool.[7]

The critical steps to be taken in the option adjusted spread process appear in Chart 1. Although each practitioner is faced with a number of specific choices (some of which are discussed below), the steps outlined in Chart 1 must be followed for almost all of the option adjusted spread models currently in use.

Raw input is provided from a number of sources. Interest rate information is gathered from the current Treasury term structure of interest rates or yield curve.

Typically, the implied one-period future interest rates (or forward rates) from the Treasury curve are used as the mean, or expected value, around which a distribution of future short-term interest rates is constructed.[8] Future mortgage rates are either constructed as a markup over the short-term rates or, in more complex models, a markup over a long-term Treasury rate that does not move exactly in concert with short-term rates. A volatility (or variance) estimate is also needed to construct a distribution of future interest rates. This parameter restricts the degree to which rates may deviate from the current term structure (the mean). Estimated prepayments are critically dependent on the volatility estimates, which may come from historical data or more exotic forms, such as implied volatilities from options contracts.

Prepayments are estimated as a function of the deviation of current coupon rates in the mortgage pool from estimated market rates and other currently available information such as the average age of the mortgage pool and other known factors (for example, the region of the country in which the mortgages originated). Future cash flows are then generated as a function of the evolution of interest rates and the demographic factors. The fact that future cash flows are dependent on the entire interest rate process is commonly referred to as *path dependency*.

Consider the case in which a downward movement in mortgage rates will prompt a prepayment. If rates increase next period and return to their original level in period two, no prepayment will occur. By the same token, if rates should fall next period and then increase to their original level, prepayment will occur. The level of rates in period two is the same in both scenarios, but the cash flow in period two is not. In this case the period two payment is either the promised payment or zero and is clearly a function of earlier interest rates (in this case interest rates in period one). Therefore, each path of rates can generate a different cash flow pattern for the mortgage.

The next step in the process is to find a constant discount factor which, when applied to every path of future short-term Treasury rates, equates the cash outflow's present value (the current market price of the mortgage) to the average present value of the cash inflows. This constant discount factor is the option adjusted spread.

The final step in Chart 1 involves shocking interest rates up and down by some amount. Combined with the current price, the new prices provide sufficient information to calculate option adjusted duration and convexity measures.

Chart 1
Steps in Option Adjusted Spread Calculation

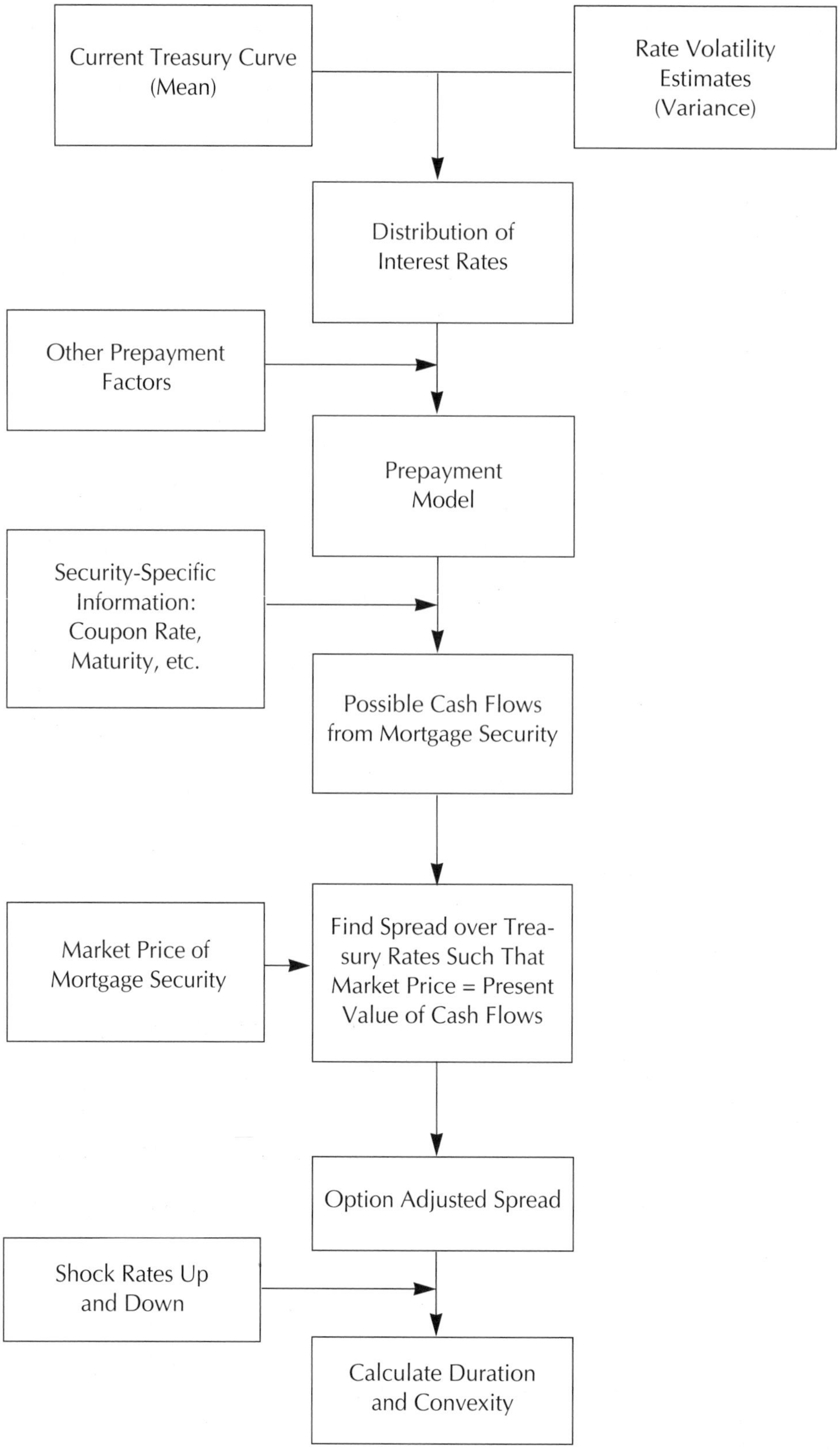

```
┌─────────────────────┐              ┌─────────────────────┐
│ Current Treasury     │              │   Rate Volatility    │
│ Curve                │──────┬───────│   Estimates          │
│ (Mean)               │      │       │   (Variance)         │
└─────────────────────┘      │       └─────────────────────┘
                             ▼
                  ┌─────────────────────┐
                  │  Distribution of     │
                  │  Interest Rates      │
                  └─────────────────────┘
                             │
┌─────────────────────┐      ▼
│ Other Prepayment     │─────▶│
│ Factors              │      │
└─────────────────────┘      ▼
                  ┌─────────────────────┐
                  │  Prepayment          │
                  │  Model               │
                  └─────────────────────┘
┌─────────────────────┐      │
│ Security-Specific    │      │
│ Information:         │──────▶│
│ Coupon Rate,        │      ▼
│ Maturity, etc.      │
└─────────────────────┘  ┌─────────────────────┐
                  │  Possible Cash Flows │
                  │  from Mortgage Security │
                  └─────────────────────┘
                             │
                             ▼
┌─────────────────────┐  ┌─────────────────────┐
│ Market Price of      │  │ Find Spread over Trea- │
│ Mortgage Security    │─▶│ sury Rates Such That   │
│                      │  │ Market Price = Present │
└─────────────────────┘  │ Value of Cash Flows    │
                  └─────────────────────┘
                             │
                             ▼
                  ┌─────────────────────┐
                  │ Option Adjusted Spread │
                  └─────────────────────┘
┌─────────────────────┐      │
│ Shock Rates Up       │──────▶│
│ and Down             │      ▼
└─────────────────────┘  ┌─────────────────────┐
                  │ Calculate Duration   │
                  │ and Convexity        │
                  └─────────────────────┘
```

Computational Choices

The procedure outlined in Chart 1 has at least two different versions, depending on the practitioners' choice of techniques for generating interest rates and discounting the cash flows.

Interest Rates. Probably the most widely used approach for generating a distribution of interest rates is the simulation method. Using forward rates embodied in the term structure as the means, the investigator inputs a variance estimate and draws a series of short-term rate paths. Resulting cash flows are generated, and the process is repeated for another drawing from the distribution of rates. The simulation approach is sometimes ad hoc in the sense that the method need not be based directly on a rigorous link to the term structure of interest rates.[9] An alternative is given by the binomial, or lattice, approach, which starts with today's term structure and assigns probabilities to scenarios wherein rates increase or decrease (or possibly remain the same). Cash flows are calculated at each point in the interest rate tree. (See the next section for an example.) A volatility estimate is needed for this technique as well, because it determines the amount by which rates are allowed to vary from point to point.

Discounting. The most intuitively appealing method for discounting involves finding the expected cash flow for each period (over all possible rates) and discounting back at rates contained in today's Treasury curve. However, the most popular method in use today (see, for example, Alan Brazil 1988) involves discounting back each cash flow at the simulated rate (as opposed to today's term structure rates). To the extent that rates and cash flows are correlated—correlation being the whole premise of rate-sensitive cash flows—the two techniques will yield different results. An example in the next section illustrates the difference between these approaches.

Properties of the Option Adjusted Spread. The foremost benefit of the option adjusted spread approach is that it provides a yield measure that more accurately reflects the timing and level of payments that an investor might expect to receive from holding a mortgage-backed security. A second advantage is that risk measures calculated from prepayment adjusted cash flows provide a better indicator of the security's true interest-rate risk properties. For example, although the price of a standard fixed-income security will vary inversely with the level of interest rates, it is possible for prepayment adjusted prices to change in the same direction, no matter which way rates move. The key to this concept is that, should rates fall, the possibility of mortgage prepayments may go up, in which case investors may bid *down* the mortgage-backed security's price. This action is, of course, the opposite of what would happen with a truly fixed-income security like a Treasury bond. This "whipsaw" effect is particularly evident in mortgage-backed securities that are selling at a premium from par value.

Finally, the option adjusted spread methodology is often put forth as one method for identifying "rich" (overpriced) and "cheap" (underpriced) mortgage-backed securities. Typically, the option adjusted spread on securities with similar adjusted durations and coupons are compared. Matching durations is an attempt to hold constant the differences in the risks of the assets. Note, however, that such comparisons tell the investor nothing to give direction about whether he or she should purchase *either* of the securities.

Suppose, for example, that the yield for a stream of expected cash flows is greater than that for a comparable duration Treasury security. This situation is analogous to the case of a positive option adjusted spread (OAS > 0). A risk neutral investor—one who demands no compensation for the variability of the cash flows (read "variability of prepayments")—would certainly find such an investment attractive. However, a positive option adjusted spread alone would not generally provide a risk averse investor with enough information to determine whether or not the extra yield would exceed the investor's desired risk premium.

Another (and equivalent) way to view this ambiguity is to recognize that if two mortgage-backed securities have the same expected cash flows but the variability is greater for, say, the second one, risk-averse investors will bid a lower price for the second mortgage-backed security. The result will be that the second mortgage-backed security has a higher option adjusted spread. The meaning is clearly not that the second security is a better one, however. In short, establishing that the expected return on a risky security is greater than the Treasury rate, or even greater than the expected return on some other security of comparable risk, does not imply that it is a good buy unless you happen to be neutral toward risk (because it could be the case that neither of the securities has a high enough premium to cover its risk). Such "risk neutral" information is exactly the sort the option adjusted spread methodology provides.

*E*xamples of Option Adjusted Spread Technology

In the following examples, noninterest rate "irrational" factors that might influence prepayments are ignored for simplicity. Moreover, for simplicity the examples will deal with a case where the term structure is flat.

Consider a mortgage-backed security for which the underlying fixed-rate mortgages are identical. The total principal balance on the pool is $1,000,000, and the mortgages carry an 11 percent coupon and have a maturity of four years. The latter assumption, while unrealistic, allows analysis of the process without changing the qualitative results. Promised payments on this annuity contract amount to $322,326 per year. Shortly after issue, rates decline in such a fashion that the mortgage pool is now selling for a current market price of $1,044,246.

It is always possible to find a rate, the static yield, that will discount back the promised cash flows to the current market price. In this case the rate turns out to be 9 percent (see the appendix). If Treasury rates are 8 percent, the "static spread" is 9% – 8% = 100 basis points. Assume that because of refinancing costs and other factors prepayment will not occur unless the spread between the coupon rate and market rates on mortgages is 300 basis points (3 percent). In this case prepayment will occur if mortgage rates are less than or equal to 11% – 3% = 8%.

Interest Rates. A simple binomial (or two-state) process is used to model changes in interest rates.[10] Rates can move up and down with equal likelihood from their current levels. The assumed change is equivalent to a rate volatility estimate. Let this be 50 basis points. In this situation, mortgage rates will be either 9.5 percent (9% + .5%) or 8.5 percent (9% – .5%) next year. In year two rates will be either 9.5 percent ± .5 percent or 8.5 percent ± .5 percent. So in year two there is a 25 percent [(.5)(.5)] chance that rates will be either 10 percent (go up twice) or 8 percent (go down twice) and a 50 percent chance the rates will return to 9 percent (that is, a 25 percent

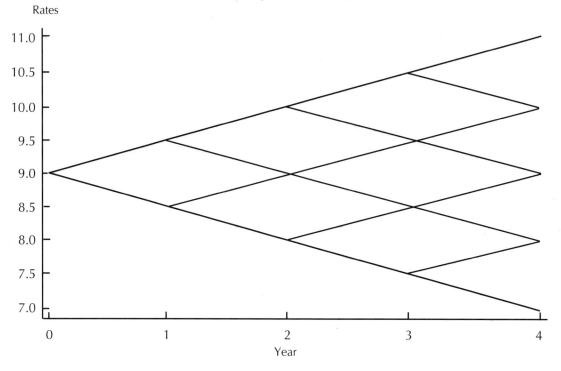

Chart 2
Interest Rate Tree
Current Mortgage Rate = 9.0%
Volatility = 50 Basis Points

chance they will increase and then decline and a 25 percent chance they will decline and then increase). Chart 2 provides a graphic representation (a "tree") of all possible rates over the four-year life of the mortgage pool.

Cash Flows. In any given year the realized cash flows will be either (a) the promised payment ($322,326), (b) the promised payment plus prepayment of the remaining principal ($322,326 + principal balance) or (c) zero. Case (b) occurs if and when mortgage rates fall below 8 percent, while case (c) is the cash flow in subsequent periods should prepayment take place.

Given the volatility estimate of 50 basis points there is no chance of prepayment in period one because rates can only fall as low as 8.5 percent. The cash flow is certain to be $322,326. However, in period two there is a 25 percent chance that rates will drop to 8 percent and prepayment will occur. Should this happen, the cash flow will be $322,326 + $551,992 = 874,318, where $551,992 is the remaining principal balance on the mortgage. Once prepayment has occurred, the cash flow in years three and four will be zero.

The expected (or average) cash flow from the pool can also be calculated by multiplying each possible cash flow by the probability that it will occur. In year one, for example, there is a 0 percent chance of prepayment because rates will always be above 8 percent. Alternatively, in year two there is a 25 percent chance the mortgage rate will be 8 percent and the corresponding cash flow $874,318. There remains a 75 percent chance the rates will be above 8 percent and the cash flow will be $322,326. Thus, the expected cash flow is $874,318 (.25) + $322,326 (.75) = $460,324. Table 1 provides the possible and expected cash flows by period.

In this special case, the option adjusted yield can be calculated by finding a discount factor that equates the discounted value of the expected cash flows (see Table 1) to the current price. The rate that solves this discounting problem is about 8.85 percent, somewhat less than the static yield of 9 percent. Finally, the option adjusted spread in this simple example is given by subtracting the Treasury rate (8 percent) from the adjusted yield; the option adjusted spread is 8.85% − 8% = 85 basis points.

This importance of the volatility measure can be seen by first considering the case in which rates in each period can change by only 25 basis points rather than 50. The mortgage rates now have no chance of falling to 8 percent before the mortgage matures.

Therefore, the expected cash flow is $322,326 in every period and the option adjusted spread will be the same as the static spread (100 basis points). Alternatively, the option adjusted spread is actually negative (−12 basis points) if the volatility estimate is doubled to 100 basis points.

Option adjusted spread estimates are also extremely sensitive to the discounting method used by the investigator. The calculation procedure described above can be viewed as a "discounted average cash flow" approach. Alternatively, as mentioned earlier, many investment houses prefer what could be called an "average discounted cash flow" (or average price) approach. This method differs from the discounted average cash flow approach because the cash flows are discounted back at the realized interest rates in Chart 1, as opposed to today's rate. In this case, low cash flows are, on average, associated with lower discount rates (the prepayment problem) and vice versa for higher rates. The net result is that the option adjusted spread will be different (typically lower). For this particular example the option adjusted spread is actually a negative 2 percent (− 200 basis points) when using the average price method.

The appendix contains equations (2) and (3), which show the mathematical distinction between the approaches.[11] This rather large difference in results comes from the fact that the high cash flows are discounted at higher rates in the average price approach.[12] The benefits are not symmetric, though, because the zero cash flow after prepayment is still zero no matter how low the discount rate is.

A final example of the option adjusted spread method involves its use in calculating the risk an in-

Table 1
Possible and Expected
Cash Flows from Mortgage by
Period

Period	Possible Cash Flow	Expected Cash Flow
1	$322,326	$322,326
2	$322,326 or $874,318	$460,324
3	$322,326 or $0	$241,745
4	$322,326 or $0	$241,745

vestor faces for relatively large interest-rate changes. A potentially useful exercise is to see how mortgage prices would change if rates are shocked up or down by some amount in the current period. For example, if Treasury and mortgage rates increased immediately by 100 basis points, there would be a zero chance that the mortgage rate could fall to 8 percent before year four (that is, $9\% + 1\% = 10\%$ and the volatility is 50 basis points a year). It is possible, using the original option adjusted spread, to calculate a new price.

Consider, for simplicity, the average cash flow method. The option adjusted spread is 85 basis points, while current mortgage and Treasury rates are 9 percent and 8 percent, respectively. Suppose rates increase immediately to 10 percent and 9 percent, respectively, and volatility remains constant at 50 basis points. Then, using the average cash flow method, the new price is $1,025,057, which is less than $1,044,246 because the present value of the future cash flows has been reduced.

Alternatively, if rates should immediately fall by 100 basis points, prepayment will occur as soon as possible (probably in period one), because the new mortgage rate is 8 percent. In this case the new price is $1,029,208, which is also lower than the original price. This whipsaw effect occurs because the lower interest rate causes earlier prepayment, more than offsetting the present value added from having a lower rate with which to discount back the cash flows. These examples should make clear that, while it is conceptually an averaging technique, the actual option adjusted spread is extremely sensitive to a variety of input and methodological decisions practitioners make.

Conclusion

The calculation of yields on mortgage-backed securities is complex primarily because of the difficulty of valuing an owner's option to prepay the mortgage. Despite their computational complexities, current ap-proaches to mortgage valuation are still just averaging techniques. As shown in this article, cash flows, and therefore returns, depend on the entire path of interest rates; that is, they are path dependent. Therefore, the interest-rate history over the life of a mortgage-backed security is an important piece of information. An additional complicating factor arises from the difficulty in determining whether a mortgage that looks "cheap" is really undervalued or whether it is selling at a discount because of above-average risk. Two other caveats merit attention. It is possible, especially for mortgage securities selling at premium above par, to encounter interest-rate changes that "whipsaw" the investor; that is, prices may fall if rates either decline or increase. The adjusted yield measures can be very sensitive to the inputs used—for example, the assumed volatility of interest rates.

The option adjusted spread has become a favored technology for dealing with this problem because it adjusts for both the timing and level of potential prepayments. In fact, the approach can be used in a variety of settings because many assets and liabilities have options of some sort embedded in their structure.[13]

While potentially useful, the option adjusted spread is not a panacea for investors hoping to find undervalued assets on a risk-adjusted basis. No formal model currently provides a basis for decomposing the option adjusted spread into compensation for risk and excess returns. Viewed properly as a yield (or yield spread over Treasury), however, the option adjusted spread measures are probably clearer indicators of the likely return than conventional static yield calculations. The trade-off here involves the option adjusted spread's sensitivity to inputs (such as volatility and the prepayment model) and the valuation framework the investigator employs. Potential purchasers, as well as regulatory personnel, should be aware of these facts. Asking potential sellers for information concerning the actual risk/return profiles of previously analyzed mortgage-backed securities would be useful in this regard.[14]

Appendix

This appendix contains the general formulas used for calculations in the text. As noted below, the actual examples usually involve simplified versions of these equations (for example, the term structure is flat).

M = market price of the mortgage-backed security

C = promised payment per period on a fixed-rate contract

Y = static yield to maturity

N = remaining maturity of the contract

The static yield is the rate that equates the present value of the promised cash inflows (Cs) to the current market price. That is, Y solves

If G is the yield on a comparable maturity (more

$$M = \frac{C}{(1+Y)} + \frac{C}{(1+Y)^2} + \ldots + \frac{C}{(1+Y)^N}$$

specifically, duration) Treasury security, the static spread is just $Y - G = S$. For the example in the text, $C = \$322,126$; $N = 4$; $M = \$1,044,246$, so $Y = 9\%$ and $S = 9\% - 8\% = 1\%$.

More notation and calculations are needed to calculate the option adjusted spread. Let f_t = one-period forward rate for government securities in period t, $f_t = (1 + R_t)^t/(1 + R_{t-1})^{t-1}$, where R_t is the current spot rate for a government security that makes one payment in period t and zero otherwise. Define r_t = actual interest rate on one-period government securities in period t. Note that this number is unknown today if $t > 1$. With this notation, $f_1 = r_1 = R_1$. Finally, let C_t = actual cash flow realized from the mortgage in period t. Notice that there are two general cases: $C_t = C$ (promised payment) if there is no prepayment, or $C_t = C$ + remaining principal balance $> C$ if there is prepayment. In this case $C_{t+1} = C_{t+2} = \ldots = C_N = 0$. For notational purposes let $E(\cdot)$ denote expectation (or expected value) of the term inside the parenthesis. The expected value of x, for example, is given by the sum of the possible outcomes for x, multiplied by the probability that each outcome will occur. There are two approaches to calculating the option adjusted spread.

Expected Cash Flow Approach

Search for a discount factor, O_c, such that O_c solves

$$M = \frac{E[C_1]}{(1+f_1+O_c)} + \frac{E[C_2]}{(1+f_1+O_c)(1+f_2+O_c)} \quad (2)$$

$$+ \ldots + \frac{E[C_N]}{(1+f_1+O_c)(1+f_2+O_c)\ldots(1+f_N+O_c)}.$$

The term $E[C_t]$, $t = 1, \ldots 4$ is given by the right-hand column of Table 1. These terms can be calculated by multiplying the possible cash flows by the probability that rates will be above or below the cutoff rate for prepayment. In particular, with equal probabilities (.5) of an increase or decrease in rates and volatility = 50 basis points, $E[C_1] = \$322,326\,(1)$. Because there is a 25 percent chance $[(.5)(.5) = .25]$ that the Treasury rate will fall to 7 percent in year two (mortgage rate = 8%), the expected cash flow in period two is given by multiplying the possible cash flows in Table 1 by their respective probabilities. This calculation gives the expected value, or $E[C_2] = \$322,326\,(.75) + \$874,318\,(.25) = \$460,324$. Likewise, because the cash flow in period three is zero if prepayment occurs, the expected cash flow in this case is $E[C_3] = \$322,326\,(.75) + \$0\,(.25)$. The expected cash flow in period four will be the same, so $E[C_4] = \$322,326\,(.75) + \$0\,(.25)$. Solving (2) for the option adjusted spread yields $O_c = 85$ basis points. Notice that when the term structure is flat, the forward rates will be the same. Thus, solving (2) is the same, in this case only, as the simpler approach used in the text—solving for the yield first and then subtracting the (constant) Treasury rate.

Expected Price Approach

Find a discount factor, O_p, that solves the following equation:

$$M = E\left[\frac{C_1}{(1+r_1+O_p)} + \frac{C_2}{(1+r_1+O_p)+(1+r_2+O_p)}\right] \quad (3)$$

$$+ \ldots + \frac{C_N}{(1+r_1+O_p)(1+r_2+O_p)\ldots(1+r_N+O_p)}.$$

In this case the rs are the realized one-period Treasury rates from the tree in Chart 2. For this example, the current Treasury rate is 8 percent and the term structure is flat; therefore, $r_1 = 8\%$. However, next-period rates will be either 7.5 percent or 8.5 percent, so $r_2 = 7.5\%$ with probability (.5) and $r_2 = 8.5\%$ with probability .5. Interest rates for future periods are calculated in a similar fashion. The possible Cs are found in the first column of Table 1. Using (3), O_p can be calculated as $O_p = -2.0\%$ or -200 basis points.

Calculating New Prices

The new prices are calculated by fixing O_c (or O_p), adding a constant amount ($\pm$ 100 basis points) to each f_t

(or r_t), and finding the new cash flows associated with these rates. The new M is then given by simply using the discount formula. For the expected cash flow approach, a 100-basis-point increase in rates will result in a zero probability of prepayment, so

$$E[C_1^+] = E[C_2^+] = E[C_3^+] = E[C_4^+] = \$322,326,$$

where C_t^+ is the cash flow for a rate increase. The discount rates in equation (2) are $(1 + f_1 + .01 + .0085)$ for period one, $(1 + f_1 + .01 + .0085)(1 + f_2 + .01 + .0085)$

for period two, and so forth. The new price can be calculated using equation (2). The rate decrease is the same problem except that, if rates should fall by 100 basis points, prepayment occurs immediately, and

$$E[C_1^-] = \$1,110,000 \text{ and } E[C_2^-] = E[C_3^-] = E[C_4^-] = 0$$

The discount factors are $(1 + f_1 - .01 + .0085)$ and so on. An analogous approach would also be used if one were applying the expected price methodology.

Notes

1. The book value of domestic bank holdings of guaranteed and nonguaranteed mortgage-backed securities was about $200 billion at the end of 1989. About $35 billion of these assets was held by banks in Alabama, Florida, Georgia, Louisiana, Mississippi, and Tennessee.

2. See Sullivan and Lowell (1988) for an introduction to the mechanics of the mortgage securities market and the major participants.

3. For convenience the terms mortgage and mortgage-backed security will, when there is no ambiguity, oftentimes be used interchangeably.

4. See, for example, Hendershott and Van Order (1987) for a formal options approach to modeling rational exercise.

5. Interestingly, duration can also be viewed as a weighted average time to maturity, where the weights for each period t are equal to the present value of period t 's cash flow divided by the total present value (the market value, or price). Shorter-term securities are those that have relatively large cash flows in earlier periods. For fixed-rate mortgages, however, the promised cash flows are a level annuity, so the weights are simply the present value factor for each period relative to the present value interest factor for an annuity.

6. It should be noted that some adjustment for early prepayments is typically incorporated into the static yield framework. For example, yield quotes provided by investment banks will often incorporate a constant prepayment rate per month for the remaining mortgage balance.

7. Those familiar with options pricing theory will realize that this method is only loosely based on conventional option pricing models. Although it is true, for example, that an option's value can, under certain circumstances, be viewed as the expected payoff over a transformed (or "risk neutral") probability distribution, the approach used here is

based on the original probabilities. In essence, such a formulation amounts to assuming that investors are, in some sense, truly indifferent to risk. See notes 8 and 11 for additional comments on this point.

8. Such a formulation is equivalent to assuming that investors demand no risk premium for holding longer-term bonds. See Abken (1990) for a review of this "expectations" hypothesis of the term structure.

9. Schwartz and Torous (1989) provide a good example of a method for explicitly linking interest rate processes to a theory of the term structure in the context of valuing mortgage-backed securities.

10. See Abken (1990) for a discussion of binomial processes in the context of the term structure of interest rates.

11. From a somewhat more technical perspective this choice of assumptions may be viewed as one of choosing between "global" and "local" risk neutrality on the part of investors. With local risk neutrality investors expect to earn the same return from all securities over any one period of time. It can be shown by repeated substitution that this results in the expected price approach discussed in the text. See Cox, Ingersoll, and Ross (1985) for a mathematical discussion of the "local" expectations hypothesis.

12. Part of the difference may also come from the fact that in this example the average realized rate is set equal to today's rate. This approach is different from the more mathematically correct one, which would be to make the average realized one-period bond price equal to today's one-period bond price.

13. See, for example, Ayaydin, Richard, and Rigsbee (1989) for a discussion.

14. For example, Toevs (1990) provides evidence on the return characteristics of various mortgage-backed securities when compared to duration-matched Treasury securities.

References

Abken, Peter. "Innovations in Modeling the Term Structure of Interest Rates." Federal Reserve Bank of Atlanta *Economic Review* 75 (July/August 1990): 2-27.

Ayaydin, Sirri, Charles Richard, and Stephen Rigsbee. "Applying an OAS Model Consistently." *Financial Managers Statement* 11 (November/December 1989): 65-75.

Brazil, Alan. "Citicorp's Mortgage Valuation Model: Option Adjusted Spreads and Option Based Durations." *Journal of Real Estate Finance and Economics* 1 (June 1988): 151-62.

Cox, John C., Jonathan E. Ingersoll, Jr., and Stephen A. Ross. "A Theory of the Term Structure of Interest Rates." *Econometrica* 53 (March 1985): 385-407.

Hendershott, Patric, and Robert Van Order. "Pricing Mortgages: An Interpretation of the Models and Results." *Journal of Financial Services Research* 1 (September 1987): 77-111.

Hummer, William B. "Say Hello to the CMO." *Bankers Monthly* 107 (December 1990): 54.

Schwartz, Eduardo S., and Walter N. Torous. "Prepayment and the Valuation of Mortgage-Backed Securities." *Journal of Finance* 44 (June 1989): 375-92.

Sullivan, Kenneth, and Linda Lowell. "Mortgage Pass-Through Securities." In *The Handbook of Mortgage-Backed Securities*, edited by Frank J. Fabozzi, 69-114. Chicago: Probus Publishing, 1988.

Toevs, Alden. "Laser Brains Rejoice: Analytical Methods Can Help Shape Market Equilibrium Prices." *Financial Analysts Journal* 46 (November/December 1990): 8-10.

The Convexity Trap: Pitfalls in Financing Mortgage Portfolios and Related Securities

James H. Gilkeson and Stephen D. Smith

The securitization of residential mortgages has been one of the biggest growth areas in credit markets during the last decade. In recent years the supply of new mortgage securities has far exceeded the supply of new corporate bonds (see, for example, Douglas T. Breeden 1991), and these instruments are being purchased in large part by financial institutions. Indeed, the relatively high returns and absence of default risk has made Government National Mortgage Association (GNMA) passthroughs, and their corresponding derivative securities, very attractive investment vehicles for banks in all size categories. Holdings of certificates of participation in residential mortgage pools and collateralized mortgage obligations by U.S. banks increased tenfold between 1985 and 1991 (from around $12 billion to $120 billion).[1] Moreover, these mortgage-related securities now make up about 8 percent of commercial bank assets.

The growing popularity of mortgage credit instruments has caused a tremendous increase in studies analyzing the unconventional cash flow characteristics of mortgage-backed securities. Unlike those of a true fixed-income security (such as a Treasury note or bond), the cash flows to mortgages, and therefore mortgage-backed securities, are influenced by the homeowner's option to prepay the mortgage without penalty. This clause makes traditional yield-to-maturity measures unreliable indicators of return because homeowners are more likely to prepay after rates have fallen. Myriad approaches have been developed to deal with this problem, including the option-adjusted spread and arbitrage-free spread measures of return (see, for example, John D. Finnerty and Michael Rose 1991, Lakhbir S. Hayre 1990, and Stephen D. Smith 1991).

This article was originally published in the Atlanta Fed's November/December 1992 Economic Review. *Gilkeson is a doctoral candidate at Duke University; Smith holds the H. Talmage Dobbs, Jr., Chair of Finance in the College of Business at Georgia State University and is a visiting scholar at the Atlanta Fed.*

While much work has been devoted to examining the relationship between the value of mortgage-backed securities and interest rates, there has been much less discussion of the interaction between mortgage values and the funding techniques traditionally used by banks. Regulators concerned about bank and thrift solvency should be aware that certain methods of financing mortgage portfolios or securitized mortgage-backed securities may expose institutions to capital losses in both high and low interest rate environments.[2]

In addition, portfolio managers should recognize that traditional methods used to hedge the interest rate risk of fixed-income securities may be counterproductive when applied to mortgage-related products. More generally, managers of financial institutions may lack adequate knowledge of the price/yield relationship associated with mortgage portfolios. It is important to understand that changes in the market values of mortgage-related assets and the liabilities used to fund them can interact in ways that cause unusual swings in the market value of equity positions. Managers need to be aware that the value of such equity (or capital) investments in mortgage portfolios, even those funded by (duration) "matched" liabilities, behaves very differently from the residual ownership claim in more traditional asset/liability combinations. Standard return measures, even those that are "adjusted" for risk, may fail to capture institutions' full exposure to interest rate fluctuations.

Practitioners are well aware that funding long-term assets with variable-rate liabilities produces exposure losses in high-rate environments. This article concerns itself with the potential gains and losses from issuing long-term liabilities to finance a portfolio of mortgages or a mortgage-backed security. It is not simply that prepayments alone cause interest rate risk. Rather, it is the asymmetric response of prepayments to rate changes that exposes the manager to risk in both high- and low-rate environments.

This article reviews the concepts of duration and convexity and ways these measures are influenced by prepayments.[3] The discussion then analyzes how equity values change with rates for alternative financing arrangements. Special attention is paid to a so-called "convexity trap" (equity losses in both low- and high-rate environments) when mortgage-backed securities are financed by fixed-rate liabilities. Finally, some solutions to the risk problem are presented. These include higher initial equity investments and various hedging instruments such as interest rate options, interest rate caps and floors, interest-only and principal-only strip securities, and traded futures contracts.

Prepayments, Mortgage Values, And Negative Convexity

An investment in a fixed-rate mortgage-backed security promises a uniform stream of payments over the life of the contract. For the moment, suppose that the mortgage either disallows prepayments or that prepayments are a fixed proportion of the mortgage pool balance. Chart 1 shows the relationship between the market value of this mortgage-backed security and interest rates. (The box on page 159 provides the example used to construct Charts 1-6 and Tables 1-2.) The absolute value of the slope of this function is often referred to as the security's duration.[4] The duration measure can be viewed as the weighted average maturity of the security, with the weights being the present value of each cash flow divided by the present value of all the cash flows (the price). Unlike maturity, which represents only the timing of the last cash flow, duration recognizes that some cash flows will be received before maturity and that these timing differences influence the security's interest rate sensitivity. Indeed, as noted earlier, the (percentage) change in price as rates change is the duration. Therefore, the slope of the line relating price to interest rates (approximately) equals the security's duration.

Notice, however, that in the case of the fixed prepayment portrayed in Chart 1, the slope (or duration) gets smaller as rates increase. This shape implies that the security's value is decreasing more slowly as market interest rates increase. The change in the duration (or rate of change in the price) is referred to as the convexity of the security, and in this case the convexity is positive. Positive convexity implies that the duration of the security is inversely related to the level of interest rates: when rates are high, later payments get less weight (in a present-value sense) than when rates are low (earlier cash flows are relatively more valuable in high-rate environments).

By way of contrast, Chart 2 shows the market value of a mortgage-backed security whose prepayment rate (realistically) increases as interest rates decline. Notice that the value is still decreasing as rates increase and increasing as rates decline. However, over most of this range of rates, the duration of the mortgage is increasing as rates increase. Similarly, the duration is decreasing as rates decline. This characteristic, called negative convexity, requires that cash flows not only increase as rates decline but that, at least for some time periods, they increase at an increasing rate. (The appendix contains a more mathematically

Chart 1
Constant-Prepayment Mortgage
(Market Value)

Value as a Percent of Par

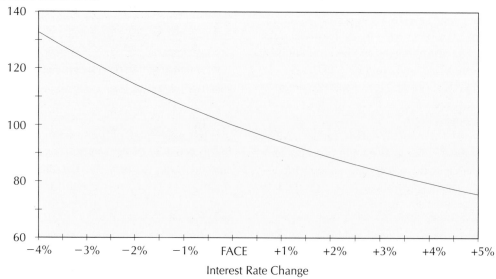

Interest Rate Change

Chart 2
Variable-Prepayment Mortgage
(Market Value)

Value as a Percent of Par

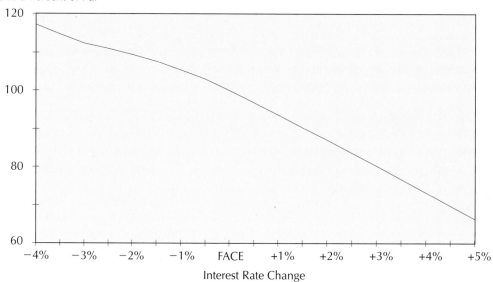

Interest Rate Change

rigorous discussion of this issue.) The intuitive explanation for this unusual value/rate relationship as rates decline is that prepayments are speeding up at exactly the time that these funds must be reinvested at low interest rates. On the other hand, there are few early cash flows in high-rate environments as prepayment rates decline or cease altogether. Therefore, the weighted maturity measure (duration) is increasing as rates rise because less weight is being placed on early cash flows when rates are high. Notice, however, that at a certain low-rate level prepayments (which cannot exceed 100 percent) begin to flatten out, and the value/rate relationship may return to one of positive convexity. In other words, at some (low enough) interest rate, an increase in prepayments is unlikely, and the mortgage portfolio behaves like a fixed-income security.

The following discussion analyzes the ways that three different financing arrangements might influence equity values, depending on whether the funds are placed in a true fixed-income security or a mortgage with varying prepayment rates. The first financing instrument considered is a fixed-term, fixed-rate certificate of deposit (CD). The duration of this instrument is chosen so that liability is initially duration-matched with both assets.[5] Chart 3A shows both the value of a constant prepayment mortgage and the value of the CD as a function of interest rates. The distance between the two curves is the market value of capital. Notice that in this case the value of equity is relatively constant, regardless of the level of rates, because the percentage change in price is the same for both the asset and the liability. The duration is also a measure of the percentage change in price for a 1 percent change in rates, and this depiction is just another way of showing that the durations of the two securities go up and down together as rates change.

Another deposit source commonly used by banks is the fixed-term, fixed-rate deposit that allows the depositor to withdraw funds after paying an early-withdrawal penalty. These deposits typically pay a lower rate than no-withdrawal deposits, allowing a bigger spread (higher equity value) at par. If rates decline, consumers have no incentive to withdraw and, if the liability's initial maturity is chosen to duration-match the asset, the market value of equity remains relatively constant. However, if rates rise significantly, consumers may rationally elect to pay the withdrawal penalty in order to reinvest their funds at the new, higher rates (see, for example, James H. Gilkeson and Craig K. Ruff 1992). At high rates, the market value of the bank's equity position may decline or even become negative unless some hedging activity is under-

taken. Chart 3B shows an example of this funding strategy.

Finally, Chart 3C shows how the bank may elect to fund a constant prepayment mortgage security using short-term, floating-rate deposits, such as money market deposit accounts (MMDAs). These accounts typically pay the lowest rates, offering the highest equity value at par.[6] If interest rates fall, the rates on these deposits fall as well and the market value of the bank's equity increases. However, if interest rates rise, the deposit rates will also rise (leaving the market-value line for deposits flat) and the market value of equity will decrease quickly. Under this funding strategy, the bank will have to hedge against rising rates. While the market value changes shown in Chart 3 (and throughout the other graphs) will not immediately show up on an institution's balance sheet (which is in book-value terms), the lower net cash flows will eventually dilute earnings and, therefore, capital.

Charts 4A-C consider the same three financing alternatives for variable-prepayment mortgages that Charts 3A-C considered for fixed-prepayment mortgages. In Chart 3A, a fixed-term, no-withdrawal deposit was shown to "lock in" a positive equity value through duration matching. Chart 4A shows that, for a mortgage that exhibits negative convexity (as discussed previously), this kind of asset-liability management is not, by itself, feasible. If rates rise, the market value of the mortgage security falls more quickly than the cost of the deposits, implying a decrease in equity value. As rates decline, the market value of the mortgage security increases more slowly than the cost of deposits, again implying a decrease in equity value.

For fixed-rate, fixed-term deposits with a withdrawal option, the upside-rate risk is similar to that associated with fixed-prepayment mortgages. However, there is also the risk that, if rates fall far enough, the slower increase in mortgage value will be overwhelmed by the faster increase in the cost of the deposit, entailing a loss of equity value. Chart 4B represents this risk.[7]

If mortgages are financed by short-term, floating-rate deposits, as shown in Chart 4C, the interest rate risks are much the same as for financing fixed-prepayment instruments. Equity value grows as interest rates decrease and falls as they rise. However, a close comparison of Charts 3C and 4C will show that, in this case, the increase in equity value is smaller and the decrease in equity value is larger for mortgages with variable prepayments. However, Chart 4C shows that the institution still has only a one-sided hedging problem when using the floating-rate funding strategy.

Chart 3
Mortgage with Constant Prepayments

Fixed-Rate Funds
(no-withdrawal option)

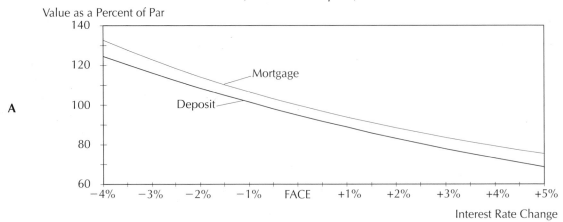

Fixed-Rate Funds
(withdrawal option)

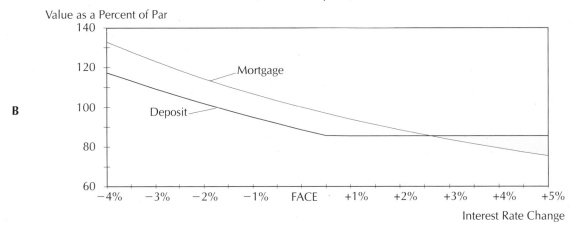

Floating-Rate Funds

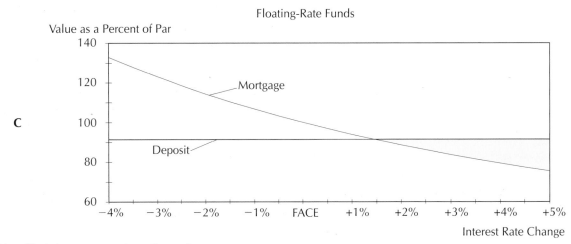

Note: Shaded areas represent negative equity.

Chart 4
Mortgage with Varying Prepayments

Fixed-Rate Funds
(no withdrawal option)

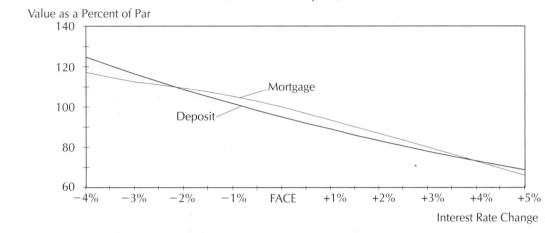

A

Value as a Percent of Par

Mortgage

Deposit

Interest Rate Change

Fixed-Rate Funds
(withdrawal option)

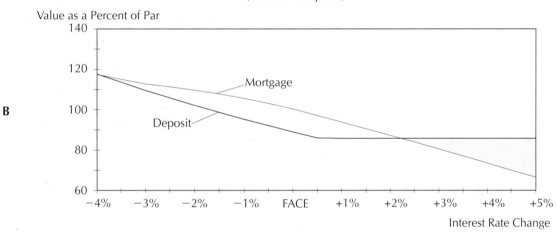

B

Value as a Percent of Par

Mortgage

Deposit

Interest Rate Change

Floating-Rate Funds

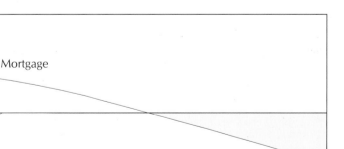

C

Value as a Percent of Par

Mortgage

Deposit

Interest Rate Change

Note: Shaded areas represent negative equity.

The Convexity Trap

It is worthwhile to take a closer look at the implications of Chart 4A, which demonstrates financing variable-prepayment mortgages with fixed-term deposits. By traditional asset-liability techniques, the asset and liability pictured are duration-matched. The market value of equity should not change as interest rates rise or fall, yet the figure clearly shows that equity decreases under any sizable interest rate movement, up or down.

This seeming paradox can be called a "convexity trap," to coin a phrase.[8] The duration-matching strategy ignores the effects of varying prepayments or, equivalently, of negative convexity. Although the duration of the mortgage and the deposit are initially matched (at the face interest rate), the convexities are of opposite signs (the mortgage is negatively convex, and the deposit is positively convex). As rates fall, the deposit curve becomes steeper as the mortgage curve gets flatter. Similarly, when rates rise, the mortgage curve gets steeper and the deposit curve flattens. The durations are no longer matched at rates other than par, implying that equity cannot be held constant except by using hedging instruments, which protect equity from large swings in interest rates, either up or down. Of course, the magnitude of potential losses in low-rate environments is limited (because nominal interest rates generally do not fall below zero). (See the box on page 159.)

Equity Cushions and Off-Balance-Sheet Hedging Instruments

Purchasers of mortgage-backed securities can try to protect themselves from losses associated with large interest rate swings in a variety of ways. The most straightforward involves reducing the leverage ratio used to fund the security. In this case, the initial equity cushion is a higher percentage of par value. Charts 5A-C compare three initial equity positions: 10 percent, 5 percent, and 3 percent of the purchase price, respectively. The liability used is the fixed-rate deposit with a no-withdrawal clause, but the same idea would apply with early withdrawal as well. The extreme cases can be seen by comparing Chart 5A with Chart 5C. With a 10 percent initial investment, the bank can withstand rate movements over a 9 percent range and still retain a positive market value of equity. Alternatively, Chart 5C shows that with a 3 percent initial in-

vestment the equity value of the position will turn negative if rates either decline by roughly 1.5 percent or increase by 3 percent. Moreover, as noted earlier, this relatively small rate window would persist even if the original par interest rate were 9 percent or 10 percent. For example, purchasers of 9 percent mortgage-backed securities who fund with 3 percent equity capital, with the remainder being funded by 7 percent fixed-rate liabilities, could encounter a negative equity position (in market-value terms) if rates should fall to around 7.5 percent. Keep in mind that the prepayment assumptions used here are relatively conservative, so the potential problem could be more severe than that shown in Chart 5C.

Other alternatives for hedging the convexity trap involve the use of off-balance-sheet instruments. For example, the portfolio manager could purchase interest rate caps and floors. An interest rate cap is an agreement whereby one party agrees, for an up-front fee, to pay a counterparty the difference between market interest rates and some base rate, in the event that future market rates should rise above the cap rate. Conversely, an interest rate floor can be purchased that pays off the difference between a base rate and market rates should future interest rates fall below the floor. Such instruments are not costless. However, the simultaneous purchase of an interest rate cap and floor at the ends of the interest rate range would provide some insurance against large rate swings and, therefore, the negative convexity of the mortgage. In this case, the net hedged position (the market value of the mortgage plus the caps and floors minus the cost of the deposit) would remain positive. Peter A. Abken (1989) and Keith C. Brown and Donald J. Smith (1988) provide good introductions to the mechanics of interest rate caps and floors.

A less esoteric, but potentially useful, approach to hedging these convexity-induced swings in value involves the purchase of put and call options on Treasury bonds. Chart 6 shows the hedged and unhedged value of equity as a function of interest rates for the duration-matched funding strategy. The unhedged curve is simply the difference between the asset and liability value curves in Chart 5B. The initial equity position is 5 percent of assets. The options are puts and calls on a thirty-year, 8 percent coupon-rate Treasury bond. The strike prices are 90 (for the put) and 110 (for the call). The hedged market value of equity function shows that purchasing such puts and calls can be used to lock in the market value of equity. The assumption used in Chart 6 is that the up-front cost of purchasing the options is 1 percent of the mortgage's par value. Therefore, the net market

Chart 5
The Convexity Trap under Varying Initial Equity Positions

10% Initial Equity

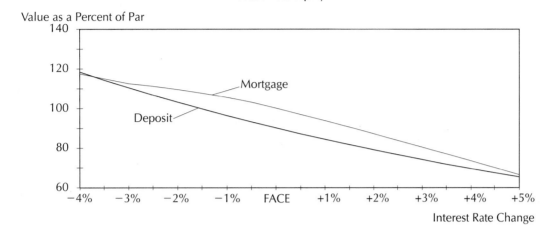

A

5% Initial Equity

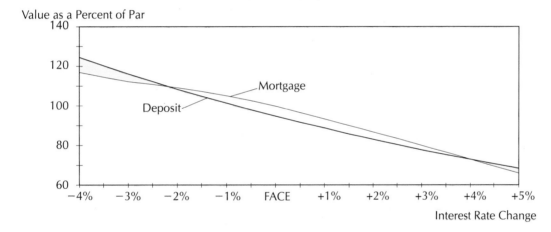

B

3% Initial Equity

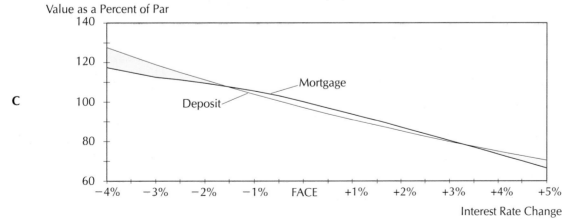

C

Note: Shaded areas represent negative equity.

Chart 6
Market Value of Equity
(Hedged versus Unhedged)

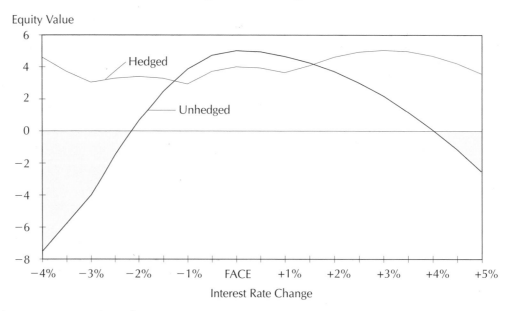

Note: Shaded areas represent negative equity.

value of equity is lower than 5 percent (5% − 1% = 4%) but still roughly constant.

A third off-balance-sheet hedge involves principal-only and interest-only securities. As their names imply, these contracts pay off only as a function of principal and interest payments on the mortgage pool, respectively. When properly priced, the market value of an interest-only security plus that of a principal-only security must equal the value of the mortgage-backed security when purchased alone. Not surprisingly, the value of interest-only securities tends to move directly with interest rates because in high-rate environments prepayments tend to slow down and more interest income is received during the life of the contract. On the other hand, the value of principal-only securities tends to move inversely with rates. When rates fall, the values tend to rise as principal repayments speed up and the discount rate factor falls. Thomas J. O'Brien (1992) provides a discussion of the valuation of interest-only securities, principal-only securities, and whole mortgages.

A final off-balance-sheet hedging alternative would be to create a short position in the Treasury bond futures market. For small interest rate changes it is possible to estimate the change in the mortgage portfolio value (including the effect of changing prepayment rates) with some precision. As stated earlier, the value of the mortgage portfolio will increase as rates fall and decrease as rates increase. Conversely, the short futures position will increase in value as rates rise and decrease as rates fall. Because futures are not subject to prepayment risks, the change in value given a particular rate movement is known. The proper strategy is to short (sell) a specific number of contracts so that, if rates rise, the loss in value to the mortgage portfolio is approximately offset by the gain in value to the futures contracts and vice versa if rates fall.

Each of these strategies has some advantages and disadvantages. The use of higher capital ratios is the most straightforward, but it involves the opportunity cost of allocating capital for this purpose. Purchasing interest rate caps and floors or T-bond puts and calls is much like purchasing an insurance policy.[9] For a fixed fee, paid up-front, the risks from both upward and downward rate movements are covered. However, these insurance-type contracts present three potential problems. First, because options tend to be short-term (at most nine months), the "insurance contract" must be rewritten in no more than nine months at an unknown future "premium." Second, options can often be the

An Example

The graphs presented in this article are constructed using representative mortgage asset and deposit liability pools and a set of conservative mortgage prepayment and deposit withdrawal assumptions. On the asset side, it is assumed that the bank holds a $1 million pool of 8 percent mortgages, all currently at par. For Charts 1 and 3A-C, a constant annual prepayment rate of 6 percent is used. This rate is equivalent to 100 percent of the Public Securities Association rate, a prepayment rate standard developed in the 1970s. Although a constant level of prepayments will cause the mortgage pool to mature faster, the convexity characteristics, as shown in these four graphs, are similar to those of a coupon-paying annuity (that is, they exhibit positive convexity).

Charts 2 and 4A-C incorporate a prepayment schedule in which prepayment rates rise as mortgage rates fall (see, for example, Smith 1991) and vice versa. Table 1 shows mortgage values, as a percentage of par, for various market rate changes. The first column shows the alternative market rates for mortgage-backed securities. Prepayments are assumed to be 6 percent at par. The second and third columns provide the constant prepayment rate and the corresponding market value of the mortgage-backed security (shown in Chart 1). The fourth column shows moderate changes in prepayment rates as interest rates change, and the fifth column provides the corresponding market value. The fifth column is represented in Chart 2. Finally, the sixth and seventh columns show "fast" prepayments and corresponding market values, respectively. If charted, the last column would look similar to Chart 2, differing in that would display more negative convexity.

The convexity trap displayed here is not dependent on mortgage rates falling to 4 percent. Table 1 could be reconstructed using a 10 percent coupon rate and the risk of negative equity would still exist for rate declines of 2 percent

to 3 percent (that is, market rates of 7 percent to 8 percent). It is the market rate relative to the coupon rate, rather than the absolute level of rates, that causes the relationship between prices and rates to be negatively convex.

On the liability side, Charts 3A-C and 4A-C compare the effect on equity of three funding alternatives. In each of the three cases, the market value of the cash flows is calculated using a discount rate equal to the current mortgage rate minus 2 percent (200 basis points). In Charts 3A and 4A, a pool of eight-and-a-half-year, 6 percent interest bank notes, making monthly coupon payments, is considered. These deposits may not be withdrawn under any circumstances. This maturity was chosen because it is duration-matched (when variable prepayment effects are ignored) with the thirty-year, 8 percent mortgage. In Charts 3B and 4B, another pool of eight-and-a-half-year, 5 percent interest bank notes making monthly coupon payments is utilized for funding purposes. These deposits may be withdrawn upon payment of a penalty equal to two years' interest (or 10 percent). Note that the market value of the deposit flattens out at 90 percent of par (which is 100 percent minus the 10 percent penalty for early withdrawal).

Finally, in Charts 3C and 4C, a pool of floating-rate deposits is used. The deposit rate is equal to the fixed-term deposit rate minus 3 percent. Note that the market values of these floating-rate deposits remain constant, at less than par, over all interest rates. These are a cheap source of funds, but they always cost the same relative to the current mortgage rate. In summary, Charts 1, 2, 3A-C, and 4A-C were not constructed using extreme data assumptions. The convexity effects of actual mortgage and deposit prices should be the same or greater than those seen here. For completeness, Table 2 shows the market value of the alternative funding sources as a function of market rates.

most expensive method of hedging interest rate risk. An option, by nature, can never be worth less than zero. The price of the option reflects this limited liability. Finally, as these instruments are based on Treasury rates, their values reflect positive convexity while, as stated earlier, mortgage portfolios often exhibit negative convexity. As can be seen in Chart 6, option-hedged equity values continue to show some volatility. The remaining convexity mismatch can, however, be corrected by purchasing a series of options at different strike prices.

It is often argued that interest-only securities and principal-only securities provide the best protection for prepayment risks because these instruments are subject to the same prepayment effects as mortgage

portfolios. Further, as the interest-only securities and principal-only securities are based on thirty-year mortgage pools, the hedge positions do not have to be frequently rewritten (in contrast to option-based strategies). However, this approach is subject to a somewhat subtle, though quite important, risk. When hedging with options or futures contracts, the only prepayment risk comes from the mortgage portfolio being hedged. While prepayment rates can be estimated for alternative future interest rates, they cannot be exactly predicted. If hedging is undertaken using interest-only securities and principal-only securities, three prepayment rate schedules must be estimated, one each for the mortgage portfolio, the mortgage

Table 1
Discounted Present Value of Thirty-Year Mortgage-Backed Security (MBS)
Cash Flows for Alternative Prepayment Rates
(8 percent coupon rate)

Current Mortgage Rate	Constant Prepayment		Moderate Prepayment		Fast Prepayment	
	Rate	MBS Value	Rate	MBS Value	Rate	MBS Value
4%	0.06	132.82	0.18	117.18	0.42	108.52
	0.06	127.74	0.18	114.72	0.42	107.38
5%	0.06	122.98	0.18	112.37	0.42	106.26
	0.06	118.53	0.16	110.96	0.36	105.88
6%	0.06	114.35	0.14	109.36	0.30	105.40
	0.06	110.43	0.12	107.52	0.24	104.75
7%	0.06	106.74	0.10	105.40	0.18	103.82
	0.06	103.27	0.08	102.92	0.12	102.39
8%	0.06	100.00	0.06	100.00	0.06	100.00
	0.06	96.91	0.054	96.81	0.054	96.81
9%	0.06	94.00	0.048	93.58	0.048	93.58
	0.06	91.24	0.042	90.31	0.042	90.31
10%	0.06	88.63	0.036	87.00	0.036	87.00
	0.06	86.18	0.030	83.66	0.030	83.66
11%	0.06	83.81	0.024	80.27	0.024	80.27
	0.06	81.58	0.018	76.85	0.018	76.85
12%	0.06	79.46	0.012	73.38	0.012	73.38
	0.06	77.44	0.006	69.88	0.006	69.88
13%	0.06	75.52	0.000	66.33	0.000	66.33

pool on which the interest-only security is based, and the mortgage pool on which the principal-only security is based. If actual prepayments vary widely across groups of mortgages the hedge may, on net, be much less effective in practice than alternative strategies.

The principal advantage of hedging with futures contracts is the low up-front cost. Futures positions are always entered into at the current market price so that the only initial cost is the exchange transaction fee. Further, as the risk of upward and downward rate movements is retained, no "insurance" fee is paid. However, futures contracts are marked to market, with the gains or losses paid each day. With options, daily gains and losses are experienced only on paper until the instrument is exercised or sold. A further problem with futures-based hedging, as with options-based hedging, is that the underlying instrument is a Treasury bond, which exhibits positive convexity. As rates change, it is necessary to adjust the hedge ratio (change the number of futures contracts held). Specifically, as rates rise (and T-bond prices fall) it is necessary to

short (sell) additional contracts. Conversely, as rates fall (and T-bond prices rise) the short hedge position must be decreased, requiring that some contracts be bought. Futures-based hedging is often referred to as a dynamic hedging strategy because of the need for continual adjustment of the hedge position. This point brings out a final concern with futures-based or dynamic hedging. What if rates move up and then move back down? According to the strategy, a manager would first short additional contracts (at the low price) and then buy back those contracts (at the high price). Buy high and sell low is not generally a profitable business strategy. A manager must, however, weigh these potential losses against the higher up-front cost of purchasing options.

In summary, there is no clear-cut best hedging strategy. Users must weigh the fixed costs of each choice against the risks of differing prepayments or high interest rate volatility. Finally, transactions and monitoring costs of frequent adjustments to the hedge ratio must be considered.

Table 2
Discounted Present Value of Potential Funding Sources

Current Mortgage Rate	Deposit Discount Rate[a]	Eight-and-a-Half Year Banknote[b]	Eight-and-a-Half Year Banknote with Withdrawal Provision[c]	Money Market Deposit Account[d]
4%	0.020	131.24	123.42	96.20
	0.025	126.78	119.13	96.20
5%	0.030	122.48	114.99	96.20
	0.035	118.36	111.01	96.20
6%	0.040	114.39	107.20	96.20
	0.045	110.58	103.53	96.20
7%	0.050	106.91	100.00	96.20
	0.055	103.39	96.61	96.20
8%	0.060	100.00	93.35	96.20
	0.065	96.74	90.22	96.20
9%	0.070	93.61	90.00	96.20
	0.075	90.59	90.00	96.20
10%	0.080	87.69	90.00	96.20
	0.085	84.91	90.00	96.20
11%	0.090	82.22	90.00	96.20
	0.095	79.64	90.00	96.20
12%	0.100	77.16	90.00	96.20
	0.105	74.77	90.00	96.20
13%	0.110	72.47	90.00	96.20

[a] It is assumed that the proper discount rate for all liabilities is the eight-and-a-half-year optionless certificate-of-deposit rate.

[b] This is a fixed-term (eight-and-a-half years), fixed-rate (6.0 percent) certificate that cannot be withdrawn.

[c] This is a fixed-term (eight-and-a-half years), fixed rate (5.0 percent) certificate that can be withdrawn. The withdrawal penalty is two years' interest (2 • 5% = 10%). The assumption used is that the balance will be withdrawn and reinvested whenever the discounted present value falls below 90 percent of par.

[d] This is a demand deposit paying the current eight-and-a-half-year rate minus 3 percent (300 basis points).

Conclusion

Mortgage-backed securities have become popular investment vehicles for managers of financial institutions. Much has been written about prepayment options and how to adjust return measures to reflect this variable. This article has provided an introduction to the interactions between variable prepayments and the choice of liabilities used to fund investments in mortgage securities. The discussion highlights the fact that variable prepayments often cause mortgage durations to react to interest rate changes in a fashion opposite that of a true fixed-income asset. The negative convexity of the mortgage creates a situation in which an institution that funds mortgage purchases with duration-matched liabilities may expose itself to capital losses should rates either increase or decrease dramatically. This convexity trap is contrasted with the alternative strategy, which uses floating-rate securities to fund the purchase of the mortgage-backed security. In the latter case the institution faces losses only if interest rates should increase. The examples presented show the possibility of negative equity values for rate decreases as small as 150 basis points below the face, or par, interest rate. Methods for hedging convexity risks are discussed, and it is shown that increasing capital ratios or off-balance-sheet instruments can offset much of the risk of negative net worth positions in mortgage-related investments.

Managers should be aware that the interest rate risk of funding mortgage-backed securities with fixed-rate liabilities is more, rather than less, complex than using floating-rate securities to fund the same mortgage purchase. This fact does not mean that mortgage-backed securities should be funded short-term and the net position left unhedged, however. Rather, managers should realize that they are carrying up- and downside risk should they fund the same mortgage-backed security with duration-matched liabilities.

In conclusion, asset/liability decisions should be made jointly. Relative value measures of mortgage-backed securities (such as the option-adjusted-spread measure) assume that the mortgage is duration-matched with some base security. This article shows that, unfortunately, for anything more than very small rate changes, such matching does not lock in the market value of capital for purchasers of variable prepayment mortgage portfolios or mortgage-backed securities. In-

deed, in this case the actual return on invested capital in the mortgage-backed security may fall below the expected return in both high- and low-rate environments. Managers should be sensitive to the convexities of alternative mortgage-backed security pools and how much of the reported excess return is compensation for this risk. Likewise, regulators should be aware that a duration-matched investment in mortgage-backed securities does not necessarily reflect the same interest rate risk as, say, a matched position in Treasury bonds.

Appendix

This appendix contains a simple presentation of the condition necessary for variable-prepayment mortgages to have the negative convexity property discussed in the text. For simplicity, let the term structure be flat and let the expected cash flow per period from the mortgage portfolio be C_t. O'Brien (1992), for example, shows what C_t would be in terms of a constant-prepayment rate and a fixed-coupon rate on the mortgage pool. Notice that if the prepayment rate is a function of market interest rates (not a constant), then C_t will vary as market rates change. If the term structure is flat, the mortgage price is just

$$P = \sum_{t=1}^{t=N} \frac{C_t}{(1+r)^t},\qquad (1)$$

where r is the market yield to maturity, Σ is the sum operator, N is the maturity, and P is the price.

Because the analysis of duration and convexity are in percentage terms, it is convenient to use the continuously compounded rate i, $i = \ln(1+r)$, where $\ln(\cdot)$ is the natural log function. Taking the derivative of $\ln(P)$ with respect to i yields a measure of duration,

$$\frac{d \ln P}{di} = -D = \sum_{t=1}^{t=N}\left[\left(\frac{d \ln C_t}{di} - t\right)w_t\right],\qquad (2)$$

where D is the duration and w_t is the present value of period t's cash flow divided by the sum of the present value of the cash flows (the price). If $(d\ln C_t)/(di) = 0$ for all periods t, as would be the case with either no prepayments ($C_t = C$) or a constant prepayment rate, equation (2) is just the standard measure of duration,

$$D = \sum_{t=1}^{t=N} (t w_t).$$

In any case, it is the change in duration with respect to interest rates that is of interest here.[1]

Taking the derivative of equation (2) with respect to i and doing some algebra results in

$$\frac{d^2 \ln P}{di^2} = \sum_{t=1}^{t=N}\left[\left(\frac{d \ln C_t}{di} - t\right)^2 w_t\right] + \sum_{t=1}^{t=N}\left[\frac{d^2 \ln C_t}{di^2} w_t\right].\qquad (3)$$

Notice that the first term on the right-hand side is the sum of squared terms multiplied by positive numbers (the w_t's). Therefore, it is always positive. So, unless

$$\sum_{t=1}^{t=N} \{[(d^2 \ln C_t)/(di^2)]w_t\} < 0,$$

the mortgage will display positive convexity (similar to a fixed-income security). In order to get negative convexity, the percentage change in the cash flows must, on average (with weights w_t) decrease at an increasing rate as interest rates rise. Put another way, the variable-prepayment function must be such that on average the cash flows are increasing at an increasing rate as interest rates fall. This property alone is not enough, of course, because the first term is always positive.

Finally, the fact that the price, P, is a monotone increasing function of $\ln P$ and r is monotone increasing in i establishes that the price itself will have the same qualitative properties with respect to i that $\ln P$ does. These facts establish the link between the pictures in the text (relating P and r) and equation (3) in this appendix.

Note

1. Note that the standard duration measure will, however, differ for the zero-prepayment and constant-prepayment rate scenarios because for $C_t = C$ (a constant),

$$w_t = [1/(1+r)^t]/\{\sum_{t=1}^{t=N} [1/(1+r)^t]\},$$

while for $C_t \neq C$,

$$w_t = [C_t/(1+r)^t]/\{\sum_{t=1}^{t=N} [C_t/(1+r)^t]\}.$$

Notes

1. Because of their tax advantages (as qualifying real estate assets for thrifts) and flexibility, one of the largest growth rates in holdings has come from a particular type of collateralized mortgage obligation—namely, real estate mortgage investment conduits, or REMICS.

2. The terms mortgage portfolio and mortgage-backed security will be used interchangeably when there is no ambiguity.

3. Bartlett (1991, chap. 7), provides an alternative introduction to these concepts in the context of mortgage-related securities.

4. Technically, the slope of the function displayed in the figures is minus the duration multiplied by the price. Duration measures percentage changes.

5. More specifically, a deposit is chosen such that the resulting duration of equity is zero. It can be shown that $D_E = D_A - (L/A)D_L$, where L/A is the liability (L) to asset (A) ratio in market value terms, D_E, D_A, and D_L are the duration of equity, assets, and liabilities, respectively. Choosing $D_E = 0$ is consistent with the idea that investors have a very short-term horizon. See, for example, Smith and Spudeck (1993, chap. 8) for a discussion of this point. As an example, consider a fifteen-year, 8 percent coupon mortgage. If prepayments are fixed at 6 percent annually, this asset has a duration of four and three-fourths years, or fifty-seven months. If the initial equity investment is 5 percent, then L/A equals .95. Setting $D_E = 0$ implies that D_L is equal to sixty months or five years. Therefore, a five-year, pure-discount CD will roughly "duration-match" a fifteen-year mortgage. The result should be a steady equity value, assuming these fixed prepayments of 6 percent annually (similar to that portrayed in Chart 3A). Keep in mind, however, that the durations of amortizing instruments (like mortgages) and nonamortizing instruments (like CDs) change at different rates through time. Therefore, hedges must be periodically adjusted. This scenario is discussed in more detail in a later section.

6. The implicit assumption is that the liquidity preference theory of the term structure is true (see, for example, Abken 1990), indicating that, on average, funding short-term is cheaper than funding long-term.

7. The withdrawal option given to depositors in this case allows the bank to offer a lower rate when compared with the case portrayed in Chart 4A. This provision allows an equity cushion vis-à-vis the no-withdrawal case.

8. The term is used because it seems representative of the price behavior associated with large changes in interest rates.

9. These strategies are almost identical, though the instruments trade on different exchanges.

References

Abken, Peter A. "Interest-Rate Caps, Collars, and Floors." Federal Reserve Bank of Atlanta *Economic Review* 74 (November/December 1989): 2-24.

_____. "Innovations in Modeling the Term Structure of Interest Rates." Federal Reserve Bank of Atlanta *Economic Review* 75 (July/August 1990): 2-27.

Bartlett, William W. *Mortgage-Backed Securities: Products, Analysis, Trading*. New York: New York Institute of Finance, 1991.

Breeden, Douglas T. "Risk, Return, and Hedging of Fixed Rate Mortgages." *Journal of Fixed Income* 1 (September 1991): 85-107.

Brown, Keith C., and Donald J. Smith. "Recent Innovations in Interest Rate Risk Management and the Reintermediation of Commercial Banking." *Financial Management* 17 (Winter 1988): 45-58.

Finnerty, John D., and Michael Rose. "Arbitrage-Free Spread: A Consistent Measure of Relative Value." *Journal of Portfolio Management* 17 (Spring 1991): 65-77.

Gilkeson, James H., and Craig K. Ruff. "The Valuation of Retail CD Portfolios." Paper presented at the Financial Management Association Meetings, San Francisco, California, 1992.

Hayre, Lakhbir S. "Understanding Option-Adjusted Spreads and Their Use." *Journal of Portfolio Management* 16 (Summer 1990): 68-69.

O'Brien, Thomas J. "Elementary Growth Model Valuation Expressions for Fixed-Rate Mortgage Pools and Derivatives." *Journal of Fixed Income* 2 (June 1992): 68-79.

Smith, Stephen D. "Analyzing Risk and Return for Mortgage-Backed Securities." Federal Reserve Bank of Atlanta *Economic Review* (January/February 1991): 2-11.

_____, and Raymond E. Spudeck. *Interest Rates: Principles and Applications*. Fort Worth, Tex.: Dryden Press, forthcoming, 1993.

Unusual Options

Path-Dependent Options

William C. Hunter and David W. Stowe

A relatively new class of options—the so-called path-dependent options—has become increasingly popular in recent years. Like other options, these contracts give their owners the right—but not the obligation—to buy or sell a specific quantity of an underlying asset (stock, bond, futures contract, commodity, and so forth) at a specified price, called the strike or exercise price, during a specific time period.

Since 1982 the use of path-dependent options has grown dramatically. A path-dependent option has a payout directly related to movements in the price of the underlying asset during the option's life. In principle, these options take many forms and can be contingent on virtually any statistic of the underlying asset's price path—for example, the high price, the low price, or the average price over some time period. Today path-dependent options are available on a host of assets including common stock, interest rate products, precious metals, commodities, foreign currencies, and stock indexes; they are often used with convertible securities issues and in merger transactions and have recently begun trading on two major exchanges.[1]

In many cases these options allow investors to limit their potential losses (and gains) and thus have a type of built-in insurance feature. They also allow investors with specialized knowledge about asset price volatility to exploit this information better in their investing and hedging activities. While factors such as cost or risk mean that path-dependent options will not satisfy every investor's needs, these options have generated interest by filling several voids or niches in derivative securities markets.

The sections that follow introduce the notion of path dependency, review the modern origins of path-dependent options, and give several examples of reasons that investors and institutions find these options attractive. The discussion also describes some essential features of three types of path-dependent

This article was originally published in the Atlanta Fed's March/April 1992 Economic Review. *Hunter is vice president and senior economist in charge of basic research in the Atlanta Fed's research department. Stowe is a former financial analyst in the department's macropolicy section.*

options—the lookback option, the barrier option, and the average-rate or Asian option. A forthcoming article in this *Economic Review* will describe in detail the valuation and pricing of these options, illustrate how they are used by individual investors and firms, and discuss their advantages and disadvantages (risks) as investment vehicles.

*T*he American Put Option

A call option conveys to its owner the right to buy the underlying asset while a put conveys the right to sell the underlying asset. An option that allows its owner to buy or sell the underlying asset (exercise the option) at any time during the life of the option is called an American option. An option allowing the owner to exercise his or her right only at the option's expiration or maturity date is called a European option.

The payoff on a European call or put option written on a share of common stock that pays no dividends depends only on the market price of the underlying common stock at maturity. That is, if T is the maturity date of the option, t is the current date, X is the exercise price, and S is the market price of the underlying common stock at time $T > t$, then the payoff or intrinsic value at T is equal to the larger of the quantities $(S - X)$ and zero for the call option and $(X - S)$ and zero for the put option. Using standard options notation, the payoff on the European call at time T is written as $max(S - X, 0)$ while the payoff on the European put at time T is equal to $max(X - S, 0)$. Payoff at time T, $(T > t)$, on the European call or put option on a stock that pays no dividends is independent of the particular path taken by the stock price during the period between the times t and T. Such standard European call and put options on a nondividend paying stock are the simplest examples of what are called path-independent options.

In contrast, an American put option written on a share of common stock has a path-dependent payoff structure. (This happens to be the case irrespective of whether the stock pays a dividend or not.) For example, looking forward from the perspective of date t, the payoff at time $T > t$ on the American put option depends not only on the price of the underlying stock at time T but also on the particular time path followed by the stock between times t and T.

An illustration will demonstrate the straightforward intuition behind the statement that the American put is an example of a path-dependent option. Assume that the underlying stock pays no dividend and that the put option is in the money—that is, the market price of the stock is less than the exercise price. The investor holding the put could exercise the option and receive an amount of cash equal to the exercise price minus the current price of the stock that he has just sold, $X - S$. In turn, this cash can be invested at the risk-free rate of interest to earn money during the remaining life of the option. At expiration the investor receives the amount $X - S$, his original investment, plus the interest earned over the remaining life of the option. An investor choosing not to exercise the put and waiting until expiration would receive only the amount $X - S$. It should be obvious that if the stock price is close enough to zero at the date the investor chooses to exercise early, he or she will be better off; the principal and interest received from investing the proceeds will exceed the difference between the exercise price and the stock price at the option's maturity date. In addition, the cases in which early exercise is optimal occur when the put is selling for $X - S$ so that selling it would be less profitable than exercising it and investing the proceeds. The key condition making early exercise preferable is that the stock price follows a path that drops close enough to zero over the life of the option to make the principal and interest earned by exercising the option greater than the exercise price minus the stock price at maturity. Thus, the payoff to the investor is seen as path dependent.

*T*he Modern Origins of Path-Dependent Options: The Lookback Option

For both standard options and securities, specific examples having characteristics similar to path-dependent options can probably be traced back at least to the early 1800s. However, the modern treatment of these securities—the rigorous valuation or pricing of these claims on the basis of dynamic hedging principles—is a more recent phenomenon, set in motion in 1979 with publication of an article by M. Barry Goldman, Howard Sosin, and Mary Ann Gatto. The authors had derived an explicit valuation formula for a hypothetical option epitomizing the age-old finance dictum of buy low (cheap) and sell high (dear)—the so-called lookback option. To allow buying low and selling high, the exercise price on the lookback option is set at the expiration of the contract instead of at contract origination (as it is for standard options). That is, at expiration the owner could "look back over the life of the option" and choose as the exercise price the most favorable price that had occurred.

If a lookback call option were exercised, the owner would be able to buy the underlying asset at the lowest price that occurred during the life of the option. Similarly, the owner of a lookback put would be able to sell the underlying asset at its highest price realized over the life of the option. It is clear that the payoff on a lookback option depends not only on the underlying asset's price on the expiration date of the option but also on the particular path followed by the price of the asset over the life of the option, hence the path dependency.

Countering the argument that their research was a purely hypothetical exercise in contingent claims valuation, Goldman, Sosin, and Gatto (1979) argued that lookback options could be of value to investors as speculative and hedging instruments and could survive as traded securities. In less than two-and-a-half years the authors were proven correct. On March 16, 1982, Macotta Metals Corporation of New York introduced and began trading lookback options on gold, silver, and platinum. The lookback call gave an investor the right to buy gold, silver, or platinum at its ex post realized low price, and the lookback put allowed the investor to sell the precious metal at its ex post realized high price.

*U*ses of Path-Dependent Options

The choice of the particular price-path statistic on which a path-dependent option is based depends on the motivation of the option writer, ranging from wanting to control some particular risk to filling some niche in the market. Some specific examples illustrate this point.

On April 22, 1982, Manufacturers Hanover Corporation sold a $100 million note offering. The sale required holders to convert the securities at maturity in 1992 into shares of the company's common stock. The conversion price would be the lower of $55.55 and the average closing price of the common stock for the thirty-day period immediately preceding the notes' maturity. By making the conversion price dependent on the average price of the common stock, the company alleviated suspicions among investors that management would fraudulently manipulate the stock price upward just before the conversion date.[2]

The "capped" stock-index option is an example of an exchange-traded path-dependent option developed to fill a special niche or appeal to specific investors in

the market. Capped stock-index options, fairly new examples of path-dependent options, are so named because they place ceilings on profitability. Because of these ceilings, capped options are cheaper than traditional stock-index options. Capped options were launched during the fall of 1991 on both the Chicago Board Options Exchange and the American Stock Exchange. Like other index options, they can be used to protect the values of stock portfolios by providing a cheaper way to obtain portfolio insurance.

Capped options trade off the Standard and Poor's (S&P) 100 and 500 Indexes on the CBOE and the Major Market and Institutional Indexes on the Amex. Like the standard call option, the value of a capped call option increases if its underlying index goes up, and a capped put option's value increases if the index declines. If the underlying index fails to attain the level specified by the option contract, known as the strike price, the options expire worthless and the sellers keep all of the premiums they collected. On the other hand, if the indexes reach the strike price, sellers must pay the optionholders the difference between the index level and the strike price but no more than a fixed cap value.

Each of these options has a cap price. For the options currently trading on the CBOE the cap price is set thirty points above the strike price for a call and thirty points below the strike price for a put, giving the options a cap value of $3,000 (thirty points times $100 per point). For those trading on the Amex the cap price is set at twenty points above and below the strike price, yielding a cap value of $2,000 (20 points times $100 per point). The purpose of the cap price is to force automatic exercise of the options. If the underlying index closes at or above the cap price for a call option or at or below the cap price for the put option, the options are automatically exercised and the cap buyers are paid the cap value two days after exercise.

The following scenario illustrates the mechanics of the capped option. An investor believes that the stock market will rally modestly from its closing value of 378 for the S&P 500 index on, say, January 12, 1992, and the third Friday in March 1992, the expiration date for the cap. The strike or exercise price on capped calls is 390, making the cap price 420 (390 plus the thirty points for the S&P 500 index). If the index closes at or above 420 between January 12 and the third Friday in March 1992, the capped call purchaser will be paid $3,000 (the net profit would be less by the amount of the premium). If the index closes at a figure less than 420 but greater than the strike price of 390—for example, 400—the purchaser will be paid an amount equal to the value of the index minus the strike price, in this case ten points times $100 per point or $1,000. On the other hand, if the index fails to reach the strike price of 390, the option expires worthless and the seller keeps the entire premium collected.

As is true for other exchange-traded options, the owners of capped options can sell them in the open market before maturity. Clearly, the payoff on the capped option depends on the particular path the underlying index follows over the life of the option; the option is path dependent. One appealing characteristic of the capped put or call option is that the seller's or writer's risk is limited to the cap amount or value while theoretically there is no limit to the risk faced by the writer or seller of a standard stock-index or -equity option. This feature of capped options, which is essentially a kind of built-in insurance, should make investors more willing to write options on the indexes offering them.

Other Popular Path-Dependent Options

The average-rate option and the barrier option are two other frequently used path-dependent options that are growing in popularity. Both are currently used most extensively in the foreign exchange markets. However, their structure is such that their use will most likely increase in domestic markets in the future. The capped option discussed above exhibits some of the essential features of a barrier option.

Barrier Options. Simply stated, a barrier option is a path-dependent option that is either canceled, activated, or exercised if the underlying instrument (the stock index in the case of a capped index option) reaches a certain level, regardless of the point at which the underlying asset is trading at maturity. Barrier options, also known as knock-out, knock-in, or trigger options, are typically straight European options until or from the time the underlying instrument reaches the barrier price.

There are four popular types of barrier options: up-and-out, up-and-in, down-and-out, and down-and-in. With the up-and-out barrier, the option is canceled should the underlying instrument rise above a certain level. The up-and-in option, on the other hand, is worthless unless the underlying instrument rises above a certain level or price, at which point it becomes a normal put option. Down-and-out options are canceled if the underlying instrument falls below a certain price. Down-and-ins are activated only when the underlying instrument's price falls to a certain level.

Because of these extinguishing or activating features, barrier options are cheaper than ordinary European options and are thus attractive to investors who are averse to paying large premiums. In addition, as illustrated in the case of the capped option, the sellers or writers of barrier options may be able to limit their downside risk.

Average-Rate Options. Average-rate or Asian options are path-dependent options, European in structure, for which the strike price is based on the average (geometric or arithmetic) price of the underlying instrument over a specified period of time, so the actual strike price is not determined until the exercise date on the contract. For foreign exchange average-rate options, the actual practice is for the average to be taken from the option's start date to a preagreed setting date. For example, suppose that a U.S. exporter buys an average-rate floating-strike call option to purchase a foreign currency for U.S. dollars at the average exchange rate over some given period, with the option expiring at the end of the period. If the average exchange rate over the period is less than the spot exchange rate at the time payment is due to the foreign importer, the exporter would profit more from exercising the option than transacting at the spot exchange rate. On the other hand, if the period's average exchange rate exceeds the spot rate, the exporter is better off converting dollars at the current spot exchange rate, in which case the option expires worthless. This example also shows that it is possible to use average rate options to hedge or limit the uncertainty associated with regular foreign cash inflows and outflows as a result of volatile exchange rates.

Many multinational corporations use average-rate put options on foreign currencies to hedge their estimated monthly foreign exchange income in an effort to achieve some budgeted average exchange rate for the year. Hence, the design of this particular option is of great value to these corporations that are in the market on a regular basis. Current accounting principles provide for foreign currency transactions to be translated at either the spot rate at the time of the transaction or the spot rate for the date of the firm's balance sheet. Any variations can be flowed through into the firm's income. For a path-dependent put, the option can be exercised if the balance-sheet rate is less than the strike (average) rate, resulting in the appearance of additional income. This additional income is calculated by multiplying the nominal amount by the difference between the strike rate and the spot rate and subtracting from this figure the amount of premium paid:

Large multinational commercial banks offer average-rate currency options to their multinational customers because these companies' usual spot dealings leave them with an average exchange rate on their books. By selling path-dependent average-rate currency options, the banks offset the average-rate foreign exchange risk exposure on their books. The premiums banks receive enhance yield by reducing their funding costs or by lowering their average exchange rate. In addition, these banks stand to earn management fees and commissions in other areas as a result of these activities, so it is worth the risk they take. Because average-rate options have lower volatility than standard European options, they are cheaper to purchase.

Valuation of Path-Dependent Options

This section attempts to offer some insights into the valuation of two path-dependent options—the lookback and the average-rate option.

Valuing the Lookback Option. As is the case for most options, the key condition required to price the lookback option in the modern tradition is that it must be possible to hedge its risk. That is, it must be shown that the cashflow obligation(s) of the writer of a lookback call option can be exactly met by the payoff from another portfolio (a hedge portfolio). Indeed, Goldman, Sosin, and Gatto (1979) showed that such a hedge portfolio could be constructed so that the lookback option can be valued without regard to the risk premium in the underlying asset's expected return. These authors showed that when the risk-free interest rate was equal to exactly one-half the underlying asset's variance, the lookback call option is identical to the purchase of a straddle (a portfolio of puts and calls on the same assets at the same strike price) on the asset. Therefore, the writers of lookback calls can simply hedge their obligation by purchasing a straddle on the same underlying asset. Because the lookback option can be hedged, it can be valued using the risk-neutral pricing technology associated with the Black-Scholes (1973) paradigm.

Valuing an Average-Rate (Asian) Option. There are two types of average-rate or Asian options: the fixed-strike and floating-strike options. The payoff on a floating-strike Asian call option at expiration is equal to the greater of either zero or the difference between the underlying asset's terminal spot price and the average value of the asset over the life of the option—that is, $max(S - Avg_S, 0)$. It is comparable to a lookback call option for which the strike price is the average value of the underlying asset as opposed to its minimum value. Because mathematical complexities have prevented development of a closed-form analytic model (such as the Black-Scholes equation) to price such an instrument, these options must be valued with a numerical approximation technique such as Monte Carlo analysis.[3]

The value of an Asian option can never be greater than the value of a regular lookback call option, for which the strike price is the achieved minimum of the asset. Thus, the price of a regular lookback option sets an upper boundary on the average-rate option's value (because the minimum value is an extreme and the average is never equal to an extreme value unless all of the values are equal).

For fixed-strike options, the second type of average-rate option, the terminal payoff is the maximum of either zero or the difference between the average value of the underlying asset and a fixed strike price—$max(Avg_S - X, 0)$. The average can be computed using either the geometric average or the arithmetic average. Again, because of mathematical complexities no closed-form equation has been developed for pricing the average-rate option written on the arithmetic average.

Under the standard risk-neutral (Black-Scholes) pricing approach, it is assumed that the natural logarithm of stock price returns are normally distributed. In valuing an Asian option written on the geometric average of an asset's value over time, this standard assumption still holds because the product of the logarithm of stock price returns is normally distributed, and this option can be valued in closed form using the Black-Scholes approach. However, the assumption breaks down for an Asian option written on the arithmetic average because the sum of the logarithm of the stock price returns over time is no longer normally distributed. As a result, it is necessary to employ other valuation techniques for an average-rate option written on the arithmetic average of the underlying asset's price.[4]

Conclusion

It should be clear from this overview of path-dependent options that risk management is not a static field. New products and financial instruments are continuously being developed to meet new needs. While many risks can be managed with traditional hedging instruments such as standard options, futures contracts, and swaps, the rapid development of exotic options like the path-dependent options suggests that the market for innovative risk-management products is in no way saturated. The demand for these new instruments is likely to continue growing as long as risk-management techniques using traditional hedging vehicles require close monitoring, involve fairly high commissions or management costs, and fail to reduce risks in the way desired.

The development of path-dependent options is, however, only one response to the demand for innovative risk-management instruments. In addition, because these instruments build on existing standardized derivative products, they may not serve the needs of every investor or institution. Their future development is likely to tend toward greater customizing for specific situations.

It is well known that a portfolio of existing standard products can replicate the payoffs on most of the new derivative products such as those discussed here. Indeed, this very fact allows creation of risk-free hedge portfolios for these contracts and also makes it possible to price them using the familiar risk-neutral pricing technology. However, the management and effort required for existing products to duplicate the payoff from the newer contracts tend to be too expensive an alternative for individual investors. Thus, the financial services firms that produce these new contracts add value to the market. These products have made a place for themselves because they are tailored to meet specific risk-management and investment needs.

Notes

1. The Chicago Board Options Exchange (CBOE) and the American Stock Exchange (AMEX) both trade path-dependent options known as "capped options." These options are described in detail below.
2. Such suspicions on the part of investors were not totally unwarranted. In a separate case, two Merrill Lynch vice presidents were fired for allegedly artificially driving up the price of options on a portfolio under their management on Christmas eve of 1981 in an attempt to maximize their bonus, which was tied to the portfolio's December 24, 1981, closing value (*Wall Street Journal*, January 21, 1982, 4). This example also points out the advantage of making this type of path-dependent option contingent on the average price of the underlying asset over some extended period rather than the closing price on some particular day, as the chances for artificial manipulation are greatly reduced. The growing popularity of tying conversion prices or ratios to time averages of prices in mergers seems to reflect similar concerns.
3. Monte Carlo simulating is a numerical approximation technique that can be used to compute option values by simulating the path taken by the price of the asset underlying the option over time. By simulating numerous such price paths, the technique allows one to compute the expected value or price of the option with increasing precision as the number of iterations or runs of the simulation are increased. This technique is described in detail in the forthcoming *Review* article examining the valuation of path-dependent options.
4. A more thorough discussion of the valuation or pricing of the lookback and the average-rate options, including a brief tutorial on the basic tenets of option pricing using the modern risk-neutral pricing technology pioneered by Black and Scholes (1973), will appear in the forthcoming *Review* article referred to above. The article explains how Monte Carlo analysis can be used to price Asian options written on the arithmetic average as well as how these options can be used to hedge foreign exchange risks from the viewpoint of individual investors and multinational corporations. The reader interested in the basics of option pricing is referred to Hull (1990) and Kolb (1991).

References

Black, Fischer, and Myron Scholes. "The Pricing of Options and Corporate Liabilities." *Journal of Political Economy* 81 (May/June 1973): 637-59.

Goldman, M. Barry, Howard Sosin, and Mary Ann Gatto. "Path-Dependent Options: Buy at the Low, Sell at the High." *Journal of Finance* 34 (December 1979): 1111-27.

Hull, John. *Options, Futures, and Other Derivative Securities.* Englewood Cliffs, N.J.: Prentice-Hall, Inc., 1989.

Hunter, William C., and David W. Stowe. "Path-Dependent Options: Valuation and Applications." Federal Reserve Bank of Atlanta *Economic Review* (forthcoming 1992).

Kolb, Robert W. *Options: An Introduction.* Miami: Kolb Publishing Company, 1991.

Path-Dependent Options: Valuation and Applications

William C. Hunter and David W. Stowe

ath-dependent options, unlike most claims whose value depends on the behavior of some other assets, are contracts entitling their holders to a cash flow that depends on the price path taken by the asset (stock, bond, commodity, and the like) underlying the contract. A relatively new class of options, their popularity has grown dramatically over the last decade, since they were first traded in 1982. That year, the trading of lookback options—so-named because at expiration the owner can "look back" over the life of the option and choose to buy or sell the underlying asset at the most favorable price that had occurred—demonstrated the value for investors of such path-dependent options as speculative and hedging instruments and proved their viability as traded securities.[1]

Standard European call and put options (giving the right to buy or sell, respectively, an underlying asset only on a particular expiration date) written on shares of common stock that pay no dividends have what are termed path-independent payoff structures. That is, their payoff is not influenced by the changes in market price of the underlying common stock between the date the option is written and its maturity date. In contrast, the payoff structures of path-dependent options are directly related to the price path followed by the option's underlying asset over the life of the option. For example, a standard American put option (one that allows its owner to sell the underlying asset [exercise the option] at any time during the life of the option) written on a common stock has a path-dependent payoff structure.

Such path-dependent options have generated interest by filling several niches in derivative securities markets. Investors find them attractive because their design matches that of some financial contracts, giving them a kind of built-in insurance feature that makes it possible to limit potential losses and gains, and because they allow investors to better use their knowledge

This article was originally published in the Atlanta Fed's March/April 1992 Economic Review. *Hunter is vice president and senior economist in charge of basic research in the Atlanta Fed's research department. Stowe is a former financial analyst in the department's macropolicy section.*

of asset price volatility in investing and hedging. Although path-dependent options do offer certain benefits, factors such as design mismatches and cost or risk mean that they will not satisfy the needs of every investor. The discussion of their pricing that follows will consider in greater depth both the advantages and risks of using these instruments.

This article focuses on two popular kinds of path-dependent options—the lookback option described above and the average-rate or Asian option—and their valuation using hedge portfolio and risk-neutral pricing techniques. Used most extensively in the foreign exchange markets, the average-rate option is European in structure and has a strike price based on the geometric or arithmetic average of the price of its underlying instrument over a specific period. The essential characteristics of these two types of path-dependent options along with the history of their development and uses as investment vehicles are described in a complementary article in the March/April 1992 issue of this *Review*. In addition to describing some basic features of the pricing models used to value these options, the sections that follow illustrate how these pricing models are implemented in practice.

The discussion also includes a brief presentation of the basic tenets of option pricing using the modern risk-neutral pricing technology developed by John Cox and Stephen Ross (1976). In addition, it explains how Monte Carlo analysis can be used to price Asian options written on the arithmetic average as well as how these options can be used to hedge foreign exchange risks from the viewpoint of individual investors and multinational corporations.

Valuation of Path-Dependent Options

Path-dependent options, like most contingent claims (that is, those whose value is tied to some other asset's behavior), can be priced using the hedge portfolio valuation methodology developed by Black and Scholes (1973) mentioned above. In simple terms, this approach implies that the cash flow obligation(s) involved in, for example, a lookback call option can be exactly met by the payoff from another portfolio—a hedge or replicating portfolio. More technically, if stocks and bonds can be used to construct a portfolio investment strategy that would provide the same cash flows as the contingent claim at the same points in time, then at any point throughout the lifetime of the contingent claim the claim's price must equal the value of the stock-bond portfolio at that time. This stock-bond portfolio hedge strategy forms the basis of the risk-neutral valuation methodology. The fundamentals of this methodology are presented in Box 1. More thorough discussions of option pricing fundamentals can be found in John Hull (1989) and Robert W. Kolb (1991). (Readers might also find helpful the standard options pricing notation collected in Box 2.)

The following discussion examines the valuation or pricing of lookback and average-rate or Asian options.

Valuing a Lookback Call Option. The lookback option is often referred to as a "minimize regret" option because it gives the purchaser the right to buy an asset at its lowest price or sell it at its highest price attained over the option's life. On a more sophisticated level, because its value is determined by the high or

---

Box 1
Valuing Standard European Call Options

Like many analytical models in finance, the basic model for pricing a standard European call option written on a share of common stock—the Black-Scholes option pricing model (named after its developers, Fischer Black and Myron Scholes 1973)—is based on a set of assumptions which, though abstract, work to simplify the valuation process. That is, it is assumed that

- there are no transactions costs, taxes, or riskless arbitrage opportunities;
- the asset underlying the option does not pay dividends;
- stock prices follow a continuous time stochastic process;
- short selling with full use of proceeds is permitted; and

- the risk-free interest rate, r, is constant and the same for all maturities.

At the time a call option on a stock expires, its worth is the greater of either the difference between the stock price at that time and the option's exercise price or zero, represented as $max(S^* - X, 0)$. Without this condition a riskless arbitrage opportunity would arise. To price the option today when there is time remaining before expiration, $T - t > 0$, the option's terminal price has to be approximated and the present value of this price computed using an appropriate discount rate.

The movements of stock prices over time can be modeled as following a random or stochastic process called geometric Brownian motion, which means that the stock price returns, which are defined as the natural logarithm of the ratio of successive stock prices, $ln(S/S_{t-1})$, are log-normally distributed. This model of stock price movement can be generalized to a continuous-time Markov process known as an Ito process. In simple terms, a Markov process is a stochastic process in which the observed value of the stock price (state variable) tomorrow depends only on its observed value today. The Ito process is characterized by a smooth predictable component—for example, the expected rate of return on the stock—and a highly erratic component that adds uncertainty or noise to the stock price movement. (See Box 3 for further discussion).

Given the properties of a log-normal distribution, the expected stock value at the option's expiration date, S^*, can be determined using the following equation:

$$E(S^*) = Se^{(\mu - \sigma^2/2)(T-t)}. \tag{B1}$$

That is, the stock price is expected to rise continuously from today, t, until time period T, by its instantaneous continuously compounded expected rate of return μ, less one-half the stock's variance. The term σ represents the standard deviation of the expected returns, and the term $(\mu - \sigma^2/2)$ is called the drift rate of the stock price process.

A key aspect of the Black-Scholes model, however, is that one does not have to be concerned with the risk-adjusted expected return on a stock, μ. It has been shown that if an investor held a portfolio containing a long position in a proportionate share of a stock, ΔS, and a short position in one call option on the stock, $-C$, then the investor would be perfectly hedged, with the portfolio generating a riskless rate of return. Perfectly hedged, the portfolio is equivalent to investing in a risk-free bond, B. This portfolio is given by

$$B = \Delta S - C. \tag{B2}$$

As is true for a risk-free bond, arbitrage will force the hedge portfolio to earn the riskless rate of return (Cox and Ross 1976). Therefore, an option's value will not be affected by a particular stock's expected rate of return, μ, since it can be replaced with the riskless interest rate, r, using the Cox-Ross risk-neutral valuation framework.

If a call option at the time of expiration has a payoff of $max(S^* - X, 0)$, the call option's value today is the present value of this expected payoff at expiration. That is,

$$c = e^{-r(T-t)}E[max(S^* - X, 0)], \tag{B3}$$

where the term $e^{-r(T-t)}$ represents continuous discounting of the terminal payoff. The call value can also be derived using equation (B2) since the payoff from investing in a call option can be replicated by purchasing a proportionate share of stock, ΔS, and borrowing at the risk-free rate, that is, short selling a Treasury security. Thus,

$$c = \Delta S - B. \tag{B4}$$

Black and Scholes derived an equation that essentially consolidates all of the steps required to compute the discounted value of a call option's expected payoff at expiration. This equation can be written as follows (see Robert Jarrow and Andrew Rudd 1983):

$$c = e^{-r(T-t)}E(S^* \mid S^* > X) \tag{B5}$$
$$prob(S^* > X)e^{-r(T-t)}Xprob(S^* > X).$$

The first term in equation (B5), $e^{-r(T-t)}E(S^* \mid S^* > X)$, represents the present value of the expected stock price at the time of the option's expiration, given that S^* is greater than the exercise price. The second term, $prob(S^* > X)$, represents the probability that the stock price will be greater than the exercise price at expiration. The third term, $e^{-r(T-t)}Xprob(S^* > X)$, is the present value of the exercise price times the probability that the stock price will be greater than the exercise price at expiration. In short, the call option is worth the value of receiving the stock at expiration, conditional on the stock price being higher than the exercise price, minus the present value of paying the exercise price, conditional on exercising the option.

The general Black-Scholes model for computing an option's value over a longer period of time can be written in the following, more convenient closed form:

$$c = SN(d_1) - e^{-r(T-t)}XN(d_2), \tag{B6}$$
where
$$d_1 = [ln(S/X) + (r + \sigma^2/2)(T - t)/\sigma \sqrt{(T - t)}, \tag{B7}$$
$$d_2 = d_1 - \sigma \sqrt{(T - t)}. \tag{B8}$$

In short, this model gives the discounted expected value of a call option at expiration. In this model, $N(d_1)$ is the cumulative standard normal distribution function giving the probability that a random variable would be less than or equal to the value d_1. It reflects the uncertainty regarding the stock's value on the option's expiration date. Given a calculation of d_1, the value of $N(d_1)$ can be found in the tables in the back of most statistics textbooks or approximated numerically. Compared to equation (B5), the term $SN(d_1)$ in equation (B6) represents ΔS, or the proportionate share of stock, and the term $e^{-r(T-t)}XN(d_2)$ represents the remainder, $c - \Delta S$, or B.

The Black-Scholes formula shows that, to value a European call option, one needs to know only the current stock price, the exercise price, the time to expiration, the volatility of the stock's returns, and the risk-free interest rate. With the exception of the volatility parameter, all of these variables can be directly observed. The volatility parameter can be estimated from historical data.

Although the Black-Scholes model employs some restrictive and likely unrealistic assumptions, it has nevertheless been shown to be quite robust when the underlying assumptions are modified.

low price of the underlying asset over the life of the contract, the lookback option has the advantage of allowing investors to better use their knowledge about an underlying asset's price volatility. As noted earlier, the key to pricing this instrument in the Black-Scholes framework is that the lookback option must be hedgeable.

In their 1979 article, M. Barry Goldman, Howard B. Sosin, and Mary Ann Gatto developed a model to value the lookback option using the Black-Scholes option pricing methodology and showed that a hedge portfolio could be constructed, allowing the lookback option to be valued without regard to the risk premium in the underlying asset's expected return. As the example in Box 1 illustrates, the domestic risk-free interest rate, r, can be used in estimating the expected terminal stock price as well as to discount the option's terminal value to the present. Goldman, Sosin, and Gatto showed that when the risk-free interest rate is equal to exactly one-half the asset's volatility (as measured by variance), the lookback call option is identical to the purchase of a straddle (a portfolio of puts and calls on the same asset with the same strike price) on the asset. In this case, the writers of lookback calls can simply hedge their obligation by purchasing a straddle on the same underlying asset.

The examples that follow employ a more general model developed by Mark B. Garman (1989) to illustrate the lookback option's essential features. The Garman model, while based on the work of Goldman, Sosin, and Gatto (1979), is simpler and offers additional insight

into the option's valuation by separating it into two underlying options. Moreover, unlike the earlier model, it can be used to value a European option on a "dividend-paying" asset such as a foreign currency option.

The Garman (1989) model for valuing a European lookback call option on a foreign currency, presented in equation (3) below, is a combination of two separate models: a European call option (see Garman and Steven W. Kohlhagen 1983), given by equation (1), and what Garman refers to as a strike-bonus option, shown in equation (2).

$$c = Se^{-r_f(T-t)}N(d_1) - Xe^{-r(T-t)}N(d_2); \quad (1)$$

$$d_1 = \frac{ln\left(\frac{S}{X}\right) + (r - r_f + \frac{\sigma^2}{2})(T-t)}{\sigma\sqrt{T-t}};$$

$$d_2 = d_1 - \sigma\sqrt{T-t}.$$

$$V_{sb} = \frac{S}{\lambda}\left[e^{-r(T-t)}(\frac{S}{L})^{-\lambda}N(d_1) - \frac{1}{\lambda}e^{-r_f(T-t)}N(d_2)\right]; \quad (2)$$

$$d_1 = \frac{-ln(\frac{S}{L}) - (\delta + \frac{\sigma^2}{2})(T-t)}{\sigma\sqrt{(T-t)}} + 2\delta\frac{\sqrt{(T-t)}}{\sigma};$$

$$d_2 = d_1 - 2\delta\frac{\sqrt{(T-t)}}{\sigma}.$$

$$Lookback_{call} = c + V_{sb}. \quad (3)$$

Equation (1) is a simple Black-Scholes valuation model for a foreign currency. The intuition behind this component of the model is explained in Box 1, with the difference that the foreign risk-free interest rate, r_f, has been introduced to represent the continuous "dividend" or interest on the foreign currency. Equation (2) is similar to equation (1) except that the strike price is replaced by the underlying asset's achieved minimum value, L, from the time the option originated, along with other modifications. In the basic Black-Scholes model for a nondividend-paying stock, the valuation is carried out in a risk-neutral setting so that a stock's expected rate of return is equal to the risk-free interest rate, r. With a foreign currency, however, the return provided by the foreign interest rate, which does involve risk, must also be taken into account. The expected proportional growth rate of the spot exchange rate, S_t, must be reduced by r_f to allow for the fact that the foreign currency can be invested to earn the foreign interest rate.

Equation (1) can be thought of as the value of an option to buy the asset at its minimum value achieved to date, from time t_0 to t. The strike-bonus option represented by equation (2) captures and prices or values the right to buy the underlying asset (the foreign currency) at the new minimum value likely to be achieved over the remaining life of the option, from time t until the expiration date T—that is, $(T - t)$.

In general, the lookback call option is similar to a basic call option. For example, as it is for the basic call option, the value of the lookback call is positively correlated with the spot price of the underlying asset, the domestic risk-free interest rate, the time remaining until the option expires, and, most importantly, the volatility of the underlying asset. In addition, in both cases the option is negatively correlated with the contract's exercise price and the foreign risk-free interest rate.

Charts 1 and 2 illustrate the price behavior of a basic European call option and a strike-bonus option, respectively, over various initial strike prices ranging from $0.80 to $1.00. In these charts the initial strike price used for the basic call and the strike-bonus option is the minimum value, L, achieved by the underlying asset since the option's origination. Chart 3 gives the value of the lookback call option (the sum of the value of the European call option and the strike-bonus option) over the same range of initial strike prices.

Although Charts 1 and 3 appear similar, the values of the basic call and lookback options (on the y-axis) differ as L is increased. The two options have approximately the same value when L is very low relative to the spot

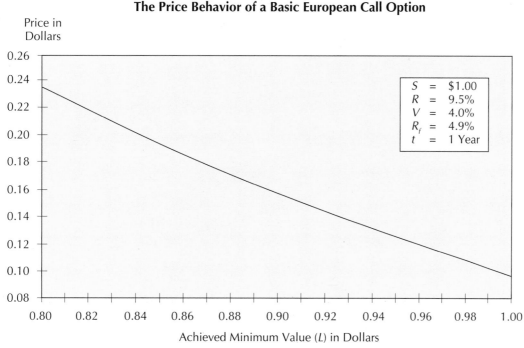

Chart 1
The Price Behavior of a Basic European Call Option

Price in Dollars

S	= $1.00
R	= 9.5%
V	= 4.0%
R_f	= 4.9%
t	= 1 Year

Achieved Minimum Value (L) in Dollars

Chart 2
The Price Behavior of a Strike-Bonus Option

Price in
Dollars

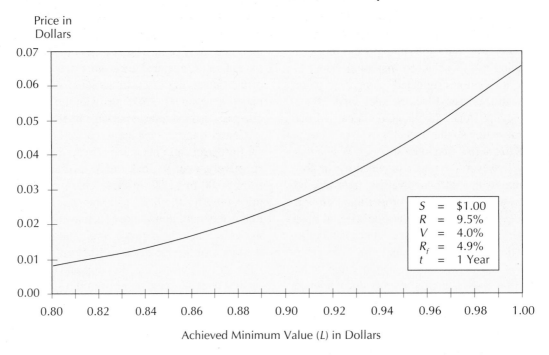

Achieved Minimum Value (*L*) in Dollars

S	=	$1.00
R	=	9.5%
V	=	4.0%
R_f	=	4.9%
t	=	1 Year

Chart 3
The Price Behavior of a Lookback Call Option

Price in
Dollars

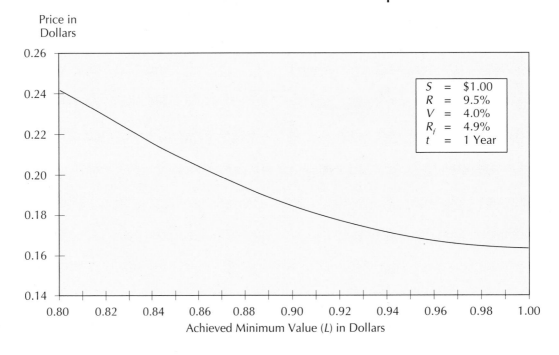

Achieved Minimum Value (*L*) in Dollars

S	=	$1.00
R	=	9.5%
V	=	4.0%
R_f	=	4.9%
t	=	1 Year

price, S. At this point, the call option is "deep in-the-money"—the price of the underlying asset exceeds the strike or exercise price, and the lookback's value is derived primarily from the basic call option's value. The strike-bonus option is relatively worthless. However, the value of the basic call option declines further than that of the lookback call option as its strike price, L, is increased to $1.00 (and is said to be "at-the-money"). Hence, the closer the achieved minimum asset price is to the spot price, the higher the value of the strike-bonus option. As the call option moves closer to being at-the-money, the value of the strike-bonus option pushes the lookback's price above the price of the basic call.

Thus, while the relationship between the lookback call option's value and the initial strike price, L, is similar to that of the basic call option, the relationship between the value of the lookback's strike-bonus component and the strike price is opposite that of the basic call option. That is, other things being equal, the value of the strike-bonus option is positively correlated with the initial strike price.

As stated earlier, the strike-bonus option gives the holder the right to buy the asset at a new minimum value anticipated from the perspective of time t. Given a very low initial minimum value, L, relative to the spot price, the probability is low that the asset's price will fall to a new minimum value and then rise again before the option expires, so the strike-bonus option has little value. On the other hand, if the option were at-the-money—the achieved minimum equals the spot price—the asset very likely would establish a new minimum price and subsequently rise before expiration. The strike-bonus option derives its value from the probability that the asset's price will achieve such a new minimum value. Therefore, for options having initial at-the-money prices, the lookback call option's value can be substantially higher than that of a comparable basic call option.

Besides the relationship between the exercise or strike price and the value of the underlying asset—the moneyness of the option—another factor influencing the value of both the basic call and the lookback call option is the underlying asset's volatility. While either option's value is positively correlated with volatility, for a lookback call option this factor is more significant because it affects the probability that the price of the underlying asset will achieve a new minimum prior to the expiration date. For instance, holding other factors constant, the value of the basic at-the-money call option priced above increased by 1.5 percent given an increase from 2.0 percent to 2.1 percent in the estimated variance of the underlying asset. In this same situation, however, the value of the strike-bonus option increased by 2.34 percent.

Valuing an Average-Rate (Asian) Option. There are two types of average-rate or Asian options: the fixed-strike and the floating-strike. The fixed-strike average-rate option is one for which the terminal payoff is the maximum of either the difference between the average value of the underlying asset and a fixed strike price or zero: $max(Avg_S - X, 0)$. The floating-strike Asian call option is similar to the lookback option given that its payoff at expiration is equal to the greater of the difference between the underlying asset's terminal spot price and its average value over the life of the option or zero—that is, $max(S - Avg_S, 0)$.

The floating-strike average-rate option is comparable to a lookback call option for which the strike price is the average value of the underlying asset, as opposed to its minimum value. The value of this option can never be greater than the value of a regular lookback call option, whose strike price is the achieved minimum of the asset, because the average is never equal to an extreme value such as the minimum unless all of the values are equal. Thus, the price of a regular lookback option sets an upper bound on the value of the floating-strike average-rate option.

The fixed-strike average-rate option is more commonly used in practice than the floating-strike option and will be the focus of this discussion. For both the floating- and fixed-strike average-rate options, the average can be computed as either the geometric or the arithmetic average. Although in practice the arithmetic average is typically used, no closed-form equation has been developed for pricing the average-rate option written on the arithmetic average because of mathematical complexities. Thus, a numerical approximation technique must be used to value an option written on the arithmetic average of the underlying asset's price (see A.G.Z. Kemna and A.C.F. Vorst 1990).[2] In the study presented here Monte Carlo simulation was the numerical approximation valuation methodology chosen. (See Box 3.)

Limiting Bounds on the Value of an Arithmetic Average-Rate Option. Theoretically the value of an option written on an asset's arithmetic average should lie between the values of a comparable European call option and an average-rate option written on the geometric average of the asset's price. The primary difference between the fixed-strike average rate option and a comparable basic call option is the volatility of the underlying spot price. Because the variance used to compute the value of the basic European call option exceeds the variance used to compute the value of the

Box 3
Monte Carlo Simulation: A Tutorial

Monte Carlo simulation is a numerical procedure used to approximate the expected value of a random variable or vector. The procedure approximates the expected value by generating random variables or vectors with a given probability density or joint probability density and, using the law of large numbers, takes the average of these values as an estimate of the expected value.

The Monte Carlo method is used to compute the expected value of a European-style call option. The value is computed by simulating the path taken by the price of the asset underlying the option over time. By simulating numerous such price paths, the technique allows computing the expected value or price of the option with increasing precision as the number of iterations or runs of the simulation are increased. The example that follows illustrates the technique.

In this exercise the objective is to compute the expected payoff of a European-style call option as of its expiration date, $E[max(S^* - X, 0)]$ and then to compute the present value of this quantity—that is, $e^{-r(T-t)} E[max(S^* - X, 0)]$. Given a model for stock price movements over time, the Monte Carlo simulation technique will allow computation of the price expected at expiration.

Each iteration or sample run of the Monte Carlo simulation gives a stock price at time T. Increasing the number of runs of the simulation increases the reliability of the estimate for S^*. (For example, 100,000 iterations would be reasonable.) The expected value of S^* is an average of the values obtained over the number of iterations.

The stock's price path can be modeled using the following equation:

$$S_{t+1} = S_t e^{r - \sigma^2/2\Delta t + S\sigma\epsilon\sqrt{\Delta t}}. \quad \text{(M1)}$$

In equation (M1), S_t is the value of the stock price today, r is the risk-free interest rate, σ is the standard deviation of stock returns, Δt represents a very small change in time (a day, for example), and $\epsilon\sqrt{\Delta t}$ is a discrete approximation to an increment in a Wiener process, in which ϵ represents a random drawing from a standardized normal distribution (a normal distribution with mean 0 and variance 1).

Suppose, for example, that the stock price today, S_t, is $50.00, Δt is 1/365 years, and the annual risk-free interest rate and standard deviation of the stock's expected return are 8 percent and 20 percent, respectively. Then, using the model in equation (M1), the stock's price one day hence can be approximated by

$$S_{t+1} = 50e^{(.08 - .02)(.0027) + (.20)(\sqrt{.0027})\epsilon}.$$

To complete the approximation of S_{t+1}, a value of ϵ needs to be randomly selected from a standardized normal distribution. (This task can typically be accomplished with an internal function available in many computer program languages.) If, for example, the random selection for ϵ is 2.1, the stock's price one day hence would be expected to be $51.11. Another random sampling for ϵ would yield a different stock price for S_{t+1}.

In practice, these steps would be repeated numerous times to get a stock price path from S_t to S_{t+n}, where S_{t+n} would be the stock price as of n days from now—that is, S^* at expiration. The option's terminal value would then be computed and this amount would be discounted back to today using the formula

$$Call = e^{-r(T-t)}max(S^* - K, 0). \quad \text{(M2)}$$

These steps would complete one sample iteration of this Monte Carlo simulation.

After performing the appropriate number of runs, the expected call option value, $Call$, is computed as the average of the estimates of the call option's value obtained over the iterations. Next, the standard deviation of the estimates of $Call$ is computed. Finally, given an expected value of $Call$ and the standard deviation of the expected value, a confidence interval—a range within which there is some level of assurance that the actual value will fall—can be constructed for the value of the option. For normally distributed variables there is a 95 percent probability that the actual value of the variable will lie within a range of ± 2 standard deviations from its sample mean.

Suppose, for example, that a European-style call option on a stock has eighty-seven days until expiration and an exercise price of $35.00. Today's stock price is $40.00, its annual volatility is 20 percent, and the yield on a Treasury bill with just over eighty-seven days until maturity is 2.96 percent. The Monte Carlo simulation consists of 10,000 iterations, giving 10,000 approximations for the present value of the call option. The mean value of the call is $5.361, and the standard deviation of the estimate was $0.0335. A 95 percent confidence interval for the value of the call can be constructed as follows:

$$\$5.361 \pm 2(.0335) = [\$5.29, \$5.43].$$

That is, there is a 95 percent probability that the actual value of this call option is within the computed range. This confidence interval can be tightened—thus obtaining a more reliable estimate—by increasing the number of iterations in the simulation or by employing a variance reduction technique (see note 4). The desired level of accuracy depends on a particular application.

In short, the Monte Carlo method simulates the random movement of stock prices and provides a probabilistic solution to the option pricing problem. Thus, by the technique's very nature, the final value derived using the

Monte Carlo simulation will not be exact, no matter how accurate the equations in the model.

The advantage of using this simulation technique is that it can accommodate complex payoffs such as those that depend on the history of the underlying asset's price over time—for example, lookback and average-rate op-

tions. However, the technique has the disadvantage of being time-consuming, depending on the number of iterations required to obtain a reasonably accurate approximation, and it may therefore be infeasible for some practical applications.

call option written on the average price of the same underlying asset, the value of the call option on the asset's average value will never be greater than the value of a standard European call option on the asset. Furthermore, because the arithmetic average is always greater than the corresponding geometric average, the value of an option written on the geometric average of an asset's price provides a lower bound for the value of an option written on the arithmetic average of the price of the same asset.

Chart 4 shows the bounds imposed on an Asian option's value written on the arithmetic average. The value of a basic European call option forms the upper bound, and the value of a call option written on the geometric average delineates the lower bound, both having the same underlying parameters (S, X, r, σ, and t).

The price of the arithmetic Asian option for a given spot price, computed using the Monte Carlo method, lies within the shaded area. The following relationships hold:[3]

$$Call_{European} \geq Asian\ Call_{arithmetic} > Asian\ Call_{geometric}.$$

The sections that follow illustrate the application of the valuation models discussed above to investment and hedging decisions in the foreign exchange markets. A Monte Carlo analysis like that used in Box 3 is employed to value the Asian option written on the arithmetic average with the exception that in the example the terminal price of the underlying asset is taken to be the arithmetic average of the n daily stock prices, where n is the number of days from time t until expiration.[4]

Chart 4
Average-Rate Option Value Boundaries
(Arithmetic Average)

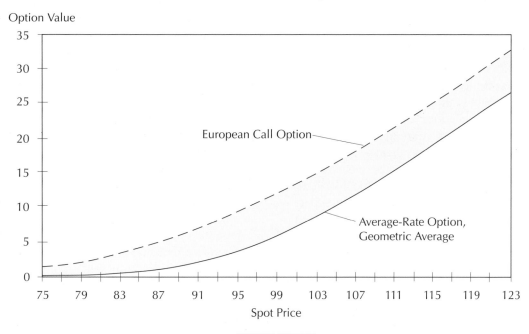

Numerical Examples. Suppose that a U.S. investor firmly believes that the Japanese economy will improve dramatically relative to other industrialized countries' economies during the upcoming year. To act on this expectation, the investor purchases a one-year call option on the Japanese yen with a strike price of $0.0073. In this context the investor is speculating or predicting that the cost of the yen in U.S. dollar terms will rise by the time the option expires—that is, the yen will appreciate against the U.S. dollar. Assume that as of the current date it costs the investor $0.0073 to buy one unit of Japanese yen (1/$0.0073 translates to a current exchange rate of 136.9 yen per one U.S. dollar) and that this cost rises to $0.0079 (126.6 yen/$) over the one-year period. At the end of the year it costs more U.S. dollars ($0.0079 − $0.0073) to purchase one unit of Japanese yen (the dollar depreciated). Because the option is very valuable at expiration, the investor's decision to purchase the one-year call option with a $0.0073 strike price turns out to have been a profitable one.

The example illustrates how an investor can use a basic currency call option in speculating on foreign currency movements. On the other hand, if the investor knew that dollars would have to be exchanged for yen at the end of the year—as might be the case for a business that imported goods from Japan with a commitment to make payment in yen—the purchase of the yen call option would constitute a foreign exchange risk hedging transaction.[5]

The following discussion illustrates more extensively how the path-dependent call option valuation models presented in this article are implemented using actual foreign exchange data on the Japanese yen and the German deutsche mark. The performance of these options is compared with that of a basic European call option written on the same currencies, and some of the risks inherent in using these instruments are pointed out.

The Data and Assumptions. Consider that on January 8, 1991, an investor is aware that one year from this date it will be necessary to purchase one million units of each of two foreign currencies: Japanese yen and deutsche marks. The investor's objective is to eliminate the upside exchange rate risk in this purchase requirement. That is, he or she wishes to avoid being adversely affected by a rise in the foreign currencies' value over the next year.

The investor is assumed to have four alternative options on the foreign currencies from which to choose: a basic call option, a lookback call option, a fixed-strike Asian option, and a floating-strike Asian option.[6] All four options are European style, and the size of each option contract is for the purchase of one million units of the underlying foreign currency. To simplify matters, all options will be initially at-the-money. In other words, on the date they were purchased (time t_0), the spot foreign exchange rates were equal to the options' strike prices.

As will be discussed further, the choice of instruments can be difficult. In terms of the cost or premium required to purchase these options, the average-rate options are inexpensive relative to the lookback option. However, depending on the behavior of the exchange rates, the investor's hedging needs, and his or her knowledge of exchange rate volatility, the more expensive lookback could be preferred.

Table 1 provides a hypothetical example of a buy-and-hold strategy on each of the four types of call options available to this investor. Each option's performance as a hedging or investment vehicle is analyzed using the Japanese yen and the deutsche mark, given the net changes in each currency's exchange rate over the one-year period.

Option transactions are initiated on January 8, 1991, to expire January 10, 1992 (367 calendar days). The basic data for this analysis are given in the first panel. So that all options will be priced at-the-money, the strike price is set equal to the initial spot exchange rate for the yen—$0.0073 per one unit of yen (the inverse of 133.3 yen per one U.S. dollar) and $0.6536 per one deutsche mark. The table also includes the domestic and foreign risk-free interest rates and estimates of asset price volatility for this time period.

The estimated initial cost of each option is shown in the second panel. The calculated premium for each option was multiplied by one million units of each currency to obtain the cost of the option contract. For both the fixed- and floating-strike average rate or Asian options, the Monte Carlo method was used in estimating value. Equations (3) and (1) were used to value the lookback and basic call options. Note the high cost of the at-the-money lookback call option relative to the basic call, as would be expected in light of the earlier discussion of the value of the strike-bonus option component of the lookback option.

The third panel shows the values of the four options at expiration. At this time the options are worth the greater of their intrinsic values, $S − X$, or zero since no time premium remains. The profit/loss on each position reported in the fourth panel represents the options' terminal values minus their initial costs.

Summary of the Results. As can be seen in the fourth panel, for the yen options all but the fixed-strike Asian call ended the period profitable. The fixed-strike

Table 1
A Hedging/Investment Application[a]

	Yen	Mark
Estimated volatility	14.14%	13.06%
Foreign interest rate	7.64%	9.13%
U.S. interest rate	6.91%	6.91%
Strike price (set equal to spot price of 01/08/91)	$0.0073	$0.6536
Average exchange rate over option's life	$0.0075	$0.6047
Minimum exchange rate achieved over option's life	$0.0070	$0.5435
Spot (terminal) exchange rate (01/10/92)	$0.0079	$0.6329
The U.S. dollar's net change	Depreciated	Appreciated

Estimated Initial Cost of Call Option Contract
(at the money)[b]

Asian (floating-strike)	$208	$14,930
Asian (fixed-strike)	$209	$15,032
Lookback call	$710	$54,000
Basic European call	$359	$25,200

Option Value at Expiration
(01/10/92)

Asian (floating-strike) max (Spot[T]—Average, 0)	$400	$28,200
Asian (fixed-strike) max (Average—Strike, 0)	$123	$0
Lookback call max (Spot[T]—Minimum, 0)	$823	$89,433
Basic European call max (Spot[T]—Strike, 0)	$542	$0

Profit/(Loss) on Option[c]

Asian (floating-strike)	$192	$13,270
Asian (fixed-strike)	($86)	($15,032)
Lookback call	$113	$35,433
Basic European call	$183	($25,200)

[a] *Option contract size is one million units of foreign currency. Time remaining until expiration (01/08/91–01/10/92) is 367 days.*
[b] *Premium times one million units of currency.*
[c] *Terminal values minus initial costs.*

Chart 5
Daily Exchange Rates, U.S. Dollar versus Japanese Yen[a]
(January 8, 1991, to January 10, 1992)

[a] *Exchange rates shown are actual exchange rates multiplied by 1,000.*

Asian option cost $86.00 more than its value at expiration (computed as the difference between the average of the daily exchange rates over 367 days and the strike price). Over the period analyzed the yen appreciated, net, from $0.0073 to $0.0079. Thus it cost more in U.S. dollar terms to purchase one yen at the maturity date than at origination. As can be seen, the basic call option struck initially at-the-money expired in-the-money, generating a profit of $183.00. The lookback call option was also profitable even though its initial cost was nearly twice that of the basic call. This value reflects the path taken by the yen over the period. As illustrated in Chart 5, the yen initially declined through June 1991 and then began to trend upward thereafter.

In the case of the deutsche mark, it is interesting that only the lookback options were profitable at expiration. The lookback call and the floating-strike average rate option generated profits of $35,433.00 and $13,270.00, respectively. The basic call option position resulted in a loss of $25,200.00 and the fixed-rate Asian option produced a loss of $15,032.00. As Chart 6 shows, over this one-year period the mark depreciated, net, against the U.S. dollar. If the dollar/mark ex-

change rate had followed a downward path over the period, all of the option positions would have expired worthless. However, the mark depreciated significantly in the first half of the year and then appreciated thereafter, ending just below its beginning rate.

As in the case with the Japanese yen, the profit associated with the lookback option can be attributed to the range achieved by the exchange rate during the period. In initially pricing the lookback call on the mark an annualized volatility estimate of 13.06 percent was used. The actual volatility over this period was a much higher 17.4 percent, and the unexpected increase in volatility positively affected the lookback option's value.

An investor who accurately forecasts the range of the dollar/mark exchange rate over the assumed investment or hedging horizon given in this example would have found the lookback call or floating Asian options attractive investment vehicles. It should be emphasized, however, that investors must understand the risks inherent in these instruments to use them effectively (as is the case with most derivative products). This point takes on added importance given that these contracts are used mostly in foreign exchange transactions. For a variety of reasons it is extremely difficult

Chart 6

Chart 6
Daily Exchange Rates, U.S. Dollar versus German Mark[a]
(January 8, 1991, to January 10, 1992)

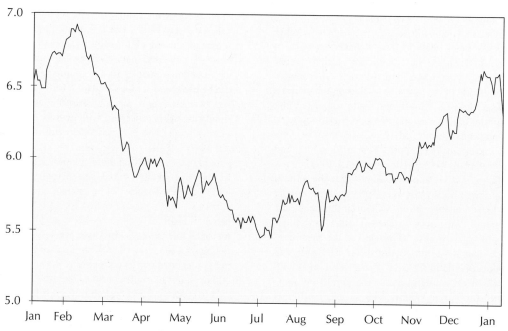

[a] *Exchange rates shown are actual exchange rates multiplied by 10.*

to forecast exchange rates, even when using large-scale structural econometric models. It is likely that such forecasting difficulties will also be encountered when attempting to forecast parameters of the price processes that determine the value of path-dependent foreign exchange options. In any number of cases other, more traditional derivative instruments such as futures and forwards or various types of swap products may represent a more cost-effective way for investors or hedgers to achieve their stated objectives. Thus, while many may find contracts including path-dependent options attractive, they will not satisfy the needs of every investor or hedger.

Conclusion

This article describes the way in which two popular path-dependent options—the lookback option and the average-rate or Asian option—are priced using modern options pricing techniques. The hedge portfolio and risk-neutral pricing approaches associated with the modern options pricing paradigm are used to price the lookback option, and Monte Carlo simulation is used in pricing the floating-strike and the fixed-strike average-rate or Asian options. A simple numerical example involving these options demonstrates the possible benefits, costs, and risks associated with their use.

Since their formal introduction in 1979, these options have experienced rapid growth. In one form or another they are now traded on exchanges, are used extensively in foreign exchange markets to hedge foreign exchange risks, and have found use in corporate mergers and acquisitions. While these options are likely to continue to find new applications and uses as hedging and/or investment vehicles, investors are advised to develop a full understanding of the risks inherent in these instruments before adding them to their investment or hedging portfolios.

Notes

1. Research published in 1979 by Goldman, Sosin, and Gatto paved the way for the modern treatment of path-dependent options. The authors had derived an explicit valuation formula for a hypothetical option with an exercise price to be set at the contract's expiration rather than at origination, as it is for standard options. Payoff on such "lookback" options would depend on the price path followed by the contract's underlying asset over the life of the option as well as on the option's expiration date. Goldman, Sosin, and Gatto suggested that such options could be of value to investors, and they were proven correct when Macotta Metals Corporation of New York began trading lookback options on gold, silver, and platinum on March 16, 1982 (Hunter and Stowe 1992).

2. The Black-Scholes environment assumes that the natural logarithms of stock price returns, $ln(S_t/S_{t-1})$, are normally distributed. In valuing an option written on the geometric average of an underlying asset's value over time, this crucial assumption still holds because the product of the logarithms of stock price returns is normally distributed. However, this assumption fails to hold in the case of an Asian option written on the arithmetic average because the sum of the logarithms of the stock price returns over time is no longer normally distributed. Therefore, there is no closed-form analytical pricing equation for the average-rate option written on

the arithmetic average (Ritchken, Sankarnsubramanian, and Vijh 1990).

3. The closed-form equation for pricing the Asian option written on the geometric average is derived in Ritchken, Sankarnsubramanian, and Vijh (1990).

4. In valuing the arithmetic average-rate option, knowledge of the valuation principles for the geometric average-rate option can be used to lower the standard error of the estimated value and therefore reduce the number of iterations required in the simulation. This procedure is known as the variance reduction technique and is described in Hull (1989) and Kemna and Vorst (1990).

5. Although the discussion to this point has focused only on the lookback call option, in the case of foreign currency options a call on one currency can be thought of as a put on another currency. That is, a call option to buy yen for U.S. dollars can be thought of as a put to sell U.S. dollars for yen. Thus, the same methodology discussed for valuing a lookback call option on a foreign currency can be used to value a lookback put option on a foreign currency.

6. Although this example considers only the use of the lookback call, average-rate, and basic European call option, in practice other hedging vehicles would also be considered or evaluated by the investor, depending on the investor's objective.

References

Black, Fischer, and Myron Scholes. "The Pricing of Options and Corporate Liabilities." *Journal of Political Economy* 81 (May/June 1973): 637-59.

Cox, John, and Stephen Ross. "The Valuation of Options for Alternative Stochastic Processes." *Journal of Financial Economics* 3 (1976): 145-66.

Garman, Mark B. "Recollection in Tranquillity." *Risk* 2 (March 1989): 16-18.

_____, and Steven W. Kohlhagen. "Foreign Currency Option Values." *Journal of International Money and Finance* 2 (December 1983): 231-37.

Goldman, M. Barry, Howard B. Sosin, and Mary Ann Gatto. "Path-Dependent Options: 'Buy at the Low, Sell at the High.'" *Journal of Finance* 34 (December 1979): 1111-27.

Hull, John. *Options, Futures, and Other Derivative Securities.* Englewood Cliffs, N.J.: Prentice-Hall, Inc., 1989.

Hunter, William C., and David W. Stowe. "Path-Dependent Options." Federal Reserve Bank of Atlanta *Economic Review* 77 (March/April 1992): 29-34.

Jarrow, Robert, and Andrew Rudd. *Options Pricing.* Homewood, Ill.: Richard D. Irwin, 1983.

Kemna, A.G.Z., and A.C.F. Vorst. "A Pricing Method for Options Based on Average Asset Values." *Journal of Banking and Finance* 14 (March 1990): 113-29.

Kolb, Robert W. *Options: An Introduction.* Miami: Kolb Publishing Company, 1991.

Ritchken, Peter, L. Sankarnsubramanian, and Anand M. Vijh. "The Economic Analysis of Path-Dependent Contracts on the Average." Case Western University, Department of Operations Research, Working Paper, 1990.

*E*valuating Embedded Options

Hugh Cohen

*I*n an effort to control interest rate exposure many banks, financial institutions, and investors are buying complicated financial instruments. Many of these are difficult to understand (and thus difficult to value) because of the embedded options they contain. This article discusses a procedure that in some instances greatly eases the way that embedded options may be valued: the technique is to value it as though it were separate from the financial contract. Treating the embedded option independently is desirable when it is accurate because it is usually simpler to ignore the details of the surrounding contract.

In this article, two examples will be used to demonstrate this method. The first is valuing the call option sometimes embedded in Treasury bonds by separating the embedded option from the contract; for this option the technique results in a correct value. The second example involves valuing the wild card option (an option that allows a trader to sell a Treasury bond between 2:00 P.M. and 8:00 P.M. at a price fixed at 2:00 P.M.) embedded in Treasury bond futures contracts. In the latter case, separating the embedded option leads to an incorrect value for it.

It is important to understand the procedure because many financial texts mistakenly value the wild card option by separation, even though doing so produces erroneous results. Additionally, callable Treasury bonds have been mispriced although they could have easily been priced correctly by separation. The discussion that follows details ways to determine if the separation technique can be correctly applied.

This article was originally published in the Atlanta Fed's November/December 1991 Economic Review. *The author is a senior economist in the financial section of the Atlanta Fed's research department.*

Callable Treasury Bonds

Callable Treasury bonds represent a significant portion of the Treasury bond market (which is composed of Treasury securities with more than ten years to maturity when issued). In the fall of 1990, the Treasury reported almost $100 billion in callable bonds outstanding, representing approximately one-fourth of the total par value of Treasury bonds (*Bulletin* 1990).

The payment stream of a Treasury bond has two parts. The bond's face value is the lump sum to be paid at maturity, which is usually thirty years from the date the bond is first issued. Semiannual coupon payments are made until the bond matures. A noncallable Treasury bond has a fixed maturity, so its payment stream is fixed. A call option gives its holder the right, but not the obligation, to buy the underlying security at a specified price, called the exercise price, over a specified period, called the exercise period. A callable Treasury bond gives the Treasury the right, but not the obligation, to accelerate the bond's maturity at any of the coupon payment dates during the five-year period before the original maturity date, provided that bondholders are given four months notice. When a Treasury bond is called, the Treasury pays the bearer the face value payment and a final coupon payment, and the Treasury is released from obligations to make later coupon payments.

The embedded call option becomes valuable for the Treasury to exercise when the bond's coupon rate is higher than the prevailing interest rate. In this scenario the Treasury can call the bond and refinance the debt by issuing a new one at the current, lower interest rate. Thus, after the call-protection period, investors in callable bonds risk losing their coupon payments at a time when interest rates are lower than coupon rates. Furthermore, if the coupon rate is lower than the prevailing interest rate the Treasury will not exercise the option, and the bondholder will be forced to continue receiving the lower coupon rate.

For the first time since December 1962, the Treasury called a bond on October 9 of this year. With interest rates at approximately 5 percent, the Treasury called $1.8 billion of callable Treasury bonds. The called issue was the August 1993 bond, with a coupon rate of 7.5 percent. (The next, and now final, coupon payment will be on February 15, 1992, because the Treasury gave the required four months' notice.) Refinancing the debt saved the Treasury approximately $18 million. At the same time it was called the bond was trading at $101.41 per $100 of face value, a surprisingly high price for a bond that could be called at face value (*Wall Street Journal*, October 10, 1991). This premium was possible partly because of disbelief by the market that the Treasury would call any bond after nearly three decades of not doing so. For whatever the reason, this callable Treasury bond was clearly mispriced.

Determining a Callable Treasury Bond's Value. One approach to determining the value of a callable Treasury bond is to begin by valuing the embedded call option as though it were stripped from the Treasury bond. Subtracting the value of this stripped call option from that of an otherwise identical but noncallable Treasury bond yields the proper value of the callable Treasury bond. To determine that they are comparable, the cash flows of the two portfolios must be analyzed and shown to be identical.

In the thirty-year callable bond described here, the first fifty coupon payments are guaranteed by the call-protection period. The final ten coupon payments may or may not be paid, depending upon whether the Treasury decides to exercise its call option, resulting in eleven possible payment streams (outlined in Chart 1). There are also eleven possible payment streams to the portfolio of a long, noncallable Treasury bond with one short call option on the final ten coupon payments and the payment of face value at maturity, with an exercise price equal to the face-value payment, as shown in Chart 2. (The investor who purchases an option is said to hold the contract long. An option's seller is said to hold the contract short.)

Because the cash flow of a callable Treasury bond and the cash flow of the portfolio composed of buying a noncallable Treasury bond and selling a separate call option on the payments during the call period are identical for every possible date on which the Treasury may exercise the call option (compare Charts 1 and 2), the value of the two portfolios must be identical to avoid arbitrage. If the two portfolios had different prices, shorting the higher-priced portfolio and longing the lower-priced portfolio would capture the difference in prices without taking any risk. Thus the embedded call option in the callable Treasury bonds may be valued as a separate contract.

For example, the value of a $100 callable Treasury bond that will mature between August 15, 2007, and August 15, 2012, with a coupon rate of 8 percent can be calculated from the following portfolio of securities: the value of a $100 noncallable bond maturing on August 15, 2012, with a coupon rate of 8 percent is $109.00. The value of a call option on the payments occurring over the final five years of this noncallable bond with an exercise price of $100.00 is $5.25. The noncallable bond's value less the value of the option is the value of the callable bond—$103.75. As will be demonstrated, not all embedded options can be accurately valued in this way.

The Wild Card Option in Treasury Bond Futures

The Treasury bond futures contract traded on the Chicago Board of Trade (CBOT) is a heavily traded contract that contains many embedded options.[1] One of these, the wild card option, is an example of an option that cannot be priced by being examined separately from the contract. Before discussing the embedded option, the following section first reviews the Treasury bond futures contract as it is traded on the CBOT.

The Treasury Bond Futures Contract. Upon entering a futures contract, the long trader, who will buy the underlying security, and the short trader, who will sell the underlying security, agree upon a futures price that will be used to calculate future cash flows. Although it can be entered into without cost, a futures contract obligates its traders to perform a series of future cash flows. The values of these cash flows are a function of the contract's settlement price, which is set by the settlement committee of the exchange at the close of trading (2:00 P.M.) to reflect the futures contract's market value at that time. After the settlement price is determined, every position in the futures contract is "marked to market." For an established long position in the futures contract, the value of the cash flow of marking to market is today's settlement price minus the previous settlement price. The cash flow for an established short position is minus one times the value of the cash flow of the long position. For a long position opened in the last trading session, the value of the cash flow of marking to market is today's settlement price minus the futures price when the position was taken. This value times minus one is the value of the

Chart 1
Cash Flow of a Callable Treasury Bond

Called at the Fiftieth Coupon Payment

Semiannual Coupon Payment Number	1	2	3	4	. . .	48	49	50	51	52	. . .	59	60
Cash Flow	+CP	+CP	+CP	+CP	. . .	+CP	+CP	+CP +FVP	0	0	. . .	0	0

Called at the Fifty-first Coupon Payment

Semiannual Coupon Payment Number	1	2	3	4	. . .	48	49	50	51	52	. . .	59	60
Cash Flow	+CP	+CP	+CP	+CP	. . .	+CP	+CP	+CP	+CP +FVP	0	. . .	0	0

Not Called

Semiannual Coupon Payment Number	1	2	3	4	. . .	59	60
Cash Flow	+CP	+CP	+CP	+CP	. . .	+CP	+CP +FVP

+CP= Coupon Payment
+FVP= Face Value Payment

Chart 2
Cash Flows of the Portfolio of One Long Noncallable Treasury Bond
And One Short Call Option on the Callable Payments
With an Exercise Price Equal to the Face Value of the Bond

When the Option Is Exercised at the Fiftieth Payment

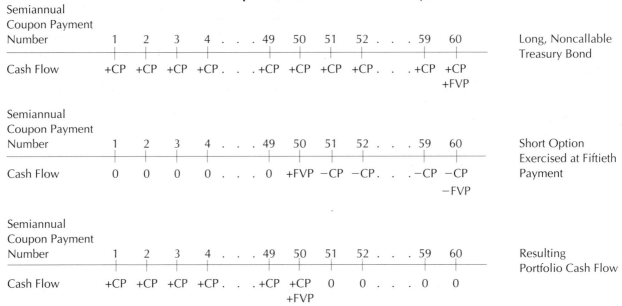

When the Option Is Exercised at the Fifty-first Payment

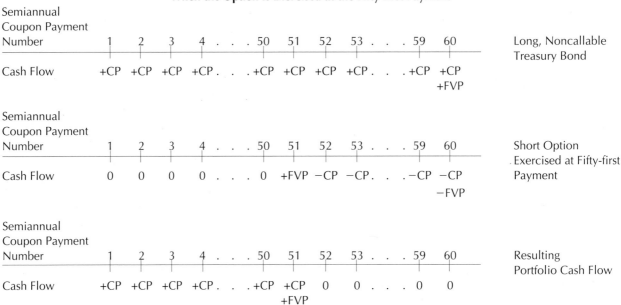

Chart 2 (continued)

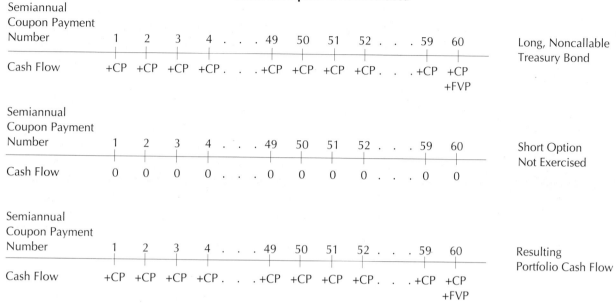

When the Option Is Not Exercised

Semiannual Coupon Payment Number	1	2	3	4	. . .	49	50	51	52	. . .	59	60	Long, Noncallable Treasury Bond
Cash Flow	+CP	+CP	+CP	+CP	. . .	+CP	+CP	+CP	+CP	. . .	+CP	+CP +FVP	

Semiannual Coupon Payment Number	1	2	3	4	. . .	49	50	51	52	. . .	59	60	Short Option Not Exercised
Cash Flow	0	0	0	0	. . .	0	0	0	0	. . .	0	0	

Semiannual Coupon Payment Number	1	2	3	4	. . .	49	50	51	52	. . .	59	60	Resulting Portfolio Cash Flow
Cash Flow	+CP	+CP	+CP	+CP	. . .	+CP	+CP	+CP	+CP	. . .	+CP	+CP +FVP	

cash flow of marking to market a new short position. Thus, a short trader profits when the settlement price decreases from the previous day, and a long position profits when the settlement price increases from the previous day. Additionally, the settlement price is used to determine the delivery price for contracts when the delivery process is initiated on that day.

To understand marking to market, consider a trader who enters a futures contract at a futures price of $100. At the end of the trading session the settlement price is $102. Because of marking to market, a long trader would receive $2, and a short trader would pay $2. If at the end of the next trading session the new settlement price were $101, a long trader would pay $1, and a short trader would receive $1. If at the end of this last trading session a short trader initiated the delivery process, the price that the long trader would pay to the short trader for the Treasury bond would be calculated using the $101 settlement price.[2]

The short trader has many delivery options, a few of which will be detailed here. The quality option gives the short trader the right to deliver any $100,000 U.S. Treasury bond, provided it has at least fifteen years remaining until maturity, if the bond is noncallable, or has at least fifteen years to its first call date

if it is callable. The short trader also has a timing option—the option to deliver the underlying Treasury bond on any business day during the delivery month. Additionally, the short trader has what is known as the wild card option. When the market closes, the settlement committee meets and establishes the settlement price for that day at approximately 2:00 P.M. (central standard time) and marking to market occurs. During the delivery month, the short trader has until 8:00 P.M. to decide whether to initiate the delivery process and to receive an invoice amount calculated using the 2:00 P.M. settlement price. Specifically, the short trader may wait until 8:00 P.M., monitoring bond markets, and then decide to deliver on the futures contract, receiving for the bond an amount calculated using the 2:00 P.M. settlement price. If the short trader decides not to initiate delivery, this same scenario is repeated the following business day until the final settlement price is posted. With the posting of the final settlement price, the wild card option expires.

Valuing the Wild Card Option. Determining the value of the wild card option embedded in the Treasury bond futures contract involves several questions. How much is it worth to the short trader to be allowed to wait until 8:00 P.M. to initiate the delivery process at the 2:00 P.M. settlement price? Suppose the option is removed from the futures contract. How much would someone not involved in the Treasury bond futures contract pay for a series of options permitting until 8:00 P.M. for a Treasury bond to be sold at a price set at 2:00 P.M.? Clearly, the option has value. If Treasury bond prices decreased significantly between 2:00 P.M. and 8:00 P.M., the bonds could be purchased at the new lower price and sold at the higher price, resulting in a profit. Alternatively, if Treasury bond prices rose over the six-hour period, the option would not be exercised, in favor of waiting until the next day when there would be another opportunity. This process could continue until the option expired. Thus, as an option separated from the futures contract the wild card option's

Table 1
The Value of Separated and Embedded Wild Card Options[a]

Wild Card Plays Remaining[b]	Embedded Wild Card	Separated Wild Card
1	.017	.199
2	.026	.312
3	.033	.371
4	.037	.421
5	.043	.454
6	.045	.486
7	.050	.528
8	.054	.559
9	.056	.590
10	.058	.612
11	.060	.627
12	.062	.653
13	.063	.666
14	.065	.680
15	.067	.697
16	.068	.700

[a] *In dollars, with a standard error of one cent. For comparison purposes, the futures price of the futures contract is approximately $88.*
[b] *The number of business days left for the short trader to exercise the wild card option.*

value comes from the opportunity to exercise the option when Treasury bond prices decline during the six-hour period.

However, it is incorrect to value the option embedded inside the futures contract in this way. Exercising the wild card option has the additional consequence of closing the futures contract position. After the wild card option has been exercised, the Treasury bond is sold from the short trader to the long trader, and the contract is fulfilled. It should be kept in mind that the wild card option belongs to the short trader of the Treasury bond futures contract, who profits from marking-to-market payments when the settlement price declines. As discussed, the value of the separated wild card option comes from the opportunity to exercise the option when Treasury bond prices decline drastically between 2:00 P.M. and 8:00 P.M.. However, if a short trader exercises the wild card option in this scenario, closing the position, the next marking-to-market payment is not made. Given that bond prices have decreased drastically, the lost marking-to-market payment appears to be a profitable opportunity sacrificed by exercising the wild card option. Thus, to value the wild card option embedded inside the futures contract the short trader must consider that exercising the wild card option may result in closing a profitable futures position. This fact is not taken into account in valuing the wild card option separately because the option's holder has no short position in the futures contract and thus would not be involved with marking-to-market payments.

Including the consequence that exercising the wild card option will close the futures contract position changes not only the value of the wild card option but the conditions under which it will be exercised. An investor may not exercise the wild card option embedded inside the futures contract, even though it results in a large positive cash flow if the marking-to-market cash flow is believed to be larger. Furthermore, an investor may exercise the wild card option when the cash flow is negative to avoid an even larger expected loss from the marking-to-market payment.

Clearly, a wild card option separated from the futures contract is of an entirely different nature than when it is embedded inside the futures contract. However, analyzing embedded options by separation, even though it may be inappropriate, is quite common. Contributing to this tendency is the fact that most textbooks discussing the wild card option of the Treasury bond futures contract actually discuss the separated wild card option, as in the following passages: "Occasionally, news that causes a significant fall in the value of bonds can occur after the market closes, but before the deadline for announcing plans to deliver. The short trader can then announce the intention to deliver, thereby locking-in the settlement price for that day, a price that does not reflect the bearish information for bonds. The next day, the bond will open at a lower price, and the short trader simply acquires the now cheaper bond for delivery at the old higher price" (Robert Kolb 1988, 198). The idea that the next marking to market will also be profitable is not addressed. Another example exactly matches the description of a wild card option separated from the futures contract: "Restricting attention to a particular deliverable bond whose invoice price is (fixed) at the 2:00 P.M. settlement price, the short effectively holds a put option on the bond (with an exercise price equal to the invoice amount of the bond) which expires at 8:00 P.M. Since there are actually many deliverable bonds, the wild card option is somewhat more complicated, as well as somewhat more valuable" (Darrell Duffie 1988).

Mispricing the wild card option can be costly to investors in two different ways. First, investors may exercise the option at times that are less than optimal because they have not taken into account the full effects of exercising it. Second, by separating the embedded option investors may agree to an incorrect futures price when they enter the contract. Valued as an embedded option the wild card option is worth significantly less than as a separated option, as shown in Table 1. Table 1 presents the results of a simulation run to value both the embedded and the separated wild card option by simulating the change in interest rates during the six-hour period when the option may be exercised. (See the appendix for a more detailed discussion of the simulation.) In the simulation, separating the wild card option from the Treasury bond futures contract results in an option worth approximately ten times that of the embedded option. It should be clear that separating the option from the futures contract does not properly value the embedded option.

Conclusion

Two examples have been presented to illustrate a problem in valuing embedded options. Often, the process used does not value the embedded option but rather, because it is simpler to calculate, a similar option separated from the contract. The separated option's value may or may not be equivalent to the embedded option's. In callable Treasury bonds the separated and embedded call options have equal value. In Treasury bond futures contracts, however, the embedded wild card option is worth considerably less than the separated one. Thus, when comparing the separated and embedded options, it is important to determine that all implications of exercising the embedded option match those of exercising the separated option. Specifically, all cash flows of one must match the cash flows of the other. Otherwise, the embedded option may be an entirely different security, and valuing it incorrectly could prove to be costly.

Appendix

A computer simulation was performed to observe the difference in value between the wild card option embedded in the Treasury bond futures contract and a wild card option separated from the contract. The term $b(t,T)$ is defined as the price at time t of a default-free zero-coupon bond that pays one dollar at its maturity, time T. It is assumed that, at any fixed point in time, prices exist for all possible zero-coupon bonds. Further, $f(t,T)$ is defined as the instantaneous forward interest rate at time T as seen from time t: $f(t,T)$ is the forward interest rate that one could contract for at time t on a default-free loan during the forward period $[T, T + dT]$. To avoid arbitrage, there exists the following relationship between bond prices (assuming the prices are smooth) and the forward rate curve:

$$b(t,T) = \exp\left[-{}_t\int {}^T f(t,\mu)d\mu\right].$$

Thinking of each payment of a Treasury bond as its own zero-coupon bond implies that noncallable Treasury bonds may be priced as the sum of zero-coupon bonds. Thus the prices of noncallable Treasury bonds can be calculated from the forward interest rate curve.

For the purpose of the simulation, it is assumed that the forward rate curve's fluctuation over time was according to the Heath, Jarrow, and Morton continuous time constant model, which was chosen because of its simplicity.[1] This model assumes changes in the forward rate curve over time to be random parallel shifts (with the inclusion of a small correction term to make the model arbitrage-free), such that

$$df(t,T) = \sigma dW(t) + \alpha(t,T)dt,$$

where

$$\alpha(t,T) = \sigma^2 t \left(T - \frac{t}{2}\right).$$

The term σ is the constant volatility over the entire forward rate curve, $W(t)$ is a standard Wiener process, and α is a function necessary to avoid arbitrage. Typically, α

Appendix (continued)

is very small. The fact that the change in the forward rate curve is independent of the value of the initial forward rate curve means that negative forward rates are possible in the future, even if the initial forward rate curve is strictly positive. However, this forward rate model was chosen because small parallel shifts in the forward rate curve seem reasonable over the six-hour period during which the wild card option may be exercised.

The simulation started at the settlement time, with one wild card play remaining, and the change in the forward interest rate curve was calculated from 2:00 P.M. to 8:00 P.M. using the continuous time constant model of Heath, Jarrow, and Morton. At 8:00 P.M. the values of both wild card options were computed from the simulated forward rate curve. The calculation of the separated wild card option's value is straightforward, being simply the difference between the value of payment received for the bond calculated from the 2:00 P.M. settlement price and the current 8:00 P.M. bond price. To do the more complicated calculation of the value of the embedded wild card option, the upper bound as detailed by Hugh Cohen (1991) was used.[2]

Once the values of both wild card options were determined at the point of having one exercise period remaining, the values at the settlement time with two wild card plays available were calculated, assuming that the option was exercised only if the payoff was greater than the expected payoff with one wild card play remaining. Working backward in this manner, the values of both wild card options were calculated over the entire delivery month.

A standard deviation of .02 was used as the annual standard deviation in the forward rates. The bonds used and their conversion factors were taken from Kolb (1988) as the bonds available for delivery on June 1, 1987. In addition, the following initial stepwise forward rate curve was used for each run of the simulation:

$$fw(0, 0.25, 0.5, 1, 5, 10, 35) = (0.076, 0.079, 0.082, 0.087, 0.089, 0.09, 0.09).$$

The values of the two wild card options are given in Table 1 as a function of the number of business days remaining for the short trader to exercise the wild card option.

Notes

1. For a complete explanation of this model see Heath, Jarrow, and Morton (forthcoming).
2. In Cohen (1991), under the assumption of the existence of an unique equivalent martingale measure, a theoretical upper bound for the value of the wild card option is established. This upper bound is used as the value of the wild card option in the simulation.

Notes

1. According to the *Wall Street Journal*, the open interest was more than 260,000 on July 11, 1991. Because each futures contract is on a $100,000 face value U.S. Treasury bond, the collective face value of the open interest is $26 billion.
2. The actual invoice amount depends on which Treasury bond the short trader chooses to deliver. Every possible deliverable bond (the terms of which are defined later) has a factor that is multiplied by the settlement price. This product plus the accrued interest of the delivered bond is the amount paid by the long trader to the short trader.

References

Bulletin of the United States Treasury, Fall 1990.

Cohen, Hugh. "The Wild Card Option in Treasury Bond Futures Is Relatively Worthless." Federal Reserve Bank of Atlanta Working Paper 91-13, November 1991.

Duffie, Darrell. *Futures Markets*. Englewood Cliffs, N.J.: Prentice Hall, 1988.

Heath, David, Robert Jarrow, and Andrew Morton. "Bond Pricing and the Term Structure of Interest Rates: A New Methodology for Contingent Claims Valuation." *Econometrica* (forthcoming).

Kolb, Robert. *Understanding Futures Markets*. Glenview, Ill.: Scott, Foresman and Company, 1988.

Applications

Forecasting Stock Market Volatility Using Options on Index Futures

Steven P. Feinstein

F inancial economists, especially those who work for the Federal Reserve, are often asked: Is the stock market going up or down? The most honest answer, and the only one that should be given, is "Yes, most likely." After the requisite resigned chuckle, a more persistent questioner will occasionally follow the first query with "How much is the market likely to fluctuate?" This follow-up is both fair and relevant. Most people who follow the market have a direct investment interest and need to know an asset's degree of risk in order to decide whether the expected return on the investment represents adequate compensation.[1] Volatility forecasts are also important to policymakers, who might use these forecasts to gauge market uncertainty and to determine when to change policy or to make announcements with minimal disruption to the financial markets.

Stock market volatility is constantly changing.[2] Therefore, investors and market watchers must continually update their volatility forecasts, which is no easy task because of the numerous factors involved. Past returns, a firm's leverage, announcements affecting a company or the whole market, option and futures expirations, holidays, expanded hours of trading, and changes in margin requirements are just some of the influences on stock volatility that have been tested.[3] Though digesting all of these elements and turning them into an integrated forecast is difficult, a short-cut method, pioneered by Henry A. Latane and Richard J. Rendleman, Jr. (1976), is available; this method allows one to infer a volatility forecast from prices of stock options. (An option is a contract that affords the buyer the right, but not the obligation, to buy or sell an asset for a prespecified price on or before some selected date. They differ from futures contracts in that a futures contract requires

This article was originally published in the Atlanta Fed's May/June 1989 Economic Review. *At the time the article was written, Feinstein was an economist in the financial section of the Atlanta Fed's research department.*

ed date. They differ from futures contracts in that a futures contract requires the purchase or sale of the underlying asset on the given date.) This "implied volatility" should inherently consider all available information on relevant factors.[4]

Stock-index options and stock-index futures began trading in January 1983. The presence of a market for stock-index options makes it possible to compute implied volatilities that pertain to the stock market as a whole rather than to a single security. A sufficient period of time has now elapsed since the introduction of stock-index options and futures that research can determine the viability of using implied volatilities based on these instruments to predict overall stock-market volatility.

This article describes the theory behind the implied-volatility method, searches for the best way to measure it, tests it for efficiency and bias, and illustrates its usefulness for anticipating change in stock-market volatility.[5] Whereas previous studies have addressed these issues using cross-sectional data from several stocks collectively over various forecast periods, this study focuses on the volatility of one vehicle, the Standard and Poor's 500 index, over several years.[6] This time-series approach can—more definitively than earlier studies—establish whether the implied-volatility approach is practical for forecasting volatility on an ongoing basis.

Implied-Volatility Theory

A stock option's price depends on the anticipated future volatility of the stock underlying the option. (See the box on page 199 for a simplified explanation of this connection.) This relationship has been formalized by Fischer Black and Myron S. Scholes (1972, 1973) in an explicit option-pricing formula that has held up quite well under extensive empirical testing.[7] The Black-Scholes option-pricing formula relates an option's price to five variables: the stock price; the strike price of the option (that is, the price that is written into the option contract); the interest rate; the time remaining before the option's expiration; and the volatility of the underlying stock price, which in this case is the standard deviation of the stock's returns.[8] The stock price, the strike price, and time to expiration are easily observed, and reasonable proxies exist for the interest rate. The option price itself is determined in the market and is likewise observable. Thus, of the six variables in the Black-Scholes formula (five inputs and one output), only the volatility cannot be directly observed.

In practice, people use forecasts for future stock volatility—the last element of the Black-Scholes formula. Market watchers, such as other investors, policymakers, and regulators, can thus extract the forecast by finding the volatility value that is consistent with the observed option price and the other variables in the option-pricing formula. The two researchers (1972) showed that sizable profits could be reaped from incorporating perfect forecasts of volatility into their formula. One can assume safely, then, that option traders would try to use all pertinent information in order to construct the best possible forecasts of future volatility.

A 1988 paper by this author showed that for at-the-money options—for which the discounted strike price equals the stock price—inserting an unbiased estimate of the standard deviation of future stock returns into the Black-Scholes formula produces an unbiased estimate of the correct Black-Scholes no-arbitrage option price, at which the strategy of trading in both options and stocks yields no unusually high profits.[9] Thus, when pricing at-the-money options, agents' forecasts of volatility should be unbiased, that is, correct on average.

Conceptually, one would like to invert the Black-Scholes formula, such that stock-option volatility could be determined from the five observable variables. Although the formula cannot be inverted explicitly, one can use iterative methods to identify the volatility value that is consistent with the observed option price. This extracted measure is the Black-Scholes implied volatility.

Properties of the Implied Volatility. Implied volatility forecasts have several advantages over historically based estimates of stock volatility, such as the sample standard deviations from a history of past stock-price variations. Historical projections are necessarily backward-looking; to be used as forecasts, these estimates require an assumption that future performance will resemble the past's. The implied volatility, alternatively, is forward-looking and, by design, a forecast of future vicissitudes.

Unlike historical estimates, the implied volatility is instantaneous—that is, it can be computed from data generated at any given moment. Since option prices quickly incorporate new information, the implied volatility responds immediately, reflecting changes in the volatility forecast. Unlike the historical estimate, which reacts slowly to changing conditions, the implied volatility can detect sudden changes in market sentiment.

Although the computations are more complex for the implied-volatility forecast than for the measure-

Why Option Prices Reflect Anticipated Stock Volatility

Full appreciation of the relationship between option prices and stock volatility requires close scrutiny of the Black-Scholes formula and an understanding of its derivation. An intuitive grasp, however, can be acquired from consideration of the option strategy known as a "straddle."

A straddle is the purchase of both a call option and a put option on the same stock. The call option will pay off if the stock price rises, whereas the put option will pay off if the stock price falls sufficiently. Suppose, for example, a stock is selling for $100. A straddle may consist of a call option with strike price $120 and a put option with strike price $80. The call and put options will usually sell for considerably less money than these amounts. Should the stock price rise beyond $120, the call will become valuable while the put becomes worthless. Should the stock price fall below $80, the put will be in the money while the call becomes worthless.

The straddle will pay off if the stock price bounces past *either* strike price. The figure below shows the potential stock prices for which the combined straddle portfolio (owning both the put and the call) generates positive payoffs. As long as the stock price moves sufficiently in either direction, whether the stock rises or falls is immaterial.

The more volatile a stock is, the more likely it is to bounce outside the range defined by the strike prices. Consequently, straddles on more volatile stocks have greater likelihood of producing revenue. Thus, the initial price of a straddle—that is, the sum of the initial put and call prices—must depend on the anticipated stock volatility. Modern option-pricing theory provides methods to value the individual components of the straddle. The dependence on stock volatility is a feature retained by each option individually.

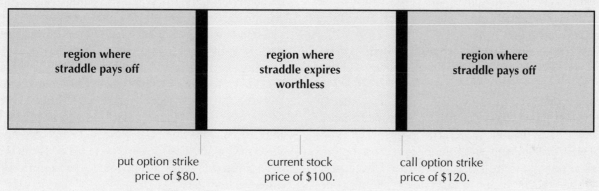

| region where straddle pays off | region where straddle expires worthless | region where straddle pays off |

| put option strike price of $80. | current stock price of $100. | call option strike price of $120. |

Should the stock prices move past either strike price, represented by the dark vertical lines, the straddle portfolio—consisting of one call and one put option—will become valuable. Should the stock value price remain in the color-shaded region, near its initial value, the straddle will expire worthless.

Since a more volatile stock is more likely to bounce past the strike prices, options on such stocks must cost more. Consequently, stock option prices reflect anticipated stock volatility.

ment of historical volatility, much less data are required. Historical volatilities are based on many observations of past stock returns, but the implied volatility requires only current values of the five observable Black-Scholes variables.

Other Consolidated Forms of Multiple Implied Volatilities

On any underlying security, simultaneous trading takes place in several call options, each differing in strike price and maturity date. A *call* option grants the right to buy a fixed amount of an underlying asset at a specified price within a given period of time; a *put* option, on the other hand, is an option contract designed to sell the underlying asset. For the Standard and Poor's (S&P) 500 futures call options, five different strike prices and three different maturity classes are usually available. (A *maturity class* refers to all options with the same expiration date.)

Each of these contracts provides its own implied volatility. Furthermore, the put options actively traded on these contracts provide implied volatilities, too. On any given trading day, an investor can purchase a put or call on an S&P 500 index future with one of three expiration dates and five prices corresponding to each of the dates. Thus, the market actually offers approximately 30 different S&P 500 index futures options at a given time, each of which can yield an implied-volatility forecast. Since the many implied volatilities that can be derived from these options rarely agree, even within the same maturity class, researchers face a dilemma: when forecasting volatility over the life span of one maturity class, which implied volatility should be trusted?

Various schemes have been suggested to incorporate the multiple implied volatilities into one optimal forecast. Each plan tries to produce a consolidated forecast in which bias is minimized and efficiency, maximized. The approaches range from choosing one particular contract's implied volatility and discarding all others to constructing various weighted or simple averages from the multiple implied volatilities. A later section of this article searches for the best implied-volatility form by examining the performance of the established consolidation methods and by considering one new technique.[10]

An Innovative Implied-Volatility Form. Averaging several implied volatilities from options with different strike prices has the desirable effect of reducing the impact of any data error or anomalous price, but this method also has an undesirable consequence. J.S. Butler and Barry Schachter (1986) showed that implied volatilities from most options should necessarily be biased, particularly for options that are well in or out of the money. (With in-the-money options, the futures price relates to the exercise price in such a manner that the purchaser profits from exercising the option; for a call option, the index price exceeds the exercise price, and for a put option, the index price is lower than the exercise price. At expiration, out-of-the-money options result in a complete loss of the investor's money.) Although this bias should not be present in at-the-money options (Steven P. Feinstein 1988), averaging implied volatilities derived from out-of-the-money options together with those from at-the-money options contaminates the theoretically unbiased at-the-money implied volatilities with systematic errors.

With this problem in mind, another strategy for reducing noise while still focusing on at-the-money options was investigated; a measure was constructed from intertemporal averaging, that is, averaging the implied volatilities from at-the-money call options observed on a small number of successive days. Some error is introduced because not completely up-to-date volatility forecasts are included; also, the implied-volatility forecasts encompass the lagged dates as well as the remaining future horizon. Yet, as long as the forecast horizon is long relative to the number of lags averaged, the informational deficiency and slight mismatch in forecast horizons should cause little damage.

The exact construction of this new form of implied-volatility forecast is given in the appendix, and the established forms are discussed in more detail in the data section that follows. The new forecast method and the established implied-volatility forms were compared on the basis of efficiency and bias. As will be shown, the new technique proved valuable.

Empirical Tests

Implied-volatility forecasts were constructed and compared with the stock-market volatility that actually transpired. A naive forecast, consisting of the sample standard deviation of stock-market returns from the 20 trading days (roughly one month) up to and including the date of the implied-volatility forecast, provided a basis for comparison. Mean squared errors and mean absolute errors were computed as measures of the forecasts' efficiency, and the various forms of implied-volatility forecasts were ranked according to these indicators. The forecasts were tested for bias by examining whether mean errors were significantly different from zero.

Time Series Design. Care was taken to ensure that all observations of forecast errors were statistically independent. Satisfying this need for independence required contructing a specially designed time series for the following reason: Since the forecast spans for all implied volatilities from the same maturity class overlap, their forecast errors are correlated. For instance, note that on any given day, the forecast span of an implied volatility is the time interval from that date out to the expiration date of the option. An implied volatility derived from an option of the same maturity class on a subsequent day will forecast over the shorter span from that later day out to the same expiration date. Thus, implied volatilities from the same maturity class taken on different days project across overlapping time intervals. Since the spans include common days, the forecasting errors in implied volatilities from the same maturity class are correlated, even when the forecasts are made on different dates. An example will further explain this problem:

The forecast error in the implied volatility derived from the June 1983 contract on April 1, 1983, is correlated with the forecast error in the implied volatility derived from the June 1983 contract on April 30, 1983; both forecast spans include May 1983, and any surprises in actual volatility during May 1983 will appear in both forecast errors. The overlap of forecast spans is illustrated in Chart 1.

To avoid this problem, one date was chosen from the life of each maturity class. Observations on these dates alone made up the time series of forecasts. The exact dates were selected so that no forecast horizons would overlap and all forecast spans would be equal in length.[11] Specifically, from each maturity class, the implied volatility from the 57th trading day prior to option expiration was included. For example, the implied volatilitiy from the June 1984 class was sampled on March 26, 1984, when the June contracts were 57 trading days from maturity. This procedure resulted in a sample of implied volatilities on the S&P 500 futures such that each observation represented a 57-day forecast with no overlap of forecast spans.[12]

Standard interval lengths shorter than 57 days can also produce time series free of overlapping forecasts. To test how implied volatilities performed over shorter horizons, this study constructed two such series of briefer forecasts. These additional time series forecast over 38- and 19-day horizons. Thus, the necessary data were available to test how well implied volatilities based on stock-index options forecast stock-market volatility over 57, 38, and 19 trading days.

The Data

Options on S&P 500 Index Futures. The empirical tests were conducted on implied volatilities from options on S&P 500 index futures. The S&P 500 is a broad-based stockmarket index that generally represents the stock market as a whole. Another advantage of this particular instrument is that the S&P 500 index future and its respective option are popular and actively traded. Consequently, the end-of-day settlement prices, which are easily obtained from daily newspapers and which are used in this study, almost always represent actual trades that took place simultaneously at the market's close. This simultaneity is necessary to compute implied volatilities precisely.

Furthermore, since the index futures option is traded as a single instrument, it avoids the problem of nonsychronization that occurs when using stock index

options. (*Nonsynchronization* refers to the fact that a stock index incorporates the last traded prices of the stocks in the index, which are not necessarily the result of recent trades.) Investors have access to all information about the underlying stocks, even news affecting infrequently traded equities, when pricing the index future. Thus, index futures are apt to reflect all available information, whereas the quoted index might not.[13] Additionally, although anticipated dividends must be subtracted from stock prices in order to price options on stocks, this correction is not needed when pricing options on stock futures. Futures pay no dividends, and so the market's pricing of the future has already, in effect, made the adjustment.

To derive implied volatilities from options on futures, one must use a slightly different option-pricing formula. The pricing formula for options on futures is quite similar to the formula for pricing options on stocks. The only difference is that the discounted future price takes the place of the stock price (Black 1976).[14]

By construction, then, the implied volatilities examined in this study were forecasts of the standard deviations of the percent changes in the discounted S&P 500 index futures. These standard deviations are closely related to the volatility of the S&P 500 index itself since the discounted index futures price must equal the dividend-corrected, full-information index price in order to preclude arbitrage possibilities.

The Raw Data. The Chicago Mercantile Exchange provided settlement prices of the futures and calls, as well as each option's strike price and expiration date. For the risk-free interest rate this study incorporated the annualized yield converted from the average of the bid and asked discounts of the particular Treasury bill that would be the first to mature after each respective option. Thus, the term of the risk-free rates coincides closely with that of the options.

For each of the 3 forecast series, 23 separate implied volatility observations were constructed, one from each of the maturity classes between June 1983 and December 1988. This study excluded the March 1983 contract, the first S&P 500 index futures option marketed, because trading on it began with less than 57 trading days to maturity.

Construction of the Actual Realized Standard Deviations. In order to assess the forecast accuracy of each implied volatility, the actual fluctuation in the S&P 500 futures subsequent to each forecast was measured. Actual volatilities were determined by computing the sample standard deviations of percent changes in discounted S&P 500 future prices.[15]

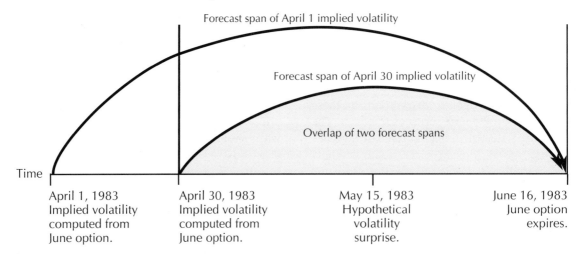

Chart 1
An Example of the Correlation of Forecast Errors

Forecast span of April 1 implied volatility

Forecast span of April 30 implied volatility

Overlap of two forecast spans

Time

| April 1, 1983
Implied volatility
computed from
June option. | April 30, 1983
Implied volatility
computed from
June option. | May 15, 1983
Hypothetical
volatility
surprise. | June 16, 1983
June option
expires. |

Suppose the implied volatilities forecast on the two dates in April are perfect forecasts with the exception that neither predicts a surprise on May 15, 1983. This surprise will appear in both measures' forecast errors. These errors would thus be correlated.

Construction of the Implied Volatilities. Each implied volatility was computed via an iterative search procedure that located the volatility value in the pricing formula that is consistent with the values of the observable variables. After implied volatilities were computed for all contracts on each selected date, the various consolidation schemes were undertaken to produce the different forms of consolidated implied volatilities.[16]

One measure—the basic implied volatility—is the volatility implied from the just-out-of-the-money call option.[17] Another, the average implied volatility, is the arithmetic average of the implied volatilities from all call options of the same maturity class.[18] A third, Latane and Rendleman's implied volatility, is a weighted average in which the weights are proportional to the derivatives of the call price with respect to the volatility.[19] Donald P. Chiras and Steven Manaster's implied volatility is a weighted average in which the weights are proportional to the elasticities instead of the derivatives.[20] The put implied volatility is derived from the just-out-of-the-money put option. The put-and-call implied volatility is the average of the implied volatilities from the just-out-of-the-money call option and the just-out-of-the-money put option.[21] Finally, the Atlanta Fed implied volatility is a new measure: the weighted intertemporal average of implied volatilities from just-out-of-the-money call

options. (This last measure is described in greater detail in the appendix.)

All implied volatilities were computed to be forecasts of per-trading-day standard deviations; this method differs from previous studies that constructed implied volatilities based on calendar days. A sample standard deviation of stock returns is a measure of standard deviation per trading day, and so to be comparable the resulting implied volatility should be per trading day as well.

The Naive Forecast—A Standard for Comparison. A conventional history-based forecast of volatility, referred to in this article as the Naive forecast, was also constructed for purposes of comparison. This measure is the sample standard deviation of discounted futures returns over the 20 days up to and including the date of each implied-volatility observation. *Actual* is the realization variable—the actual sample standard deviation of discounted stock futures returns over the respective forecast intervals.

The full data set contained a series of 23 observations of each of the implied-volatility forms and for each of the three forecast horizons described above: 57, 38, and 19 days. Corresponding Actual and Naive measures complete the data set. The 57-day basic and Atlanta Fed implied-volatility forecasts, the Naive forecast, and the Actual measure are presented in Table 1. The 57-day basic implied-volatility forecast and the Actual measure are graphed over time in Charts 2 and 3.

Full versus Precrash Sample. The time series include the stock-market crash of October 1987. The crash is evident in the actual realization variable following the 57-day December 1987 forecast. Furthermore, the 38- and 19-day December 1987 implied volatilities and Naive forecasts were made just after the market break, when option volumes were low and option prices were much higher than they had ever been. Table 1 indicates that implied volatilities for the 57-day forecast were indeed much higher following the crash than before, but they gradually moderated from those extreme levels. So that the crash's effects on the measures could be analyzed, all of the tests were performed on the entire data sample and then again on just the precrash sample, that is, the sample period preceding but not including the December 1987 contract. Means and standard deviations of all measures are presented in Tables 2 and 3. The statistics are given for both the entire sample period and for the precrash sample.

Results of the Tests

How the Various Implied Volatilities Performed. Tables 2 and 3 reveal that the various consolidation methods produce similar forecasts. Yet the mean squared forecast errors presented in Table 4, which show the efficiency of the different projections, reveal a definite pattern. The Atlanta Fed intertemporal average exhibited smaller mean squared errors—indicating greater accuracy—among the 57- and 38-day forecasts, and this result held for both the full sample and for the precrash sample.

The results were different among the 19-day forecasts. The basic as well as the put-and-call implied volatilities outperformed that of the Atlanta Fed over the full sample, and the latter displayed the highest mean squared error over the precrash sample. Among the 19-day implied-volatility forecasts, the basic form showed minimum mean squared errors over both samples, and understandably so. Relative to the shorter forecast horizon, the error introduced in the other samples by averaging implied volatilities that were not up-to-date is greater than any errors in the basic format stemming from errors in variables. The implication from the 19-day forecast results is clear: for longer-term forecasts intertemporal averaging of implied volatilities is helpful, but for shorter forecasts

the lone current implied volatility from the just-out-of-the-money option dominates. Averaging among the multiple contrasts with different strike prices appears to provide no benefit over simply selecting the just-out-of-the-money option.

Comparisons between the Implied Volatilities and the Naive Forecast. Table 4 also compares the various implied volatilities and the historically based forecast. The 57- and 38-day implied volatilities outperformed the Naive forecast over both the full and precrash samples, and the 19-day implied volatilities did better than the Naive forecast over the full sample. Only in the precrash period, among the 19-day forecasts, did the Naive forecast outperform the group of implied volatilities.

There are several possible explanations for failure of the implied-volatility forecasts among the 19-day projections in the precrash period. Perhaps the possibility of a large market shift has always been accounted for in the determination of implied volatilities. When such a break did occur in October 1987, this consideration was validated and the implied volatilities outperformed the Naive forecast. Markets seem to have been anticipating a crash, in the form of a "crash premium" in options prices, which produced large positive forecast errors. This scenario, however, does not adequately explain why the Naive forecast outperformed the implied volatilities only over the short horizon.

Another explanation might be that the Naive predictor functions well over short horizons in normal circumstances, causing it to outperform the implied volatilities among the 19-day forecasts in the precrash sample. After the crash, however, the Naive forecast could not reliably predict a return to normality. Other possible explanations exist, and future research will be directed at addressing this phenomenon. The matter is primarily of academic interest, though. The crash occurred, and over *all* available data the implied-volatility forecasts of long, medium, and short lengths performed better on the basis of mean squared error than did the Naive alternative.

Mean Absolute Errors. The mean squared error just discussed assigns greater weight to larger errors than to smaller ones. Consequently, over a period such as 1983-88 in which one enormous market shift transpired, the rankings could be based primarily on how well each forecast performed near the crash. To test that possibility, mean absolute errors were computed, and the forecasts were ranked accordingly. The mean absolute error statistic, which is the mean of the absolute values of the errors, weighs all errors equally. Table 5 presents these statistics and the rankings.

Table 1
Selected 57-Day Implied-Volatility Forecasts and Realizations
(standard deviation of daily percent returns)

Date	Maturity Class	Actual Volatility	Naive Forecast	Basic Implied Volatility	Atlanta Fed Implied Volatility
3/25/83	6/83	0.009499	0.011625	0.010791	0.010670
6/24/83	9/83	0.009158	0.010762	0.009684	0.009325
9/23/83	12/83	0.006917	0.006858	0.008598	0.008647
12/22/83	3/84	0.008069	0.007162	0.006768	0.006646
3/26/84	6/84	0.007894	0.007256	0.008194	0.008242
7/2/84	9/84	0.010431	0.007442	0.007562	0.007672
10/2/84	12/84	0.008636	0.009235	0.008943	0.008920
12/21/84	3/85	0.007875	0.009512	0.008035	0.008239
4/1/85	6/85	0.006050	0.006548	0.007570	0.007557
7/1/85	9/85	0.006344	0.005609	0.006394	0.006371
10/1/85	12/85	0.006583	0.008745	0.006862	0.006852
12/30/85	3/86	0.009730	0.007854	0.008712	0.009400
4/1/86	6/86	0.011083	0.009217	0.012115	0.012186
6/30/86	9/86	0.012601	0.010009	0.010401	0.010393
9/30/86	12/86	0.009273	0.015980	0.012199	0.011917
12/29/86	3/87	0.009985	0.007493	0.009912	0.009863
3/30/87	6/87	0.013617	0.010685	0.012707	0.012358
6/29/87	9/87	0.009013	0.006973	0.011430	0.011508
9/29/87	12/87	0.057259	0.012423	0.012459	0.012589
12/28/87	3/88	0.016797	0.018950	0.019941	0.019174
3/28/88	6/88	0.012347	0.010582	0.016645	0.015559
6/27/88	9/88	0.010308	0.012757	0.013649	0.012955
9/27/88	12/88	0.007728	0.007137	0.010946	0.010901

Source: Computed at the Federal Reserve Bank of Atlanta from data provided by the Chicago Mercantile Exchange.

The rankings for the long- and medium-range forecasts are virtually the same as those previously stated, with the set of implied volatilities besting the Naive forecast in both the full and precrash samples. Among the short-range forecasts, however, the rankings showed an important difference: The Naive predictor showed the lowest mean absolute error in both the full sample and the precrash sample. Since, relative to mean squared error, the mean absolute error statistic deemphasizes performance of the predictors around the time of the October 1987 crash, the difference between the two rankings would seem to pinpoint the crash as the time when the historically based forecast suffered relative to the implied volatilities, thus adding support to the hypothesis that the Naive forecast is effective over short horizons in calm conditions but will fail in a more turbulent environment.

Which consolidated implied-volatility form worked best on the basis of mean absolute error? Again, the rankings among the implied volatilities were topped by measures constructed exclusively from at-the-money call options. The Atlanta Fed implied volatility was the most accurate forecast among the 57- and 38-day forecasts. The basic implied volatility gave the best short-term implied-volatility forecast.

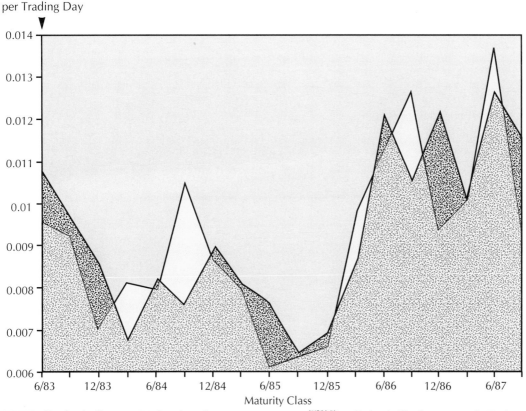

Chart 2
57-Day Implied-Volatility Forecast vs. 57-Day Realization
(Precrash Data Sample: June 1983 through September 1987 Contracts)

Standard
Deviations
of Returns
per Trading Day

Maturity Class

Realized volatility over 57 days from forecast observation through contract expiration

Implied volatility forecast made 57 days prior to contract expiration

In most periods prior to the crash, the basic implied-volatility forecast generally appears to have anticipated stock-market volatility shifts.
Source: See Table 1.

Tests for Bias. Tests were performed to determine if the mean errors were significantly different from zero. A significantly positive mean error would indicate that the forecast was biased upward, predicting too great a volatility. Significantly negative mean error would indicate a downward bias and an underestimation of future volatility. Table 6 presents the results of the tests.

The 57-day forecasts showed no significant bias, and most of the 38- and 19-day implied volatilities did not exhibit bias prior to the crash. Over the entire sample period, however, the implied volatilities did indeed show significant or nearly significant bias, indicating

that the implied-volatility forecasts moved up too much when they rose after the crash. The full-sample mean forecast errors of the 38-day implied volatilities were positive and approximately four times greater than the mean errors before the crash. The mean error in the full sample for the 19-day implied volatilities approximately doubled that in the precrash sample. Perhaps thinner trading in options following the crash led to mispricing, or maybe option prices rose to account for the possibility of a repeat market break that never materialized. Only time will tell whether this systematic positive bias is a persistent phenomenon or one confined to the aftermath of the crash.

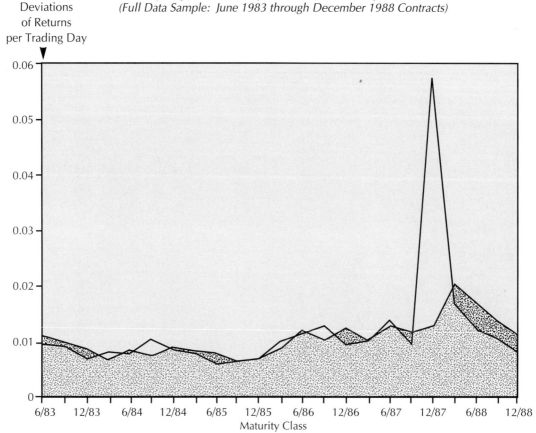

Chart 3
57-Day Implied-Volatility Forecast vs. 57-Day Realization
(Full Data Sample: June 1983 through December 1988 Contracts)

Standard
Deviations
of Returns
per Trading Day

Maturity Class

Realized volatility over 57 days from forecast observation through contract expiration

Implied volatility forecast made 57 days prior to contract expiration

The volatility in the period during which the crash occurred was of a much higher magnitude than previous volatility or forecasts. Following the crash, the implied volatility correctly forecast falling volatility.

Source: See Table 1.

Note that the Naive predictor never exhibited significant bias, but this outcome could be more a result of greater dispersion among the Naive predictor's forecast errors than a result of on-target forecasting. In both cases where the Naive forecast appeared unbiased and the implied volatilities appeared biased, errors in the historically based forecast exhibited far greater dispersion.

Using Implied Volatilities to Predict Volatility Changes

Although 38- and 19-day implied-volatility forecasts appear to be biased predictors of future swings in the market, these measures served quite well as harbingers of the *direction* of change in stock-market volatility. Whereas the Naive forecast assumes that the future will mirror the past, an implied-volatility forecast can be applied to predict whether future market performance will be more or less turbulent than in the past. A test was devised to see how useful the implied volatilities were for this purpose.

For this test, a drop in volatility is defined as occurring when a forecast span exhibits lower volatility than did the 20 days prior to the forecast date. A rise takes place when the span displays greater volatility than did the previous 20 days. The ratio of the realized or actual standard deviation to the Naive forecast will then indicate whether the period experienced a rise or a fall. If the former divided by the latter is

Table 2
Means of Implied-Volatility Forecasts and Realizations

	57-Day Forecasts		38-Day Forecasts		19-Day Forecasts	
	All Data	Precrash	All Data	Precrash	All Data	Precrash
Actual Volatility	0.011617	0.009042	0.009431	0.008727	0.008965	0.008451
Naive Forecast	0.009601	0.008831	0.013853	0.009326	0.009779	0.008664
Basic	0.010457	0.009270	0.012349	0.009388	0.010405	0.009197
Atlanta Fed	0.010345	0.009265	0.012036	0.009342	0.010601	0.009363
Average	0.010596	0.009384	0.012482	0.009554	0.010682	0.009415
Latane-Rendleman	0.010615	0.009410	0.012536	0.009628	0.010736	0.009505
Chiras-Manaster	0.010608	0.009346	0.012504	0.009488	0.010845	0.009424
Put	0.010621	0.009364	0.012555	0.009503	0.010684	0.009328
Put-and-Call	0.010539	0.009317	0.012452	0.009445	0.010545	0.009262

Source: See Table 1

Table 3
Standard Deviations of Implied-Volatility Forecasts and Realizations

	57-Day Forecasts		38-Day Forecasts		19-Day Forecasts	
	All Data	Precrash	All Data	Precrash	All Data	Precrash
Actual Volatility	0.010040	0.001998	0.003422	0.001827	0.003073	0.002271
Naive Forecast	0.003121	0.002370	0.016701	0.003009	0.005253	0.001747
Basic	0.003196	0.001929	0.010236	0.002323	0.003874	0.001889
Atlanta Fed	0.002957	0.001869	0.008700	0.002168	0.003970	0.002133
Average	0.003184	0.001904	0.010115	0.002325	0.003973	0.001854
Latane-Rendleman	0.003172	0.001897	0.010100	0.002285	0.003947	0.001853
Chiras-Manaster	0.003266	0.001924	0.010216	0.002407	0.004160	0.001917
Put	0.003343	0.001982	0.010246	0.002385	0.004198	0.001905
Put-and-Call	0.003267	0.001952	0.010239	0.002349	0.003983	0.001891

Source: See Table 1

greater than one, volatility has climbed; if the ratio is less than one, volatility has declined. In addition, the ratio of the implied volatility to the Naive forecast indicates whether a fall or a rise was predicted. If the implied volatility divided by the Naive forecast is greater than one, a forecast of greater volatility is issued. If that ratio is less than one, a fall in volatility is predicted.[22]

The 23 57-day spans in the full data sample contained 14 upswings and 9 downturns in volatility. The Atlanta Fed implied volatility correctly predicted the direction of these changes 19 times.[23] Six of the 9 falls and 13 of the 14 rises were correctly predicted, a success rate unlikely to have happened completely by chance. The probability of this outcome would be only 0.1 percent if the predictor were equally likely to succeed or fail. Around the 38-day forecasts, 16 falls and 7 rises took place. The Atlanta Fed implied volatility correctly predicted 17 of these changes—11 falls and 6 rises, a result that had only a 2.9 percent probability of occurring strictly by chance. For the 19-day forecasts, 11 falls and 12 rises took place; the Atlanta Fed implied volatility correctly predicted 17 of the 23 changes, 6 falls and 11 rises.

57-Day Forecasts

All Data		Precrash	
Atlanta Fed	0.0000898366	Atlanta Fed	0.0000020959
Basic	0.0000911502	Basic	0.0000021930
Average	0.0000913429	Chiras-Manaster	0.0000022796
Latane-Rendleman	0.0000913626	Average	0.0000023230
Put-and-Call	0.0000915179	Latane-Rendleman	0.0000023640
Chiras-Manaster	0.0000916063	Put-and-Call	0.0000024107
Put	0.0000919392	Put	0.0000026653
Naive Forecast	0.0000925160	Naive Forecast	0.0000057465

38-Day Forecasts

All Data		Precrash	
Atlanta Fed	0.0000411145	Atlanta Fed	0.0000037958
Average	0.0000613298	Basic	0.0000045031
Latane-Rendleman	0.0000613702	Put-and-Call	0.0000045916
Basic	0.0000622101	Latane-Rendleman	0.0000046010
Put-and-Call	0.0000628733	Average	0.0000046580
Chiras-Manaster	0.0000629718	Put	0.0000047388
Put	0.0000636279	Chiras-Manaster	0.0000048418
Naive Forecast	0.0002089594	Naive Forecast	0.0000074591

19-Day Forecasts

All Data		Precrash	
Basic	0.0000091484	Naive Forecast	0.0000054929
Put-and-Call	0.0000100337	Basic	0.0000062446
Atlanta Fed	0.0000102795	Put-and-Call	0.0000063854
Average	0.0000104832	Average	0.0000065595
Latane-Rendleman	0.0000105135	Put	0.0000065824
Put	0.0000110382	Chiras-Manaster	0.0000066718
Chiras-Manaster	0.0000120698	Latane-Rendleman	0.0000067284
Naive Forecast	0.0000133162	Atlanta Fed	0.0000070297

Source: See Table 1.

The indicator succeeded in forecasting a greater percentage of the rises than the falls, but the implied volatilities were more likely to be correct when predicting a fall than when predicting a rise, as can be seen by studying the results from a different perspective. The 57-day implied volatilities predicted rises 16 times, and 13 of these forecasts turned out to be correct. On the other hand, six of the seven "fall" predictions turned out to be accurate. The 38-day implied volatilities predicted falls 12 times, and on 11 occasions falls actually occurred. Among the 11 predictions of rises, only 6 were correct. The 19-day implied

volatilities predicted rises 16 times, 11 times correctly. Six of the seven predictions of falls were accurate.

Thus, the implied volatility "fall" forecasts were correct more often than the "rise" forecasts, an effect that is plausibly related to the positive bias detected in the 38-day and 19-day forecasts. If forecasts are biased upward, they will predict upturns too often and fail to predict some declines. When a fall is projected, however, the forecast reliability is great. Overall, though, the implied volatilities were useful in predicting changes in stock-market volatility, succeeding more than two-thirds of the time. This result cannot be

Table 5
Mean Absolute Errors and Rankings for Implied-Volatility Forecasts

57-Day Forecasts

All Data		Precrash	
Atlanta Fed	0.003317	Atlanta Fed	0.001122
Basic	0.003463	Basic	0.001158
Put-and-Call	0.003556	Chiras-Manaster	0.001210
Average	0.003576	Put-and-Call	0.001223
Chiras-Manaster	0.003590	Average	0.001246
Latane-Rendleman	0.003592	Latane-Rendleman	0.001269
Put	0.003658	Put	0.001299
Naive Forecast	0.003750	Naive Forecast	0.001914

38-Day Forecasts

All Data		Precrash	
Atlanta Fed	0.003275	Atlanta Fed	0.001471
Basic	0.003617	Basic	0.001554
Put-and-Call	0.003712	Put-and-Call	0.001601
Average	0.003715	Put	0.001648
Latane-Rendleman	0.003719	Chiras-Manaster	0.001673
Chiras-Manaster	0.003787	Average	0.001675
Put	0.003806	Latane-Rendleman	0.001686
Naive Forecast	0.005504	Naive Forecast	0.001982

19-Day Forecasts

All Data		Precrash	
Naive Forecast	0.002274	Naive Forecast	0.001820
Basic	0.002305	Basic	0.001851
Put-and-Call	0.002426	Put-and-Call	0.001892
Average	0.002469	Average	0.001924
Atlanta Fed	0.002490	Put	0.001934
Latane-Rendleman	0.002511	Chiras-Manaster	0.001949
Put	0.002547	Latane-Rendleman	0.002000
Chiras-Manaster	0.002644	Atlanta Fed	0.002004

Source: See Table 1.

wholly attributed to positive bias coupled with a rising trend in volatility, since nearly as many falls as rises took place over the period.

Conclusions and Suggestions for Future Research

This study demonstrates the usefulness of implied volatilities in forecasting stock-market vicissitudes. When forecasting 57 and 38 days into the future, im-plied volatilities were more efficient than the history-based sample of standard deviation of past returns (the Naive forecast). Among 19-day forecasts, however, the Naive forecast appeared to do better than the implied volatilities before the stock market crash of 1987, although the implied volatilities outperformed the Naive forecast after the crash.

Apparently, the Naive predictor functions best over short horizons when the market is calm. This result is quite reasonable in light of the Naive predictor's design, which is based on the past. One has no way of knowing ahead of time, however, whether calmness

Table 6
Results of t-tests on Implied-Volatility Forecasts

	Mean Errors		t-statistics of Hypothesis that Mean Error = 0	
	57-Day Forecasts		57-Day Forecasts	
	All Data	Precrash	All Data	Precrash
Naive Forecast	−0.00201	−0.000210	−1.00573	−0.404260
Basic	−0.00116	0.000228	−0.57436	0.715403
Average	−0.00102	0.000342	−0.50399	1.056126
Latane-Rendleman	−0.00100	0.000367	−0.49476	1.128814
Chiras-Manaster	−0.00100	0.000303	−0.49714	0.941579
Put	−0.00099	0.000321	−0.49008	0.920722
Put-and-Call	−0.00107	0.000275	−0.53214	0.824701
Atlanta Fed	−0.00127	0.000222	−0.63513	0.660540
	38-Day Forecasts		38-Day Forecasts	
	All Data	Precrash	All Data	Precrash
Naive Forecast	0.004421	0.000598	1.506796	1.028655
Basic	0.002917	0.000660	1.867351	1.499926
Average	0.003050	0.000826	1.984053	1.900026
Latane-Rendleman	0.003104	0.000900	2.024598	2.120899
Chiras-Manaster	0.003072	0.000760	1.970059	1.687388
Put	0.003123	0.000775	1.995856	1.746285
Put-and-Call	0.003020	0.000717	1.932285	1.628309
Atlanta Fed	0.002605	0.000614	2.085444	1.410572
	19-Day Forecasts		19-Day Forecasts	
	All Data	Precrash	All Data	Precrash
Naive Forecast	0.000814	0.000212	1.073707	0.417751
Basic	0.001440	0.000746	2.539720	1.433457
Average	0.001717	0.000964	2.934312	1.861818
Latane-Rendleman	0.001771	0.001054	3.058654	2.038533
Chiras-Manaster	0.001880	0.000973	3.019127	1.863861
Put	0.001719	0.000876	2.837983	1.666446
Put-and-Call	0.001580	0.000811	2.699463	1.553787
Atlanta Fed	0.001636	0.000912	2.783363	1.554338

Source: See Table 1.

will persist. Thus, the implied volatility is a necessary adjunct even when forecasting over very short horizons. Moreover, the Naive predictor is least reliable when volatility is changing, and this is just when a reliable predictor is needed most.

The Atlanta Fed implied volatility was the most efficient form of implied-volatility forecast when projecting over 57- and 38-day horizons, while the basic implied volatility was the most efficient among the 19-day implied-volatility forecasts. Remember that both the Atlanta Fed and the basic implied volatilities are constructed exclusively from just-out-of-the-money options, providing empirical support for the proposition that such options offer the most reliable implied-volatility forecasts. The forms that used away-from-the-money options fared worst, as predicted.

No statistically significant bias could be detected in the 57-day implied-volatility forecasts. The same can be said for the 38-day and 19-day forecasts prior to the 1987 crash with the one exception of the Latane and Rendleman implied-volatility form. In the data sample that included the crash, however, the implied-volatility forecasts displayed significant positive bias. Apparently, since the crash, implied-volatility forecasts have been too high relative to subsequently realized actual stock-market volatility.

This bias may be due to a flaw in the option-pricing mode, or it may reflect mistakes made by options market investors after the crash. Even in view of this result, implied volatilities might still have been the best forecasts attainable with all then-available information, and, furthermore, they might have been statistically unbiased in an a priori sense. Those postcrash implied volatilities may have correctly incorporated the possibility of another stock-market crash, yet the implied volatilities now appear to have been biased because that scenario did not happen.[24] There is no way to know. Whether the short- and medium-term implied volatilities will continue to appear biased can only be determined with continued monitoring and testing of future data.

The final test in this study demonstrated how an implied-volatility measure can be used as a leading indicator of stock-market volatility changes. The 57-day Atlanta Fed implied-volatility indicator was quite successful in predicting whether stock-market volatility would rise or fall.

Aside from the direct uses discussed in this study, implied volatility has a variety of other applications for both investors and policymakers. Since active trading now takes place in futures and options on fixed-income securities and on foreign currencies, in addition to stock indexes, implied volatilities from those options can be used to forecast the volatility of bond prices and exchange rates. Future testing should include these applications. Implied volatilities can also provide investors with up-to-date measures of the riskiness in various investment markets.

Also, policymakers can use these indicators to assess market uncertainty and to plan policy changes or announcements accordingly. Authorities can determine whether new policy has calmed or unsettled the markets. This information cannot be inferred from a price response alone since a large price swing might simply reflect adjustment to a new, stable level. Similarly, a small price response might disguise considerable uncertainty and a lack of consensus about equilibrium prices. The implied volatility, on the other hand, will indicate the new level of uncertainty in the form of traders' forecasts of future price stability.

Appendix
The Design of the Atlanta Fed Stock-Market Volatility Indicator

The Atlanta Fed implied-volatility indicator is a weighted average of current and lagged implied volatilities from just-out-of-the-money call options. The implied volatility from the one just-out-of-the-money call option on the current day is averaged together with the one implied volatility from the just-out-of-the-money option from each of the previous four days.

Averaging several closely related implied volatilities makes the resultant measure less sensitive to errors in measuring variables or to any temporary price anomalies. Including away-from-the-money options, however, should theoretically contaminate the resultant measure with systematic bias. (See Butler and Schacter 1986 and Feinstein 1988 for more on this topic.) Intertemporal averaging offers the benefit of averaging without having to rely on away-from-the-money options.

Intertemporal averaging has a drawback, nonetheless. Lagged implied volatilities are informationally deficient, that is, they contain a few days less information than current implied volatilities. Moreover, lagged implied volatilities forecast over slightly different spans. A lagged implied volatility's forecast span includes its immediate future, a few days that are not in the forecast span of the most current implied volatility. If the days following the lagged implied volatilities are anticipated to be unlike those in the remainder of the forecast span, this mismatch in spans could introduce noise into the averaged measure.

The problems with intertemporal averaging can be minimized by proper design of the averaging weights. Since lagged implied volatilities are as likely as the current implied volatility to suffer from errors in the raw variables, they should be given—at most—equal weight in the averaging. But, because lagged implied volatilities are deficient with respect to the information they contain, they reasonably should be given less weight and those weights should decline with the length of the lag.

A five-day information deficiency is more serious relative to a short forecast than to a long forecast. Similarly, a five-day mismatch of forecast spans is more serious when the forecast horizon is near than when it is distant. Thus, the pattern of weights should be related to the length of the forecast span. The weights should decline gradually with lag length when the horizon is distant, but for a nearby horizon the decline should be steep. For example, in constructing a 19-day implied volatility forecast, the average should place the greatest weight on the most current implied volatility, but in constructing a 57-day forecast the average should be more equally weighted.

The following weighting scheme, which has these properties, was developed and used to construct the Atlanta Fed implied volatility:

$$\omega_L = \frac{\left(\frac{Y}{60}\right)^L}{\sum\limits_{i=0}^{4} \left(\frac{Y}{60}\right)^i}$$

where ω is the weight assigned to the lagged implied volatility; L is the lag length, ranging from zero to four; and Y is the length of the forecast span, that is, the number of trading days between the forecast date and option expiration. The weights ω decline geometrically with lag length L, and the base factor varies with forecast span Y. The weights are normalized to sum to one.

The formula for the Atlanta Fed implied volatility is thus given by:

$$\sum\limits_{L=0}^{4} \omega_L \cdot IV_L$$

where IV_L is the implied volatility from the just-out-of-the money option observed on the Lth day prior to the current day.

Notes

1. See Feinstein (1987) for definitions and descriptions of stock-market volatility and a discussion of its costs.
2. See, for example, Officer (1973) or Feinstein (1987).
3. See Black (1976b) regarding the effects of recent stock returns and firm leverage; Pattel and Wolfson (1979, 1981) regarding the effects of announcements; Stoll and Whaley (1986) and Feinstein and Goetzmann (1988) regarding option and future expiration effects; Fama (1965) and French (1988) regarding holidays and trading hours; and Hardouvelis (1988) regarding margin requirements.
4. The reader unfamiliar with option fundamentals can find the necessary introduction in Feinstein and Goetzmann (1988).
5. A forecast is unbiased in the statistical sense if it is expected to be correct on average, which is a rather nice property to expect from a forecast. If, over time, a forecast method consistently produced forecasts that erred by some nonzero amount, that method's projections would be deemed biased. The "bias" would be the quantity, either negative or positive, by which the forecasts usually missed. No forecast method, however, can be counted on to produce perfect forecasts every time. Efficiency, in the statistical sense, measures the size of a forecasts' errors. A more efficient forecast usually has smaller errors.

   Unbiasedness and efficiency are desirable qualities in a forecast, but sometimes there is a trade-off between the two. A biased forecast that is very efficient is often better than an unbiased forecast which is inefficient. That is, a method that produces forecasts which are systematically too high or too low (biased) but quite close to the correct value (efficient) may be preferable to a method that produces forecasts that are on average correct but usually off by a large magnitude. This article describes the bias of the implied volatilities but ranks the measures by efficiency. Further discussion on optimal choice of a forecast is beyond the scope of this paper.
6. Cross-sectional studies were conducted by Latane and Rendleman (1976), Chiras and Manaster (1978), Schmalensee and Trippi (1978), and Beckers (1981).
7. Tests of the Black-Scholes model include those by Macbeth and Merville (1979).
8. In the original formulation of their model Black and Scholes required that the stock volatility be constant and known. Merton (1973), however, showed that the volatility need not be constant and that the pricing formula is easily generalized to account for volatility that changes with time. Yet in Merton's formulation, too, the stock volatility is assumed to be nonstochastic.
9. That is, the strike price discounted at the risk-free rate over the term of the option. The *risk-free* rate is the interest rate on risk-free bonds, such as those issued by the U.S. Treasury.
10. Also, different implied volatilities can be derived by using option pricing models other than the Black-Scholes model. These models either specify different assumptions regarding the process that drives stock prices, or they attempt to account for some factor ignored by the Black-Scholes model. Most of these models include additional unobservable variables, and so they require ad hoc assumptions in order to produce implied-volatility forecasts. Rubinstein (1985) showed, however, that under reasonable assumptions about the additional unobservable variables, the alter-

native models based on different stock processes produce implied volatilities that coincide with the Black-Scholes implied volatility for at-the-money moderate-term options. Consequently, little is lost by restricting the analysis in this article to Black-Scholes implied volatilities.

The early exercise futures option-pricing model developed by Whaley (1986) has no more variables than the Black-Scholes model and thus provides implied volatilities without ad hoc assumptions. When implied volatilities constructed from this model were tested, the measure did not deviate significantly from the at-the-money Black-Scholes implied volatility and performed virtually the same in each test. Thus, Whaley's numbers are not presented here since these results can be inferred from the Black-Scholes form.

11. This construction was necessary to avoid the heteroskedasticity attributable to the fact that implied volatilities from the same maturity class on different dates forecast over spans of varying length. The variances of the forecast errors will differ when the length of the forecast intervals differ.

12. This length, 57 days, was the shortest interval between contract expirations and thus the longest interval length for which forecast spans did not overlap. If the interval were longer, 60 trading days for instance, the 60-day span forecast by the December 1984 implied volatility would overlap the forecast span of the March 1985 implied volatility. The March 1985 forecast would have been made three days before the December contract expired. Using 57 days, no forecast spans overlap, and so all forecast errors should be uncorrelated.

13. This point is central in Kawaller, Koch, and Koch (1988).

14. That is, the future price discounted at the risk-free rate over the term of the option.

15. Note that the sample standard deviation is actually only an estimator for the "true" standard deviation parameter of the stock return process, and a biased one at that. The true volatility parameter of a stock process cannot be directly observed and so must be estimated; however, when investors speak of stock volatility, they are usually referring to the observable sample standard deviation. For the purposes of this article, the ability of the implied volatility to forecast the variable of common interest is assessed, that is, the subsequently realized sample standard deviation of stock market returns, corrected for bias. The bias correction involves premultiplying the sample standard deviation by a factor that was near one for the cases presented in this article. The formula for the correction factor is given in Cox and Rubinstein (1985): 256. Whenever *sample standard deviations* are mentioned in this article, the reader should understand that the bias-corrected version is intended.

16. Options with volume below 50 trades or prices below 50 cents were dropped prior to consolidation. When volume is low, the future and option prices are less likely to be synchronous. When price is low, the bid-ask spread and transaction costs tend to distort the pricing.

17. See Beckers (1981).

18. See Schmalensee and Trippi (1978).

19. See Latane and Rendleman (1976). This derivative is the sensitivity of the call price level changes in the volatility.

20. See Chiras and Manaster (1978). This elasticity is the sensitivity of percent call price changes to percent changes in the volatility.

21. This method is close to that used by the Chicago Mercantile Exchange in the "Volatility Corner" feature in their periodical *Market Perspectives*.

22. Frank King, associate director of research at the Atlanta Fed, originally suggested this application of the implied-volatility forecasts.

23. To promote computational and expositional parsimony, the test was performed only on the Atlanta Fed implied-volatility form, which generally had the best results in the efficiency tests.

24. This is an example of the well-known "peso problem" in testing for unbiasedness of forecasts. See Frankel and Meese (1987) for a good discussion of the peso problem.

References

Beckers, Stan. "Standard Deviations Implied in Option Prices as Predictors of Future Stock Price Variability." *Journal of Banking and Finance* 5 (September 1981): 363-81.

Black, Fischer. "The Pricing of Commodity Contracts." *Journal of Financial Economics* 3 (January/March 1976a): 167-79.

_____ . "Studies of Stock Price Volatility Changes." *Proceeding of the American Statistical Association* (1976b): 177-81.

Black, Fischer, and Myron S. Scholes. "The Valuation of Options Contracts and a Test of Market Efficiency." *Journal of Finance* 27 (May 1972): 399-418.

Black, Fischer, and Myron S. Scholes. "The Pricing of Options and Corporate Liabilities." *Journal of Political Economy* 81 (May/June 1973): 637-59.

Butler, J.S., and Barry Schachter. "Unbiased Estimation of the Black/Scholes Formula." *Journal of Financial Economics* 15 (March 1986): 341-57.

Chicago Mercantile Exchange. *Rules of the Chicago Mercantile Exchange*. Chicago Mercantile Exchange, 1983.

_____ . *Market Perspectives*. Various issues.

Chiras, Donald P., and Steven Manaster. "The Information Content of Option Prices and a Test of Market Efficiency." *Journal of Financial Economics* 6 (June/September 1978): 213-34.

Cox, John C., Jonathan E. Ingersoll, and Stephen A. Ross. "The Relation Between Forward Prices and Futures Prices." *Journal of Financial Economics* 9 (December 1981): 321-46.

Cox, John C., and Mark Rubinstein. *Option Markets*. Englewood Cliffs, N.J.: Prentice-Hall, 1985.

Fama, Eugene F. "The Behavior of Stock Market Prices." *Journal of Business* 38 (January 1965): 34-109.

Feinstein, Steven P. "Stock Market Volatility." Federal Reserve Bank of Atlanta *Economic Review* 72 (November/December 1987): 42-47.

_____ . "A Source of Unbiased Implied Volatility Forecasts." Federal Reserve Bank of Atlanta Working Paper 88-9 (December 1988).

Feinstein, Steven P., and William N. Goetzmann. "The Effect of the 'Triple Witching Hour' on Stock Market Volatility." Federal Reserve Bank of Atlanta *Economic Review* 73 (September/October 1988): 2-18.

Frankel, Jeffrey A., and Richard Meese. "Are Exchange Rates Excessively Variable?" National Bureau of Economic Research Working Paper No. 2249 (May 1987).

French, Kenneth R. "Stock Returns and the Weekend Effect." *Journal of Financial Economics* 8 (August 1980): 55-69.

Hardouvelis, Gikas. "Margin Requirements and Stock Market Volatility." Federal Reserve Bank of New York *Quarterly Review* 13 (Summer 1988): 80-89.

Kawaller, Ira G., Paul D. Koch, and Timothy W. Koch. "The Relationship between the S&P 500 Index and S&P 500 Index Futures Prices." Federal Reserve Bank of Atlanta *Economic Review* 73 (May/June 1988): 2-10.

Latane, Henry A., and Richard J. Rendleman, Jr. "Standard Deviations of Stock Price Ratios Implied in Option Prices." *Journal of Finance* 31 (May 1976): 369-81.

Macbeth, James D., and Larry J. Merville. "An Empirical Examination of the Black-Scholes Call Option Pricing Model." *Journal of Finance* 34 (December 1979): 1173-86.

Merton, Robert C. "Theory of Rational Option Pricing." *Bell Journal of Economics and Management Science* (Spring 1973): 141-83.

Officer, Robert R. "The Variability of the Market Factor of the New York Stock Exchange." *Journal of Business* 46, no. 3 (1973): 434-53.

Patell, James M., and Mark A. Wolfson. "Anticipated Information Releases Reflected in Call Option Prices." *Journal of Accounting and Economics* 1 (August 1979): 117-40.

_____ . "The *Ex Ante* and *Ex Post* Price Effects of Quarterly Earnings Announcements Reflected in Option and Stock Prices." *Journal of Accounting Research* 19, no. 2 (1981): 434-58.

Rubinstein, Mark. "Nonparametric Tests of Alternative Option Pricing Models Using All Reported Trades and Quotes on the 30 Most Active CBOE Option Classes from August 23, 1976 through August 31, 1978." *Journal of Finance* 40 (June 1985): 455-80.

Schmalensee, Richard, and Robert Trippi. "Common-Stock Volatility Expectations Implied by Option Premia." *Journal of Finance* 33 (March 1978): 129-47.

Stoll, Hans R., and Robert E. Whaley. *Expiration Day Effects of Index Options and Futures*. Monograph Series in Finance and Economics, Monograph 1986-3. Solomon Brothers Center for the Study of Financial Institutions, Graduate School of Business Administration, New York University, 1986.

Whaley, Robert E. "Valuation of American Futures Options: Theory and Empirical Tests." *Journal of Finance* 41 (March 1986): 127-50.

Covered Call Options: A Proposal to Ease LDC Debt

Steven P. Feinstein and Peter A. Abken

This article was originally published in the Atlanta Fed's March/April 1990 Economic Review. *At the time the article was written, Feinstein was an economist in the financial section of the Atlanta Fed's research department. Abken is a senior economist in the financial section of the Atlanta Fed's research department.*

*M*any less developed countries (LDCs) struggling to pay off massive loans possess an untapped, exportable resource for which a demand exists in developed nations. Revenue from such a resource would not only help to service debts but also further the indebted developing countries' economic advancement. This potential source of debt relief is not a physical commodity but rather a type of financial asset—namely long-term, high strike price call options on their chief export commodities.

The proposal in this article offers interested parties such as commodity users or speculators the opportunity to bid on the right to purchase a certain quantity of a chief export commodity for a prespecified price on a given future date. In making these call options available, LDCs would in effect be selling commodity price insurance—insurance that pays off if the commodity price rises beyond some high level. For example, a bidder might purchase the right (but not the obligation) to buy Mexican oil at $27 a barrel on a given date five years hence, even though the price of oil at the time of bidding is only $17.25. Should the prevailing market price remain below the "strike" level of $27, the option owner would simply elect not to carry out the transaction.[1] Should oil rise to $30 a barrel by the agreed-upon expiration date, though, the bidder could purchase the oil at $3 below prevailing prices. Although the LDC must then relinquish goods for less than the going rate, revenue from the earlier option sales would have ameliorated matters during a period of low prices. The loss of potential profits would come at a time of high prices when the selling country could best afford it.

Using call options in meeting debt obligations is not an entirely new idea. Numerous articles in academic journals have suggested construction of financial instruments that tie a borrower's liabilities to a commodity price, and the recent Mexican loan restructuring (described below) includes such a feature.[2] In other plans, however, options have been bundled together with bonds. By selling options separately, as proposed here for the first time, an LDC can generate substantial revenue without renegotiating all its outstanding debts.

Such an "unbundled" approach is possible with this proposal because it calls for selecting a strike price high enough to ensure that the debtor will face the future obligation only when fulfillment of all other obligations is relatively easy. This feature would obviate the need to gain the endorsement of existing creditors prior to selling the options. Keeping the options separate from debt instruments also affords the LDC greater flexibility in the management of its revenue flow and debt. A program of selling options when commodity prices are low and redeeming them when prices are high can help an LDC smooth revenue across periods of high and low commodity prices. A further advantage is that the market for the unbundled option is likely to be wider than the market for options coupled with debt.

The World Debt Problem—A Review

Since 1982 the high indebtedness of many developing nations has placed a severe strain on both the LDCs and the world banking community. According to the most recent accounting, LDCs owe $1.3 trillion to foreign banks, governments, and international agencies.[3] Not only have LDCs struggled to service this debt, but exposure to these troubled loans has threatened the strength of commercial banks.

The roots of the problem can be traced to the volatility of commodity prices and interest rates over the last two decades. The oil price increases of 1973 and 1979 led to a massive redistribution of wealth from oil importers to oil exporters, primarily those in the Middle East. These "petrodollars" accumulated in commercial banks around the world as surplus funds awaiting investment opportunities. Because of their apparent excellent potential to develop rapidly, Latin American economies were deemed to be excellent credit risks. As a result, these countries received enormous loans from commercial banks.

The loans were predominantly short-term, with interest rates tied to the London Interbank Offer Rate (LIBOR).[4] By 1980 three-fourths of the debt owed by Latin American countries was set at variable rates; 40 percent was due for repayment within one year, and 70 percent within three years.[5] From 1971 to 1980, LIBOR was on average 0.8 percent (80 basis points) less than the rate of U.S. wholesale price inflation; developing countries were effectively borrowing at very low or even negative real interest rates.[6] Later, however, rates on LDC debt surged as the United States tightened monetary policy in an attempt to control inflation. LIBOR averaged 9.2 percent (920 basis points) above the U.S. inflation rate from 1981 to 1982.[7] As rates rose, debt service obligations soared.

The worldwide recession that accompanied higher interest rates further hurt LDCs. Reduced demand for their exports and plummeting commodity prices compounded their misfortune. As the value of imports began to overwhelm that of exports, current account payment balances of the highly indebted countries turned sharply negative.[8] By the end of 1982, 34 developing countries were unable to service their debt fully.[9] As oil exporters, Mexico and Venezuela were special cases. As oil prices leveled off and then began to drop, however, these two countries also began to have difficulty making payments on the substantial debt they had accumulated against future oil revenues.

The predicament has taken a heavy toll on the LDCs. In net terms Latin America and the Caribbean *exported* capital in each of the last eight years; the 1989 net outflow amounted to $24.6 billion (see Barbara Durr 1989). As a result, domestic investment and development have suffered. Growth over the last decade has slowed to a crawl, making repayment of the foreign debt even more difficult and less likely.[10] Moreover, standards of living have declined. Between 1980 and 1987, per capita consumption of the LDCs fell nearly 12 percent (see Giancarlo Perasso 1989, 535). If the quality of life for the citizens of LDCs is to improve, many believe, capital must flow into these countries on net, not in the opposite direction.

Lenders have also suffered. In 1982 the sum of LDC loans on the books of U.S. banks was over 180 percent of the capital in those banks (Jeffrey Sachs 1989a). Since then, the market value of LDC loans has fallen sharply below book value. For example, by March 1990, Peruvian loans could be sold for only six cents on the dollar, and the market valued Mexican debt at 40 percent of face value.[11] Consequently, bank earnings have suffered, and bank stocks have reflected deteriorating loan portfolio values (Sachs 1989a).

Nonetheless, considerable progress has been made toward alleviating the crisis. Banks have reduced their LDC loan exposure and increased capital, thereby easing fears of bank insolvency. By 1988, aggregate exposure stood at less than 80 percent of capital (Sachs 1989a). This improvement afforded some breathing room and made it possible for banks to offer debt relief. Recently, U.S. Treasury Secretary Nicholas Brady's initiative to reduce LDCs' debt burden helped Mexico restructure its commercial bank debt. Mexico received concessions on principal and interest, along with new loans (Peter Truell 1990).

The LDC debt problem, however, is far from over. No single approach is likely to work across the board, and in most cases debt reduction will probably be part of future financial arrangements. Yet developing countries that rely solely on debt reduction may find it difficult to borrow in the future. Nor is rescheduling old loans and securing new loans a satisfactory long-term solution. Many experts now agree that the problem is one of solvency rather than a lack of liquidity available to the LDCs (Anna J. Schwartz 1989). In other words, these nations' economic prospects are sufficiently bleak that markets doubt LDCs can make good on their past financial obligations. Consequently, as long as stretching payments out over longer horizons preserves the net present value of LDCs' liabilities, such a tactic will not end the crisis.

Highly indebted countries must therefore search for ways to restore their solvency. Essentially, in order to pay off their huge debts, they must raise more revenue. Better economic planning and measures to stem domestic capital flight are the sorts of actions that will have lasting positive effects (A. Schwartz 1989 and Rudiger Dornbusch 1987). Some policymakers and analysts advocate debt-equity swaps as means by which LDCs can pay off loans without incurring new liabilities; however, these transactions represent permanent sales of an LDC's productive resources (such as forests, mines, and factories) and so cannot provide revenue on a continuing basis. Consequently, such swaps serve only as temporary palliatives. Furthermore, the manner in which debt-equity swaps are executed usually results in money supply expansion in the LDC, thus fueling inflationary pressures.[12]

A New Proposal

Selling high strike price call options on export commodities is one way LDCs could generate revenue without selling their productive resources or renegotiating existing debt. Thus commodity price volatility, which contributed to the debt crises in the first place, could provide a partial key to its solution. It is precisely the volatility of LDC export prices that makes high strike price call options valuable today, just as uncertainty makes various forms of insurance more desirable.

Because a call option affords the buyer the right, but not the obligation, to buy at a given price on a given date, investors find it profitable to exercise the option only in the event that the commodity's market price rises above the strike price. Thus, an LDC that sells high strike options incurs an obligation that needs to be fulfilled only if commodity prices increase substantially—a circumstance in which fulfillment of all obligations would be easier for the LDC.

Selecting a high strike price for the call options enhances the instrument's marketability. High strike price call options need not be designated as "senior" obligations (those that must be met in advance of existing debt) in order to attract buyers. Although call option transactions entail some risk of default, the option's value remains high, even when default risk and junior designation are taken into consideration, because the chance of default is small when the commodity reaches the high strike price. (See the example of option pricing in the box on page 222.) As junior obligations, option sales would not require approval by existing creditors—an obstacle that frequently blocks additional loans to highly indebted countries.

Since LDCs would be issuing call options on their own export commodities, the countries would bear little financial risk in meeting their obligations. When calls are covered, the issuer simply sells the available commodity to the option holder for the strike price. When call options are not covered, that is, when the underlying commodity is not in the possession of the issuing party, the issuer takes the chance of having to purchase quantities of the commodity at high prices to fulfill the contract.

LDCs could either sell covered calls to new investors or swap them for a portion of outstanding debt. To ensure a fair price to the LDC for the calls, the sale and distribution could be conducted via a closed-bid auction in a manner similar to the Morgan Guaranty Mexican debt-swap of February 1988. LDCs could set a minimum acceptable price in advance, or they could retain the right to reject low bids.

The covered call is a simple use of options. Additional flexibility could be achieved through use of combinations of options, which would, for example, keep an LDC from sacrificing all of the additional revenue forgone if prices rose above the strike price.

Table 1
Estimated Value of Vulnerable Oil Options
For Various Terms and Strike Prices

(Johnson-Stulz Pricing Method: Spot Oil Price = $17.25;
Oil Price Volatility = 28 percent per year; Initial Pool Value = $10.77 per option;
Pool Volatility = 42 percent per year; Correlation between Oil Price and
Pool Value = .5; Interest Rate = 8 percent per year)

Strike price per barrel	Years until expiration:					
	2	3	4	5	6	7
$25	$1.27	$2.01	$2.59	$3.04	$3.39	$3.65
26	1.11	1.83	2.42	2.88	3.23	3.51
27	.96	1.67	2.25	2.72	3.09	3.38
28	.84	1.51	2.10	2.57	2.96	3.25
29	.73	1.44	1.95	2.43	2.84	3.13
30	.63	1.25	1.82	2.30	2.70	3.01
31	.55	1.14	1.69	2.17	2.57	2.89
32	.48	1.04	1.58	2.06	2.46	2.78

A more elaborate use of options could tailor the payoff contingencies to better suit the LDC and potential investors.

One such strategy is the call option spread, which would provide a cap on the payout in the event of a very high commodity price. A spread is conceptually equivalent to the LDC's selling a call at a given strike price and simultaneously buying a call at a higher strike price.[13] This combination entitles the investor to an increasing payout as the commodity price rises in the range between the two strike prices. If the commodity price rises further, though, the cap comes into play. LDC governments might prefer this arrangement for political reasons. Setting a cap on the contingent liability would also be advantageous in the case of agricultural commodities, for which quantity risks caused by uncertain harvests are significant.

Supporting Theory

As is now clear, the LDC is not the only party to bear commodity price risk; the LDC's creditors share that risk. While periods of high prices are characterized by large capital inflows and rapid growth, low prices strain LDC economies and often result in debt crises as the revenue needed to service outstanding debt dries up. At the same time debt held by the LDC's creditors fluctuates in value according to the LDC's creditworthiness, which in turn depends on the commodity price. If the risk of price fluctuation subjects both the LDC and the creditor to the specter of default during low-price times, and if default is costly to the two parties, then some sort of revenue smoothing is advantageous to both parties. One way to smooth revenue across high- and low-price periods is for the LDC to sell "claims" on the high-price period. High strike price options are exactly such a claim. They allow the LDC to transfer money from potential high-price periods into an immediate low-price period.

According to option pricing theory, the more volatile the commodity price is, the more such an option is worth. Consequently, the use of LDC covered calls is most feasible in exactly those cases where it is most necessary.

An Example of an LDC Covered Call

While the features and theoretical underpinnings of LDC covered calls are straightforward, a realistic example can clarify the features outlined. Mexico owes $100.3 billion to foreign interests.[14] Payment of principal and interest exceeded $15 billion in

Table 2
Estimated Revenue to Mexico
For Issues of Options with Various Terms and Strike Prices
(billions of U.S. dollars)

(Based on Johnson-Stulz vulnerable option valuation; assumes options cover 470 million barrels, approximately one year's exports; all other assumptions are as given in Table 1)

Strike price per barrel	Years until expiration:					
	2	3	4	5	6	7
$25	$.60	$.94	$1.20	$1.40	$1.60	$1.70
26	.52	.86	1.10	1.40	1.50	1.70
27	.45	.79	1.10	1.30	1.50	1.60
28	.39	.71	.99	1.20	1.40	1.50
29	.34	.68	.92	1.10	1.30	1.50
30	.30	.59	.86	1.10	1.30	1.40
31	.26	.54	.79	1.00	1.20	1.40
32	.23	.49	.74	.97	1.20	1.30

1988, an amount equal to 46 percent of export revenues.[15] Yet Mexico consistently produces between 880 million and 1.1 trillion barrels of oil each year. Since 1982 over 470 million barrels per year have been exported.[16] Proven reserves amount to 70 billion barrels. Thus, the supply and production of Mexican oil is reliable.

Under conditions prevailing in the second quarter of 1989, when the market price for Mexican oil stood at $17.25 per barrel, an option to sell oil five years later at a price of $27 would have been worth approximately $2.72 (see Table 1).[17] This figure is computed using Herb Johnson and René Stulz's (1987) pricing model, which is similar to the Black-Scholes model but also accounts for default-risk.[18] The box on page 222 describes the methodology and explains the assumptions and parameter values used.

With a price of $2.72 for an option on one barrel of Mexican oil, a sale of call options on one year's quantity of oil exports could net Mexico $1.28 billion in current revenue (Table 2). A sale of options on five years' exports would bring $6.4 billion.[19] This revenue would be sufficient to retire 6.37 percent of Mexico's foreign bank debt at face value, and more than 15.9 percent at current market discounts. By comparison, the recent Mexican financing package negotiated under the Brady plan framework extinguished $7 billion in commercial bank debt. In

addition, a fixed reduced interest rate was secured on over $22 billion in claims. However, this debt relief was partially offset by new loans totaling nearly $1.4 billion from banks and about $5.75 billion from official sources to provide for principal repayments and guarantee interest (see Jorge C. Castaneda 1990 and Truell 1990). The Mexican government has expressed an interest in further reducing their commercial bank debt over time, and the revenue raised by the proposal presented here could allow such reductions without a drawdown in reserves.

The sale of options is not a sale of oil; it merely sets the highest price that Mexico can charge the option purchaser for oil during the expiration year. Should the price of oil remain low, Mexico would be free to sell oil in any manner it chooses. Only if the price rebounds and exceeds the $27 strike price would Mexico be obliged to sell oil to the option holders for $27 per barrel. At that price, though, the flow of revenue would be sizable, and Mexico's financial situation would be greatly improved. In either case, the sale of covered calls would provide Mexico with added revenue now, revenue that could be used to ease the current financial crisis.

Table 1 presents the Johnson-Stulz prices for vulnerable Mexican oil options—that is, those subject to default risk—using various combinations of strike prices and maturities. Table 3 presents Black-Scholes

Table 3
Estimated Value of Default-Free Oil Options
For Various Terms and Strike Prices

(Black-Scholes Pricing Method: Spot Oil Price = $17.25;
Oil Price Volatility = 28 percent per year; Interest Rate = 8 percent per year)

Strike price per barrel	Years until expiration:					
	2	3	4	5	6	7
$25	$1.41	$2.45	$3.47	$4.43	$5.33	$6.18
26	1.23	2.23	3.22	4.17	5.08	5.93
27	1.06	2.02	2.99	3.93	4.83	5.69
28	.92	1.83	2.78	3.71	4.60	5.45
29	.80	1.66	2.58	3.49	4.38	5.23
30	.69	1.51	2.39	3.29	4.18	5.02
31	.60	1.37	2.22	3.11	3.98	4.82
32	.52	1.24	2.07	2.93	3.79	4.63

prices, which assume no default risk but correspond to the same parameter values. (These parameters are given in the box and in the tables.) The difference between the Black-Scholes and Johnson-Stulz prices is the credit spread, that is, the reduction in the value of the option that is due to the risk of default. As a percentage of the option price, the credit spread is lower for higher strike prices. The attractiveness of the option is that its contingent liability is paid only when funds are plentiful and thus effectively does not compete with existing debt for available funds.

Mexico is not the only example of a country that could benefit from selling call options on an export commodity. Brazil, for example, could sell options on soybeans and coffee. Chile and Peru might sell options on copper, and Bolivia, tin options. Any commodity-exporting country could make use of a similar strategy. Table 4 lists several LDC candidates and their principal export commodities.

The Proposal from the LDCs' Perspective

A sale of high strike price covered calls would provide an LDC with much-needed revenue when revenue is otherwise scarce. Unlike a debt-equity swap—which involves permanent sale of productive resources, often at depressed prices—the LDC covered call entails no loss of control or ownership over productive resources. Sale of LDC covered calls, on the other hand, relinquishes only some potential profits for a fixed amount of time—that is, the difference between the market price of the commodity and the option's strike price (if the difference is positive) for a prespecified quantity of output.

The obligation would be "costly" to the LDC in high-price periods because the LDC would fulfill its obligation by selling at a lower-than-market price; however, that price would be much higher than the market price had been at the time the option was written. Thus, the transaction would still be profitable to the LDC and would further enhance its welfare, despite its obligatory nature. Furthermore, if the LDC had unused production capacity, exercise of the options would provide additional customers and greater total revenue.

Should the commodity price not rise above the strike price, the option would expire unexercised and the LDC would face no further encumbrance. In order to supplement income during the continued low-price state, the LDC might then wish to issue additional covered calls against another future period's production.

The Proposal from the Creditor's Perspective

Sales of covered calls by LDCs would benefit creditors for several reasons. The new instrument embodies some attractive investment features. LDCs' selling covered calls represents a feasible alternative to demanding new loans from creditors. The revenue covered calls provide LDCs would enhance the value of the other LDC debt held by the creditors. Although covered calls require no servicing prior to expiration, unlike debt forgiveness, they have inherent value; thus the accounting treatment is more favorable to banks than is outright debt forgiveness.

Another advantageous feature of an LDC covered call is its ability to let the investor/creditor share more fully in the fortunes of the LDC during times of increasing commodity prices. A portfolio of loans to an LDC carries considerable exposure to commodity price risk, but offers limited reward should prices rise. LDC covered calls would grant creditors access to greater upside potential. Just as commodity prices are theoretically unbounded, the potential gain from owning an LDC covered call would be unlimited.

Although the option would expire worthless should commodity prices not recover, the same could be said of LDC debt. Nonperformance on loans is quite possible during the low-price periods in which an option would expire out of the money. Thus, LDC debt and LDC covered calls have certain downside features in common. Certainly there are price scenarios in which LDC debt would perform better than LDC covered calls; nevertheless, some creditors/investors might prefer the different risk-return profile of the option.

Another potentially attractive feature of LDC covered calls could be their greater liquidity relative to LDC bank debt and equity stakes. As a standardized security, LDC covered calls should be easier to sell than bank debt and equity holdings. Indeed, an active market for LDC covered calls might develop in response to their availability. Banks would then have an avenue to reduce their LDC exposure, should they wish to, by swapping bank debt for calls and then selling those calls in the market.

The proposal should also appeal to creditors because of the effect it would have on the entire portfolio of LDC investments. The options would only pay off when LDC funds are plentiful, and the initial sale or swap of the options would reduce the LDC's debt burden. Hence, the LDC could better service all of its obligations regardless of the behavior of commodity prices. The LDC would potentially have more funds

Table 4
Selected Heavily Indebted Countries and Their Chief Export Commodities

Country	Commodity	Export Revenue from Commodity as a Percent of Total Exports, 1982-88
Argentina	Wheat	10.8
	Corn	7.8
Bolivia	Natural Gas	49.3
	Tin	25.1
Brazil	Soybeans	9.5
	Coffee	8.4
Chile	Copper	45.4
Colombia	Coffee	39.8
	Fuel Oil	13.4
Ecuador	Crude Oil	54.7
	Bananas	9.4
Côte d'Ivoire	Cocoa Beans	29.7
	Coffee	18.3
Mexico	Petroleum	57.0
Morocco	Phosphates	18.5
Peru	Copper	16.8
	Zinc	9.5
Philippines	Coconut Products	10.8
Uruguay	Wool	19.7
Venezuela	Petroleum	86.0

Source: International Monetary Fund.

for development and thus face enhanced future financial prospects. Accordingly, the value of all the LDC's outstanding debt could appreciate.

Clearly, purchase of LDC covered calls is preferable to debt forgiveness from the creditors' point of view. Like debt forgiveness, selling LDC covered calls would relieve the debtor of some debt service obligations and make service of remaining debt more manageable. This change would enhance the value of remaining debt, just as debt forgiveness does. By receiving LDC covered calls, however, creditors would maintain a claim on LDC funds that might become available at a later date. Furthermore, whereas banks must write off debt that is forgiven, receipt of calls would preserve some capital since LDC covered calls are a valuable asset.

An Explanation of the Johnson-Stulz Pricing Model

The Johnson-Stulz method is useful for valuing "vulnerable" options, that is, options that face some risk of default. The method relies on various assumptions similar to those required by the Black-Scholes methodology, which is commonly used to price exchange-traded and other default-free options. Both models assume that the price of the underlying asset (oil in the Mexican example) moves randomly and smoothly through time and that the percent change over any instant of time is independent of the change at any other point in time.[1] Therefore, the intrinsic value of the option—that is, the difference between the strike price and the underlying asset price—also moves smoothly. Black and Scholes showed that a portfolio consisting of the underlying asset and a short position in bonds could exactly replicate the option. Because the replicating portfolio and actual option offer the same payoff at expiration, their values must be the same any time before expiration. Otherwise, arbitrage profits could be realized. The Black-Scholes methodology essentially prices the option by adding up the observable prices of the assets in the replicating portfolio.

The Johnson-Stulz method differs from the Black-Scholes method in that it assumes the option writer has limited assets available to meet the potential liability of the option. Mexico, for example, has a limited pool of funds with which to cover its option obligations upon exercise. If the pool value falls below the option obligation, the option owners do not receive the full option payoff upon expiration.[2] Instead, they receive the available funds in the pool. In other words, at expiration the vulnerable call pays the minimum of the option's intrinsic value or its share of the pool (the total pool divided by the number of options issued).

In pricing the option used in the example, the pool was valued in the following manner: for a given period, Mexico's current account surplus, which was sometimes negative, was added to the previous period's foreign currency reserves, and required debt service was subtracted.[3] This number, however, was often negative since Mexico partially financed large trade deficits and debt service by obtaining new loans. To apply the Johnson-Stulz method, it was necessary to adjust the pool, normalizing it to equal zero at the level at which default would be likely.

The unadjusted pool reached its historical minimum in the third quarter of 1981; the next year Mexico suspended interest payments. Since that time the total quantity of foreign debt has risen. Moreover, both the ratio of debt service to GNP and the ratio of external liabilities to GNP have similarly been much higher in several of the years since the time of the payments moratorium.[4]

Thus, the rapid rate of capital outflow, rather than the excessive level of debt amassed, apparently was the main factor prompting Mexico's interest suspension in 1982. To normalize the pool, therefore, it was assumed that Mexico would make payments on the options as long as the pool value remained above its historical minimum. If that minimum were ever again achieved, it would lead to default. To normalize the pool in this way, the historical minimum (-$5.4 billion) was subtracted from each entry in the time series of pool values.[5] Finally, the pool per option was computed by dividing the total pool value by the number of options issued.

Table 1 presents Johnson-Stulz prices for Mexican oil options using various combinations of strike prices and maturities. The computation uses data from the second quarter of 1989. The oil price was $17.25 per barrel at that time. The total value of the pool was $5.1 billion, or $10.77 per option if options are issued on one full year's worth of exports, 470 million barrels. Parameter inputs were estimated using quarterly data from 1982 to 1989. The standard deviation of percent changes in the pool value is 43 percent per year. The volatility of the oil price is 28 percent per year.

The prices in Table 1 may overstate the true value of these options for the following reason: the oil price may not follow a random walk as the Johnson-Stulz, like the Black-Scholes, model assumes. Oil prices may revert to some long-run level, which may vary over time. If this were true, the oil prices would not be as variable over time as the models predict, and so the computed prices would be too high. However, there is no firm empirical evidence that oil prices are mean-reverting. Nevertheless, the Johnson-Stulz prices, though possibly high, are closer to the true value of the default-risky options than the Black-Scholes prices. Further modeling research should achieve more reliable values for these options.

The Johnson-Stulz methodology takes into account the relationship between the value of the pool and the underlying commodity. When oil prices are high, the funds available to Mexico to service outstanding debt and pay off options are more plentiful. The correlation coefficient between these two variables is 0.5, estimated over the sample period running from 1982 to 1989. The higher this correlation, the lower the option default risk will be. A high positive correlation would be expected for countries like Mexico whose economies depend largely on single export commodities. Thus, high strike price covered call options are attractive instruments for these countries, since the relationship between commodity price and the country's financial resources mitigates default.

1. More precisely, the asset price is assumed to follow a diffusion process (a continuous-time geometric Brownian motion). This assumption is standard in option pricing models. For the sake of greater realism, it would be desirable to allow discrete jumps in the process, which, for example, might be due to oil price shocks. However, such a model poses serious technical problems in valuing vulnerable options. These details will be addressed in future research.

2. Since Mexico would own the oil on which the option was written, however, a default on the options would entail selling the oil to a third party on the spot market rather than selling to the option owner at the strike price.

3. Data were provided by the International Monetary Fund and Banco de Mexico.

4. The Economist Intelligence Unit (1989), 35.

5. Since this computation involved subtracting a negative number, it in effect added to the pool. This recognizes the historical record that the unadjusted pool could become negative without resulting in a default.

The Market for LDC Covered Calls

Users of the LDC's export commodity face price risk exactly opposite of that borne by the LDC: users suffer when prices are high and prosper when prices are low. Purchase of an LDC covered call would be a form of insurance against excessive price hikes. It would insulate the user against severe fluctuations in the commodity price, thereby facilitating investment planning and marketing decisions. Should the price remain low, the option would expire worthless, much in the same way an accident insurance policy returns nothing when no accident occurs. During low-price periods, however, the option owner would continue to enjoy the low price of the essential commodity.

Processors and distributors of oil products, along with the U.S. Department of Energy, which purchases oil to supply the nation's strategic reserves, might be potential buyers of LDC covered calls on oil. Agents who wish to speculate on the price of oil might also be interested, and they would add liquidity to the market. Investment managers could use LDC covered calls to hedge over the long term against the adverse effects commodity price shocks can exert on investment portfolios. Currently, few instruments are available that allow agents to speculate or hedge prices over the long term.

Potential Problems

This plan is subject to criticism in several areas, and certain details would have to be worked out. For example, creditors and investors might fear that an LDC would renege on its obligation should the price of oil rise substantially above the option strike price. This behavior is unlikely, however, since it would be akin to default on a loan. An LDC's initial sale of LDC covered calls in order to retire debt would exhibit a willingness to honor international financial agreements. For countries striving to do so during hard times, reneging during easier circumstances seems unlikely.

The LDC would have to bear inflation risk. Worldwide inflation over the life of the option might lower the real value of the strike price at which the commodity would have to be sold. If this occurred, however, the same inflation that would make fulfillment of the option obligation costlier to the LDC would also relieve the LDC of some of its debt burden. Inflation increases the real cost of the option obligation but decreases the real cost of the debt obligations. As long as the term of the options were similar to or shorter than the interval at which banks reprice loans in response to inflation and changing interest rates, the two countervailing inflation effects could offset one another. In this way, LDC covered calls could possibly offer creditors and debtors a hedge against inflation risk.

Logistical details need to be addressed on a case-by-case basis. For instance, to avoid simultaneous exercise of all options, which would put a tremendous strain on the LDC's ability to deliver the commodity, the option could be written so that a forward delivery contract would be sold to the holder, with the delivery date determined by the order in which the exercise request is received.

Conclusion

High strike price covered call options are a market-oriented solution that should be explored further and given serious consideration as a response to the current LDC debt crisis. Because their use offers LDCs a new source of revenue without adding to an already difficult debt burden, sale of call options would benefit both LDCs and the holders of existing LDC debt. By smoothing income across periods of high and low commodity prices and providing insurance against periods of excessively high commodity prices, this financial instrument holds advantages for LDCs, consumers of their export commodities, and investors. Thus, it presents a promising new approach to easing debt obligations and furthering economic advancement in highly indebted countries.

Notes

1. The type of option proposed here is the "European" option, which cannot be exercised until maturity.
2. E. Schwartz (1982) cited two instances where commodity-linked bonds—which grant the lender the option to take a given quantity of a commodity instead of the principal at maturity—had been issued. O'Hara (forthcoming) described how commodity-linked bonds could be used to shift commodity price risk from LDCs to risk-neutral banks. Many other examples exist.

   The "value recovery clause" in the recent Mexican debt package allows banks to receive additional payments starting in 1996 should the price of oil be above $14 per barrel in constant 1989 dollars by that time. The additional payments will be subject to a cap proportional to the amount of old loans each bank tenders in exchange for the new fixed-interest bonds.
3. The World Bank (1989a), 2.
4. LIBOR is the rate of interest on large loans between creditworthy international banks. It is commonly used as the base rate for floating-rate international loans, much in the manner that the prime rate is often used as the base for floating rates on loans in the United States.
5. The World Bank (1988), xi.
6. See Schuker (1988), 134.
7. Ibid.
8. Developing countries amassed current account surpluses totaling $11.9 billion (U.S.) over the five years from 1971 through 1975. Over the period 1981-86, LDCs amassed deficits totaling $242.7 billion (International Monetary Fund, 1987 Yearbook, 136).
9. See Schuker (1988), 134.
10. Latin America's per capita output fell 7 percent in the 1980s, whereas it had grown 40 percent in the 1970s. See Farnsworth (1990).
11. See "LDC Debt News" (1990), 12.
12. See Sachs (1989b), 92, and DiLeo and Remolona (1989).
13. In practice, it would not be necessary to issue two options; one contingent claim contract can be written with the same features.
14. See "Country Risk-Watch" (1989/90), 94-95.
15. The World Bank (1989b), 254.
16. See Banco de Mexico.
17. World Oil Price Table, Weekly Petroleum Status Report.
18. For a description of the Black-Scholes model, see Black and Scholes (1973).
19. This is the sum of the values of five series options covering export production for the period between three and seven years into the future. Three-year options would cover the oil to be produced three years from now, four-year options would cover production four years from now, and so forth.

References

Banco de Mexico. "Indicadores del Sector Externo." *Indicadores Economicos*, updated monthly.

Black Fischer, and Myron Scholes. "The Pricing of Options and Corporate Liabilities." *Journal of Political Economy* 81 (1973): 637-59.

Castaneda, Jorge C. "Mexico's Dismal Debt Deal." *New York Times*, February 25, 1990.

"Country Risk-Watch." *The International Economy* 3 (December 1989/January 1990): 94-95.

Dileo, Paul, and Eli M. Remolona. "On Voluntary Conversions of LDC Debt." Federal Reserve Bank of New York, unpublished manuscript, July 24, 1989.

Dornbusch, Rudiger. "International Debt and Economic Instability." Federal Reserve Bank of Kansas City *Economic Review* (January 1987): 15-32.

Durr, Barbara. "Debt, Inflation Continue to Hamper Latin America." *Financial Times*, December 22, 1989.

The Economist Intelligence Unit. *Mexico: Country Profile, 1989-90*. Annual Survey of Political and Economic Background. London: The Economist Intelligence United Limited, 1989.

Farnsworth, Clyde. "U.S. Falls Short on Its Debt Plan for Third World." *New York Times*, January 9, 1990.

International Monetary Fund. *International Financial Statistics*. Washington, D.C.: IMF, various issues.

Johnson, Herb, and René Stulz. "The Pricing of Options with Default Risk." *Journal of Finance* 42 (June 1987): 267-80.

"LDC Debt News." *American Banker*, March 20, 1990, 12.

O'Hara, Maureen. "Financial Contracts and International Lending." *Journal of Banking and Finance* (forthcoming).

Perasso, Giancarlo. "The Pricing of LDC Debt in the Secondary Market: An Empirical Analysis." *Kyklos* 42, fasc. 4 (1989): 533-55.

Sachs, Jeffrey. "New Approaches to the Latin American Debt Crisis." Essays in International Finance, no. 174. International Finance Section. Department of Economics, Princeton University. Princeton, New Jersey, July 1989a.

_____ . "Making the Brady Plan Work." *Foreign Affairs* (September 1989b): 87-104.

Schuker, Stephen A. *American "Reparations" to Germany, 1919-33: Implications for the Third-World Debt Crisis*. Princeton Studies in International Finance, no. 61. International Finance Section. Department of Economics, Princeton University. Princeton, New Jersey, July 1988.

Schwartz, Anna J. "International Debts: What's Fact and What's Fiction." *Economic Inquiry* 27 (January 1989): 1-19.

Schwartz, Eduardo. "The Pricing of Commodity Linked Bonds." *Journal of Finance* 37, no. 2 (1982): 525-39.

Truell, Peter. "Mexico, Creditor Banks Complete Pact Covering $48 Billion of Debt." *Wall Street Journal*, January 11, 1990.

The World Bank, *World Debt Tables, 1987-88: External Debt of Developing Countries*. Vol. 1, *Analysis and Summary Tables*. Washington, D.C., 1988.

_____ . *World Debt Tables, 1989-90: External Debt of Developing Countries*. Vol. 1, *Analysis and Summary Tables*. Washington, D.C., 1989a.

_____ . *World Debt Tables, 1989-90: External Debt of Developing Countries*. Vol. 2, *Country Tables*. Washington, D.C., 1989b.

Capital Requirements for Interest Rate and Foreign Exchange Hedges

Larry D. Wall, John J. Pringle, and James E. McNulty

Over the past decade, off-balance-sheet financial instruments used to hedge risk associated with interest-rate and foreign-exchange-rate fluctuations have proliferated. The growth in both the types of instruments and their sophistication can be traced to the increased volatility of interest rates and foreign exchange rates during the late 1970s and early 1980s, and to the rise in international financial transactions. New technologies have also been an important catalyst, making it possible to communicate and process the information necessary to manage contracts and evaluate the instruments.

Domestic depository institutions are prime participants in the markets for interest-rate and foreign-exchange-rate contracts. Commercial banks and savings and loan associations can use these instruments not only to control their own exposure but also, in large part, to help commercial and institutional customers manage their financial risk. However, participation in the interest-rate and foreign-exchange-rate market can significantly alter a depository's riskiness. An institution can use such contracts not only to minimize its exposure to risk but also to speculate and, hence, increase its risk. Providing these instruments to customers may also subject an institution to greater risk if the products are not properly hedged. Moreover, products such as interest-rate and currency swaps can generate credit risk since the counterparty to the contract could default on its obligations.

Bank and thrift regulators in the United States are aware of the potential of these off-balance-sheet instruments to alter depositories' risk exposure substantially. Commercial bank regulators have formally incorporated the credit risk associated with interest-rate and foreign-exchange instruments into their risk-based capital standards. These standards focus solely on

This article was originally published in the Atlanta Fed's May/June 1990 Economic Review. *Wall is a research officer in charge of the financial section of the Atlanta Fed's research department, Pringle holds the C. Knox Massey Professor of Business Administration Chair at the University of North Carolina at Chapel Hill, and McNulty is an associate professor in the Department of Finance, College of Business, Florida Atlantic University.*

credit risk, however: bank's capital requirements do not explicitly consider the impact of interest-rate risk and foreign-exchange risk, although regulators have expressed a desire to include these components as soon as a practical method can be determined.

Thrift regulators, on the other hand, have explicitly incorporated interest-rate instruments in calculating interest-rate risk for thrifts' capital requirements. They do not consider foreign-exchange instruments, though, primarily because very few thrifts have significant exposure in this area; nor do they include credit risk associated with interest-rate instruments.[1]

A review of the capital requirements now in place surrounding these instruments suggests the advantages of accounting for their impact on an institution's riskiness through capital standards and not merely as an aspect of credit risk. The impracticality of using off-site monitoring as a method of evaluation seems to be a major obstacle to linking an institution's involvement in these markets with capital requirements. This article reviews existing capital requirements for foreign-exchange-rate and interest-rate instruments and proposes an approach that is less cumbersome, more accurate, and potentially more cost effective. The discussion begins by summarizing key features of the most widely used contracts to control interest-rate and foreign-exchange-rate risk.

*I*nterest Rate and Foreign Exchange Instruments

A wide variety of interest-rate and foreign-exchange instruments has emerged to meet risk management needs. In addition to providing the usual kinds of contracts, commercial banks and other financial intermediaries have been ingenious in customizing these instruments to meet clients' particular needs. The following discussion will outline some of the key features of common contracts.[2]

All interest-rate and foreign-exchange instruments are linked in that the value of these contracts is a function of foreign-currency exchange rates or interest rates and thus outside the control of the participants. For this reason they are sometimes called derivative assets. Another common feature of all of these instruments is that they are a zero-sum game—that is, the amount of payments received by one party must equal those made by the other party.[3]

An important difference distinguishing various contracts is that some are traded on exchanges where-

as others are negotiated by the two participants. Exchange-traded contracts offer the advantage of minimal credit risk because the exchange itself is a party to the contract. When a firm buys, for example, a call option on an exchange, its contract is with the exchange rather than the seller, and the exchange assumes responsibility for making payment on the call. Partly because of the reduction in credit risk, exchange-traded contracts are also more liquid, making it easier to enter into or close out a position.

Exchange-traded contracts are, however, less flexible. These contracts' fixed maturities may or may not be appropriate for controlling a firm's exposure. A further disadvantage of exchange-traded contracts is that they may require the posting of margin—funds set aside to cover potential losses. In this way exchanges are able to eliminate the credit risk of their contracts. Contracts are "marked to market" periodically, in most cases at least once every trading day, by transferring funds from the margin to the other party whenever adverse moves occur in the market price of the contract. For most (but not all) nonexchange contracts no collateral is posted, nor is there any transfer of funds before the settlement date.

Options, Futures, and Forward Contracts. Virtually all interest-rate and foreign-exchange-rate instruments can be created from some combination of put and call options. A call option gives its purchaser the right—but not the obligation—to *purchase* a given type of asset at a prespecified price (the exercise price) at a prespecified date in the future (the expiration date).[4] For example, an investor may own an option to purchase Japanese yen at the rate of 155 yen per dollar on or before October 1. If the yen's market price on the expiration date is 170 per dollar, the owner will exercise the option since the market value of the yen is greater than the exercise price on the option. If, however, the dollar buys 135 yen on October 1, the holder will not exercise the option because yen may be purchased at a lower price in the market. The buyer typically pays the price of an option (its premium) up front. A put option, on the other hand, gives its owner the right to *sell* an asset at a fixed price on a prespecified date in the future. The put option is otherwise analogous to the call option. Both types of options are traded on exchanges and may be purchased from certain financial intermediaries as well if exchange-traded options are inadequate.

Another important off-balance-sheet hedging instrument is the futures contract. Traded on an exchange, futures contracts obligate one party to purchase an asset at a fixed price at a prespecified date in the future. For example, a Treasury bill futures contract may require one party to purchase, on the prespecified date of November 1, for the prespecified amount of $920, a $1,000 Treasury bill that matures in 360 days. The party that buys the Treasury bill is said to have "gone long" in Treasury bill futures, while the party which agrees to sell is "short." In contrast to options, which involve no obligation to the buyer after the initial purchase, futures contracts entail risk for both sides.

A futures contract can be created from a combination of a call and put option. Taking the long side of a future maturing on September 15 with a current price of $905, for example, is identical to buying a call contract and selling a put contract in which both options mature on September 15 and have a strike price of $905.

Closely related to the futures contract is the forward contract. Unlike the futures contract, however, the forward contract is not traded on an exchange, typically requires no posting of margin, is not marked to market prior to maturity, and can be tailored to any maturity.

Caps, Floors, and Collars. Options, futures, and forward contracts all involve a single transaction at some point in the future. Bonds and many other contracts that a firm might wish to hedge, on the other hand, involve multiple payments in the future. Several instruments developed in the 1980s are designed to reduce the number of contracts required to hedge multiple payments. One popular contract is an interest-rate cap.[5] In a cap agreement, should the market rate exceed the cap rate, the writer (seller) pays the purchaser an amount equal to the market rate minus the cap rate; in return, the borrower pays a one-time fee in advance. The effect of the cap then is to set a maximum cost on the firm's outstanding debt.

Suppose, for instance, a firm issues debt with an interest rate of LIBOR (London Interbank Offer Rate) and buys a LIBOR cap of 10 percent with the notional principal of the cap equal to the principal on the loan.[6] As long as the LIBOR rate remains below 10 percent, the business will pay that rate on its debt and receive nothing from its cap. Should the LIBOR rate exceed 10 percent, the firm would receive a payment from the cap dealer. If LIBOR is at 11 percent, for example, the firm must pay interest equal to 11 percent of the loan principal to its debtholders but will receive a payment equal to 1 percent of the notional principal. Because the net value of the two payments is 10 percent, the business's net interest payments are capped at 10 percent. Interest rate caps are "over-the-counter

instruments"; that is, they are not traded on an exchange but may be purchased from some large commercial and investment banks.

Caps resemble options in two respects: the buyer of the cap must make an up-front payment, and after the contract is signed only the cap writer is at risk. Major differences exist between the two contracts, nonetheless. Whereas an option typically entails purchasing an asset at a fixed price, a cap involves paying only an interest differential. Another distinction is that the payments under a cap are linked; if the seller of a cap defaults on one payment, then the rest of the payments under the cap are terminated, though the buyer can still sue for the net present value (including the future interest earnings) of the future payments.

A floor is an option-like interest-rate risk management tool similar to a cap, except that a floor sets a minimum rather than a maximum rate. Thus in a floor agreement, should the market rate drop below the floor, the writer (seller) pays the purchaser an amount equal to the floor rate minus the market rate. Floor agreements can be particularly useful to those investing in floating-rate debt instruments who nonetheless have fixed-rate obligations. Consider, for example, an insurance company that wants to fund the purchase of a floating-rate asset with receipts from the sale of fixed-rate annuities. If the interest rate on its asset drops below the rate on its annuities, the insurance firm will incur a loss. A floor arrangement, however, would assure the firm that the combined return from the debt and the agreement will exceed its cost of its annuities. Floor agreements, like caps, are traded over the counter rather than on exchanges.

Collar agreements combine buying a cap and writing a floor in which the cap rate differs from the floor rate. A collar is useful to contain the effective interest costs of a floating-rate debt issue within a narrow band. Suppose a firm issues debt with an interest rate of LIBOR and enters into a collar, with the floor rate set at 9 percent and the cap rate set at 11 percent. If LIBOR rates drop below 9 percent, the firm will pay a total of 9 percent: the debtholders will receive LIBOR, and the other party to the collar, 9 percent minus LIBOR. The business will pay LIBOR, and no payments will be made under the collar agreement should LIBOR stand between 9 and 11 percent. If LIBOR exceeds 11 percent, the firm's net cost will be 11 percent: the debtholders will receive LIBOR and the writer of the collar will pay the firm LIBOR minus 11 percent. Firms wishing to cap their interest payments without paying an up-front fee to cover the cost of the cap may choose collars (because the cost of purchasing a cap can be offset by the income from writing a floor).[7] Collars are an over-the-counter instrument.

Swaps. Interest-rate swaps, in which two parties exchange interest-rate payments, are another popular risk management tool. The most common version of the interest-rate swap requires one party to pay a fixed rate of interest while receiving a floating interest rate from the other party. A fixed-to-floating-rate interest-rate swap can effectively convert a floating-rate obligation to a fixed-rate obligation (or vice versa). An interest-rate swap is similar to a collar in which the floor and cap rates are equal. A swap might also be viewed as a linked set of forward contracts. Interest-rate swaps are usually arranged so that no up-front payment is required from either party.

Interest-rate swap agreements are not traded on an exchange. In order to reduce the credit risk associated with a swap, the parties do not actually exchange the full value of the interest payments. Instead, the difference between the fixed and floating rates is calculated, and a single net payment is written by the party owing the greater amount of interest.

Another type of swap is a currency exchange in which two parties agree to trade payments in different currencies at a predetermined exchange rate. For example, Southeast Manufacturing might borrow Swiss francs in the Eurobond market and use a currency swap to convert the obligation to dollars. In such an agreement the company could pay an initial amount in Swiss francs equal to the principal on the loan, make periodic interest payments in U.S. dollars, and make the last payment of interest and principal in U.S. dollars. In return, the firm would receive U.S. dollars at the initial date and receive interest and principal in Swiss francs. The swap not only effectively changes the borrowed Swiss francs to dollars but also provides a prearranged exchange rate for converting Southeast's dollars into francs. These in turn will be used to pay interest and repay the principal at the end of the loan. Currency swaps, like interest-rate swaps, are not traded on an exchange.

Regulation of Interest Rate and Foreign Exchange Instruments

Exchange-traded interest-rate and foreign-exchange instruments are regulated by the exchanges and, domestically, by the United States Commodity Futures Trading Commission. No U.S. government

organization directly regulates transactions of instruments not traded on an exchange. Although both commercial bank and thrift regulators have established regulations to temper the impact of these instruments on the safety and soundness of banks, none of the federal regulators of depository institutions have responsibility for the markets in these instruments.

Thrifts and Interest-Rate Risk Management. Although thrifts have traditionally had mismatched asset and liability maturities that call for measures to contain interest-rate risk, most hedging techniques were not specifically authorized for thrifts by regulation until the early 1980s.[8] In 1981, for the first time, thrifts were officially permitted to use futures and options to control their interest-rate risk. Futures, however, proved a poor hedging instrument for many thrifts. A look at thrifts' experience with futures illustrates why regulators began to encourage swaps as an alternative way of managing interest-rate risk.

Using financial futures to hedge interest-rate risk requires a thrift to take a short position in the futures market. Because most thrifts suffer losses when interest rates increase (since a large share of their assets are at fixed, long-term rates), they need an off-balance-sheet hedge that rises in value when interest rates increase. Futures agreements provide for the purchase or sale of a debt security, in which the value of the underlying security decreases as rates go up. The optimal futures hedge for a thrift therefore involves a promise to sell the asset at a fixed price in the future. This places the thrift in a "short" position. What happened between 1982 and 1986, of course, was that interest rates fell substantially so that the value of the underlying asset increased. As a result, many thrifts experienced huge losses on their futures hedge positions. Even the most well constructed short hedge in the financial futures market will produce losses if interest rates drop because the hedge position has been established precisely to produce gains that will protect the institution if rates rise.

Another drawback of futures positions is that, unlike swaps, they must be marked to market daily. Thrifts, like most financial institutions, follow accounting practices whereby assets generally are counted at their book value rather than market value. However, market losses on futures positions have to be recorded as such immediately, although their recognition in the income statement is normally deferred over the time remaining to maturity of the instrument being hedged. In addition, margin calls on futures contracts to offset losses to the exchange creates an immediate cash outflow for the thrift.

The combination of large deferred losses and cash outflows as a result of *declining* interest rates created tremendous psychological problems for an industry that had just experienced huge setbacks because of *rising* interest rates during the 1979-82 period. These losses convinced many boards of directors, as well as regulators, that futures are not appropriate hedging tools for thrifts.[9] Nor do many thrifts possess the level of expertise necessary to manage futures positions. The fact that Treasury bill futures contracts extend only two years forward also makes the futures markets impractical for institutions that want to hedge long-term liability costs.

The interest-rate swap market, and to a lesser extent the market for caps and collars, became a natural alternative for thrift financial managers seeking to avoid these problems. Thrift regulators' endorsements of such "cash market" hedging as interest-rate swaps and interest-rate caps, in lieu of futures hedging, provided thrifts with another stimulus to switch to swaps as a way of managing interest-rate risk. Caps, collars, and swaps do not entail margin calls, and other problems such as basis risk (arising from changes in the spread between rates) are more manageable. Many thrift financial managers thus became more comfortable with swaps than with other hedging techniques.

Research has confirmed the suitability of swaps for hedging mortgage portfolios. Robert Crane and Peter Elmer simulated the performance of a number of asset and liability structures for a financial institution under 1,500 different interest-rate scenarios. The strategy that proved best on a risk-return basis was to fund fixed-rate assets (in this case, 15-year mortgages) with deposits that had been extended in maturity through interest-rate swaps. In fact, swaps performed so well in these simulations that they reduced the risk of 15-year fixed-rate mortgages below that of a strategy based on adjustable-rate lending.

Maturity Matching Credit. One regulatory development that stimulated the growth of the swap market was the maturity matching credit, one of the earliest formal risk-based capital requirements, instituted by the Federal Home Loan Bank Board in 1987. The maturity matching credit reduced the capital requirements for thrifts if their asset-liability gap (the amount by which its liabilities of a given maturity exceed assets of the same maturity) ranged between 15 and 25 percent of total assets. Institutions whose cumulative one- and three-year gaps were both below 15 percent would qualify for a credit equal to 2 percent of assets, while those with gaps in the 15 to 25 percent range would receive credit on a sliding scale.

Thus a thrift with gaps less than 15 percent, which would otherwise have been required to hold capital equal to 5 percent of assets, could lower its requirement to 3 percent. The maturity matching credit provided undercapitalized thrifts with a strong incentive to hedge, thus giving a further boost to participation in the swap market.

Table 1 shows how a swap would qualify a thrift to receive maturity matching credit. This hypothetical institution has total assets of $100 million, $70 million of which has a maturity more than three years. The thrift has $10 million in assets of one year or less and $40 million in liabilities of one year or less. Thus its one-year asset-liability gap is a negative $30 million—30 percent of its assets. Its cumulative three-year gap is a negative $40 million, or 40 percent of assets. Because both its one- and three-year gaps exceed 25 percent of its assets, the institution would not qualify for the maturity matching credit and thus would be required to hold capital at 5 percent of assets.

By entering into a $25 million interest-rate swap as the fixed-rate payer, the institution would be able to reduce both its one-year and three-year gaps below 15 percent so that it would qualify for the full 2 percent credit. This adjustment occurs because the swap extends maturity of the short-term liabilities (most likely deposits or repurchase agreements) beyond three years. The line "adjustment of liabilities for hedging" in Table 1 shows that short-term liabilities have been reduced by $25 million while long-term liabilities have increased by the same amount, lowering the one-year gap to a negative 5 percent and the three-year gap to a negative 15 percent of assets.

A survey of southeastern thrifts in mid-1989 by Craig Ruff showed that those most likely to engage in hedging were the ones with net worth ratios between 3 and 6 percent of assets—precisely the type of thrift that would benefit from the maturity matching credit.

Additional Regulatory Initiatives. Two 1989 regulatory initiatives by the Federal Home Loan Bank Board will probably further encourage thrifts to use swaps. Thrift Bulletin 13, which set out specific responsibilities for management and boards of directors in controlling interest-rate risk, requires each insured thrift's board of directors to set specific limits on the institution's exposure to changes in interest rates. These limits apply to both the percentage change in net interest income and the percentage change in the market value of the net worth of the institution. Thrift Bulletin 13 also requires that each institution with over $500 million in assets perform a simulation

Table 1
Gap Analysis
First Federal Savings and Loan Association

	Maturity on Time to Repricing:			
	Under One Year	One to Three Years	Over Three Years	Total
Before Hedging:				
Assets	10	20	70	100
Liabilities and Net Worth	40	30	30	100
GAP (A - L)	−30	−10	40	
Cumulative GAP	−30	−40	0	
After Hedging:				
Assets	10	20	70	100
Liabilities and Net Worth	40	30	30	100
Adjustment of Liabilities for Hedging*	−25	0	25	0
Liabilities after Hedging	15	30	55	100
GAP (A - L)	−5	−10	15	
Cumulative GAP	−5	−15	0	

*The hedge is a $25 million interest-rate swap that converts variable-rate liabilities into fixed-rate liabilities.

analysis to estimate its exposure to changes in interest rates.

The rationale for this regulation was that boards of directors should act as the first line of defense against excessive interest-rate risk. Although it has declined since 1984 when the Federal Home Loan Bank Board first began to measure it, most thrifts continue to have a large amount of interest-rate exposure. Regulators expect directors who see numerical estimates indicating high interest-rate exposure at their institution to force management to restructure the balance sheet or engage in off-balance-sheet hedging.

Another 1989 regulation likely to promote hedging is the risk-based capital proposal, which connects thrifts' capital requirements to the impact changes in interest rates are likely to have on the market value of the institution's net worth. Specifically, it states that thrifts must hold capital equal to one-half of the change in the market value of net worth that would result from a 200-basis-point (or 2 percentage point) change in interest rates.[10] Institutions with large amounts of interest-rate risk thus need to hold more capital, and hedging the interest-rate risk through caps, collars, or swaps becomes an attractive alternative.

Apart from 1989 risk-control initiatives, the Financial Institutions Reform, Recovery, and Enforcement Act of 1989 (FIRREA) includes a provision requiring the Office of Thrift Supervision (OTS) to establish risk-based capital regulations no less stringent than those imposed on nationally chartered banks (Title III, Section 5). Although the FIRREA provision does not require OTS standards to equal national bank standards exactly, its enforcement could mean that commercial bank regulations for interest-rate and foreign-exchange instruments might also be imposed on thrifts.

Regulation of Commercial Banks' Use of Hedging Tools

Because commercial banks have historically been far less exposed to interest-rate changes than most thrifts, regulation of bank participation in the interest-rate and foreign-exchange instruments market has followed a different course. Although large commercial banks routinely take foreign-exchange risks, losses from such involvement have not been a significant factor undermining the financial stability of any major bank in recent years. Bank regulators have been concerned primarily with credit risk. Though they have been increasingly sensitive to off-balance-sheet items, U.S. bank regulators did not consider them formally until 1986. Capital regulations adopted in the United States in 1981 and still in effect through 1989, for example, applied only to on-balance-sheet assets. In 1988, however, the Group of Ten countries, plus Luxembourg and Switzerland, reached an accord, called the Basle Agreement, on new procedures for evaluating capital.[11] The new standards extend to off-balance-sheet activities and weight both on- and off-balance-sheet activities according to their credit riskiness.[12] Interest-rate and foreign-exchange-rate risk are not, however, explicitly incorporated into the capital guidelines.

Although the Basle Agreement applied only to large banking organizations with international operations regulated by the signatories, U.S. regulators have decided to impose the requirements on all domestic commercial banks as well. These standards have since been further extended to cover the European Community (EC) and the European Free Trade Association (EFTA).[13] One important limitation of the agreement is that the capital standards do not necessarily apply to firms not regulated by central banks or other commercial bank overseers. U.S. investment banking and insurance companies, for example, are not regulated by U.S. federal bank regulatory agencies and, hence, are not bound by the capital regulations governing swaps—a situation with potentially significant competitive implications (Joanna Pitman 1988).

The new capital guidelines, which are to become fully effective at the end of 1992, will require banks to maintain a ratio of at least 8 percent total capital to risk-weighted on- and off-balance-sheet items. By the end of 1992, banks will also have to maintain a core capital ratio of at least 4 percent. Core (tier 1) capital, as defined by the Basle Agreement, consists of the book value of common and perpetual preferred equity, minority equity interest in consolidated subsidiaries, and retained earnings less goodwill. Supplementary (tier 2) capital includes items like general loan loss reserves, mandatory convertible debt, perpetual debt, subordinated debt, and limited-life preferred stock. Total capital is the sum of core and supplementary capital. Transitional arrangements provide for banks to arrive at a total capital ratio of at least 7.25 percent by the end of 1990, with core capital elements totaling at least 3.25 percent.

Risk Weighting. On-balance-sheet assets are assigned to various risk categories that are weighted to reflect the extent of uncertainty. Assets with virtually no credit risk, such as cash and central government securities from the industrialized countries belonging to the Organization for Economic Cooperation and Development, are assigned a weight of zero and thus require no capital. Other assets, including most bank certificates of deposit, receive a 20 percent weight, while home mortgages receive a 50 percent weight. Assets of normal credit risk, such as claims on the private sector, fixed assets, and real estate, are assigned a 100 percent weight.

Off-balance-sheet items are first converted into credit risk equivalent values based on the type of instrument. For example, a credit conversion factor of 100 percent is applied to direct credit substitutes such as standby letters of credit, which obligate banks to supply credit at some unspecified future time. These are then generally multiplied by the risk weights applicable to the counterparty for an on-balance-sheet transaction.

Because off-balance-sheet activities are converted into risk equivalents of on-balance-sheet items exclusively on the basis of credit risk, no capital requirements are imposed on exchange-traded options and futures that contain risk for the exchange by requiring daily payment of variation margin. Also excluded from the calculations are options, caps, and floors written by a bank. These instruments involve no credit risk to the bank since the purchaser's part of the agreement is completed with the initial payment and entails no further obligation that could lead to default.

The credit risk involved in interest-rate and foreign-exchange instruments can be calculated in one of two ways: the current exposure method places most of the weight on the present market value of the interest-rate or foreign-exchange instrument, whereas the original exposure method assigns risk based on the swaps' maturity and does not account for subsequent changes in market value. Though most of the Group of Ten bank supervisors favored the current exposure method, the Basle Agreement allows supervisors to choose either procedure. According to the agreement, bank regulators may permit individual banks to adopt either method, with the understanding that once a bank chooses the current exposure method it cannot switch back to the original exposure method.

The current exposure approach divides credit risk related to an interest-rate or a foreign-exchange instrument into two parts: the actual current exposure and the potential for an increase in exposure, depend-

Table 2
Calculation of Credit-Equivalent Amounts for Interest-Rate Swaps
under Risk-Based Capital Guidelines,
Current Exposure Methos

Type of Contract and Remaining Maturity	Potential Exposure			+	Current Exposure		=	Credit Equivalent Amount (Dollars)
	Notional Principal (Dollars) x	Potential Exposure Conversion = Factor	Potential Exposure (Dollars		Replacement Cost*	Current Exposure (Dollars)**		
1) 120-day forward foreign exchange	5,000,000	.01	50,000		10,000	10,000		60,000
2) Fixed/floating interest-rate swap, single currency, 7 months	5,000,000	0	0		−5,000	0		0
3) Fixed/floating interest-rate swap, single currency, 4 years	10,000,000	.005	50,000		−200,000	0		50,000
4) Fixed/floating interest-rate swap, single currency, 4 years	10,000,000	.005	50,000		150,000	150,000		200,000
5) Fixed/floating interest-rate swap, single currency, 7 years	5,000,000	.005	25,000		325,000	325,000		350,000
6) Cross-currency, floating/floating foreign-exchange swap, 7 years	5,000,000	.05	250,000		350,000	350,000		600,000

* These numbers are purely for illustration.
** The larger of zero or positive mark-to-marker value.

ing on changes in interest rates or foreign-exchange rates. Because the bank would incur losses if the counterparty defaulted and the net present value of the net instrument payments would have positive value to the bank, the actual current credit exposure is viewed as equal to the marked-to-market value of the interest-rate and foreign-exchange instrument. If the interest-rate or foreign-exchange instrument has negative value to the bank, then the bank is not currently subject to credit risk since counterparty default would not result in bank losses. Therefore, the value of the current exposure is set at zero. The potential increase in credit exposure due to interest-rate changes is equal to 0.5 percent of the notional principal of an interest-rate instrument for instruments that mature in more than one year. If the interest-rate instrument matures in one year or less, the potential increase in exposure is set equal to zero.

Because bank regulators view foreign-exchange rates as potential more volatile than interest rates, a higher capital requirement is imposed on exchange-rate instruments.[14] For those that mature in less than one year the potential increase in exposure is set at 1 percent of the instrument's notional principal. Foreign exchange instruments maturing in more than one year require a potential increase in credit exposure equal to 5 percent of the instrument's notional principal.[15]

An example of the computation of the credit equivalent amount is provided in Table 2. The first contract is a 120-day forward foreign exchange agreement. Since the contract matures in under one year, the potential exposure is equal to the notional principal (assumed to be $5 million) multiplied by a credit conversion factor of 0.01, resulting in an exposure of $50,000. The contract is also assumed to have a current replacement cost of $10,000. The second contract is a single-currency, fixed-to-floating interest-rate swap that matures in seven months. The swap matures in less than one year, so its potential exposure is set at zero and only the current exposure is considered. The seven-month swap has a negative replacement cost because the bank would receive a payment for entering into such a swap. Since the regulations do not count negative replacement cost, this swap has a credit equivalent exposure of zero.

The third transaction illustrates calculation of credit equivalent exposure for an interest-rate swap with negative replacement cost but more than one year to maturity. In this case the credit equivalent amount is equal to the potential exposure of the swap. The next two fixed-to-floating interest-rate swaps (4 and 5) illustrate that the potential conversion factor remains at 0.005 regardless of the remaining maturity on a swap. Remaining maturity is less important for swaps under the current exposure method because any increase in replacement cost will be reflected through the calculation's current exposure component when the swap is next valued for capital adequacy purposes. The last contract is a cross-currency, floating-rate-to-floating-rate currency swap that matures in seven years. Because this contract's potential exposure is far larger than on the seven-year interest-rate swap, the credit conversion factor is 0.05 rather than the 0.005 factor applied to interest-rate swaps.

Although it is less accurate, the original exposure method is computationally easier. It may also be more consistent with the other risk-based standards in that it avoids the need to mark to market. The original exposure method sets the credit exposure equal to the notional principal of the swap multiplied by a conversion factor that depends on each swap's maturity. The agreement permits each regulator to choose whether the conversion factors will be based on the original maturity of the swap or its remaining maturity. The conversion factor for swaps maturing in less than one year is 0.5 percent. An additional 1.0 percent is added to the conversion factor for each additional year. The capital requirement for contracts contingent on foreign exchange is 2 percent for those maturing in one year or less, with another 4 percent added for each additional year.

Once a credit-equivalent amount is calculated, interest-rate and foreign-exchange contracts are treated differently from other off-balance-sheet activities. The credit-equivalent amounts of such contracts are all multiplied by a 50 percent credit-risk weighting, regardless of the counterparty's credit risk, reflecting regulators' judgment that most participants in the swap market are reliable. The Basle Agreement notes, however, that the credit risk weighting on swaps could be raised if the average credit quality of swap counterparties deteriorates or if swap losses increase.

Netting of Swap Payments. An important element in determining capital requirements for a bank's swap portfolio is the contractual agreement to net swap payments across multiple swaps between two parties. Each party does not present payments; instead, the party that owes presents the net amount due after the various transactions are tallied. This system lessens the likelihood that one party will default after receiving a full payment from the counterparty. The Basle Agreement generally permits banks to net contracts subject to novation, an arrangement that automatically amalgamates swaps payable in the same currency at the same time into a single net payment. Netting by novation may be implemented in stages in those countries where national bankruptcy laws allow liquidators to unbundle transactions within a given period under a charge of fraudulent preference.[16] The Basle Agreement does not permit netting where the contracts are merely subject to close-out clauses, in which outstanding obligations on all swaps are accelerated and netted to determine a single exposure in the event of bankruptcy, for example. The supervisors approve of both novation and close-out clauses but contend that these have not yet been adequately tested in the courts. Netting of contracts under close-out clauses may be permitted in the future in jurisdictions where it is upheld in the courts.

Regulation of Interest-Rate Risk. Although capital regulations for banks do not explicitly incorporate the impact of interest-rate risk, regulators are nevertheless concerned about this source of risk. Guidelines for large banks generated by the Office of the Comptroller of the Currency (OCC) stress four components of risk management, according to the analysis of David Scott: a policy on interest-rate risk approved by each bank's board of directors; limits on total risk exposure, preferably stated in terms of income at risk from an interest-rate movement of specified size; a measurement system that adequately captures the riskiness of a bank's portfolio; and development and use of good management reports. James Houpt (see especially p. 9) expressed similar views about Federal Reserve regulatory policies. Neither Houpt nor Scott seems inclined to require all banks to assess the sensitivity of the equity value to changes in interest rates. Indeed, Houpt argues that "in many cases liquid and otherwise solvent institutions can 'ride out' market fluctuations without ever feeling the effect of sizable rate changes on their bottom lines" (9). Both also suggest that it would be difficult and probably too costly for regulators to gather sufficient information for accurate off-site analysis of banks' interest-rate risk.

Proposals for Interest Rate Risk and Capital Guidelines

Making exposure to interest-rate changes a formal part of the risk-based capital system would be desirable for three reasons. First, U.S. regulators have made a considerable effort to secure international agreement on standards in order to assure a level playing field for organizations operating in more than one country. Accounting for interest-rate risk in capital requirements would further promote equality across various countries. Second, formal guidelines should help organizations plan for the future. Third, appropriate standards could discourage banks from exposure to excessive interest-rate and foreign-exchange risk.

In developing an interest-rate risk component to capital standards, regulators must determine which risk measure to use. Several considerations suggest the focus should be on market values rather than accounting values. Economically insolvent organizations have a great incentive to take large risks: such a bank will capture most of the gains while the FDIC incurs most of the losses if a venture fails. In addition, the argument that banks can "ride out" a change in rates is mistaken. Consider, for example, a bank that has become economically insolvent because rates have risen. Managers of such an institution almost certainly will tell regulators that they expect rates to fall, returning the bank to solvency. Interest rates might indeed fall, but they might just as well increase, in which case the bank would lose even more value. No evidence suggests that bank supervisors or managers can out-guess the consensus forecast of the market reflected in current interest rates.[17]

Two alternatives are available for analyzing the effect of rate changes on bank equity values: (1) duration analysis and (2) simulation analysis. Duration analysis in its simplest form condenses a bank's exposure into a single number. A weakness of this approach is that it does not easily incorporate the options implicit in many bank contracts (such as mortgage loans with prepayment privileges) nor does it address the irregularities introduced by caps, floors, and other off-balance-sheet contracts. Simulation analysis, on the other hand, requires regulators to specify the rate changes that will be analyzed. For example, regulators may require a bank to assess the effects of a 100-basis-point increase in rates and the effects of a 100-basis-point decrease.

The problem of off-site monitoring must also be addressed in developing an interest-rate risk component. The Office of Thrift Supervision requires thrifts to report over 600 items dealing with maturity and yields of assets, liabilities, and off-balance-sheet items in order to monitor thrifts' interest-rate exposure (Houpt). Bank regulators would doubtless require at least this level of detail in reporting and possibly more to analyze some of the larger bank's interest-rate exposure accurately.

Scott and Houpt argue with some merit that the costs of such detailed reporting are likely to exceed the benefits in many cases. Moreover, even if regulators could obtain sufficient detail on a quarterly basis at reasonable cost, it is not clear that the figures would adequately reflect a bank's interest-rate exposure between quarterly statements. The ease of buying and selling many assets, such as securitized mortgages, combined with the low cost of entering into off-balance-sheet transactions, makes it possible for an institution's exposure to change dramatically in a very short time. Indeed, a large bank that actively "supplies" interest-rate risk management products to corporations could easily change the magnitude and even the direction of its exposure to interest rates within days (if not hours) after quarterly financial records are closed. Thus, quarterly financial filings may not only be excessively costly but may also fail to measure risk accurately.

One alternative to off-site risk evaluation based on quarterly financial statements would be standards grounded in each institution's internal risk limits. This procedure would be in keeping with current regulatory policies that require institutions to set and follow internal risk standards. The first step in using internal risk criteria would be to establish a trade-off between exposure to interest-rate fluctuations and capital requirements. In such a system, changes in equity value would include the effect of interest-rate fluctuations on the market value of a bank's assets, liabilities, and off-balance-sheet items. Each bank would then specify its maximum exposure to an interest-rate change and set up information reporting systems to ensure against accidentally exceeding these limits. Of course, the bank would also be required to conduct its operations in such a way that it did not intentionally violate its own guidelines for interest-rate exposure.

If capital standards were based on an institution's internal risk limits, internal reporting requirements could be tailored to the sophistication of each bank's activities. While banks relying on short-term funding and loans with minimal off-balance-sheet items might need very little information about exposure, money-center banks might require highly refined reporting systems. This approach would also offer banks some trade-off between their capital requirements and the complexity of their information-gathering tools. Banks with lower internal tolerances for risk exposure could ensure compliance through sophisticated reporting procedures while other banks might choose to set higher tolerances that could be monitored with less refined systems.

The effectiveness of this approach, which is similar to Thrift Bulletin 13, would depend on careful bank examination. Bank supervisors would have to evaluate an individual bank's information system in relation to its interest-rate risk model to ensure against accidental violations of the exposure limit, and determine that the bank has in fact complied with its own risk guidelines. The capital requirements could levy an automatic penalty (higher capital or fines) for accidental breaches and a more severe one for deliberate infractions.

Reliance on internal standards would keep organizations from increasing their interest-rate risk between quarterly financial statements to evade capital requirements since internal guidelines would apply at all times. One potential problem with this strategy is that a bank's preferred risk positions might change over time. This shift could be accommodated, however, by letting organizations change their standards. To decrease interest-rate risk, a bank would need only to notify regulators that it planned to reduce its level of permitted risk. Raising the internal risk criteria would require compliance with the capital guidelines for the higher risk level.

The approach outlined here for linking interest-rate risk to capital standards is also appropriate for foreign-exchange exposure. Since a bank's foreign-exchange-rate exposure can change significantly, a system not solely reliant on quarterly financial statements is desirable. Capital requirements based on a bank's internal risk standards would compel institutions to maintain prespecified limits for foreign-exchange risk at all times.

Conclusion

The market for interest-rate and foreign-exchange instruments evolved rapidly during the 1980s in response to the needs of commercial banks, thrifts, and their customers. Regulators' awareness that the potential of these instruments to increase as well as decrease the risk exposure of insured depositories has also grown. Recognizing that these hedging tools can adversely alter interest-rate risk, thrift regulators have incorporated interest-rate instruments in their capital standards. Bank regulators have responded by considering the credit risk that is associated with interest-rate and foreign-exchange contracts in risk-based capital guidelines.

Though bank regulators are developing guidelines that will enable banks to self-manage their risk exposure, they have not yet evolved a method for including interest-rate and foreign-exchange exposure in their risk-based capital guidelines. A procedure such as the one proposed here, which uses a bank's internal risk limits to establish links between this kind of risk exposure and capital criteria has two important advantages: first, it would reduce the costs of complying with the capital requirements by allowing banks a choice between the expense of developing more sophisticated information-gathering systems and maintaining higher capital levels; second, it offers a more reliable basis for a bank's capital requirements by accounting for an institution's exposure at all times, not just as it is reported in quarterly financial statements.

Notes

1. The need to measure interest-rate and foreign-exchange risk is not unique, and even some of the proposals to increase market discipline would benefit from incorporating estimates of interest-rate and foreign-exchange risk. For example, the Shadow Financial Regulatory Committee proposes that banks be required to maintain higher levels of total capital, and Wall would require banks to issue puttable subordinated debt. Both of these plans require a suffi-ciently large capital cushion to ensure that losses by a bank over a short period of time cannot exceed a depository's equity and subordinated debt. Neither of these proposals explicitly addresses the issue of interest-rate and foreign-exchange-rate risk measurement.

2. Neither a complete review of the features of these contracts nor a comprehensive discussion of the various types of contracts is within the scope of this study. See Smith,

Smithson, and Wilford (especially chapter 3) for a more thorough discussion of interest-rate and foreign-exchange contingent contracts.

3. The fact that the exchange of cash flows is a zero-sum games does not necessarily imply that the instruments do not create value for their users. For example, see Wall and Pringle (1988) for a review of possible gains to interest-rate swap users.

4. An option that can be exercised only on a specific date is referred to as a European option. American options may be exercised any time through a specific date in the future. Exchange-traded options are generally American options. However, Merton has proven that the value of an option is maximized by deferring exercise until the last day if the underlying asset does not make any payment prior to the expiration date. The discussion below focuses on European options since the conditions for deferring exercise frequently hold for interest-rate and foreign-exchange-rate options.

5. See Abken for a more detailed discussion of caps, floors, and collars.

6. The notional principal is used for certain interest-rate contingent agreements to determine the dollar value of the payment. The role of the notional principal in determining the payment under a cap agreement is analogous to the use of the principal amount of a loan in the calculation of interest payments on the loan. The primary difference between the principal on a loan and the notional principal of a cap is that the notional principal never changes hands. The term notional principal is used in a similar manner for floor, collar, and interest-rate swap agreements.

7. Abken provides examples.

8. The discussion of thrift regulation is based in part on Mc-Nulty.

9. While the official regulatory attitude toward futures has not changed since the early 1980s, many, if not most, re-gional thrift regulatory officials take a dim view of futures for the reasons mentioned here.

10. This is one part of a three-part capital requirement that includes a credit-risk component similar to that used for commercial banks and a collateralized borrowing requirement.

11. The Group of Ten consists of Belgium, Canada, France, the Federal Republic of Germany, Italy, Japan, the Netherlands, Sweden, the United Kingdom, and the United States of America.

12. See Keeton for an analysis of the effect of the risk-based capital guidelines on banking organizations' capital requirements.

13. The European Community consists of Belgium, France, Italy, Luxembourg, the Netherlands, the Federal Republic of Germany, Denmark, Ireland, the United Kingdom, Greece, Spain, and Portugal. The European Free Trade Association includes Austria, Norway, Sweden, Switzerland, Finland, and Iceland.

14. See Board of Governors of the Federal Reserve System and Bank of England and Muffett.

15. For a critique of a draft version of the swap requirements see Smith, Smithson, and Wakeman.

16. Fraudulent preference exists if a debtor favors one creditor over others in settling bankruptcy claims, thus transferring property without a fair consideration in exchange. For an extensive discussion of swap netting see Shirreff.

17. Moreover, even if some group of supervisors could demonstrate a superior ability to predict interest rates, this edge would not necessarily help the regulatory agencies. Private investors would happily bid away any regulator who can consistently out-guess the market on future rate changes.

References

Peter A. "Interest-Rate Caps, Collars, and Floors." Federal Reserve Bank of Atlanta *Economic Review* 74 (November/December 1989): 2-23.

Alfriend, Malcolm C. "Interest Risk-Based Capital Standard: History and Explanation." Federal Reserve Bank of Richmond *Economic Review* 74 (November/December 1988): 28-34.

Arak, Marcelle, Laurie S. Goodman, and Arthur Rones. "Credit Lines for New Instruments: Swaps, Over-the-Counter Options, Forwards and Floor-Ceiling Agreements." Federal Reserve Bank of Chicago, *Conference on Bank Structure and Competition*, 1986, 437-56.

Belton, Terrence M. "Credit Risk in Interest Rate Swaps." Board of Governors of the Federal Reserve System unpublished working paper, April 1987.

Bennett, Dennis E., Deborah L. Cohen, and James E. McNulty. "Interest Rate Swaps and the Management of Interest Rate Risk." *Housing Finance Review* 3 (Spring 1988): 249-64.

Board of Governors of the Federal System and Bank of England. "Potential Exposure on Interest Rate and Exchange Rate Related Instruments." Unpublished staff paper, 1987.

Crane, Robert C., and Peter J. Elmer. "Adrift in FRM's." *Secondary Mortgage Markets* 3 (Fall 1986): 2-7.

Felgran, Steven D. "Interest Rate Swaps: Use, Risk and Prices." *New England Economic Review* (November/December 1987): 22-32.

Henderson, Schuyler K. "Exposures of Swaps and Termination Provisions of Swap Agreements." In *Swap Finance*, vol. 2, edited by Boris Antl, 125-41. London: Euromoney Publications Limited, 1986.

Henderson, Schuyler K., and Armel C. Cates. "Termination Provisions of Swap Agreements under U.S. and English Insolvency Laws." In *Swap Finance*, vol. 2, edited by Boris Antl, 91-102. London: Euromoney Publications Limited, 1986.

Houpt, James V. "A Regulatory Perspective on Interest Rate Risk: A Fed View." *Issues in Bank Regulation* 13 (Fall 1989): 7-10.

Jackson, Dominique. "Swaps Keep in Step with the Regulators." *Financial Times*, August 10, 1988, 22.

Keeton, William R. "The New Risk-Based Capital Plan for Commercial Banks." Federal Reserve Bank of Kansas City *Economic Review* 74 (December 1989): 40-60.

McNulty, James E. "Interest Rate Risk: Lessons Learned and Questions Unanswered." *Journal of Retail Banking* 9 (Fall 1987): 29-34.

Merton, Robert C. "The Theory of Rational Option Pricing." *Bell Journal of Economics and Management Science* 4 (Spring 1973): 141-83.

Muffet, Mark. "Modeling Credit Exposure on Swaps." Federal Reserve Bank of Chicago, *Conference on Bank Structure and Competition*, 1987, 473-96.

Neal, Kathleen, and Katerina Simons. "Interest Rate Swaps, Currency Swaps, and Credit Risk." *Issues in Bank Regulation* 11 (Spring 1988): 26-29.

Pitman, Joanna. "Swooping on Swaps." *Euromoney* (January 1988): 68-80.

Ruff, Craig. "Off-Balance-Sheet Hedging Activity: Fourth District Thrifts." Federal Home Loan Bank of Atlanta, September 1989.

Scott, David. "A Regulatory Perspective on Interest Rate Risk: An OCC View." *Issues in Bank Regulation* 13 (Fall 1989): 3-6.

Shadow Financial Regulatory Committee. "An Outline of a Program for Deposit Insurance Reform." Statement 41, February 1989.

Shirreff, David. "Netting Nightmare." *Risk* 3 (March 1990): 15-23.

Smith, Clifford W., Jr., Charles W. Smithson, and Lee Macdonald Wakeman. "Credit Risk and the Scope of Regulation of Swaps." Federal Reserve Bank of Chicago, *Conference on Bank Structure and Competition*, 1987, 166-85.

Smith, Clifford W., Jr., Charles W. Smithson, and D. Sykes Wilford. *Managing Financial Risk*. New York: Ballinger Publishing Company, 1990.

Smithson, Charles W. "A LEGO® Approach to Financial Engineering: An Introduction to Forwards, Futures, Swaps, and Options." *Midland Corporate Finance Review* 4 (Winter 1987): 16-28.

Wakeman, Lee Macdonald. "The Portfolio Approach to Swaps Management." Chemical Bank Capital Markets Groups unpublished working paper, May 1986.

Wall, Larry D. "A Plan for Reducing Future Deposit Insurance Losses: Puttable Subordinated Debt." Federal Reserve Bank of Atlanta *Economic Review* 74 (July/August 1989): 2-17.

Wall, Larry D., and Kwun-Wing C. Fung. "Evaluating the Credit Exposure of Interest Rate Swap Portfolios." Federal Reserve Bank of Atlanta Working Paper 87-8, December 1987.

Wall, Larry D., and John J. Pringle. "Interest Rate Swaps: A Review of the Issues." Federal Reserve Bank of Atlanta *Economic Review* 73 (November/December 1988): 22-40.

_____ . "Alternative Explanations of Interest Rate Swaps: A Theoretical and Empirical Analysis." *Financial Management* 18 (Summer 1989): 59-73.